This book is a masterful contribution to the literature on the psychological treatment of depression. In exquisite detail, and full of wonderful metaphors and moment-by-moment description of the process of therapy, it will become required reading for all therapists who seek to help people find a way through their struggles with depression.

> —Prof. Mark Williams, professor of clinical psychology and Wellcome Principal Research Fellow at the University of Oxford, holding a joint appointment in the Departments of Psychiatry and Experimental Psychology

Depression is the number one mental health problem seen in clinical practice and any clinician interested in practicing acceptance and commitment therapy is going to want to have this book within easy reach. Zettle provides a well thought out, easy to understand approach to treating the depressed client using the ACT framework. Capitalizing on his many years of clinical experience using the ACT model, Zettle offers numerous practical insights into managing the ongoing process of therapy, and uses brief case examples to highlight key points. The session by session ACT protocol described in the second half of the book will be a fantastically useful aid to clinicians in the field.

> —Kirk Strosahl Ph.D., coauthor of *Acceptance and Commitment Therapy: An Experiential Approach to Behavior Change* and *A Practical Guide to Acceptance and Commitment Therapy*

This professional book is the first to outline the conceptual roots, empirical basis, and practical application of acceptance and commitment therapy (ACT) for unipolar depression. In a clear and accessible style, the author guides mental health professionals and students alike in the strategic application of ACT as a supplement or alternative approach to available treatments for depression. Readers learn how to integrate and use acceptance and mindfulness strategies with commitment and behavior change strategies to help depressed clients live better, not simply to feel better. The book includes several well-crafted examples, clinical dialogues, and practical exercises, and a step-by-step integration of the material into a twelve-session protocol It is a vital clinical resource for professionals who are committed to helping restore the lives of those who are stuck and wallowing in depression and misery.

> —John P. Forsyth, Ph.D., associate professor of psychology and faculty director of the Anxiety Disorders Research Program at the University at Albany, SUNY, and author of *Acceptance and Commitment Therapy for Anxiety Disorders* and *ACT on Life Not on Anger*

This book provides more than an excellent explication of applying ACT to depression. Zettle's presentation of the fundamental ACT principles and processes is so clear and comprehensive that readers will almost certainly see the potential application of them to many other forms of human suffering in addition to depression. I give this book my highest recommendation.

—Hank Robb, Ph.D., ABPP, past president of the American Board of Counseling Psychology and founding board member of SMART Recovery™

I enthusiastically endorse Zettle's ACT for Depression. Well-written and comprehensive, this text is a valuable addition to the ACT literature. Addressing one of the most widespread difficulties encountered in clinical practice, this resource details a robust treatment which will be well-received by practicing clinicians with both behavioral and non-behavioral backgrounds alike.

—R. Trent Codd, III, Ed.S., LPC, LCAS, president of the Cognitive-Behavioral Therapy Center of WNC, P.A., in Asheville, NC

Having been present at the birth of ACT approximately thirty years ago, Zettle articulates ACT's basic principles with the ease and clarity that can only come from a seasoned veteran. The rationale and techniques for applying ACT to depression are sensitive, satisfying, and establish Zettle as a true expert on depression as well as a master clinician. The book succeeds at offering both a clear, concise articulation of ACT for depression in terms of core, functional processes, allowing clinicians to apply ACT flexibly and functionally as well as a session-by-session manual for clinicians to follow when the needs for structure and support are a priority. It is easy to read with out sacrificing the philosophical and theoretical complexity of the approach. I recommend it for novice and experienced ACT clinicians as well as other clinicians and clinical students wishing to add acceptance and commitment techniques to their clinical repertoires.

— Jonathan W. Kanter, Ph.D., assistant professor of psychology, director of the Depression Treatment Specialty Clinic, and coordinator of the University Psychology Clinic at the University of Wisconsin-Milwaukee

A C *for* Depression
T

A Clinician's Guide to Using Acceptance &
Commitment Therapy in Treating Depression

ROBERT D. ZETTLE, PH.D.

New Harbinger Publications, Inc.

Publisher's Note

Selected metaphors adapted from Steven C. Hayes, Kirk D. Strosahl, and Kelly G. Wilson, *Acceptance and commitment therapy: An experiential approach to behavior change*, copyright © 1999 by the authors. Used with permission of Guilford Press.

"Goals Action Form" adapted from Steven C. Hayes, Kirk D. Strosahl, and Kelly G. Wilson, *Acceptance and commitment therapy: An experiential approach to behavior change*, copyright © 1999 by the authors. Used with permission of Guilford Press.

Adaptations of exercises (Raisin exercise and Mindful Walking exercise) and handouts (Mindfulness of the Breath; Sitting Meditation: Mindfulness of Sounds and Thoughts; and Homework Record Form—Session 1) are from Zindel V. Segal, J. Mark G. Williams, and John D. Teasdale, *Mindfulness-based cognitive therapy for depression: A new approach to preventing relapse*, copyright © 2002 by the authors. Used with permission of Guilford Press.

Lyrics from Saint Valentine's Angel (1973) by Donovan are used with the permission of Peer International Corporation.

Valued Living Questionnaire copyright © 2002 by Kelly Wilson. Reprinted with permission of the author.

Personal Values Questionnaire by J.T. Blackledge and Joseph Ciarrochi. Reprinted with permission of the authors.

ACT Initial Case Conceptualization Form adapted from and used by permission of Jason Lillis and Jason Luoma, copyright © 2005.

Distributed in Canada by Raincoast Books

Copyright © 2007 by Robert D. Zettle
New Harbinger Publications, Inc.
5674 Shattuck Avenue
Oakland, CA 94609
www.newharbinger.com

All Rights Reserved
Printed in the United States of America

Acquired by Catharine Sutker; Cover design by Amy Shoup;
Edited by Jean Blomquist; Text design by Tracy Carlson

Library of Congress Cataloging-in-Publication Data

Zettle, Robert D.
  ACT for depression : a clinician's guide to using acceptance and commitment therapy in treating depression / Robert D. Zettle.
    p. ; cm.
  Includes bibliographical references.
  ISBN-13: 978-1-57224-509-9 (pbk. ; alk. paper)
  ISBN-10: 1-57224-509-3 (pbk. : alk. paper)
  1. Depression, Mental--Treatment. 2. Acceptance and commitment therapy. I. Title.
  [DNLM: 1. Depressive Disorder--therapy. 2. Cognitive Therapy--methods. WM 171 Z61a 2007]
RC537.Z48 2007
616.85'2706--dc22

                    2007036484

09 08 07

10 9 8 7 6 5 4 3 2 1   First printing

To my father, John A. Zettle (1918-2002), who left this world a better place than in which he found it.

Contents

Dear Reader:

Welcome to New Harbinger Publications. New Harbinger is dedicated to publishing books based on acceptance and commitment therapy (ACT) and its application to specific areas. New Harbinger has a long-standing reputation as a publisher of quality, well-researched books for general and professional audiences.

It is often said that depression is the common cold of psychopathology. This saying provides a common sense metaphor for how shockingly pervasive depression is, but it does not do justice to its horrific impact. A cold does not often lead to loss of relationships, to poor social functioning, or even to suicide. Depression does all these things and more.

There are good, empirically supported treatments for depression, both psychosocial and pharmacological, but that too fails to do justice to the large numbers of patients who do not respond to existing treatments, drop out of treatment, or relapse. There is a crying need for new approaches that might lead to better outcomes, better treatment matching, and better understanding of the nature and range of successful processes of change.

You are holding a volume that has potential in all of these areas. *ACT for Depression* is written by Robert Zettle. He comes to this project with credentials that uniquely qualify him to author this volume. He is Steve Hayes's first doctoral psychology student, the first researcher ever to do a randomized controlled trial of ACT, and an early psychology intern trained by Aaron Beck, the father of cognitive therapy. A skilled clinician and trainer with a broad and deep background, Zettle has crafted a book that helps the reader understand practical methods for applying an ACT model to this difficult psychological problem.

Practical, clear, and groundbreaking, this book provides an explanation of the psychopathology underlying depression, walks through how to assess these processes, and shows how these can lead to a coherent approach to case formulation with clients who are depressed. Not just an intellectual exercise, the results of case formulation link point-to-point to treatment methods within an ACT model. Dr. Zettle shows how to foster each of the key processes that are argued to be important, and then provides a well-crafted twelve-session protocol that is bound to be widely used in research and practice. He also gives clear guidance about special issues such as suicidality and comorbidity.

As part of New Harbinger's commitment to publishing sound, scientific, clinically based research, Steven C. Hayes, Georg H. Eifert, and John Forsyth oversee all prospective ACT books for the Acceptance and Commitment Therapy Series. As ACT Series editors, we review all ACT books published by New Harbinger, comment on proposals and offer guidance as needed, and use a gentle hand in making suggestions regarding the content, depth, and scope of each book. We strive to ensure that any unsubstantiated claim or claims that are clearly ACT inconsistent are flagged for the authors so they can revise these sections to ensure that the work meets our criteria (see below) and that all of the material presented is true to ACT's roots (not passing off other models and methods as ACT).

Books in the Acceptance and Commitment Therapy Series:

■ Have an adequate database, appropriate to the strength of the claims being made

■ Are theoretically coherent—they will fit with the ACT model and underlying behavioral principles as they have evolved at the time of writing

- Orient the reader toward unresolved empirical issues

- Not overlap needlessly with existing volumes

- Avoid jargon and unnecessary entanglement with proprietary methods, leaving ACT work open and available

- Keep the focus always on what is good for the reader

- Support the further development of the field

- Provide information in a way that is of practical use to readers

These guidelines reflect the values of the broader ACT community. You'll see all of them packed into this book. They are meant to ensure that professionals get information that can truly be helpful, and that can further our ability to alleviate human suffering by inviting creative practitioners into the process of developing, applying, and refining a more adequate approach. Consider this book such an invitation.

Sincerely,
Steven C. Hayes, Ph.D., Georg H. Eifert, Ph.D., and John Forsyth, Ph.D.

Acknowledgments

A series of events—some expected, some simply fortuitous—led to my writing of this book. These events began in the fall of 1976 when I began my doctoral program in clinical psychology at the University of North Carolina at Greensboro. Also new to the department that fall was a just-hired assistant professor by the name of Steve Hayes. Perhaps for no "darn good reason" as Steve would say, he was assigned as my advisor. My life would never be the same. Steve was not only my advisor but also my mentor, friend, and "academic father." I was his first doctoral student. I would especially like to acknowledge Steve's early tutelage and nurturance. This book surely would not have been possible without it.

Both Steve and I fairly quickly recognized that we shared the sense that behaviorism needed a new way of looking at language and verbal behavior. We needed to move beyond the work of Skinner in order to effectively address the wide array of suffering experienced by human beings. By the time I was ready to conduct dissertation research in late 1981, Steve had already compiled a draft of a manual for a new treatment approach, known at the time as "comprehensive distancing." This approach, instead of looking at the content of language, looked at the context of language or verbal activity, that is, how the process of thinking impacts our actions and emotional reactions. My dissertation, which compared what would later be known as ACT to cognitive therapy in the treatment of depression, was the first randomized clinical trial evaluating this new approach. This book continues the work of applying ACT to depression that was begun over a quarter of a century ago.

In addition to Steve, I want to thank several people who, in many different ways, helped me in my writing of this book. In no particular order, they include Hank Robb, who helped track down the Joseph Campbell quote he is so fond of reciting; Jason Lillis and Jason Luoma for allowing me to include an adaptation of their ACT Initial Case Conceptualization Form; J. T. Blackledge and Joseph Ciarrochi for granting permission to include a copy of their Personal Values Questionnaire; and Kelly Wilson for permitting me to include the Valued Living Questionnaire.

I would like to express my gratitude to Wichita State University for granting me a sabbatical in the fall of 2006. This made it possible for me to fully devote my time to writing this book and to concentrate on it without the usual distraction of departmental committee meetings and the like. I am also grateful to the staff of New Harbinger for approaching me about undertaking this project and for their invaluable assistance in helping me make this book much more understandable and readable. My special thanks to Catharine Sutker, acquisitions director, for her help in shepherding a "rookie" like me through the somewhat intimidating process of writing a book, and to Heather Mitchener, editorial director, and Carole Honeychurch, senior editor, for their useful suggestions in revising earlier drafts.

Finally, I would also like to express my appreciation to all of my clients who, while struggling with depression, have trusted me to serve as their therapist over the years. I can only hope that you have learned as much from me as I have from you.

CHAPTER 1

What Is ACT for Depression and What Makes It Unique?

Let's begin with the good news and bad news about depression. First, the bad news. Depression is widespread and appears to be on the rise. Often referred to as "the common cold" of psychological disorders (Pilgrim & Bentall, 1999), depression represents one of the most frequent outpatient psychiatric complaints (Mitchell, Pyle, & Hatsukami, 1983). Although it is expected to be surpassed by HIV/AIDS by 2030 (Mathers & Loncar, 2005), unipolar major depression presently ranks as the leading cause of disability worldwide among individuals over the age of four (Murray & Lopez, 1996). Current prevalence rates for major depression in this country (Kessler, Chiu, Demler, & Walters, 2005) are roughly twice as high for women (21.3 percent) as for men (12.7 percent) and appear to have been increasing steadily over the past half century (Seligman, 1990). Over this same time span, the median age of onset, now the late teens to early twenties, has become progressively lower (Kessler et al., 2003).

Not surprisingly, the calculable financial and human costs of depression also appear to be accelerating. Major depression is estimated to cost businesses in the United States $70 billion annually in lost productivity among affected employees and in health care and related expenses (Tanouye, 2001). Additionally, depression may contribute to employee turnover and attrition. The financial costs, however, pale in the light of the incalculable human costs of depression—the loss of personal vitality and viability; the strain on personal, familial, and professional relationships; and the very real possible loss of life itself, as about 15 percent of individuals who have been diagnosed with major depression will commit suicide (Maris, Maltsberger, & Yufit, 1992).

In contrast to this sobering backdrop of bad news, however, is some good news. In particular, depression appears to be one of the more readily "treatable" of all psychological disorders. At least three psychological approaches to treatment of depression—cognitive therapy (Beck, Rush, Shaw, & Emery, 1979), interpersonal therapy (Klerman, Weissman, Rounsaville, & Chevron, 1984), and behavioral activation (Jacobson et al., 1996; Jacobson, Martell, & Dimidjian, 2001)—have been recognized as interventions with "well-established" empirical support for their efficacy based upon favorable research findings (Chambless et al., 1996, 1998; Task Force, 1995) comparing them with antidepressant medication (Antonuccio, Danton, & DeNelsky, 1995; Antonuccio, Thomas, & Danton, 1997), alternative psychological approaches, and/or attention-placebo conditions (in which clients are merely afforded the opportunity to talk about their depression with an empathetic therapist). Although not as thoroughly investigated, two other therapeutic approaches that are generally construed as cognitive behavioral in their focus—psycho-educational programs (Lewinsohn, Hoberman, & Clarke, 1989) and the incorporation of mindfulness-based components within cognitive therapy (Segal, Williams, & Teasdale, 2002)—have also enjoyed empirical support in the alleviation of depression and/or prevention of its reoccurrence.

Purpose of This Book

This book presents yet another treatment option, acceptance and commitment therapy or ACT (pronounced as one word, "act," not A-C-T) for addressing varied forms of human suffering, including depression (Hayes, Strosahl, & Wilson, 1999). While ACT, which has been developed over the past twenty to twenty-five years (Zettle, 2005), can be thought of as a collection of related treatment techniques, I believe it is much more useful to view it as an overarching approach in which a wide array of therapeutic techniques, procedures, and exercises are embedded—some of which have been uniquely developed, while others have been borrowed from other psychotherapeutic approaches and traditions.

Although ACT incorporates some techniques that are not usually associated with behavior therapy, it is typically regarded as part of the "third" or "new wave" of interventions within behavior therapy (Hayes, 2004). (For more on the three waves of interventions, see Overview of ACT below.) This third wave also includes mindfulness-based cognitive therapy (MBCT) as well as related approaches, such as dialectical behavior therapy (Linehan, 1993a), functional analytic psychotherapy (Kohlenberg & Tsai, 1991), and integrative behavioral couples therapy (Jacobson & Christensen, 1996). Before providing an overview of ACT and a discussion of what distinguishes it from other cognitive behavioral approaches to the treatment of depression, I would like to offer a few comments about the intended audience and purpose of this book.

This book is primarily written for mental health professionals who are interested in better familiarizing themselves with ACT and, more specifically, for those counselors and therapists specializing in the treatment of unipolar depression who would like to expand their clinical practice to include ACT. To a lesser degree, I also hope that members of the general public who know all too well what it is like to struggle with depression may find the book personally useful, especially when combined with the recent self-help book of Hayes and Smith (2005) based upon ACT principles. While chapter-length overview presentations of brief ACT for depression (Zettle & Hayes, 2002) and practical guidelines for its implementation have appeared in print (Zettle, 2004) previously, this book is the first to combine a conceptual explication of how ACT for depression both resembles and differs from other empirically supported cognitive behavioral approaches to depression (such as cognitive therapy, behavioral activation, and MBCT) with a more extensive detailing of how the actual application and implementation of ACT differs from them as well. As such, I seek to address the dual goals of not only how to think about ACT for depression but, more importantly, how to do it as well. With its greater focus on how to implement ACT, I intend this book to supplement rather than replace earlier publications about ACT in treatment of depression. Because of its explicit focus on depression, this book is also not meant to serve as a substitute for the original ACT text (Hayes et al., 1999), which provides much more extensive and detailed attention to the philosophical and theoretical foundations of the approach than I will offer here.

A Case-Conceptualization Approach

Those of you familiar with Eifert and Forsyth's (2005) work in applying ACT to anxiety disorders will notice significant overlap with this book, particularly in the first two chapters, which present an overview of ACT and its guiding principles. However, the manner in which practical guidelines subsequently are organized and structured across the two books differs to a considerable degree. This is not to suggest nor imply that one approach is better in any sense of the term than the other. As you will see, the overriding goal of ACT is to increase *psychological flexibility*, or the ability to freely choose various ways of leading a vital and valued life, and it is as applicable to the behavior of those of us who practice it as it is to that of our clients. You should not be surprised, then, that in staying true to this objective, there may be multiple ways in which to conduct ACT effectively. Whether or not this, indeed, turns out to be the case, is an empirical question that has yet to be investigated. My recommendation here that ACT be applied flexibly and in a nonlinear rather than sequential fashion is based more on personal preference, values, and associated philosophical grounds than on scientific findings.

Many of the practical suggestions offered by Eifert and Forsyth (2005) in applying ACT to anxiety disorders are sequenced on a session-by-session basis. By contrast, practical guidelines in this book are organized more conceptually around the six core processes (the "hexaflex") that comprise a model of psychopathology according to ACT (Hayes, Strosahl, Bunting, Twohig, & Wilson, 2004) and the associated therapeutic strategies that target them (Strosahl, Hayes, Wilson, & Gifford, 2004). While a prototypical sequence of how ACT techniques and components may be applied in treatment of depression will be offered in chapter 9, a *case-conceptualization approach* that is linked back to how the core pathogenic processes may contribute in different ways to the depression of each client (Hayes, Strosahl, Luoma, Smith, & Wilson, 2004) initially will be presented to guide the selection and administration of associated treatment techniques and strategies.

Scope and Focus of This Book

I should point out that the scope of this book is limited to the application of ACT-consistent principles and techniques to the conceptualization, assessment, and treatment of unipolar depression. Specifically, we will not extend ACT to the treatment of depressive episodes within cases of bipolar disorder for at least two reasons. First, skill in conducting ACT is more readily acquired by doing it rather than merely reading about how to do it, and I have no clinical experience in applying ACT to the treatment of depressive episodes within cases of bipolar disorder. Second, no published reports of treating bipolar depression with ACT exist at this time.

Strictly speaking, it is more appropriate to view the focus of this book as the application of ACT in working with clients who offer unipolar depression as a presenting problem rather than as a directive on how to "treat" depression with ACT. As you will see, the agenda of ACT is not so much to treat depression so that clients who experience it can begin to live without it, as it is to enable clients to become liberated enough from their struggles with depression to begin to lead meaningful and vibrant lives with it. Levels of depression have been shown to decrease when this occurs (Zettle & Hayes, 1986; Zettle & Rains, 1989), even though increasing psychological flexibility in order to lead a more valued life, and not symptom reduction, is the primary therapeutic goal of ACT.

Because depression exhibits high rates of comorbidity with other psychological problems, particularly anxiety disorders (Mineka, Watson, & Clark, 1998), clients who seek treatment of depression often have other psychological concerns that also may be addressed by the application of a transdiagnostic approach such as ACT that targets common processes that may account for co-occurring forms of human suffering. Regarding depression or any other problem in living as a "thing to be treated" borders on reification and is antithetical to the ACT-perspective of viewing any psychological event as a dynamic, ongoing act-in-context. Moreover, holding depression as an entity may contribute to client fusion with a damaged conceptualized self (such as, "I *am* depressed"). It also furthers the structural/topographical (versus functional) approach embodied by the current diagnostic system (*Diagnostic and statistical manual of mental disorders* [4th ed.]; American Psychiatric Association, 1994) of which high rates of comorbidity are an ostensible artifact (Achenbach, 1990–1991). However, to be consistent with the syndromal approach of the *DSM*, books like this one, research literature, and psychiatric databases are, of necessity, organized around diagnostic categories and, as a matter of convenience, I will consequently frequently use the phrase "treatment of depression," despite my personal qualms in doing so.

Overview of ACT

Within a broader historical context, as I mentioned previously, ACT can be regarded as a member of the "third wave," or generation, of cognitive behavioral therapies. I will only offer a summary of the generational changes within behavior therapy here. If interested, please consult Hayes (2004) for a more detailed account of these issues.

The First Wave of Behavior Therapy

The first generation of behavior therapy, which can be dated as far back as the 1920s (Jones, 1924), sought to modify problematic behavior by the application of basic principles of classical/respondent conditioning à la Pavlov (for instance, Wolpe, 1958) and/or operant conditioning, in which behavior change is linked to reinforcing consequences (for example, Baer, Wolf, & Risley, 1968). The potential contribution that language and cognition played in the initiation, maintenance, exacerbation, and alleviation of abnormal behavior (particularly among verbally skilled adults) could be acknowledged, while at the same time it could be largely ignored as long as the problems being treated were either conceptualized as classically conditioned (such as specific phobias) or, if operantly conditioned, were exhibited by populations with developmental disabilities (such as autism and/or mental retardation) that displayed limited verbal abilities.

The Second Wave of Behavior Therapy

As the first wave of behavior therapy matured and extended to a wider array of clinical populations with more diverse presenting problems, the need to somehow incorporate language-based processes within behavior therapy became more obvious. In the 1970s, cognitive therapy emerged (see A. T. Beck, 1976, for example) as a distinct approach in response to this challenge along with related efforts to create a cognitive behavioral modification/therapy hybrid by combining purported cognitively based processes and techniques, such as use of coping self-statements (for example, "If I take things one at a time, I can avoid feeling overwhelmed"), with existing respondent and operant conditioning principles and strategies (Mahoney, 1974; Meichenbaum, 1977).

Despite clear technical and some conceptual differences between the first and second waves of behavior therapy, they nevertheless shared a common objective of focusing on what can be regarded as a strategy of *first-order change*, that is, attempting to alter the form, frequency, and or content of abnormal behavior. Consistent with this agenda, the first wave of behavior therapy primarily emphasized the use of either respondent or operant conditioning principles to directly modify emotional reactions, à la systematic desensitization, or deficits (such as in skills of daily living) and excesses of motor behavior (like self-injurious and self-stimulatory behaviors) as in applied behavior analysis. The second wave in essence merely included cognition, whether in the form of irrational beliefs, negative self-talk, dysfunctional attitudes, depressogenic attributions, or schemata as another type of behavior, or third response mode, that could also be targeted successfully by first-order change techniques. In particular, restructuring procedures became a preferred strategy for altering personal beliefs (such as "I'm incompetent") that depressed clients might have about themselves.

The Third Wave of Behavior Therapy

By the start of the new millennium, empirical shortcomings as well as philosophical reservations about the second wave of behavior therapy gave rise to ACT and other third-generation approaches emphasizing a *second-order change* agenda in which focus is shifted away from altering the form or content of abnormal behavior to the context in which it occurs. In particular, by the late 1990s, findings from both process and component analyses of cognitive behavioral therapies raised legitimate questions about whether or not second-wave approaches worked in the way they were said to work (Ilardi & Craighead, 1994) and if the purported cognitive-change techniques they incorporated were even essential for their therapeutic success (Gortner, Gollan, Dobson, & Jacobson, 1998; Jacobson et al., 1996; Zettle & Hayes, 1987). In addition, philosophically, *contextualism*, or the view that abnormal behavior is most usefully understood within the situational and historical backdrop in which it occurs, in general (Hayes, Hayes, Reese, & Sarbin, 1993), and *functional contextualism,* which emphasizes the pragmatic goals of influencing behavior change, more specifically (Biglan & Hayes, 1996; Hayes, Hayes, & Reese, 1988), concurrently began to be increasingly recognized and offered as an alternative to the mechanistic worldview in which both the first and second waves of behavior therapy were grounded. In contrast to functional contextualism, a mechanistic wordview is more concerned with the ability to predict abnormal behavior from psychological models and theories of it than with how to effectively prevent and/or modify it (Hayes & Brownstein, 1986).

ACT and Second-Order Change

Although perhaps somewhat open to debate, the overriding commonality that unites ACT with other behavior therapeutic interventions of its generation is a shared emphasis on a second-order, contextualistic approach to therapeutic change. Specifically, as applied to the treatment of depression, the goal of contextualistic approaches is not to change dysfunctional beliefs (for instance, "I can't do anything right") by altering their content or form (for example, "I can at least do some things right") through the application of disputational and/or cognitive restructuring strategies, although there is strong evidence to suggest that instances of clients believing their own depressing thoughts does plummet with ACT (Zettle & Hayes, 1986). Nor is it the goal of ACT to instigate changes in overt behavior, such as increasing pleasurable activities, for the purposes of regulating mood and/or restructuring ways of thinking, although it certainly actively supports behavioral change that moves clients in valued life directions. Rather than targeting the form or frequency of particular psychological components of depression, ACT pursues the second-order change agenda of altering the functions that they serve by going outside of "the system" in which they normally operate. From this perspective, the "problem" with depression is not so much dysphoric mood or depressive thoughts themselves, but the contexts that link such private events into an overall pattern of ineffective living. For example, if the system of contexts that supports holding thoughts, feelings, and other private events as causes for overt behavior can be weakened, it may be unnecessary to change or alter them for depressed individuals to become unstuck and move forward in life. For instance, clients may claim that they could go ahead and make valued changes in their lives like switching careers or going back to school if they felt more self-confident. Rather than trying to instill self-confidence, the Acceptance and Commitment therapist questions the usefulness of this formulation by perhaps asking whether it would be possible for such clients to make the contemplated life changes *and* lack confidence that it would work out for them. In short, ACT suggests the real possibility of being able to transform the functions that private events, such as sadness and pessimistic thoughts, serve by altering the broader context within which depression occurs. Unfortunately, as we will see, many of the contextual factors to be altered are both ubiquitous and social-verbal in nature due to the functional properties of human language and cognition.

Relational Frame Theory and ACT

ACT is certainly not the only approach to behavior therapy to argue that we need to better understand the roles that cognitive processes and language play in human suffering and its alleviation if we are to improve upon our ability to serve our clients. As already discussed, similar recognition of this limitation served as the impetus for cognitive therapy and related second-wave interventions. What, however, sets ACT apart not only from cognitive therapy but other third-wave approaches as well is its linkage to relational frame theory (RFT; Hayes, Barnes-Holmes, & Roche, 2001). RFT approaches human language and cognition from the perspective of functional contextualism and emphasizes the situational factors in which thinking develops as well as how potentially to change the impact that it exerts on other areas of psychological functioning.

It is beyond the scope and purpose of this book to provide more than a historical overview and summary of RFT and offer a few examples of its extension to depression. If you are interested in knowing more, consult the Hayes et al. (2001) text for further details on RFT more generally and the chapter within it by Wilson, Hayes, Gregg, and Zettle (2001) in particular for more on its application to clinical psychological issues. In large measure, RFT emerged in reaction to some of the shortcomings of Skinner's (1957) original effort to provide a contextualistic account of verbal behavior. Perhaps foremost among these was Skinner's predominant focus on human language from the perspective of the speaker. Relatively neglected was listening and, more specifically, an analysis of when both speaking and listening occur with the "same skin" (that is, self-talk or thinking). Even though Skinner's book was published during the same time period that the first wave of behavior therapy was beginning to emerge, it is not surprising in retrospect that his account of verbal behavior had no discernible impact on it.

Cognitive models and theories of depression and other disorders (A. T. Beck, 1976; Beck & Emery, 1985) that accompanied and supported the second generation of cognitive behavioral therapies attempted to more adequately address the role of thinking in human psychopathology. However, as already discussed, such accounts, for both empirical and philosophical reasons, were ultimately also seen as wanting. Perhaps one useful way to think of RFT is that it represents an attempt to address the limitations of both Skinnerian and Beckian approaches to human language and cognition while also maintaining their respective strengths. Specifically, the scope and depth of cognitive/language-based phenomena and processes that RFT seeks to account for subsume those addressed by models offered in support of cognitive therapy, but, like Skinner's approach to verbal behavior, it does so from a contextualistic rather than mechanistic perspective (Pepper, 1942). Perhaps most importantly as we will see, the use of language or relational framing is conceptualized like any operant behavior to be influenced by the contexts in which it occurs and develops. This is in contrast to mechanistic accounts that typically attribute language development to an acquisition device (Chomsky, 1965) or other innate, mentalistic entities.

Nature of Relational Framing

RFT fundamentally holds that human language and cognition are based on relational frames. Although I personally prefer the gerund form, "relational framing," to underscore that behavior is being talked about, for convenience, I will use the more common noun form, *relational frame*. Think of a *relational frame* as responding to stimuli based upon arbitrary relationships that are drawn between them. For example, there is no natural relationship between saying the word "ball" in the presence of certain spheroid objects. Rather, the relationship between the two must be arbitrarily established but is itself under contextual control as the word "ball" can also be used in speaking about a type of party.

The behavior involved in forming relational frames entails responding to one stimulus based on its relation to another stimulus or stimuli. For example, in teaching the concept of "bigger" to a child, a golf ball, baseball, and basketball might be arranged in various pairs with the child asked to point to the "bigger" object on each trial. After experiencing this several times—whether deliberately instigated or occuring more spontaneously and naturally—the child learns to respond "relationally" based upon the relative size of comparable objects, or "stimuli." Infrahuman organisms such as apes, rats, and pigeons also demonstrate a similar capacity (Reese, 1968). What has not been shown in nonverbal organisms (either infrahumans or human subjects that lack language), however, is the ability to then take such relational responding and place it under arbitrary contextual control. For instance, when shown a penny, a nickel, and a dime and asked to point to the "bigger" coin, a young child may reliably point to the nickel when it is paired with either the dime or the penny. An older child with a history of spending money, however, is more apt to respond to the coins on the basis of their monetary value (in that the dime is "bigger" in value than the nickel and the penny, although it is physically smaller than the former and of the same approximate size as the latter) rather than simply their size.

According to RFT, this type of relational responding ("bigger") can itself be regarded as part of a larger functional response class of comparative framing—that is, more and more objects can be compared on the basis of their size, of one item being "bigger" than another. As such, not only can inanimate objects be compared relationally with each other, but so can human beings. This may be done by size—"He's bigger than I am"—or by other relative valuations such as "Everybody else is better than I am." Not only are such evaluations expected according to RFT, they are virtually inevitable once comparative framing is up and running. One way to respond to such a negative self-evaluation—"Everybody else is better than I am"—is to rationally weigh the evidence both for and against it as, for example, might be done in cognitive therapy. An alternative approach, according to ACT, is to not challenge the veracity of the thought, but to merely recognize it for what is (an evaluation) rather than what it appears to be (an objective, albeit erroneous description that must be disputed and corrected).

Properties of Relational Framing

By definition, all relational framing exhibits three properties or features that have been implied thus far: mutual entailment, combinatorial entailment, and transformation of stimulus functions. Let's look at each of these more closely because each can play a role in depression.

Mutual Entailment

The first property of relational framing is *mutual entailment* or *bidirectionality*. To illustrate this property, let's return to the example of the child with the golf ball, baseball, and basketball. If, in a particular context (e.g., in the backyard with Mom and Dad), the child learns that the golf ball relates in a particular way to the baseball, then this must also "entail" some kind of relation between the baseball and the golf ball. So, if the baseball is bigger than the golf ball, then the golf ball must be smaller than the baseball. This is mutual entailment or bidirectionality—that is, the relation between the golf ball and the baseball is mutual; it goes in both directions. A common type of mutual entailment that occurs in depression, which we will discuss more extensively in chapter 2, arises from negative self-evaluations. For example, the statement "I am worthless" places "I" and "worthless" in a relational frame with each other such that "I" = "worthless" and "worthless" = "I."

Naming represents perhaps the simplest frame of coordination with the name of an object participating in a *frame of coordination* (or *equivalence*) with the referent or object itself (for instance, "This is a book"). Coordination is a relational frame that establishes identity or functional similarity between the two stimuli involved. The name of the object is "book," but the name is not literally the same as the object itself. The word "book" participates in a frame of coordination with the actual book—the object with a cover and pages, the object to which the name "book" refers. As I just suggested, a particularly psychologically damaging type of relational framing that occurs in depression involves making negative self-referential pronouncements (for example, "I'm stupid"). Even the affective impact of a formulation such as "I'm depressed" would be expected to be amplified, that is, negatively intensified, from an RFT perspective because of the *relational networks*, that is, relations among relations, that contribute to the verbal construction of emotions.

As Skinner (1953, chap. 17; 1974, chap. 2) has speculated, the use of a number of emotional terms and labels such as "depression" may have arisen as metaphorical extensions. The bodily sensation of being "weighed down" experienced in psychological depression may be quite similar to that experienced when a direct physical force or pressure is exerted, as when one is being held down by another person. Through bidirectionality and the transfer of stimulus functions, the thought "I'm depressed" may carry with it the same heavy, encumbered sensations encountered under physical restraint. The term "stimulus functions" as it is being used here denotes that some of the feelings of being "weighed down" elicited by the word "depressed" are transferred to the self when it is described as "depressed."

Combinatorial Entailment

The second property or feature that defines relational framing is *combinatorial entailment*, which basically means that objects that have been individually "entailed" (that is, related) to each other (as illustrated with the golf ball, baseball, and basketball above), may be combined (or compared) in new ways. Within a given context, if you learn that A relates to B in a certain way, and B relates to C in a certain way, then—in this particular context—A must also relate to C in a certain way. Let's go back to the golf ball, baseball, and basketball. If the golf ball (A) is smaller than the baseball (B), and the baseball is smaller than the basketball (C), then we know that the golf ball (A) is also smaller than the basketball (C). When we look at combinatorial entailment in depression, we see how clients who compare themselves to others may, through the process of combinatorial entailment, construct an inferior self-concept. For instance, "John has his life together better than I do," "Mary has her life together better than John does," and therefore "Mary is yet another person who has her life together better than I do."

Transformation of Stimulus Functions

The third and final defining property of relational framing is that it enables the *transformation of stimulus functions*. Accordingly, a change or alteration in the function of one of the stimuli that participates in a frame of coordination will result in that same stimulus function being transferred to other stimuli within the frame. Recall that naming is a common form of coordinational framing, so let's say that I acquired a terrible fear of medium- to large-sized dogs after being viciously bitten by a Rottweiler. Then, for example, the mere word "Rottweiler" may send me into an emotional tailspin quite similar to what I'd experience if I actually ran into a Rottweiler on the street. That's an example of the transformation of stimulus functions. Moreover, because Rottweilers also may participate in a frame of coordination with other similarly sized dogs, my conditioned emotional reaction may also be extended to other canine breeds—both seeing them as well as hearing their names—such as Weimaraners, Dobermans, and German shepherds. Likewise, in depression, reminders of a personal loss such as the death of a loved one or a divorce may be avoided—by, for example, turning off a radio when what was once "our song" begins to play—to preclude reexperiencing the transformed emotional pain. Unfortunately such reminders can include thoughts, images, memories, and other psychological experiences that we cannot turn off or from which we cannot successfully run away. Note that such experiences cannot be readily explained by a simple appeal to classical conditioning (Dougher, Hamilton, Fink, & Harrington, in press). When the relationship was alive and well, hearing "our song" likely elicited a positive emotional reaction. Now that the relationship no longer exists, the stimulus function of the song has been transformed dramatically into something negative and painful.

The Goal of ACT: Psychological Flexibility

The ultimate goal of ACT in working with clients with depression, as mentioned earlier, is not to eliminate their depression. Rather, it is the promotion of psychological flexibility, which, according to Hayes, Strosahl, Luoma, et al. (2004),

> … involves the ability to defuse from provocative or evocative private content, accept private experience for what it is, stay in touch with the present moment, differentiate a transcendent self from the contents of consciousness, make contact with valued life ends and build patterns of committed action in pursuit of those ends. (p. 60)

Core Processes That Contribute to Psychological Flexibility

The six core processes that contribute to psychological flexibility (the hexaflex, see figure below) according to ACT are:

- Self as context

- Defusion

- Acceptance

- Contact with the present moment

- Values

- Committed action

Conversely, each of the six core positive processes also entails a corresponding, opposing, pathogenic process—for example, fusion opposes defusion, experiential avoidance opposes acceptance, and so on—that contributes to psychopathology, human suffering, and other manifestations of psychological inflexibility. The two sets of core processes can be usefully thought of as representing end points along six continuous dimensions. However, as we will see, the mere absence of a pathogenic process, such as experiential avoidance, does not ensure that the countervailing positive process (in this case, acceptance) will flourish. As we further consider the two sets of opposing processes throughout this book, sometimes we will find it more useful to emphasize the positive ones and at other times to stress their pathogenic counterparts. This is because the objective of ACT is not only to weaken the processes that contribute to psychological rigidity, but also to strengthen the positive ones that support psychological flexibility.

Before further fleshing out the hexaflex model, a few more comments about the goal of psychological flexibility and how ACT approaches it more globally may be useful. Psychological flexibility/inflexibility fundamentally relate to an expansion versus narrowing of a behavioral repertoire. However, because psychological flexibility, and by extension its flip side (psychological inflexibility), is defined functionally, it can assume varied forms. Depending on the context, psychological flexibility may entail the generation and implementation of varied responses in the face of a given problem or obstacle as might

Core Processes that Contribute to Psychological Flexibility

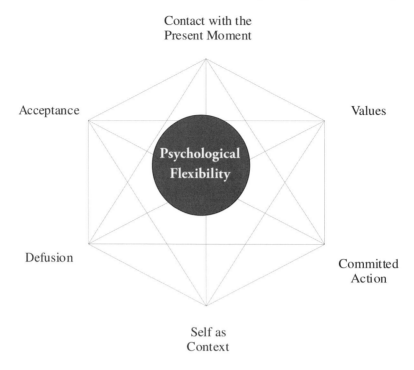

occur in brainstorming. Accordingly, when clients are stuck, it may be useful to ask, "Is there any other way you can respond to X?" However, there may be other situations in which psychological flexibility must take the somewhat stereotypical form of persistently placing one foot in front of the other to move in a valued direction (such as in writing this book).

Acceptance and Commitment as Superordinate Processes

The formal name of ACT itself—acceptance and commitment therapy—denotes the two superordinate processes that foster psychological flexibility and subsume the six subordinate positive processes within the hexaflex model. Consistent with RFT, the name per se also implies the opposing effects that human language can have on psychological flexibility. If I may be granted a license to mix metaphors here, human language according to RFT is a two-edged sword with both a "dark side" and a "light side." The overarching purpose of ACT is to minimize the life-draining, repertoire-narrowing effects of language's "dark side" while simultaneously maximizing the vitalizing, repertoire-expanding impact from its "light side." By relational framing, we humans may create a dreaded future that is even more depressing than what life hands us in the here and now. However, through language, we can also formulate and follow plans that allow us to approach our long-held hopes and dreams in the face of adversity, and by doing so, provide value and meaning to our lives. We can't live without language and relational framing. A central challenge faced by ACT is that of how to live fully *with* them.

Acceptance is the opposite of the deliberate efforts of experiential avoidance to alter the form or frequency of certain private experiences—such as unwanted thoughts, feelings, bodily sensations, memories, images, and the like—or the circumstances in which they occur. Acceptance counteracts language's self-destructive aspects, or "dark side," and encompasses the abandonment of deliberate, verbally mediated efforts to control dysphoric mood, self-deprecating thoughts, suicidal urges, and other unwanted psychological experiences that are part of clinical depression. (The term "acceptance" being used here to denote the superordinate process reflected in ACT's title differs from "acceptance" as one of the six positive and subordinate processes within the hexaflex that contribute to psychological flexibility. Acceptance as a superordinate process not only subsumes "acceptance" as a subordinate process, but also the positive processes of defusion, mindfulness, and self as context.)

Commitment, by contrast, embraces the beneficial dimensions of human language through valuing and the intentional pursuit of courses of action consistent with and directed by personal, verbally construed values. In representing the "light side" of human language, commitment as a superordinate process subsumes both committed action and values within the hexaflex. The order of the two terms in ACT is perhaps not coincidental. Acceptance is not a goal in its own right, but is practiced in the service of commitment to leading a valued life. Acceptance without commitment is a shallow victory, and commitment is not sustainable without acceptance.

The "Dark Side" of Human Language

Let's look more closely now at the core pathogenic processes that support depression through their contributions to the "dark side" of language. What have been collectively referred to in ACT as "mindfulness and acceptance processes" (Hayes, Strosahl, Bunting, et al., 2004) are designed to undermine the ways in which language contributes to psychological inflexibility. We will discuss each of the negative psychological processes involved in turn, with the opposing processes that support psychological flexibility and which ACT seeks to strengthen denoted parenthetically.

Fusion (vs. Defusion)

Fusion refers to the domination of stimulus functions derived from relational frames over behavioral regulation arising from contact with direct contingencies (for instance, responding to the meaning of words rather than merely to how they sound). In short, evaluations and other verbal constructions of the self as well as the world outside of ourselves become melded or fused with direct experiences to such a degree that the psychological impact of such language-based processes overshadows those that are experientially based. Our minds effectively trump our direct experience so that our experience becomes not whatever is being directly contacted in the present moment, but that which our words have built. For example, I may respond to the self-evaluation "I'm stupid" as if it were a factual description (not unlike that of "I'm sitting") rather than recognizing and simply acknowledging it as the mere by-product of a relational process (that is, "I notice that I have the thought that I'm stupid"). Stated somewhat differently, the negative self-evaluation is treated as a given and is "bought into," leaving little wiggle room for psychological flexibility and alternative ways to respond to it.

The positive core process that counters fusion is defusion. Defined most broadly, *defusion* expands a behavioral repertoire by responding in any alternative manner to fused material.

Those of you familiar with cognitive therapy may recognize fusion as somewhat similar to what is often referred to as "emotional reasoning" (Burns, 1980, p. 46). The mere presence of an emotional reaction is taken as evidence of its truthfulness (such as "I must be stupid because I feel stupid"). However, ACT goes considerably further than cognitive therapy in recognizing that fusion is not limited to emotional reactions or moods. It can also encompass verbally accessible thoughts, images, impulses, memories, and other private events as well as other larger verbal constructions such as reason giving and the telling of one's life story. Moreover, ACT also suggests, even when applied to thinking alone, that there are strategies other than cognitive restructuring that may provide more direct and efficient means of defusion.

Experiential Avoidance (vs. Acceptance)

Fusion sets the stage for experiential avoidance. Through the bidirectional and transformation-of-stimulus function properties of relational framing, merely thinking about a depressing sequence of events, such as those surrounding the loss of a loved one, may exert the same emotional punch as occurred when, for example, the loved one died. As a consequence, we may attempt to not only actively suppress or avoid thinking about the loss, but also avoid placing ourselves in situations that would remind us about it, such as being in the company of friends or acquaintances who may raise it as a topic of conversation. Occasionally experiential avoidance is quite useful, at least in the short term. Unfortunately it typically does not appear to work in the long run; it limits psychological flexibility, takes time and energy away from leading a valued life, and generates what is commonly referred to in ACT as "dirty pain." *Dirty pain*, which will be discussed more fully in chapter 2, is the emotional distress and discomfort that results from unsuccessful attempts to control unwanted psychological experiences. Acceptance—not as passive toleration or resignation but as an active, freely chosen process—is offered as an alternative to experiential avoidance. Because "acceptance" is often interpreted by clients as toleration or resignation, you will often find it helpful to use the term "willingness" instead. *Willingness* is not a feeling and it is not the same as "wanting." Rather it refers to the act of actively choosing to experience unwanted psychological events without attempting to control them.

Rumination (vs. Contact with the Present Moment)

While we will cover the possible role that rumination plays in the maintenance and exacerbation of depression at some length in the next chapter, I want to make a few comments about its overall negative impact in limiting psychological flexibility here.

Rumination most simply refers to the process of living in (fusion with) a verbally constructed past and/or future rather than functioning psychologically in the here and now. Past transgressions, missed opportunities, and personal shortcomings may be continually mulled over and replayed (for instance, "If I had treated my husband better, maybe he wouldn't have left me"), while ways of avoiding an equally unappealing future may be contemplated (for example, "Maybe if I can figure out why I feel this way, I'll find a way out"). In some respects, rumination bears some resemblance to problem solving, but, unlike problem solving, it largely serves to narrow psychological flexibility and is incompatible with making contact with the present moment. The problems can't be solved because they either exist in the past or haven't yet occurred.

Attachment to a Damaged Conceptualized Self (vs. Self as Context)

Not only does our own language construct a conceptualized past and future, but it also builds and maintains a sense of who we are. In the case of depression, unfortunately, negative conceptualizations about the self (for example, "I am depressed," "I am a person who always seems to screw things up," and so on) abound and may be rigidly defended. When we form a strong identity with a conceptualized self through frames of coordination (for instance, "me = incompetent" and "incompetent = me"), we may respond to the efforts of others (including therapists), as well as outside direct experiences that might challenge such a formulation, as if our very sense of physical well-being is under attack. As Hayes et al. (1999, p. 182) have suggested, if "me = conceptualization," "eliminate conceptualization = eliminate me" and even attempts to forge a more positive self-concept may be actively resisted. As will be seen, the goal of ACT is to facilitate defusion from the conceptualized self rather than directly alter its content by, for instance, attempting to convince depressed clients that they really are competent through the use of disputational strategies and/or behavioral homework. Additionally, an alternative contentless and transcendent sense of self as context is fostered to provide a nonthreatened perspective from which the content of one's life, including that of the conceptualized self itself, may be viewed and responded to in a psychologically flexible manner.

The "Light Side" of Human Language

We'll now take a closer look at the two core processes that embody the "light side" of human language and which ACT seeks to further strengthen. What have been viewed in the aggregate within ACT as "commitment and behavior change processes" (Hayes, Strosahl, Bunting, et al., 2004) are in the service of bolstering how language supports psychological flexibility. Contact with the present moment and self as context, both of which have already been discussed as participating in mindfulness and acceptance processes, may also be regarded as components of the superordinate process of commitment and behavior change (Hayes, Luoma, Bond, Masuda, & Lillis, 2006) but will not be expanded upon in what follows.

Valuing

Within ACT, *values* are defined as "verbally construed global life consequences" (Hayes et al., 1999, p. 206). Clients often seek treatment for depression because their depression itself is held as an obstacle or barrier to the fulfillment of values. For example, a recent client stated, "If I weren't so depressed, I could be a better grandmother." Such a statement suggests a type of valuing that can help in the identification of related goals and commitment to value-directed courses of action (for instance, "Are there goals you can shoot for right now—without having to wait for your depression to go away—that would move you in the direction of being a better grandmother?"). The number of core values for each client may be rather limited, but each may be approached through a myriad of goals, thereby increasing psychological flexibility. If necessary, active efforts can be undertaken to uncover values that may have gone unrecognized (quite likely reflecting a type of experiential avoidance) for some period of time by challenging clients to articulate what they want their life to stand for. Because the immediate contingencies surrounding behavior often support dysfunctional actions and passivity (for example, staying home alone vs. taking the grandchildren to the zoo), temporally framing values may come to control more functional behavioral changes that unfold as part of an ongoing process (for instance, investing a modest amount of money today to help fund a grandchild's future college expenses). In short, values may function much like a lighthouse beacon in providing not only an orienting point but also in illuminating pathways to take when approaching it.

Committed Action

Once values have been identified and clarified, rules that specify related goals and the behavior necessary to attain them can be formulated and followed. Changes in overt behavior, provided they are linked to and directed by values, play an important role in ACT. Merely changing behavior for the sake of doing so or as a means of cognitive restructuring are not priorities in ACT. Goals that vary across a temporal dimension serve as the links between values and committed courses of action. Values are not things or objects that can be obtained or acquired, but goals can be. Plans and other types of verbal constructions can then be formulated that move goal-seeking behavior in a valued direction. "Being a loving grandmother," for example, is not a goal but a value. Taking the grandchildren to the zoo tomorrow and accumulating a fund to help cover their costs of attending college constitute short- and more long-term goals respectively and move client behavior in a valued direction. Psychological flexibility is increased as a given value, and related goals could be linked to an almost unlimited number of specific behaviors (for example, "In how many different ways could you be a loving grandmother?").

What Makes ACT Unique?

In some ways, we have already addressed this question to a considerable degree. Another way to underscore the unique features of ACT is to compare it to and contrast it with cognitive therapy, MBCT, and behavioral activation as alternative, broadly defined cognitive behavioral approaches to the treatment of depression.

Cognitive Therapy

Cognitive therapy is the only approach of the three against which the relative efficacy of ACT has been compared directly thus far.

Outcome Research

In an initial comparative outcome study, eighteen depressed women were randomly assigned to receive twelve weekly sessions of either cognitive therapy or an early version of ACT (Zettle & Hayes, 1986). Participants in both conditions improved significantly from pretreatment through a two-month follow-up period, although those receiving ACT were judged by a blind, independent evaluator using the Hamilton Rating Scale for Depression (Hamilton, 1960) to be significantly less depressed at follow-up. A second randomized clinical trial, however, detected no differences in the efficacy of two variants of cognitive therapy and ACT when both were delivered in a group format (Zettle & Rains, 1989), suggesting that the therapeutic impact of ACT in treatment of depression may be attenuated when it is not individually administered.

Process Research

While the existing, albeit rather limited, research thus far suggests that the efficacy of ACT compares favorably to that of cognitive therapy, analyses of process measures from the two comparative outcome studies strongly suggest that the two interventions initiate therapeutic change through differing mechanisms. In the Zettle and Hayes (1986) study, participants completed the Automatic Thoughts Questionnaire (ATQ; Hollon & Kendall, 1980) at pretreatment, posttreatment, and follow-up as well as before each weekly therapy session. Because the ATQ assesses both the frequency and believability of depressing thoughts, it was possible to determine whether differential reductions in each varied as a function of treatment condition. Participants in both therapies reported significant, but equivalent, reductions in the frequency of negative thoughts across the course of the study.

A different pattern, and one consistent with ACT's emphasis in undermining experiential avoidance, was revealed by an analysis of ATQ believability scores. In particular, at posttreatment, ACT participants reported significantly greater reductions in their belief in negative thoughts than those who received cognitive therapy. In other words, ACT participants were not less likely than their cognitive therapy counterparts to report experiencing depressing thoughts, but were significantly less likely to believe them. Moreover, a recent reanalysis of the ATQ data (Hayes et al., 2006) further suggests that ACT effected therapeutic change through defusion as changes in the believability scores were determined to successfully meet all the requirements for mediating reductions in both self-reported and interviewer-related measures of depression among those treated with ACT (MacKinnon, 2003).

Additional evidence that ACT, unlike cognitive therapy, works by weakening verbal/social support for depression is offered by the findings from a reasons questionnaire also included as a process measure in the Zettle and Hayes (1986) study. To assess the possible supportive role of reason giving in dysfunctional behavior, participants initially were asked to provide separate reasons for overeating and being suicidal, and subsequently to rate "how good" each was. Reasons were reliably categorized by judges as either "internal," referring to private events as the cause of the dysfunctional behavior (such as "I felt hopeless") or "external," involving environmental events (for instance, "I got fired from my job"). Only ACT participants displayed a significant reduction in validity ratings for internal reasons from pretreatment through follow-up.

A final piece of evidence that suggests ACT and cognitive therapy operate through discrepant processes comes from the Zettle and Rains (1989) comparison. Only participants treated with cognitive therapy reported significant reductions from pretreatment through follow-up in their agreement with "depressogenic beliefs" as assessed by the Dysfunctional Attitude Scale (DAS; Weissman & Beck, 1978). At first glance, such findings appear to conflict with the analysis of ATQ believability scores but may be attributable to differing instructions in the two instruments. Although both measures ostensibly seek to assess the degree to which respondents believe (fuse with) depressing cognitive material, the ATQ does so by instructing participants to "indicate how strongly, if at all, you tend to believe that thought when it occurs," while the DAS asks them to denote how much they "agree or disagree" with each listed belief. It is entirely consistent with the model upon which ACT is based that successfully treated depressed clients might still agree with depressive beliefs provided that any dysfunctional control exerted by them is effectively weakened. In short, agreement with a depressive belief as assessed by the DAS may not reflect fusion with it. For example, a depressed client may still agree that "If I do not do well all the time, people will not respect me," but such a psychological event may no longer be avoided (for instance, "I'm willing to do what needs to be done to move forward in life *and* have the thought that people don't respect me"). At the very least, the differential DAS results further underscore the divergent mechanisms through which cognitive therapy and ACT apparently attain therapeutic change, especially when viewed in the context of additional research that has noted significant reductions in DAS scores when depression is successfully reduced through pharmacotherapy (Reda, Carpiniello, Secchiaroli, & Blanco, 1985; Simons, Garfield, & Murphy, 1984; Simons, Murphy, Levine, & Wetzel, 1986).

ACT and Cognitive Therapy

To summarize, although based on limited research, ACT appears similar to cognitive therapy in its impact on outpatient unipolar depression. In most other important respects, including the associated processes through which such an impact appears to unfold, clear distinctions can be drawn between the two approaches. Strategically, cognitive therapy pursues a mechanistic, first-order change agenda, while ACT emphasizes second-order change from a functional contextualistic perspective. The targets of change within cognitive therapy are dysfunctional beliefs and related distorted ways of thinking, whereas ACT does not elevate thoughts per se over other private events (such as mood, impulses, or bodily sensations) in seeking to alter the contexts in which they occur. Finally, clear tactical differences also distinguish ACT from cognitive therapy. In particular, restructuring techniques, such as the completion of dysfunctional thought records (Beck et al., 1979) are not used in ACT to initiate first-order change in cognitive variables to reduce dysphoric mood. Moreover, behavioral homework assignments are not employed for the purposes of cognitive restructuring and mood regulation, but occur in the service of increasing psychological flexibility by helping clients to regain contact with living a full and meaningful life.

Mindfulness-Based Cognitive Therapy

The primary commonality between MBCT and ACT is that both constitute second-order change approaches within the third wave or generation of cognitive behavioral therapies. Two factors appear to have been central in the development of MBCT (Segal et al., 2002). The first was the recognition that one of the challenges in dealing with depression is to effectively address relapse rates. At least half of those clients who are successfully treated for an initial episode of depression will relapse (Paykel, Ramana, Cooper, Hayhurst, Kerr, & Barocka, 1995), with each subsequent episode increasing the likelihood of depression's recurrence (Consensus Development Panel, 1985). The second factor critical to MBCT's development was the conclusion that the central change process within cognitive therapy is apparently not one of restructuring depressing thoughts but of enabling clients to distance themselves from them. Accordingly, as its name suggests, MBCT appropriately emphasizes meditation-like techniques and exercises in teaching clients to relate differently (mindfully) to their own depressing thoughts.

Role of Distancing/Decentering

"Distancing," or what has come to be more commonly referred to as "decentering" (Segal et al., 2002), can be viewed as a defusion process and consequently is not foreign to ACT. In fact, an earlier version of ACT was known as *comprehensive distancing* (see Zettle, 2005, 2006), following A. T. Beck's (1970) assertion that "distancing" is the "first, critical step" within cognitive therapy (Hollon & Beck, 1979, p. 189) that enables clients to respond to their negative thoughts as mere beliefs rather than facts. Despite their similarities, distinct strategic and tactical differences exist between MBCT and ACT. Perhaps most importantly, the developers of MBCT recommend that its strategic use be limited to preventing depression relapse and even speculate that its application to treatment of an initial, acute episode of depression would be ineffective (Segal et al., 2002, p. 318), favoring cognitive therapy instead. By extension, it seems reasonable to expect that they would also take issue with the premise of this book that the viability of ACT as a treatment option for current depression is sufficiently supported by existing research.

Because of tactical differences between MBCT and ACT, restricting the former to the prevention of depression relapse seems justifiable, although eventually subjecting this assumption to an empirical evaluation seems warranted. From the perspective of ACT, MBCT almost exclusively emphasizes the acceptance half of the approach—what were previously outlined as the mindfulness and acceptance processes integral to ACT—and does so with a more limited range of tactics than typically used in ACT. Relatively neglected by MBCT is the commitment dimension of ACT. The therapeutic component of increasing activities is not introduced until near the conclusion of the eight-session MBCT protocol offered by Segal and his colleagues (2002) and appears to be more in the service of mood regulation than being linked to and guided by values. ACT is similar to MBCT in likewise promoting mindfulness, but it goes beyond MBCT to also incorporate commitment and behavior-change processes as part of therapeutic change.

ACT and Mindfulness-Based Cognitive Therapy

To summarize, ACT shares the emphasis that MBCT places upon mindfulness and acceptance processes, although ACT uses a wider range of techniques and procedures in promoting them. However, ACT clearly places more weight than MBCT does in supporting committed behavior change as an integral part of therapy and any activity instigation is not used for the purpose of mood regulation. Because MBCT, unlike ACT, has not been recommended in treating initial presenting episodes of depression, the two approaches have never been directly compared.

Behavioral Activation

As a treatment for acute depression, behavioral activation (Dimidjian et al., 2006; Martell, Addis, & Dimidjian, 2004) in large measure represents a return to behavior therapy's roots (Ferster, 1973), stimulated by a component analysis of cognitive therapy that suggested that the behavioral homework assignments it incorporates account for cognitive therapy's efficacy (Jacobson et al., 1996). To a substantial degree, the relationship between behavioral activation and ACT is the mirror image of that between MBCT and ACT. Behavioral activation, like the commitment side of ACT, recognizes the therapeutic benefits of instigating changes in the activity levels of depressed clients. However, it does not include meditation practices or explicitly incorporate any other treatment components that directly address the mindfulness processes reflected by the acceptance half of ACT.

In effect, as a first-order change strategy, behavioral activation seeks to increase client activities that will lift dysphoric mood by contacting natural reinforcing contingencies supporting adaptive behavioral change. Such key activities can include those that lead to a sense of mastery (such as comes from finishing a task like completing a report) and/or pleasure (such as visiting friends). Like MBCT, behavioral activation also differs from ACT in not explicitly linking an increase in overt activities to the pursuit of value-directed goals, although it appears to more closely approximate ACT's emphasis on commitment and behavior change to a greater degree than MBCT by using idiographic functional analyses to help guide activity scheduling.

ACT and Behavioral Activation

To summarize, both ACT and behavioral activation agree on the therapeutic importance of instigating overt behavioral change with depressed clients. They differ in that ACT explicitly links activities to client values and, unlike behavioral activation, incorporates therapeutic procedures designed to strengthen mindfulness and acceptance processes. Because the two approaches have never been compared with each other, no conclusions can be drawn about their relative levels of efficacy in treating depression.

Summary

The title of this chapter posed two fundamental questions about ACT. The first asked "What is ACT?" ACT for depression is a therapeutic approach, rather than a set of techniques, that is part of the third wave within behavior therapy. ACT is based upon relational frame theory as a functional contextualistic account of human language and cognition. Accordingly, ACT seeks to minimize the ways in which language contributes to psychological rigidity and human suffering while also strengthening the ways in which it can support valued living and psychological flexibility. As a second-order change approach, ACT for depression does not seek to change depressive ways of thinking or regulate dysphoric mood, but instead tries to target the contexts and processes that prevent continued valued living in the presence of such private events.

The second key question that we addressed in this chapter is this: "What makes ACT unique?" When viewed in conjunction with cognitive therapy, MBCT, and behavioral activation, what defines ACT as a unique second-order change approach is the way in which it synergistically integrates, in new and creative ways, both of the critical, active ingredients that appear to account for the efficacy of cognitive therapy for depression. ACT, like MBCT, incorporates mindfulness procedures, albeit to a lesser degree, along with other techniques and components to foster acceptance. In addition, like behavioral activation, ACT emphasizes the important role of becoming and remaining active in transforming the lives of clients from ones of depression to ones of vitality and purpose.

In closing this chapter, the limits of ACT in addressing depression should be acknowledged. As already discussed, I do not recommend the extension of ACT to cases of bipolar depression. Even among clients experiencing unipolar depression, it seems doubtful that ACT should be the treatment of choice if the presenting problem is primarily a function of a social skills deficit (Hersen, Bellack, Himmelhoch, & Thase, 1984; Lewinsohn & Gotlib, 1995). At this point, further research is needed to ascertain whether or not combining ACT with a primary intervention, such as social skills training, would provide more efficacious treatment in instances where the case formulation and conceptualization (see chapter 5) suggest that depression largely results from a deficit in interpersonal/social skills.

CHAPTER 2

What Makes Depression So Depressing?

As discussed in the previous chapter, unipolar clinical depression constitutes one of the most common forms of human suffering. Whether or not similar levels of depression are ever encountered by nonhumans to a comparable extent is perhaps a question that will never be adequately resolved. However, an affirmative answer would seem doubtful, suggesting that the support clinical depression receives from language makes it a uniquely human phenomenon (Cryan & Holmes, 2005). That various types and forms of relational framing contribute to the acquisition, maintenance, and exacerbation of human suffering is, of course, a basic premise of the overall model on which ACT is based.

A Primary Pathway to Depression

In attempting to understand how language may make depression depressing, I'd like to draw some parallels between the pathways that transform anxiety into disordered behavior and related processes that may serve similar functions with depression. For example, Eifert and Forsyth (2005) have persuasively argued that fear and anxiety per se are not disordered or unhealthy and, in many contexts, may be quite adaptive. Anxiety becomes problematic with deliberate efforts to avoid, regulate, or in other ways control the experience of it. Accordingly, it is not anxiety itself that is problematic, but how we respond to and relate to it. A similar process may be the primary, although by no means the exclusive, pathway that gives rise to unipolar clinical depression.

Normal Mood Fluctuations

Epidemiologists have recognized that dysphoric mood and other symptoms commonly associated with depression are perhaps most meaningfully viewed as lying on a continuum (Kaelber, Moul, & Farmer, 1995). However, there also seems to be little debate, even among those who have maintained that the experience of low mood and sadness may be normal and adaptive (Neese, 2000), that at some point on the continuum, depression escalates to clinical proportions and becomes dysfunctional. As already suggested, I believe a case can be made that the "dark side" of language is what is responsible for taking dysphoria that occurs quite adaptively as a natural consequence of normal mood fluctuations and transforming it into what Winston Churchill referred to as the "black dog" of depression (Storr, 1988). Before doing so, I'd like to further elaborate on the potential adaptive functions of dysphoric mood.

Adaptive Functions of Dysphoric Mood

The proposition that anxiety per se is adaptive seems much less of a stretch than attempting to make a similar case for at least mild levels of depression as encountered by both humans and nonverbal organisms. Because we need to distinguish among divergent points lying on a depressive continuum, I'll use, of necessity, different terms in discussing their relationship to each other (otherwise, according to RFT, they are equivalent). Accordingly, I will use *dysphoria* here to refer to mild, adaptive levels of depressive symptoms experienced by human as well as infrahuman organisms, and *depression* to denote a dysfunctional disorder that compromises valued living.

One of the earliest and most widely cited accounts of a possible adaptive role for dysphoria was offered by Klinger's (1975) incentive-disengagement theory. Organisms that encounter barriers to goal attainment initially and appropriately increase their efforts. As a normal reaction to loss or if the obstacle cannot be overcome, dysphoria occurs and serves to terminate the goal-seeking behavior, thereby conserving resources. However, if the organism cannot disengage, dysphoria may escalate and, in the case of humans, culminate in clinical depression. From a broader evolutionary perspective, Neese (2000) has more recently proposed that dysphoria may serve an additional adaptive function within a wider range of "unpropitious situations in which efforts to pursue a major goal will likely result in danger, loss, bodily damage, or wasted effort" (p. 14). More specifically, dysphoria is posited to not only lead to the adaptive disengagement of ineffective goal seeking, but also prevent the premature pursuit of alternatives. Thus, from this viewpoint, while anxiety inhibits dangerous actions, dysphoria inhibits futile ones. Following a loss and/or failed attempt at goal attainment, taking a break and temporarily "regrouping" may represent a more optimal strategy than simply stubbornly and unsuccessfully forging ahead.

"Clean" vs. "Dirty Pain"

From the perspective of ACT, what we have referred to in this discussion as dysphoria may be regarded as *clean pain*, an unpleasant, yet adaptive, psychological experience that may occur in response to life's "unpropitious situations" (Hayes et al., 1999, p. 136). Not all goals in leading a full, vital, and engaged life will be attained, and personal losses and failures (for example, death of loved ones, financial setbacks, failed/strained interpersonal relationships, etc.) will inevitably also occur along the way. Moreover, even the successful attainment of goals would be expected to result in dysphoria if they are not tightly linked to values, an issue that will be expanded upon later on in this chapter. Dysphoria thus appears to be an inevitable part of the human condition as a natural, and even psychologically healthy, consequence of both leading and not leading a full life.

What is not psychologically healthy is the increasingly negative spiral of *dirty pain*, or psychological trauma (Hayes et al., 1999, 251) that results when we attempt to avoid, escape from, or otherwise control dysphoria, anxiety, and other forms of clean pain. The unwillingness to experience psychologically clean pain transforms it into the psychological trauma of dirty pain (Hayes et al.). For example, let's say you or I have not reached a goal, such as receiving a job promotion or getting married. Naturally we experience the dysphoria and accompanying negative self-evaluations that come with failing to attain an important goal. However, once we begin to run away from our dysphoria and, as expected from ACT and RFT, our efforts prove to be unsuccessful, we experience even more dysphoria and, through a closed-loop process, it continues to grow and negatively spiral into the dirty pain of clinical depression. Dirty pain and the suffering associated with it arise from the unwillingness to accept dysphoria, anxiety, and other forms of clean pain. In short, dysphoria (and the inability to experientially avoid it) has now itself become depressing. Although clinical depression is perhaps most closely linked to failed efforts to experientially avoid dysphoria, it may result more generally from pursuing the broader agenda of "not feeling bad" (Hayes, 2005), where dysphoria may not be the only, or even primary, unwanted affective state from which the depressed client is running.

The Role of Rumination

Several language processes, such as thought suppression, rumination, and reason giving, have been implicated in the escalation of dysphoria into clinical depression (Zettle & Hayes, 2002). Among these suspects, rumination appears to be the chief culprit based upon an expanding body of converging empirical evidence that points to the central role it plays in the initiation, exacerbation, and maintenance of depression. *Rumination* most generally refers to the verbal process of attempting to answer self-posed questions about the meaning, causes, and consequences of depression (for instance, "Why am I feeling this way and what does it mean?"). More specifically, rumination appears to consist of two identifiable components—one that focuses on psychological experiences including aspects of the conceptualized self, and the other that does so in an analytical and critically evaluative fashion (Roberts, Gilboa, & Gotlib, 1998).

Related Research Findings

While it is beyond the scope of this chapter to provide an exhaustive review of the research literature linking rumination and depression, some summarization of the major findings seems in order. Individual as well as gender differences in coping styles exist (Nolen-Hoeksema, 1990), and those who are more apt to resort to a "ruminative style" have been shown to be more susceptible to experience depression in response to various life stressors (Nolen-Hoeksema, 2000; Nolen-Hoeksema, Larson, & Grayson, 1999). For example, among college students who survived an earthquake, those who displayed a ruminative style in dealing with dysphoric mood were more likely to be depressed seven weeks later than their nonruminating peers (Nolen-Hoeksema & Morrow, 1991). Fortunately, a natural disaster such as an earthquake, is a stressful event that relatively few of us will encounter in our lifetimes. The same cannot be said about experiencing the death of a loved one. Even after controlling for initial depression levels, bereaved adults with a ruminative style were more likely to evidence higher levels of depression when assessed six months later (Nolen-Hoeksema, Parker, & Larson, 1994).

As mentioned in the previous chapter, rumination at least has the appearance of problem solving, but with the misplaced focus of attempting to minimize a "problem"—for example, the clean pain of uncomplicated bereavement—that is not there to be solved. Not only does rumination as an experiential avoidant strategy backfire by engendering more depression instead of less dysphoria, it also apparently further contributes to psychological inflexibility by inhibiting potentially effective problem solving. In a pair of related studies (Ward, Lyubomirsky, Sousa, & Nolen-Hoeksema, 2003), ruminating and nonruminating college students were compared in their evaluation of and commitment to self-generated plans to address two potentially aversive situations (changes in campus housing and to the undergraduate curriculum). Both projects found that ruminators were less confident in and satisfied with their own proposed solutions, less likely to commit to them, and more likely to want more time to "research" them before possibly acting upon them. In short, rather than moving toward effective action, ruminators exhibited even more psychological rigidity by becoming paralyzed by further mulling over of issues, uncertainties, and self-doubts.

Similar contributions of rumination to depression have also been documented further through two programs of experimental research. The first has compared the differential reactions of dysphoric college students reporting above-normal, but subclinical, levels of depression, as assessed by the short (Beck & Beck, 1972) or regular forms (Beck, Ward, Mendelson, Mock, & Erbaugh, 1961) of the Beck Depression Inventory (BDI), to their nondysphoric peers (with BDI scores within the lower levels of the "normal range") to inducements to engage in either rumination or distraction. Specifically, during rumination induction, participants are asked to direct their attention to emotion-focused ("what your feelings might mean"), symptom-focused ("the physical sensations in your body"), or self-focused ("your character and who you strive to be") thoughts, while those in the distraction condition are instructed to attend to externally focused thoughts (for example, "the expression on the face of the Mona Lisa" or "a truckload of watermelons") (Lyubomirsky, Tucker, Caldwell, & Berg, 1999). Compared to distracting dysphorics and both nondysphoric groups, dysphorics who are induced to ruminate evidence less willingness to engage in pleasant distracting activities and a reduced ability to generate effective solutions to interpersonal problems (Lyubomirsky & Nolen-Hoeksema, 1993, 1995), as well as a greater pessimism about positive events in their future and an increased free recall of past negative life events (Lyubomirsky & Nolen-Hoeksema, 1995; Lyubomirsky, Caldwell, & Nolen-Hoeksema, 1998). Paradoxically, dysphorics who ruminate believe they gain valuable insight into the nature of their struggles (Lyubomirsky & Nolen-Hoeksema, 1993), but are then even less likely to actually implement any solutions that are formulated while doing so (Lyubomirsky et al., 1999). In effect, rumination leads to even more fusion with a verbally constructed world and less effective engagement with life outside oneself. Furthermore, the world that is constructed and the problems that inhabit it are disconnected with the here and now and mired in either a regretted past or dreaded future.

Many of the findings that have emerged from experimentally investigating the impact of rumination on dysphoric college students are consistent with the results of related research with participants experiencing clinical depression. Of the two components that comprise rumination, that of engaging in analytic thinking and evaluative framing has been shown to specifically contribute to the overgeneral recall of categorical autobiographical material by clinically depressed subjects (Watkins & Teasdale, 2001). For example, rather than remembering a specific mistake from the past (such as forgetting to mail an income tax return on time), an entire category of previous errors, like "all the other times I've screwed up by forgetting something," is recalled.

In a follow-up study, depressed and nondepressed participants were induced to engage in either "analytical" or "experiential" self-focusing on their psychological experiences and bodily sensations (Rimes & Watkins, 2005). The analytical condition emphasized the evaluative component of rumination by asking participants to think about "the causes, meanings, and consequences of each symptom/sensation" (p. 1676), while the experiential induction instructed subjects to merely focus their attention on the experience of each symptom/sensation. Although the experiential induction was not explicitly conceptualized as a mindfulness-like procedure, framing it in this manner seems justifiable given its emphasis on "just noticing" symptoms and sensations. The two types of self-focused thinking had an equivalent, but nonsignificant, impact upon negative self-evaluations and dysphoric mood of nondepressed participants. By contrast, the analytical, ruminative type of self-focus was the only one of the two to increase self-judgments of worthlessness/incompetency and dysphoric mood among the group of clinically depressed participants.

To summarize, a converging body of correlational/prospective as well as experimental research with nondepressed, dysphoric, and depressed participants has implicated rumination as a key contributor to the pathway that leads from dysphoria to depression. In this respect, rumination appears to be as central to clinical depression as worrying is to generalized anxiety (Watkins, Moulds, Mackintosh, 2005). A recent comparison of the two processes suggests that they may differ in their content (that is, specific ruminative thoughts may differ from particular worries) and in their relative temporal focus (rumination is more focused on the past and worrying more on the future), but they serve a similar experiential avoidant function (Watkins et al.). More specifically, worry appears to represent an attempt to reduce the unpleasant physiological arousal that is part of the experience of anxiety (Borkovec, Ray, & Stober, 1998), while rumination involves ineffectual efforts to ward off dysphoria by trying to figure it out (Holowka, Salters-Pedneault, & Roemer, 2005; Smith, Hughes, & Alloy, 2006). However, both processes appear to be equally adept at transforming naturally occurring psychological reactions into dirty pain–inducing traumatic experiences.

"Self-Worth" as an Evaluation of "Life Worth"

As just discussed, one of the consequences of rumination is an increase in self-blame, self-criticism, and other forms of negative self-evaluation (Lyubomirsky et al., 1999; Rimes & Watkins, 2005). The conceptualized self that emerges is one that is judged to be damaged and lacking in worth (for example, "There's something wrong with me," "I don't deserve to be happy," etc.). An impoverished conceptualization of the self and related affective experiences have long been recognized as one of the defining features of depression. According to A. T. Beck (1967), a derogatory view of the self comprises one third of the "cognitive triad" that typifies depressive thinking, and "feelings of worthlessness" (p. 327) and "low self-esteem" (p. 349) are included among the criteria for a major depressive episode and diagnosis of dysthymic disorder, respectively, within the *DSM–IV* (1994).

From the perspective of ACT, the "self" that is being evaluated as lacking in worth is a *conceptualized self*, that is, one constructed from a network of self-referential relational frames. Some of these frames are both descriptive and "factual" in nature (for instance, "I am a forty-year-old married woman"), whereas others are clearly evaluative (such as "I'm worthless"). A damaged conceptualized self per se is not regarded as problematic and is unlikely to contribute to psychological inflexibility in the absence of fusion with it. Unfortunately, some degree of fusion is likely to be associated with any type of negative self-evaluation. It is especially troublesome when the attachment to and identification with the damaged conceptualized self is so solidified that psychological contact with a transcendent sense of self is effectively precluded. Through frames of coordination and combinatorial entailment, if "I (possible self as context) = "me" (conceptualized self) and "me = worthless," then "I = worthless." In short, when such fusion occurs, we have no alternative type of self-experience and perspective from which a contentless and transcendent sense of self can "just notice" the content of our lives, including that of the conceptualized self. Instead, when our sense of "I-ness" becomes one by fusion with the damaged conceptualized self, a negative self-evaluation is not held as a mere psychological event (that is, "I have the thought/evaluation that I am worthless") but as an immutable fact ("I *am* worthless"). Psychological inflexibility sets in, and depression becomes more embedded as an evaluative self-referential frame is responded to in the same manner as one that is descriptive in nature.

Depressed individuals may recognize the ostensible desirability of changing the conceptualized self, but they also may be in contact with the futility that attempting to change one's self-worth is akin to deliberately altering one's age or gender. ACT for depression does not share the agenda of enhancing self-worth or improving the self-concept. This is not primarily because attaining such goals might prove to be especially difficult and are, therefore, not recommended, but, more importantly, because such a strategy, even if it were successful, is regarded as being unnecessary. Rather than rehabilitating the conceptualized self with which depressed clients are fused, emphasis is instead placed on fostering experiential contact with a transcendent sense of self as context from which self-referential thoughts and feelings can be viewed as being independent of the self.

A second type of problematic fusion in which the conceptualized self participates is that between self-worth and life worth. The low "worth" of the conceptualized self—its stimulus function—may be transferred to that of life more generally through equivalence framing (such that "self-worth" = "life worth"). When this occurs, life itself becomes devalued and may be "put on hold" until the conceptualized self is repaired. This process is perhaps best exemplified by depressed clients who identify "feeling better about myself" as their primary therapeutic goal.

A Case Example

A recent client with this expressed goal—feeling better about himself—is perhaps illustrative. The client, who was in his late forties, reported a lifelong struggle with self-esteem that only abated temporarily following the attainment of specific external goals. Examples included obtaining his undergraduate and graduate degrees, a recent job promotion, and being commended by his boss for skillfully completing a difficult task at work. He would enjoy a short-lived boost to his self-esteem only to soon find himself in an even more terrifying and precarious position as the ante kept rising. Following such accomplishments, the client's evaluation was that he would have to attain even more prestigious and challenging goals to merely maintain his newly acquired level of self-esteem in the face of escalating expectations held by himself as well as those around him. Moreover, there was now even more at stake should he fall short of those heightened expectations as how he lived and saw his life had become tightly fused with his newly won, albeit fragile sense of self-worth.

The client was asked not to consider what his life would be like if he was able to maintain his desired level of self-worth, but how it might be different if he no longer struggled with it. His response was that he would lead a fuller, richer life by being more spontaneous in his relationship with his wife, more daring and assertive at work, and more open to a possible career change. When asked to choose between sustaining a high level of self-esteem and not having the more meaningful life he described versus experiencing a fluctuating level of self-worth and leading that more invigorating life, he opted for the latter.

Suicide as the Ultimate Escape Act

Unfortunately, for all too many individuals who struggle with depression, the pathway that we have been examining in this chapter leads to the contemplation of suicide as a means of terminating such suffering. Although as many as 15 percent of those who have been diagnosed and treated for major depression commit suicide (Angst, Stassen, Clayton, & Angst, 2002; Maris et al., 1992), it should be pointed out that suicidal thoughts and attempts are surprisingly common within the general population (Chiles & Strosahl, 2005) and not limited to those experiencing depression (Henriksson et al., 1993). While suicide, like any behavior, may be determined by multiple factors, the purposive attempt to terminate aversive psychological states such as depression, guilt, and anxiety appears to be one of the more common motives (Bancroft, Skrimshire, & Simkins, 1976; Baumeister, 1990).

It has been argued in this chapter that dysphoria may constitute a naturally occurring and adaptive reaction by both human and infrahuman organisms to failure and loss. Despite claims that have been made to the contrary, such as those involving Norwegian lemmings (cf. Maltsberger, 2003), suicidality as a *verbal action*, or behavior that is only possible as a consequence of framing events relationally (Hayes, 1992), appears to be uniquely human and to be the culmination of the languaging processes that move dysphoria along the pathway to clinical depression. In particular, because even those who are suicidal have never experienced their own death, the behavior of killing oneself cannot possibly have been shaped by contact with the direct consequences of doing so. Rather, as a type of *rule-governed behavior*, or action that is controlled by language, suicidality is under the control of the verbally constructed, instead of direct-experience based, consequences of death (Hayes). One such consequence produced by the formation of temporal frames relating life and death is the avoidance of further suffering (for example, "life = suffering," "death = no life," "no life = no suffering," "death = no suffering"). Accordingly, suicide in such a context may be regarded as the ultimate act of escape.

It seems appropriate to mention here that there has been some disagreement among practitioners of ACT about the usefulness of regarding at least some instances of "experiential avoidance" as "experiential escape" (Wilson, 2006). On this point, I have argued elsewhere (Zettle, 2004), that experiential escape appears to play a greater role than that of avoidance in affective disorders, insofar as those who struggle with depression can be seen as attempting to terminate, albeit unsuccessfully, an existing aversive psychological state. Suicide as a form of experiential escape provides not only a means of seeking respite from an external world that is seen as cruel and uncaring, but also, perhaps even more importantly, from a conceptualized self that is judged to be inadequate, incompetent, unattractive, and guilty (Baumeister, 1990). Indeed, suicide can and does occur within the context of an external world that from all outward appearances seems quite benevolent and hospitable, as the fictionalized case of Richard Corey suggests (Robinson, 1921, p. 35).

From the perspective of ACT, deliberate efforts to rehabilitate a damaged conceptualized self ultimately would be expected to fail, and the option of murdering it subsequently may seem to be the only viable alternative means of escape, especially given the cognitive rigidity and psychological inflexibility that accompanies suicidality (Baumeister, 1990). Perhaps somewhat ironically, ACT agrees that the absence of a conceptualized self would permit greater psychological flexibility and, in that sense, advises that you "kill yourself every day" (Hayes & Smith, 2005, p. 190). Suicidal individuals thus seem to be in touch with the potential for leading a more vital and meaningful life if freed from the tyranny of the conceptualized self, but see its literal, rather than mere figurative death, as the only means of such liberation. As we will discuss at greater length in chapter 8, ACT holds that defusion from the conceptualized self, fostering contact with a transcendent sense of self as context, and distinguishing between these two aspects of self provide a more life-sustaining and invigorating alternative.

Unipolar Depression Within DSM–IV

Within *DSM–IV* (1994), unipolar depression is diagnosable as one of three depressive disorders: (a) major depressive disorder, (b) dysthymic disorder, and (c) depressive disorder not otherwise specified (NOS). A differential diagnosis between major depressive disorder and dysthymic disorder cannot be made by relying upon distinguishing topographical features as they share similar signs, such as low energy or fatigue, and symptoms, such as depressed mood and insomnia/hypersomnia. Rather, the two disorders are differentiated based upon their severity, chronicity, and persistence. Major depressive disorder, by definition, is more severe, but also more likely to be experienced in an episodic manner than the more chronic but less debilitating form that depression takes in dysthymic disorder. By default, unipolar depression that fails to meet the criteria for either major depressive disorder (for instance, the period of mood disturbance does not show at least five of the nine symptoms required for a major depressive episode) or dysthymic disorder (such that it hasn't lasted at least two years) is diagnosable as depressive disorder NOS.

Implications for Treatment Utility

Unfortunately, the distinctions that the *DSM* makes in the differential diagnosis of depressive disorders in general appears to be of limited treatment utility (Hayes, Nelson, & Jarrett, 1987) in enabling mental health professionals to provide more efficacious psychological services for clients with a presenting complaint of depression. More specifically, in determining both if and how to apply ACT, knowing which specific depressive disorder is "accurate" with a given client is virtually useless as the distinctions upon which differential diagnosis is made (such as severity, chronicity, and persistence of the mood disturbance) are ones that do not help guide treatment decisions. A case-conceptualization strategy embedded within a functional dimensional approach to psychiatric diagnosis (Hayes, Wilson, Gifford, Follette, & Strosahl, 1996) would seem to provide a more useful alternative than merely knowing a *DSM* diagnosis, although the degree to which this is the case would need to be evaluated empirically.

An Alternative Approach to Classification

A functional approach to the classification of clinical problems would certainly look quite different than the syndromal approach of the *DSM*. Specific diagnoses that can be differentiated based upon distinguishable symptoms (obsessive-compulsive disorder vs. major depressive disorder, for instance) might be determined to serve a similar function, such as that of experiential avoidance (Hayes et al., 1996). Not only may disorders that are "structurally dissimilar" be functionally identical, but those that are "structurally identical" may prove to be functionally dissimilar. For example, both substance abuse and depression may help clients avoid painful psychological experiences (Petersen, 2007), but not all cases of depression serve an experiential avoidant function. Thus, as mentioned in the previous chapter, it should not be assumed that ACT is equally applicable to all presenting cases of depression. It is entirely possible and consistent from a functionalistic perspective that two hypothetical depressed clients could display the exact same configuration of signs and symptoms and, therefore, appropriately receive an identical *DSM* diagnosis, yet be experiencing depressions that are functionally distinguishable.

Accordingly, a primary issue to address in considering ACT is to first ascertain as much as possible if a given client's presenting problem of depression appears to be serving an experiential-avoidant function. If it is, then a case-conceptualization approach that links back to the six core processes that contribute to psychological flexibility (see the hexaflex, figure 1 in chapter 1) is recommended in applying ACT in a prescriptive manner responsive to the idiosyncratic needs of each client. However, if the presentation of depression appears to be serving a different function—as the result, for example, of a social skills deficit—then an alternative therapeutic approach, such as social skills training (Hersen et al., 1984; Lewinsohn & Gotlib, 1995), should be considered as the primary intervention with ACT perhaps serving an ancillary role.

Alternative Pathways to Depression

As just reiterated, ACT is suggested as a viable treatment option in all instances in which clients present with depression that appears to be serving an experiential-avoidant function. The degree to which the inverse of each of the six core processes that comprise the hexaflex contributes to depression, though, varies on a case-by-case basis. In a corresponding manner, it is also my experience and contention that more than one pathway can activate and implicate the pathogenic processes that lead to depression and psychological inflexibility. This chapter began with the explication of perhaps the most common pathway to depression and ends here with a consideration of several alternatives. Before doing so, it should be noted that none of the alternative pathways are proposed as being mutually exclusive with the primary one discussed earlier nor with each other. All roads may lead to Rome, and multiple pathways can dead-end at depression.

Pursuit of Value-Incongruent Goals

Mental health professionals have often made a distinction between *reactive depression* and *endogenous depression*, where the former is thought to be precipitated by environmental events and sudden life changes and the latter to be driven instead by internal, biologically based processes (Beckham, Leber, & Youll, 1995). Cases of reactive depression, moreover, generally have been held to be triggered by negatively valenced life events such as divorce, job loss, or death of a loved one. It has long been recognized, however, that some instances of reactive depression apparently and paradoxically occur after successful rather than failed goal attainment and loss (Carlisle, 1938). Ironically, the newly attained goal that seems to precipitate the "success depression" is often one that represents the culmination of a long, ongoing, and effortful quest, such as a long-sought-after job promotion or career advancement. As Joseph Campbell is credited with having said, "Midlife is when you reach the top of the ladder and find that it was against the wrong wall" (Shellenbarger, 2005, p. 265).

Success Depression

Martin Seligman (1975) was the first to provide a systematic cognitive behavioral account of success depression through an extension of his learned helplessness theory. Other explanations from a more social-psychological take on learned helplessness theory (Berglas, 1990) and a psychodynamic perspective have also been proposed (Carlisle, 1938). Thus, I am not suggesting that the discussion that follows here is the only viable accounting of success depression that can be offered. More importantly, though, it does suggest an alternative pathway from the perspective of ACT that can lead to clinical depression.

Only the pursuit and attainment of goals that are themselves congruent with key values would be expected to support a full and meaningful life free of depression. For instance, being promoted to the head of the company may be a dispiriting experience, and depression would be a natural consequence, if such a goal is not linked to currently held values. No matter how skillfully and successfully the ladder is climbed, doing so would be expected to be unfulfilling if it is propped against a wall devoid of values. There would appear to be several smaller "trails" that may flow into and contribute to this larger pathway. Values are not immutable, and valuing as a dynamic, behavioral process may change over time. Religious conversions are one example of this (Williams, 2006), but less dramatic instances are probably more common. What we valued in our early twenties (for example, being socially popular) may not be what is cherished in middle-age (for instance, maintaining good health and being a good grandparent). Accordingly, the attained goal that triggers the success depression may have been value-congruent when a commitment initially was made to pursue it, but its status was altered as valuing changed over the period of time required for its acquisition. The fact that the goal in question is no longer linked to valuing may only become painfully apparent once it is attained. At this point, some values clarification and identification may be required therapeutically before more fulfilling life goals can be specified.

Role of Rule-Governance

Other "trails" that may contribute to the pursuit of value-incongruent goals appear to be linked more tightly to the control by language through rule-governance. *Rules* from the perspective of RFT have been defined functionally as frames of coordination between two relational networks that control behavior (Barnes-Holmes, O'Hora, Roche, Hayes, Bissett, Lyddy, 2001) but can be regarded more simply for the purposes of this discussion as language or verbal stimuli that exert a controlling influence over behavior. Instructions, advice, suggestions, commands, and requests are some of the common forms that rules may take. For example, "Go west, young man" and "Insert tab B into slot A" are both instances of rules. Because we as verbally skilled humans have both speaking and listening repertoires, we may follow rules that we ourselves have formulated as well as rules issued to us by others. Tracking and pliance are the two functional units of rule following (Zettle & Hayes, 1982) that seem to be most relevant to understanding why goals that are not linked with values would still be actively pursued.

Tracking. *Tracking* is rule-governed behavior under the control of an apparent correspondence between the rule and the way the world is arranged independently of the delivery of the rule (Barnes-Holmes et al., 2001, Zettle & Hayes, 1982). A rule that controls tracking is known as a *track*. For example, we would expect someone to follow (track) the advice of "The quickest way to get to Wichita from Kansas City is to take the turnpike" (as a rule or track) if, in fact, getting to Wichita quickly is desired, irrespective of the specific form in which the advice was received. Because the world of the turnpike between Kansas City and Wichita exists independently of the advice about taking it, hearing someone say it as opposed to reading it in a travel guide should have the same effect. For a moment, imagine the psychological impact of following a track somewhat like "Graduate from college, get married, buy a house, and you will be happy in life" only to find that happiness is not the end result. One option at that point is to step back and reevaluate. Unfortunately, another course of action is to add something else to the happiness formula (for example, have a child, get that big job promotion) and press on because if you stop following that track, you may frame it as "being wrong." In short, at least some cases of depression seem to result from clients preferring to "be right" *and* not to have their lives work for them over having the experience of "being wrong" *and* leading fulfilled lives.

Pliance. *Pliance* is rule-governed behavior under the control of apparent socially mediated consequences for a correspondence between the rule itself (termed a *ply*) and the relevant behavior. For example, taking the turnpike from Kansas City to Wichita not because it is the quickest way of doing so, but merely because I suggested it, especially if I have selectively reinforced your following of my advice in the past, provides an instance of pliance. Unlike this example where the ply is stated by someone else (in this case, me), recall that, as is the case with tracking, we can formulate plys for ourselves and then follow them rigidly. For example, the verbal construction "If I don't feel happy, it means there's something wrong with me" may lead to the rigorous, yet ultimately unfulfilling, pursuit of happiness. Self-formulated plys limit psychological flexibility and lead to the type of behavioral insensitivity to external contingencies of reinforcement that has been documented in laboratory investigations of rule-governance (see for example, Catania, Matthews, & Shimoff, 1982; Hayes, Brownstein, Haas, & Greenway, 1986; Hayes, Brownstein, Zettle, Rosenfarb, & Korn, 1986; Hayes, Zettle, & Rosenfarb, 1989; Shimoff, Catania, & Matthews, 1981). The unyielding and rigid pursuit of happiness, for instance, may be continued for a long time, even though doing so produces very little immediate payoff.

Many plys can be identified by the use of imperative terms such as "should," "ought," or "must," although not reliably so, insofar as plys are defined functionally (by their impact upon behavior) and not by their formal properties (such as the way they are worded or spoken). Suppose a client formulates and adheres to the following ply: "I *must* appear to be successful to feel worthwhile." Such a rule creates a coordinated verbal network in which "attaining concrete goals = appearing successful" and "appearing successful = self-worth." Consequently, the client may vigorously and successfully pursue goals that are not congruent with personal values but instead are in the service of maintaining a worthy conceptualized self. However, it's also entirely possible, with the passage of time and the accumulation of more successes, that the client frames appearing to be successful as equivalent to being deceptive ("appearing successful = being deceptive"). If being deceptive also participates in a frame of coordination with low self-worth ("being deceptive = low self-worth"), a verbal network is established that results in the "impostor syndrome," which ("appearing successful = low self-worth"), in turn, has itself been found to be related to depression (Kolligan & Sternberg, 1991). Once such a "strange loop" is created, further efforts to bolster the threatened conceptualized self by notching even more successes may only fuel more despair and depression.

Failure to Pursue Value-Congruent Goals

Those in pursuit of value-incongruent goals may appear to be leading a full, engaged life but still suffer with depression. Consistent with the primary pathway that may lead to depression presented at the start of this chapter in which efforts to control dysphoria backfire, the same also applies to those who actively, albeit unsuccessfully, seek value-congruent goals. The same, however, cannot be said for those who have simply given up and have withdrawn from the pursuit of goals consistent with their values, leaving them à la Thoreau (1854/1995) to lead "lives of quiet desperation." In some instances, individuals appear to be acutely aware of what specific outcomes would constitute such goals but see themselves as incapable of approaching them (that is, "Why waste my time?"). This may especially be the case if a rather limited array of goals are linked to core values. For example, while completely financing a grandchild's college education may not be an attainable goal, other more readily achievable, short-term goals might be identified that also would be in the service of the value of "being a good grandparent" (such as spending more time with the grandchild).

A greater therapeutic challenge is presented when clients claim that they do not know what their values are or, alternatively, that they have no values. ACT does not take statements of this sort literally, especially the one declaring an absence of values, but rather seeks to understand the experiential-avoidant function served by such verbal behavior. Not knowing what our values are precludes the painful realization that we are not moving our lives in a direction consistent with them. Ignorance is far from bliss in this context, but it at least may effectively avoid short-term suffering, though at the cost of restricting psychological flexibility and remaining stuck in depression. It may be speculated that a history of failing to successfully attain value-congruent goals has occurred in such instances. The depressed client obviously once had values and still does, perhaps even the same ones that have been "forgotten," but psychologically contacting the distance between such values and the client's current life situation is too emotionally painful. From the perspective of ACT, where you find values, you will find suffering; and where you find suffering, you will find values (Wilson, 2005). A client's statement that "I once had hopes and dreams for myself, but I've been hurt and disappointed so many times that I no longer even allow myself to dream" exemplifies the dynamic relationship between values and the painful consequences of abandoning them. We will address ways of responding therapeutically to presentations of depression that have apparently resulted from this pathway in greater detail in chapter 4.

Depression as a Form of Experiential Avoidance

According to the primary pathway presented at the start of this chapter, depression is a consequence of pursuing an agenda of "not feeling bad" in general and, more specifically, that of running away from dysphoria. In addition to being produced by experiential avoidance, depression itself may also serve an avoidant function by preventing us from coming into contact with even more basic and threatening psychological experiences. Clients under such circumstances may prefer remaining comfortably numb and immobilized within their depression to taking risks that pose even potentially greater psychological dangers. For example, becoming and remaining depressed may keep clients so effectively disengaged socially that fears of intimacy and interpersonal rejection can be successfully avoided ("'Tis better never to have loved, than to have loved and lost").

Additionally, depression may offer protection in certain instances against the disappointment of goal-attainment failure (for example, "I'd rather not even try for a promotion at work than try and fail"). The hypothetical, conceptual self that could have earned the promotion were it not for the depression thereby maintains a semblance of competency. Although it obviously warrants further empirical investigation, the insidious effects of depression potentially serving a behaviorally and dispositionally based self-handicapping strategy (Higgins & Berglas, 1990; Snyder, 1990) cannot be completely dismissed. A verbally constructed network supporting depression in this possible role might go something like the following:

I have experienced depression, am experiencing it now, and will continue to experience it.

I am depressed.

People who are depressed have reduced productivity and don't receive job promotions.

As long as I am depressed, my productivity at work will remain down, so there is no point in seeking a promotion.

The Priority of "Being Right"

Some of the psychological consequences of being right were alluded to earlier in our discussion of how rules may be rigidly followed in the pursuit of value-incongruent goals. The priority of being right, however, takes on added importance in understanding depression when it expands to more extensive verbal networks. The most extensive such verbal or relational network that all of us construct is our own life story. It consists of factual, autobiographical information (for instance, where we grew up, went to school, etc.), but more importantly, it also includes interwoven frames that create a cogent, coherent life narrative by relating the facts to each other, to our past psychological history and current experiences, and to our conceptualized self. While certain autobiographical facts are immutable, the story that we construct and tell about them is not. Thus, psychological flexibility is possible as multiple stories are capable of being told of the same life. The telling of one's life story can be thought of as *reason giving*, or the offering of an explanation or justification for something, on a grand scale. Just as multiple reasons can be given for a specific action, they (in the form of more than one life story) can also be offered for how one has lived and is currently living one's life.

Psychological flexibility is precluded and depression may inevitably result when fusion occurs with life stories that are particularly traumatic and which induce dirty pain. In such instances, clients may become so closely identified and invested in the narrative they have constructed that ostensibly explains why they are depressed, that they are left with no "wiggle room" to get better. Indeed, to move on with their lives *and* be depressed may be held as tantamount to being wrong and renouncing the life story that provides a plausible explanation for the depression in the first place. In simplistic RFT terms, if depression participates in a coordinated network with the life story (such that "depression = life story"), depression is locked into place until the story changes. If the story itself is held tightly as a factual account and not as a constructed narrative, changing it must mean that the client is, and in all likelihood for some time has been, "wrong" about those facts.

The life story may be especially resistant to being retold if the traumatic events that are part of it are attributed to the actions or inactions of others. Self-righteousness that emerges in such circumstances may add to the therapeutic challenge as "getting better" is now not only incompatible with "being right" about the life story, but also with the portions contained within it about "being wronged" (for example, "Given the way I was mistreated, I have every right to be depressed"). The depression itself may be essentially wielded as a constant reminder to transgressors of the damage they have inflicted. In short, being right and holding others accountable trumps getting better. Taken to its extreme, this process may, unfortunately, yield yet another motive for suicide—namely, that of revenge. In particular, certain relational networks may serve an augmenting function for suicidal behavior that may already be present at some strength because of other factors (Chiles & Strosahl, 2005). *Augmenting* is the third and final functional unit of rule-governed behavior (Zettle & Hayes, 1982) and exerts its impact upon behavior by altering the degree to which certain events function as reinforcers or punishers. An *augmental* as discussed here is verbal behavior that makes the act of suicide more attractive. Chiles and Strosahl offer the following chilling example: "I want my mother to suffer for all the damage she did to me" (p. 138). More will be offered on how ACT addresses suicidality, in general, and in cases like that just cited, in chapter 10.

Summary

Not all cases of unipolar depression appear to be serving an experiential-avoidant function and are, therefore, recommended as treatable with ACT. Even those that do may have emerged through varying pathways and, accordingly, may be treated somewhat differently consistent with a case-conceptualization approach within ACT. An unwillingness to accept dysphoria that naturally results from loss and failed goal attainment and to instead attempt to actively run away from it is suggested as the primary pathway that makes depression so depressing. Alternative and overlapping pathways are also possible but are not distinguishable from each other based upon the differing depressive disorders within the *DSM*. The same primary pathway presented in this chapter may lead to any of the depressive disorders, and two hypothetical cases of major depression (or even of dysthymic disorder and depressive disorder NOS, for that matter) could result from different pathways.

Simply knowing a given client's depressive diagnosis thus seems to be of limited treatment utility in the application of ACT. As we have seen in this chapter, various pathways may lead to depression. To the extent that these pathways activate and implicate the negative processes that contribute to psychological inflexibility, understanding the specific pathway or combination of them that results in depression with each client would appear to be more useful. What is seemingly of even greater usefulness, however, is an assessment and conceptualization of the degree to which each of the pathogenic processes are involved in each case of depression. We will explicate these processes first introduced in chapter 1 in greater detail in the following chapter.

CHAPTER 3

Pathogenic Processes in Depression

In chapter 1, we introduced a number of processes from an ACT perspective that are held to contribute to depression specifically and other forms of human suffering more generally. You will remember that these pathogenic processes have corresponding core processes that contribute to psychological flexibility. The following list names the pathogenic processes in depression (with their corresponding psychological flexibility–inducing processes in parentheses):

- Fusion (defusion)

- Experiential avoidance (acceptance)

- Rumination (contact with the present moment)

- Attachment to damaged conceptualized self (self as context)

The purpose of this chapter is to further explicate and familiarize you with the pathogenic processes in order to serve as a link between chapter 1 and chapter 4, which deals with their assessment.

One possible way to think of ACT is that its objective is to weaken and undermine pathogenic processes, such as fusion and experiential avoidance, associated with the "dark side" of human language, while simultaneously strengthening antagonistic processes, such as defusion and acceptance, as well as those, such as valuing and committed action, that are reflective of the "light side" of human language. Construing ACT in this manner is certainly not incorrect, but seems rather narrow and is perhaps not the most useful way of doing so. This is because the six processes depicted in the hexaflex (see fig. 1 in chapter 1) are only of critical importance insofar as they contribute to psychological flexibility.

For example, defusion per se, or stated alternatively, "for its own sake," is not an appropriate therapeutic goal. Depending upon the circumstances and the particular thinking involved, fusion may, in fact, prove to be quite useful. "Buying into" self-efficacy expectations (Bandura, 1997), like the Little Engine That Could ("I think I can—I think I can"), may help support successful perseverance in the face of adversity (Piper, Hauman, & Hauman, 1978). For your depressed clients, the thought "My life can get better" is most likely a useful one, whereas that of "My life won't get any better" is not. Defusion from the former thought would not be appropriate, but quite likely would be for the latter, especially if it kept the client stuck. Defusion in the service of increased psychological flexibility is a relevant therapeutic objective to the degree that psychological flexibility, in turn, is functionally related to leading a full, meaningful, and valued life.

Psychological Flexibility vs. Inflexibility

Previous research has documented a significant and expected relationship between psychological flexibility as assessed by the Acceptance and Action Questionnaire (AAQ; Hayes, Strosahl, Wilson et al., 2004) and levels of self-reported depression (Garst & Zettle, 2006). Moreover, another recent project in my research lab (Gird & Zettle, 2007) suggests that subjects exhibiting high levels of psychological inflexibility or rigidity as assessed by the AAQ respond to dysphoria in ways that exacerbate their overall level of emotional distress and parallel the process discussed in the previous chapter whereby clean pain is transformed into dirty pain. Specifically, psychologically rigid subjects reacted with significantly greater distress to an induction of dysphoric mood than their more flexible counterparts, even though the initial levels of induced mood between the two groups were comparable.

As discussed in chapter 1, it is important for you to bear in mind that psychological flexibility and its opposite, psychological inflexibility or rigidity, are defined functionally in relationship to serving valued courses of action. Psychological flexibility frees us up to pursue a myriad of ways of leading a vital, engaged life, whereas psychological rigidity keeps us bogged down.

Form vs. Function

Because psychological flexibility and inflexibility are defined functionally, at times they may take identical forms, and this may make it hard for you to distinguish one from the other. A good example is provided by persistence. Sometimes patiently and persistently continuing to put one foot in front of the other is what is required to maintain true to one's values (Wilson & Murrell, 2004). The admirable lives of Dr. Albert Schweitzer and Mother Teresa unambiguously "stood for something" and thus exemplify this process, even though both were ultimately unsuccessful in eradicating disease, hunger, poverty, and other forms of human misery. By contrast, at other times and in other circumstances, staying the course and doggedly continuing to do what has always been done is dysfunctional and contributes to the dirty pain of clinical depression. Rumination, for instance, is unlikely to be useful no matter how persistently it is pursued.

Psychological flexibility is associated with the expansion of a behavioral repertoire and psychological inflexibility with its restriction. However, as just seen with the example of perseverance, depending upon the context, a narrowed range of responding may be more reflective of psychological flexibility than rigidity. For example, college students evidencing higher levels of psychological flexibility as measured by the AAQ were more likely than their psychologically inflexible peers to persist on challenging tasks (Zettle et al., 2005; Zettle, Petersen, Hocker, & Provines, 2007). Similarly, displaying a pattern of varied and possibly rapidly shifting actions may be more reflective of psychological inflexibility than the expansive behavioral repertoire that characterizes psychological flexibility. Consider the frenetic activities that typify a manic episode and the emotional lability of clients who may warrant a diagnosis of borderline personality disorder.

At perhaps the simplest level, the overarching critical question for you to ask of your clients with depression in determining whether a given activity, whether it be in the form of overt behavior or thinking, represents psychological flexibility versus rigidity is one of "Is this working for you?" "Has this behavior (for instance, spending much of your waking hours lying in bed, wondering about what you might have done differently in your marriage, etc.) moved you closer to or further away from the type of life you ultimately want to have for yourself?" A more extensive way of addressing the same fundamental issue, and one that specifically incorporates the six core processes that contribute to psychological flexibility, has been suggested by Hayes, Strosahl, Bunting, et al. (2004):

> [G]iven a distinction between you as a conscious human being and the psychological content that is being struggled with (self as context) …
>
> are you willing to experience that content fully and without defense (acceptance) …
>
> as it is and not what it says it is (defusion), AND …
>
> do what takes you in the direction (committed action) …
>
> of your chosen values (values) …
>
> at this time and in this situation (contact with the present moment)? (pp. 13–14)

Answering "yes" to this question increases psychological flexibility; responding "no" to it supports psychological inflexibility.

Types of Psychological Inflexibility

As discussed, psychological flexibility and inflexibility or rigidity can each occur in various guises. Nevertheless, some of the forms that each takes appear to be more typical than others. Accordingly, it may be useful to further consider the different ways that psychological inflexibility, in particular, may be manifested in depression in order to more readily recognize it, ultimately weaken it, and replace it with psychological flexibility.

Perseverative Thought and Behavior

The negative relationship between aversive affective states (such as anxiety or fear) and threatening conditions, on the one hand, and behavioral fluidity, on the other, has long been recognized and is well documented. For example, aversive conditioning with rats not only results in "response fixation" (Farber, 1948) in which avoidant and escape behaviors assume a stereotypical and repetitive form, but also in the "conditioned suppression" of other actions that fail to serve an avoidant/escape function (Estes & Skinner, 1941). In effect, the repertoire becomes narrowed such that the only behaviors that are not suppressed are those that allow escape from or avoidance of the aversive stimulus. Moreover, the remaining escape/avoidance responses take on a fixed and stereotypic form.

Nonhuman Examples

Other preparations with rats that are more analogous to circumstances that may precipitate a reactive depression in humans also have been shown to produce repertoire-constricting effects. Rats that are initially trained to make a discriminated response, such as jumping to the correct platform in using the Lashley jumping apparatus (Feldman, 1957; Maier, 1949) or pressing the only lever of two within a Skinner box associated with delivery of a reinforcer and avoidance of shock (Lal, 1966), are subsequently presented with an unsolvable problem. The cue that functioned as the discriminative stimulus in the initial training is now presented randomly so that making the previously reinforced response to it is no longer reliably followed by delivery of food or water and/or the avoidance of shock. According to Klinger's (1975) incentive-disengagement theory discussed in the previous chapter, the animals would be expected to eventually adaptively conserve their resources by failing to respond altogether under such circumstances, and this is indeed what occurs. If they are then, however, forced to make a response, perseveration, or repeating the same action over and over again, occurs. Rats who are induced to respond from the jumping apparatus will continually opt to leap to the left, for example, even though, the "correct" option of jumping right is clearly within view. Problem-solving efforts that continue in the face of insoluble problems and "unpropitious situations" à la Neese (2000) thus typically assume fixated and rigid forms. Rumination that unsuccessfully persists in an attempt to control dysphoria or feelings of guilt, remorse, and other unwanted private events is perhaps the most telling example of this in human depression.

Human Examples

Much of the initial research just considered that has investigated the impact of aversive conditions (such as the avoidance of shock and presentation of unsolvable problems) on behavioral flexibility did so by observing the overt responses of infrahuman organisms. As already suggested, functionally similar effects should be and are seen with depressed human beings. However, because of our ability to use language, psychological inflexibility in human depression would be expected to be manifested in perseverative thinking as well as overt behavior.

While more will be said shortly about how rumination more generally relates to and contributes to psychological inflexibility, it seems useful here to first highlight what appears to perhaps be the key perseverative cognitive component within rumination. Pyszczynski and Greenberg (1987) in explaining rumination have argued that especially clients who experience reactive depression become stuck in a self-regulatory cycle of thinking about how to regain what has been lost. Persistent dwelling on a personal loss cycles into negative self-evaluation, blame, and the type of fusion with a damaged conceptualized self discussed in the previous chapter. Unfortunately, what has been lost—particularly as occurs in the death of a loved one, for example—is often not replaceable, and clients are thus faced with an unsolvable problem. Comments by your clients like "I'll never get over losing her" and "My life hasn't been the same since he died" reflect this reality, particularly if they are stated over and over again. Considerable defusion and acceptance work may be needed to address such thinking if the clients involved are to become unstuck.

Your therapeutic task becomes even more challenging if considerable self-blame is also present (for example, "If only I had taken better care of him/her") and your clients are living in a regrettable past. Depression under such circumstances seems clearly linked with the inability of clients to give up when it would be more adaptive to do so. It may be necessary with such clients to allocate considerable time and effort within ACT to underscore the futility of holding the loss and self-allocated responsibility for it so tightly.

Rumination, as suggested previously, may be viewed as an attempt to solve an unsolvable problem. The type of perseverative thinking seen in rumination, however, also has appeared in examining eventual successful strategies used by dysphoric and depressed subjects in solving various problems, suggesting that cognitive rigidity may be a more general feature of depression. For instance, Martin, Oren, and Boone (1991) found level of depression to be predictive of perseverative responses in comparing the performance of dysphoric, depressed, and control subjects on the Wisconsin Card Sorting Test (WCST; Grant & Berg, 1948). The results of an earlier study that employed a similar card sorting task, but one that permitted a more fine-grained analysis of problem-solving behavior, further suggest that more perseverative errors displayed by depressed inpatient subjects may be attributed to their difficulty in abandoning disconfirmed hypotheses (Silberman, Weingartner, & Post, 1982). Depressed subjects formulated as many card sorting hypotheses as their control counterparts but overall performed poorer on the task as they were much slower to reject a hypothesis once it had been disconfirmed. Similar perseveration in the form of repetition errors and carrying out redundant tests of problem-solving hypotheses has also been observed in comparing how dysphoric and control subjects correctly identify a faulty unit contained within a matrix of wiring diagrams (Channon & Baker, 1996).

Final forms of perseverative thinking and behavior displayed by depressed subjects have been documented in the generation of random numbers and playing of a computer game. Depressed psychiatric inpatients showed more perseveration in generation of random numbers than control subjects and fellow inpatients diagnosed with personality disorders, but less repetition of the same sequence of numbers than those diagnosed as schizophrenic (Horne, Evans, & Orne, 1982). An interesting related finding is that the generation of nonrandom number sequences is positively correlated with the severity of psychiatric disturbance and that a change to randomness is associated with therapeutic improvement. Finally, mildly depressed college students displayed less variability in their responses in playing a computer game than their nondepressed peers, although their behavior became indistinguishable when the contingencies were changed without warning to reinforce variable sequences of responding (Hopkinson & Neuringer, 2003).

To summarize, taken in the aggregate, the existing research that has addressed the issue supports the common clinical observation that depressed clients frequently engage in perseverative thinking and overt behavior (A. T. Beck, 1967). Some of the more obvious and perhaps clinically relevant examples have already been mentioned, and others will be cited in some of the remaining sections of this chapter. Less dramatic and more subtle forms of behavioral rigidity that you may see in your depressed clients may include the same brief and stereotypical responses to questions—for example, repeatedly answering "Fine" or "All right" when asked how their weekend or a specific activity went. One suggestion is to query for further details and to ensure that we as therapists also don't become stuck in our own routines by varying the form of the questions: ask "What did you like best about your weekend?" rather than "How was your weekend?" Although I have no data on their potential usefulness, the possibility of varying appointment times, changing therapy rooms, seating arrangements, and even suggesting that a client who habitually shows up wearing the same wardrobe dress differently seem worthy of consideration. In short—especially in light of research suggesting that nondepressed individuals who are high-response perseverators report more stable levels of guilt and that high levels of neuroticism are only predictive of depression when combined with behavioral inflexibility (Robinson, Wilkowski, Kirkeby, & Meier, 2006)—anything that induces your clients to think and act differently may have the potential to help them, even if only momentarily, break out of the psychological rigidity that has locked their depression in place.

Rumination

Although much has already been said about how rumination contributes to the psychological inflexibility seen in clinical depression, its key status perhaps warrants a few more observations. Measures of rumination and depression are correlated with each other (Smith et al., 2006), but they can obviously exist independently of each other. It's possible for some degree of rumination to occur outside of depression, and not all of your depressed clients will ruminate to the same extent. Accordingly at least two projects have investigated the relative contributions that rumination and depression, both singly and in combination, make to behavioral rigidity.

Watkins and Brown (2002) used the same random-number-generation task developed by Horne et al. (1982) to evaluate the differential impact of a rumination versus distraction induction on the performance of depressed and control subjects. An interactive effect was found in that, compared to the distraction induction, induced rumination resulted in increased perseverative number generation for the depressed subjects only. No difference was found between the two comparison groups in the distraction induction condition, suggesting that depressives who are prone to ruminate are most likely to display inflexibility. Correlational research with the WCST, however, also suggests that rumination, independently of depression, may contribute to perseveration (Davis & Nolen-Hoeksema, 2000). College students who scored high on a self-report measure of rumination committed significantly more perseverative errors on the WCST than their low-ruminating counterparts even after differences in level of depression were controlled for statistically.

Assessment Considerations

There are several ways to determine if your depressed clients engage in a high level of rumination. A formal, objective means is to administer an instrument like the Response Styles Questionnaire (RSQ; Nolen-Hoeksema & Morrow, 1991), designed to assess rumination. Another option is to simply ask them a question like "How much time do you find yourself thinking about why you are depressed and about what it may all mean?" Or alternatively, "If you find yourself with some spare time on your hands, how do you usually spend it?" Because rumination is such a high-probability activity among many depressed clients, a final and informal way to detect it is to simply listen to the spontaneous comments of your clients. Even though verbal behavior should always be viewed functionally, statements like "I wish I could figure out why I feel this way" and "I just keep trying to understand what I may have done to deserve this" are likely tip-offs.

Reason Giving

Most, if not all of us, quite naturally search for possible causes of unpleasant psychological experiences like depression. One of the apparent intended purposes of rumination is to derive answers to the question of "Why am I depressed?" (Zettle & Hayes, 2002). On occasion, you may encounter clients who have not yet arrived at a set of possible reasons for their depression prior to presenting themselves for therapy, may experience considerable distress surrounding this, and may even present the question they have been struggling with as a central issue to be addressed in treatment—for example, "I have so much going for me. I don't know why I'm so depressed." Insight-oriented approaches to therapy would likely take such a comment/question quite seriously by devoting a considerable amount of time, effort, and energy in attempting to directly answer it. An ACT approach to depression also takes such talk seriously, but because of what it may suggest about the pathway to depression taken by clients who say it. As discussed in the previous chapter, such cases of "success depression" likely result from the pursuit of value-incongruent goals and, from a case-conceptualization approach, may be dealt with differently in therapy.

At least in my clinical experience, it is more common for depressed clients to enter therapy with the by-products of their pretherapeutic ruminations already in hand. Cases in which clients have already arrived at purported reasons for their depression, at first glance, might appear to be somewhat easier to treat insofar as no therapeutic time needs to be devoted to answering the question of "why?" Unfortunately, this does not hold for several reasons. For one, considerable fusion is often present with whatever reasons clients have determined are the causes of their depression. Stated somewhat differently, clients have bought into and firmly believe in the validity of the reasons as the cause of their depression (for instance, "If I had not lost my job, I wouldn't be depressed").

The problem here is not so much fusion with reasons as causes per se, but that it is also usually accompanied by additional fusion with how the purported causes and treatment of depression are framed (for example, "In order to successfully treat depression, its causes must be identified and removed"). Causes by definition have already occurred, although in some instances they may still be ongoing, and, therefore, are typically inaccessible even when they involve environmental events like the loss of a job or breakup of a romantic relationship. Unfortunately, holding reasons for depression as its causes becomes even more of a therapeutic challenge when the reasons involve private events such as negative, unwanted thoughts and related feelings of guilt, sadness, regret, and the like that cannot be successfully eliminated. On this point, all of us seem to be inclined to cite our own thoughts and feelings as reasons for undesirable behavior and, moreover, to regard them as "good" and valid explanations (Hayes, 1987). Reason giving for depression, particularly when private events are referenced, constitutes yet another form of psychological rigidity that locks depression in place. If the reasons for my depression, as I see it, are the self-blame and guilt surrounding some past life event, I can't move until those feelings are removed. Yet according to the model upon which ACT is based, the more effort that is put into running away from such emotions, the more solidified they become.

Assessment Considerations

Reason giving for depression, like rumination, can be detected in both more objective and less formal ways. While more will be offered on the assessment of reason giving in the next chapter, research that has involved its formal assessment in relationship to depression supports the clinical observations already made about the process and the contribution it makes to psychological inflexibility. In an undergraduate sample, a paper-and-pencil measure of reason giving for depression, the Reasons for Depression Questionnaire (RFD; Addis, Truax, & Jacobson, 1995; Thwaites, Dagnan, Huey, & Addis, 2004), was found to be significantly related to both depression and psychological inflexibility, as assessed by the BDI and AAQ, respectively (Garst & Zettle, 2006). A regression analysis indicated that the RFD and AAQ both independently and significantly accounted for variability in BDI scores, consistent with the conceptualization of reason giving as a process that contributes to psychological flexibility but which is not synonymous with it.

Related Research

Not surprisingly, the suggested relationship between reason giving and rumination also has received empirical support as individuals who give more reasons for depression have been found to ruminate more in response to depressed mood (Addis & Carpenter, 1999). Of even greater importance, depressed clients who score high on the RFD have been found both to be more difficult to treat than other depressives and to exhibit higher levels of posttreatment depression even when controlling for pretreatment levels (Addis & Jacobson, 1996). Consequently, knowing how tightly your clients hold on to the explanations they have settled on for their depression may have prognostic implications as well as implications for how you can adjust ACT to be most responsive in addressing this dimension of psychological inflexibility.

Storytelling

To a large degree, storytelling in depression can be usefully regarded as a higher level of reason giving in which clients incorporate multiple explanations for depression with autobiographical facts into a network of relational frames that provides some level of coherence and meaning to their lives. As such, the narrative that is told may in effect function to offer reasons for reasons. For example, a recent client, when asked to offer her thoughts about her depression, cited a failed second marriage and then went on to spontaneously explain not only why that would make her depressed ("I don't know why, but I guess I've always wanted to be needed"), but also why she held herself responsible for the divorce initiated by her husband ("If I would have been a better wife and more attentive to his needs, he wouldn't have divorced me").

As with relational framing that occurs at the level of individual depressive thoughts as well as at the level of reason giving, that which is involved in storytelling in and of itself is not problematic. A life story that is held lightly and even potentially one with which there is a great deal of fusion are not problematic if psychological flexibility is promoted. Unfortunately that rarely seems to be the instance in clinical depression, although the degree to which fused storytelling contributes to psychological rigidity will vary from client to client and must, therefore, be assessed on a case-by-case basis. Guidelines for doing so will be presented in the next chapter. Unsolicited comments by your clients, however, may offer a clue. A spontaneous statement by the client described in the previous paragraph as part of her life story is illustrative: "I guess I'm just stubborn—at least that's what my sister and my previous counselor have said I am—about blaming myself for the breakup of my second marriage. They seem to think my husband was just as much at fault as I was, and maybe even more, but I know that just isn't true." Responding to the client's comments by rationally evaluating the evidence for and against the client versus the husband being responsible for the divorce is unlikely to be useful from the perspective of ACT. What the client said, however, does need to be taken seriously insofar as it likely reflects a high level of fusion with storytelling and related psychological rigidity that will help direct the focus of treatment.

Cognitive Fixation and Suicidality

Cognitive fixation, or being able to think about something in only one way, and rigidity in thinking have been associated with vulnerability for suicide (Reinecke, 2006) and represent yet additional forms that psychological inflexibility may assume. As detailed in the previous chapter, not all depressed clients are suicidal and not all suicidal individuals are depressed. Nevertheless, if you do considerable work with depressed clients, you will in all likelihood see more than your fair share of individuals who at least seriously consider suicide. More will be offered on management of suicidality from an ACT perspective in chapter 10, and my purpose in mentioning it here is to relate it more broadly to psychological inflexibility.

A fairly extensive literature has characterized the thinking of suicidal individuals as highly rigid, inflexible, and one-sided (Arffa, 1983; Ringel, 1976). While some have conceptualized the type of cognitive rigidity associated with suicidality as a trait, it seems more useful to instead regard it as a more transient correlate or marker of suicidality (Baumeister, 1990), suggesting that suicidal thoughts themselves may be a reflection of psychological inflexibility. To the extent that the contemplation of suicide constitutes an attempt to terminate personal suffering, it represents a rigid and inflexible means of doing so (Chiles & Strosahl, 2005). Viewed with the context of research showing that depressed women produce fewer potential solutions to interpersonal problems than their nonde-pressed counterparts (Lapp, Marinier, & Pihl, 1982), suicide may be held as a preferred problem-solving strategy as relatively few competing alternatives are generated.

As with any action, the behavior of thinking about and/or attempting suicide may be determined by multiple controlling variables. Nevertheless, there appears to be both suffi-cient empirical support as well as conceptual reasons from an ACT perspective to initially regard any talk of suicide as yet another manifestation of psychological inflexibility. If further assessment indeed suggests that this is the case, it may be dealt with in much the same manner that ACT addresses other forms of behavioral rigidity.

Recall that in chapter 1 we talked about six core processes that ACT seeks to strengthen in fostering psychological flexibility. It seems useful in discussing them further here as well as in subsequent chapters to group them into three associated pairs:

- Defusion and acceptance

- Commitment and behavior change

- Mindfulness and self as context

In particular, processes involving defusion can be linked with those that support acceptance in counteracting the negative contributions of fusion and experiential avoid-ance to the "dark side" of language. Processes concerned with commitment and behavior change represent the second grouping. It is possible to view these processes as being in opposition to the pathogenic processes of lacking values and behavioral passivity or inac-tion, but it seems more useful to pair them together, as suggested in chapter 1, because of their role in emphasizing the "light side" of human language. The final set of paired positive processes involving mindfulness and self as context can be usefully thought of as "common processes" that are invoked to at least some degree by the other two pairs. However, this does not imply, as we will see in chapter 8, that it is not meaning-ful to speak of techniques and procedures within ACT that are specifically designed to strengthen mindfulness and self as context.

Processes Involving Defusion and Acceptance

Collectively, processes involving mindfulness and acceptance within ACT are designed to undermine the opposing pathogenic processes of fusion and experiential avoidance that support psychological inflexibility. For ease of discussion, we will consider fusion and experiential avoidance separately in turn. It should be recognized, however, that distinc-tions among any of the processes denoted within the hexaflex (see fig. 1 in chapter 1) are arbitrarily drawn and are not derived from some independent discovery and mapping of reality. Rather, they are the creation of ACT therapists (Hayes, Strosahl, Bunting, et al., 2004) and accordingly should be held as lightly as any other languaging. Nonetheless, differentiation among processes contributing to psychological flexibility represented within the hexaflex has thus far proven useful and for this reason will be continued here, although it is hoped that the hexaflex will ultimately be replaced by a heuristic of even greater utility.

Fusion

To briefly reiterate, fusion is technically defined as the domination of relationally derived stimulus functions over those that emerge from direct contact with external contingencies. Stated somewhat differently, fusion occurs when *how* we talk about something (such as a job interview that was "awful") is more powerful in determining our psychological reaction to it than the event itself. Reason giving and storytelling are both types of languaging in which their by-products overshadow direct experiential control. The reasons offered for depression are certainly not causes in any scientific meaning of the term, and the related life stories that are told are not literal facts, but rather a created narrative that seeks to present a coherent version of them.

Another level of fusion associated with depression that seems more pervasive than that involving reason giving and storytelling occurs with individual thoughts, particularly negative self-evaluations, such as "I'm stupid." Although you can use more formal means of detection such as self-monitoring and the administration of paper-and-pencil instruments like the ATQ (Hollon & Kendall, 1980) to identify specific fused thoughts, simply listening to what your clients spontaneously (and usually, repeatedly) say about themselves is recommended instead. Responding to a thought like "I'm stupid" more as a descriptive fact rather than a mere evaluation has a repertoire-narrowing impact in several ways. If I *am* stupid, opting not to engage in activities in which intelligent responding is required appears to be a very wise move—much like I would not leap out of a tall building because I can't fly. To the extent that fusion/defusion can be viewed most usefully as end points on a continuum, different degrees or levels of fusion with negative self-evaluative thoughts are possible. A given thought that is a candidate for fusion may be "mulled over" in a ruminative fashion (for example, "Is it really true that I am stupid?") or, alternatively as we will see, may also first become a target for suppression. In any event, time, effort, and energy that could be expended in more life-affirming activities are squandered on behaviors that decrease rather than increase psychological flexibility.

Experiential Avoidance

Experiential avoidance as a process antagonistic to acceptance, like fusion, can take different forms. Daydreaming, distracting oneself, and ingesting alcohol and other types of drugs to ward off unpleasant memories are common forms of experiential avoidance. As I just suggested, a particularly common avoidant strategy at the level of negative self-evaluations is thought suppression. Depressed individuals see negative thoughts as a primary cause of their unhappiness and report frequently attempting to deliberately put them out of their minds by suppressing them (Wenzlaff, 1993). Thought suppression is perhaps widely used because both our direct experience with it and related research on the phenomenon suggest that thought suppression may be quite effective, at least in the short-term. In the absence of competing rule following, our behavior, like that of other organisms, is contingency-shaped, that is, controlled by the immediate consequences of our actions. A systematic program of research on thought suppression more generally indicates that unwanted thoughts can be successfully excised from awareness for short periods of time, but that a rebound effect typically occurs in which the targeted thought returns with renewed strength (see Wegner, 1994).

Thought Suppression

Research specific to depression suggests that deliberate attempts to not think depressing thoughts is ultimately even less successful for several reasons. Efforts to suppress a given thought typically entail distraction by deliberately thinking of an alternative thought (by, for instance, thinking of a red truck in suppressing thoughts of a blue car). When we are depressed, however, we gravitate toward using other negative thoughts as distractors in place of the unwanted thought we are attempting to suppress. For example, focusing on how unattractive we look to divert our attention away from thinking about how stupid we are is unlikely to leave us feeling any less depressed. Not surprisingly, depressive thinking that is suppressed reemerges sooner when other unwanted thoughts are used as distractors (Wenzlaff, Wegner, & Roper, 1988) and, moreover, reinduces the dysphoric mood that was present when the suppression initially occurred when it does reemerge (Wenzlaff, Wegner, & Klein, 1991). Related research, furthermore, suggests that the bonding that apparently occurs between the suppression of depressive thoughts and dysphoric mood is such that reoccurrence of the mood also reinstates the suppressed thinking (Wenzlaff et al., 1991), reflecting a spiraling relationship between these private events. The final and perhaps most compelling piece of evidence about the futility of attempting to escape from depressing thoughts is that efforts to suppress them appear to lead to rumination and increased depression (Wenzlaff & Luxton, 2003).

Suppression may be the most common experiential escape strategy used in coping with depression, but it is hardly the only one. We will consider other internal control strategies, such as daydreaming, as well as forms of experiential avoidance/escape that are more external and situationally focused, including those that may occur in the therapeutic setting itself, in the next chapter.

Processes Involving Commitment and Behavior Change

In the aggregate, valuing and the engagement in related committed action can be grouped together as processes in the service of expanding a behavioral repertoire and psychological flexibility. Conversely, the opposing pathogenic processes that encompass the dominance of verbal/relational control over valuing and under- or overactivity in place of committed action help keep clients stuck in their depression (Hayes et al., 2006). It is these latter two processes that will be our focus here in leading up to a discussion in the next chapter of how you can assess for their presence.

Dominance of Verbal Control

The specific type of verbal control that all too often trumps valuing likely involves pliance. Recall that pliance is rule following under the control of arbitrarily and socially mediated consequences for a correspondence between behavior and actions specified by the rule. For example, a child who is advised to dress warmly before going outdoors in the winter may be praised for complying and scolded for not doing so. Insofar as aversive control tends to be used more often in managing behavior than positive reinforcement, pliance as a response class is more likely to have been established under such conditions and accordingly serves an avoidant function. Loosely speaking, as children we learned to follow parental advisement about what to wear not in order to earn the praise of our parents but to avoid their admonishments.

Consider the implications of extending this analysis to valuing where what your clients say they care about is under the aversive control of pliance. In short, their verbal behavior represents rigidly following a rule about what *should* matter to them and thus may be more a reflection of what they were taught to say while growing up, what they think they should say now as adults, and what they think you as the therapist want to hear than the type of life they desire for themselves in the long term (Hayes et al., 2006). None of this should be taken to suggest that having the same values as one's parents is necessarily a bad thing. Indeed, for many of us, it seems to have worked out fairly well. The more important point to be made is that values cannot be freely chosen under conditions that support escape and avoidance behavior, underscoring the challenge in ACT of shifting the control of valuing from *aversive* to *appetitive control* (Wilson & Murrell, 2004). Behavior under aversive control moves away from something undesirable, such as in escape or avoidance, whereas behavior under appetive control approaches that which is desirable. The type of valuing ACT seeks to support entails moving toward what is important in life rather than running away from its unpleasantries. Seeing what the behavior of valuing looks like in a *free operant situation* (Ferster, 1953) in which there are no constraints upon it and you can do "whatever you damn well please" is not possible unless such conditions are, in effect, created within the context of therapy.

Assessment Considerations

The challenge of identifying and clarifying valuing is heightened by the fact that while values are not verbally constructed, they are verbally accessible (Hayes et al. 1999, p. 206), and it generally takes less effort to lie with our mouths than it does with our feet. In this respect, the degree to which there is a correspondence between clients' professed values and their overt behavior may provide at least one clue about valuing that is not contaminated by the very process of attempting to assess it. For example, a client's claim that he values familial relationships but he seldom visits or even otherwise communicates with family members should be a cause for legitimate skepticism and further evaluation. Obviously to determine the extent to which verbal/relational control dominates over valuing, valuing itself must be assessed. Further suggestions for successfully undertaking this tricky process within ACT will be offered in the next chapter.

Uncommitted Action

A reading of your client's values when freed from aversive control is of importance not so much for its own sake, but to the extent that doing so will also help you identify actions that are not linked to valuing and thus fail to enhance psychological flexibility. Just as behaviors that are value directed can take different forms, the same is true for uncommitted actions that are disconnected from valuing. The most easily recognized guise assumed by uncommitted action within depression, of course, is behavioral passivity and inaction as "markedly diminished interest … in all, or almost all activities …" (p. 327) and "low energy or fatigue" (p. 349), are part of the diagnostic criteria for major depressive disorder and dysthymic disorder, respectively (*DSM–IV*, 1994). At the same time, however, don't confuse uncommitted action in the form of behavioral passivity with slowed movement and speech typical of psychomotor retardation. Relative to the hare, the tortoise moved quite slowly, albeit in a valued direction.

At the other extreme, uncommitted action can also take the form of an abundance of overt behavior, although this should not be confused with what some mental health professionals have referred to as an "agitated depression" (Akiskal, Benazzi, Berugi, & Rihmer, 2005). As suggested in the previous chapter, a pattern of sustained behavior, like that seen in a success depression, may not be congruent with the client's values and may serve an avoidant function: for example, "As long as I continue to engage in apparently productive activities [climbing up that ladder], I don't have to stop and face the pain of a life devoid of meaning [realizing the ladder is against the wrong wall]." Once you have identified your client's values, the next key question is to what degree are they being followed, and if not, why not? An overall low level of behavior does not necessarily mean that there is less committed action occurring nor a high activity level that there is more. Further assessment and case conceptualization is called for in both instances.

Common Processes Involving Mindfulness and Self as Context

Contact with the present moment and self as context can be construed as common processes that occur within each of the two sets of paired processes—those involving defusion and acceptance as well as those concerned with commitment and behavior change—just reviewed (Hayes et al., 2006). I'm highlighting them within their own section here largely for ease of discussion. The relationship between mindfulness and contacting a transcendent sense of self, on the one hand, and processes involving defusion/acceptance and valuing/committed action, on the other, is perhaps best clarified by considering their opposing pathogenic processes. The opposite of mindfully living in the present is dwelling on the past and/or future, and the opposite of self as context is identification with a damaged conceptualized self.

Living in the Past/Future

Preoccupation with either the regretted past or dreaded future is incompatible with fully and mindfully contacting the present. Because of the major role played by rumination in limiting psychological flexibility, most of our focus thus far has been appropriately on the deleterious impact of fusion with thoughts and memories about the past. However, as A. T. Beck (1967) emphasized, one-third of the "negative cognitive triad" that typifies depression involves projections about the future as well. A verbally constructed future may be inhabited that is even less promising and fulfilling than either the past or present (for instance, "Things may change in the future, but only for the worse").

The fusion that occurs with thoughts about the future as well as the past, in effect, creates "facts" that we find "unacceptable," which we then unsuccessfully attempt to run away from, suppress, or otherwise control. Until regrets about the past and worries about the future can be responded to in a mindful and accepting manner, there is not sufficient wiggle room left for valuing and committed action. Valuing may still be intact—I still care about what I've always cared about—but even if it is, committed action is effectively precluded. In part, this may be because so much time, energy, and effort is spent on mulling over the past and being preoccupied about the future that very little is left for engaging in activities that are value related. For example, your depressed client may opt to stay home and ruminate rather than go to the movies with friends. A critical question to ask of your depressed clients in this regard is about how they choose to use spare time they have.

Committed action also may not occur because a preoccupation with the past and/or future generates fused thoughts as well as unwanted feelings and mood states that function as barriers. This process is perhaps more likely and easily seen surrounding fused thinking and related emotional reactions about the future. At the starkest level, if a client is fully fused with the thought "I have no future," opting to act as if one does seems rather foolish. An even greater concern is that such fusion may also be associated with increased levels of hopelessness that have been found to be a major psychological risk factor for suicide (Beck, Kovacs, & Weissman, 1975; Brown, Beck, Steer, & Grisham, 2000). The old saying that "suicide is a permanent solution to a temporary problem" rings hollow for those contemplating suicide, as killing themselves is seen as successfully resolving a permanent and enduring problem. While the management of suicidality by itself can constitute a major clinical challenge (Chiles & Strosahl, 2005), as emphasized earlier in this chapter, it seems most useful from the perspective of using ACT with depressed clients to view it within a broader context as a marker for psychological inflexibility and various processes that contribute to it.

Fusion with a Damaged Conceptualized Self

One of the processes that supports suicidality specifically and psychological rigidity more generally is tight identification with a view of the self that is fundamentally flawed or damaged in some way. Again, as A. T. Beck (1967) noted from his clinical experience in working with depressed clients, repetitive, highly critical self-evaluations (such as "I'm stupid" or "I can't do anything right") comprise another part of the negative cognitive triad descriptive of their thinking. Fusion with such thoughts creates not only a dreaded future they cannot live in but also a conceptualized self they cannot live with, and from which its murder is seen as the only escape.

Mindfulness and acceptance processes are severely limited if a damaged self-identity dominates over a transcendent sense of self. In effect, there is no place or posture from which, as Kabat-Zinn (1994) has stated, "paying attention in a particular way: on purpose, in the present moment, nonjudgmentally" (p. 4) is possible. From the perspective of the conceptualized self, we are continually threatened and under assault from negative, automatic self-evaluations and are incapable of responding in a nonjudgmental fashion to them. Self as context is necessary to be able to "just notice" not only nonself-referential thoughts and related emotions that occur as part of clinical depression, but also, perhaps even more importantly, fused characteristics of the conceptualized self as well.

What is known more colloquially as a "poor self-concept" also compromises valuing and the capacity for associated committed action. The act of freely choosing what we value and fully committing ourselves to engaging in related activities that enliven those values can only be made by a sense of self that is able to watch our struggles with depression, while at the same time standing apart from it—à la the Chessboard Metaphor that is often used within ACT to engender a more robust self as context (Hayes et al, 1999, pp. 190–192). There are seemingly few givens in depression, but one that perhaps comes the closest is fusion with a flawed sense of self. The fundamental issue for you to address on a client-by-client basis is thus not whether identification with a negative conceptualization of the self is present but rather how tightly it is held.

Summary

The primary goal of ACT is the promotion of psychological flexibility. To accomplish this, processes antagonistic to those portrayed in the hexaflex and which contribute to psychological rigidity, of necessity, must be weakened. The pathogenic processes emphasized in this chapter that contribute to depression from the perspective of ACT—fusion, experiential avoidance, rumination, attachment to a damaged conceptualized self—have not been "discovered," but thus far have been found to be useful in thinking about depression and how to work effectively with clients who struggle with it. The six core processes that contribute to psychological flexibility—defusion, acceptance, self as context, contact with the present moment, values, and committed action—and the three groupings into which they can be paired—defusion and acceptance, commitment and behavior change, mindfulness and self as context—while instrumental in all cases of depression for which ACT is an appropriate treatment option, are likely to be involved to varying degrees. Some of your depressed clients, for instance, may have their greatest difficulty in defusing from a negative self-concept, whereas others may find committing to value-directed actions to be their most formidable challenge.

In order to determine the extent to which each of the negative processes that contribute to psychological inflexibility are implicated with the depression experienced by your clients, evaluation on a case-by-case basis is required. Such ideographic assessment is necessary for the individualized approach to case formulation and conceptualization within treatment of depression with ACT being advocated in this book. We will cover the assessment of the negative or pathogenic processes in the next chapter, and how to conceptualize the information obtained into client-specific formulations and treatment approaches will be the focus of chapter 5.

CHAPTER 4

Assessment of Core Processes

Historically, assessment within behavior therapy has lagged behind and taken a back-seat to the development of interventions (Ciminero, 1986). None of the classic texts from the first wave of behavior therapy (such as Franks, 1969; Kanfer & Phillips, 1970; Yates, 1970) devoted a single chapter exclusively to behavioral assessment. Assessment did not fair much better during the second generation of behavior therapy either. While Meichenbaum (1977) at least included a specifically titled chapter concerned with assessment in his book, other authors of important books on cognitive behavioral modification (Mahoney, 1974) and cognitive therapy (Beck et al., 1979) from the same era did not. Around this same period of time, however, the first books solely focused on behavioral assessment were published (Ciminero, Calhoun, & Adams, 1977; Cone & Hawkins, 1977; Hersen & Bellack, 1976), although the nature and evaluation of its relationship to behavior therapy remained somewhat unclear.

An ACT Approach to Assessment

Within this historical context, the assessment approach that I recommend in this chapter is somewhat atypical for several reasons. Let's take a look at those reasons now.

Integrating Assessment and Behavioral Change

First, this is an *iterative approach,* in which you repeatedly ask your clients questions, often in different words, that help reveal how the core processes operate in their lives, how strong they are, and what alternative approaches to treatment might be effective. However, in contrast to other assessment approaches in which assessment is primarily used to assist in diagnosis and/or the evaluation of treatment outcome, these assessment questions are tightly integrated with the behavioral-change dimensions of ACT (that is, helping clients live their lives fully despite the depression rather than trying to relieve the symptoms of depression). In essence, assessment and treatment begin at the same time. Because of this, your assessment of the core processes will not necessarily proceed in a linear fashion, such as fusion first, experiential avoidance second, and so on. Instead, the approach is, if you will, more holistic and, as you will see in what follows, much closer to the actual give and take of an initial therapy session. In this chapter, we will cover how you can initially assess pathogenic processes with your depressed clients, before we discuss how to alter them in subsequent chapters. Please be aware that the particular sequence I offer here does not imply that assessment procedures and treatment techniques within ACT can somehow be rigidly separated, one from the other, in a linear fashion. Rather, what I recommend is a dynamic approach in which an initial assessment informs the beginning of treatment, and the impact of that intervention in turn informs the continuing process of assessment, and so on back and forth. As noted in chapter 1, whether or not such an approach enjoys treatment utility (Hayes et al., 1987) over a more traditional, sequential approach to assessment and treatment within ACT is an empirical question that can only be answered with further research.

Fostering the Therapeutic Relationship

A second difference is that you conduct the assessment while simultaneously developing and fostering the therapeutic relationship with your client. The third wave of behavior therapies, in general, have been more cognizant than their predecessors of the critical role played by the relationship and interaction between client and therapist in psychological change (especially see Kohlenberg & Tsai, 1987, 1991). It is no coincidence that Hayes et al. (1999) in their book devoted an entire chapter (chapter 10) to the effective ACT therapeutic relationship. Because we are all verbal organisms, the same "dark side" of human language that contributes to the struggles of our clients ensnares us as therapists as well. No one is immune, and such common human experiences create a natural level of empathy that can be openly communicated to our clients. While self-disclosure should always be undertaken with discretion, a genuine, heartfelt recognition that you wrestle with some of the same issues your clients face, in most instances, is recommended (for example, "My mind works the same way yours seems to in always reminding me of when I've messed something up"). Because the division between assessment and treatment is made more for purposes of discussion than it is based on functional distinctions, you can, as I mentioned above, begin attending to the therapeutic relationship from the first interaction with your clients; you do not need to wait until pretreatment assessment has been completed and therapy itself is ready to start.

Assessing Flexibly

A third and final possible defining characteristic of the assessment approach detailed within this chapter involves the order in which it evaluates each of the core processes. While I suggest a starting point and order in which to assess these processes, I encourage you to hold this rather lightly and be flexible in your assessment approach. Any of the processes could be selected as the first to be assessed. Because they are interrelated and all contribute to psychological flexibility/inflexibility, focusing on one of the processes (fusion, for example) quite often "pulls" for others (such as valuing). For instance, you and your client may find yourselves seemingly being sidetracked by one process as you hone in on another. If you notice this, it doesn't mean that your approach is wrong. Follow the process that is doing the pulling, and if necessary, go back to assessing the process from which you were pulled. For example, thoughts that your client fuses with or buys into—such as "I'm stupid" and "I can't do anything right"—are only problematic insofar as they interfere with valued living. Separating out more troublesome from less troublesome thoughts thus naturally pulls for some discussion and consideration of valuing. You might, in a situation like this, ask your client, "As you see it, what have you missed out on in life that is important to you because of getting caught up in these thoughts?" Eventually assessing each of the core processes to arrive at an initial case formulation and conceptualization is more important than the particular order or sequence in which you evaluate them.

(On a practical note, because of the integrative nature of this assessment process, you will not find major headings below for all of the core processes. Some are best addressed within other core processes or concepts—for example, contact with the present moment and self as context are discussed under Three Senses of Self. In those cases, the specific core process will be noted with a minor heading.)

The Starting Point: The Client's Life Story

Most therapeutic approaches begin with clients being asked about the purpose of their initiating treatment, and ACT is no exception. Simply asking, "What brings you here today?" is usually enough to start the client's life story and allow you to sit back and listen. An active, empathetic listening approach is recommended in which it is appropriate to engage in reflection and summarization of the emotional and informational content of what you are hearing.

Initial Assessment of Fusion

Your primary objective in eliciting your clients' experiences with depression is to focus more on core processes that are reflected in what they say rather than in the content of their life story per se. For example, you may be able to detect fusion with specific automatic thoughts, reason giving, and storytelling, more from the degree of conviction and emotionality with which something is said than from what is being stated. A fused thought is an emotionally laden one, or what cognitive therapists commonly refer to as a "hot cognition" (J. S. Beck, 1995, p. 82). Accordingly, if clients become tearful and it is not clear what verbal construction is behind the emotion, they can be gently asked (for example, "I notice that you are starting to cry. Can you tell me what you are thinking about right now?"). Your ultimate purpose in doing so is not to identify thoughts for subsequent restructuring or disputation but for likely defusion. If necessary, ask your clients to elaborate or expand upon certain details of their life story, again not so much for the purpose of getting the facts straight or an exhaustive account of them but, more importantly, in order to evaluate the degree to which the client is fused with the particular version of the facts that is being told.

Identification of Depression Pathways

In some cases, you may also find it useful to ask clients to clarify the chronology of certain life events in order to better understand the pathway that led to their depression and the additional core processes that may have contributed to it. Some clients are obviously more talkative than others, but by actively listening to the client's life story, you can usually conclude a preliminary assessment of fusion and the likely pathway(s) that resulted in depression by the end of the first appointment. Assessment of the core processes within the ACT model is not a race, and storytelling can always be revisited if necessary.

While how clients tell their life story is generally of greater relevance than what is told, consider the content of what is said to help identify depression pathways that entail the priority of "being right" and/or "playing the martyr." As suggested in chapter 2, life stories in which your clients make frequent references about why they are justified in being depressed, given the mistreatment they have endured at the hands of others, are often revealing, especially if they are told in a very emotional manner. Statements like "It's no wonder I'm depressed given the way everyone has turned their back on me" suggest the need for considerable defusion work surrounding the life story and reason giving. This recommendation is in no way meant to minimize or trivialize the trauma your clients may have experienced. However, the events themselves are not the same as the story that gets told about them. Especially if the client is fused with the life story, it is even more critical that you as the ACT therapist do not do likewise, but instead hold it lightly.

Experiential Avoidance and Creative Hopelessness

Perhaps largely because of the way the Hayes et al. (1999) ACT book is organized, engendering creative hopelessness has come to be seen as the first clinical method typically introduced in conducting ACT. *Creative hopelessness* is the natural result of experiencing the unworkability of attempting to control unwanted thoughts and feelings. From an assessment perspective, inducing creative hopelessness will also often provide you with an initial opportunity to assess the strength of experiential avoidance and is a prime illustration of the dynamic and integrative relationship between assessment and therapeutic processes within ACT alluded to earlier. You may garner a preliminary reading of the overall level of experiential avoidance engaged in by your clients, and even some of the various forms it frequently takes, through listening to their life stories. Take particular note of some of the more common spontaneous references made by your clients of what they may have already tried (such as pharmacotherapy, previous psychotherapy, reading of self-help books, etc.) in coping with depression and to what effect.

Assessment of Suicidality

Even if some of the more common and widely accepted forms of attempting to control depression are cited in the life story, you still need to explicitly ask your clients about other experiential-avoidant efforts. I recommend this not only so you can conduct a more thorough initial evaluation of experiential escape/avoidance, but also so you can set the stage for engendering creative hopelessness. One all-too-common experiential escape/ problem-solving strategy that should be assessed with all your depressed clients is suicidality. In an empathetic and calm, matter-of-fact manner, ask your clients about any previous suicide attempts as well as any current thoughts of suicide (for instance, "It's not unusual and is quite understandable when we struggle with depression to find ourselves having thoughts of suicide. Could you tell me about your experiences with that?"). It is especially useful to know and ask about the broader context and the client's psychological and emotional state associated with any past and current suicidality. The fundamental issue for you to address in processing the client's responses is one of understanding the function(s) served by any past and current suicidal behavior.

As discussed previously, because not all suicidal thoughts and behavior are in the service of experiential escape and problem solving, you must determine if this is their primary function for each client on a case-by-case basis. If necessary, ask your clients to reflect upon their own suicidality by saying something like, "What were you hoping to accomplish by trying to kill yourself?" If it becomes apparent that the suicidal behavior is linked to emotional control, it is also useful to know, for at least two reasons, the specific aversive affective states (such as guilt, sadness, hopelessness, shame, etc.) from which the client sought escape. First, it is helpful to know the specific emotional problems for which suicide emerged as a solution so that you can subsequently address alternative ways of responding and coping with them. Second, if the particular psychological state from which the suicidal client sought escape was hopelessness, there are, at least in my view, potential implications for the engendering of creative hopelessness at this point in treatment.

Titrating Creative Hopelessness

As Hayes et al. (1999, chap. 4) point out, it is essential to be clear that your goal as an ACT therapist in engendering creative hopelessness is not to induce a feeling or emotional reaction by clients but rather the repertoire-expanding action of being liberated from an emotional-control agenda that has not worked. However, this does not preclude the possibility that clients—especially for whom suicidality has served, and perhaps still serves, as an escape from hopelessness as a feeling state—may respond to efforts to induce creative hopelessness as a behavior with more of the same emotion (for instance, "Now even my therapist seems to think there is no hope for me"). For this reason, I follow a "titrating" approach—that is, I adjust the intensity level of interventions used to induce creative hopelessness to what I feel is appropriate for a particular client. I typically go after creative hopelessness less rigorously and present a more modest dose of techniques to induce it in working with clients who feel (or have felt) that suicide is an escape from depression. I am somewhat more rigorous in inducing creative hopelessness with clients who are not suicidal or, if they are, whose suicidality has not served an experiential escape function. This is a tricky dance to undertake. On the one hand, you want to engender enough creative hopelessness for clients to abandon the continued pursuit of their counterproductive experiential change agenda and thereby increase psychological flexibility by opening themselves up to the possibility of responding differently to their depression. On the other hand (and at the same time), you want to prevent them from reverting back to suicidality as a preferred problem-solving strategy.

I want to make it clear that there is presently no empirical support for adjusting the level of creative hopelessness to be induced with depressed clients in the manner I recommend here. Consequently you are advised to hold the recommendation lightly, especially insofar as I acknowledge that it may function more to minimize my own insecurities than promote more efficacious treatment. (As emphasized earlier, the language machine stalks all of us!) For this reason, you may wish to experiment somewhat in your work with ACT by comparing for yourself the somewhat more measured approach I suggest here for engendering creative hopelessness against the relatively more rigorous strategy for doing so outlined in chapter 4 of the Hayes et al. (1999) text.

It is not unusual to revisit treatment issues within ACT and additional doses of creative hopelessness–engendering techniques and procedures, such as the Chinese Handcuffs (pp. 104–105), Person in the Hole ("Man in the Hole" in Hayes et al., 1999, pp. 101–104), and Tug-of-War with a Monster (p. 109) metaphors from the ACT book (Hayes et al., 1999) can be reemphasized and presented again later, if necessary. Should this be the case, I believe that such subsequent efforts to weaken experiential escape/avoidance are more likely to be successful if preceded by some defusion work surrounding hopelessness-related thoughts. For example, clients might be asked to respond to their feelings of hopelessness and related thoughts as objects by participation in the Physicalizing Exercise (Hayes et al., pp. 170–171).

Emotional Control Strategies

Regardless of which approach you take to induce creative hopelessness, it is still important to identify additional emotional control strategies used by your clients above and beyond those that involve seeking professional assistance, reading self-help books, and, as just discussed, thinking about and possibly even attempting suicide. The two approaches to engendering creative hopelessness differ not in the degree to which they seek to exhaustively detect all types of experiential control, but in the extent to which they drive home to clients the unworkability of whatever efforts are identified. Repeatedly asking your clients "What else have you tried to help yourself feel less depressed and how has it worked for you?" may be necessary to ensure that no emotional control strategies are overlooked. To accomplish this, it seems useful to divide these additional efforts into internal, external, situation-specific, and in-session emotional control strategies.

Internal Control Strategies

The experiential control strategy that is most likely to be used by your depressed clients—namely, rumination—has already been discussed at length and sufficient ways of assessing and detecting it suggested (see chapters 2 and 3). Daydreaming, thought suppression, and other forms of cognitive distraction represent additional internal control strategies that may be detected by asking a question such as "To what degree have you tried to put depressive thoughts and feelings out of your mind by trying to think about other things?" As I alluded to earlier, your identification of the specific thoughts being avoided in such instances will also be helpful in guiding subsequent defusion work.

Less common internal control strategies are likely to vary considerably from client to client and may only be identifiable through more active collaboration with them. For example, even within the titrating approach for inducing creative hopelessness, I invariably present the Person in the Hole Metaphor (Hayes et al, 1999, pp. 101–104), although often in a somewhat toned-down version. Afterward, clients are given the homework assignment of identifying additional ways they engage in "digging." A recent depressed client reported at the beginning of our next session that she now realized that she had been using reading for most of her adult life as an experiential escape strategy. She elaborated that she always enjoyed reading, even as a child, but that as an adult she found herself spending more and more time immersed in it as way of not having to deal with depressing life issues. Also, she noted that her reading had increasingly become more rigid and inflexible in nature (for example, "I found myself feeling like I *had* to read"). Prior to beginning ACT, she had rationalized the function of her reading—she would only allow herself to read nonfiction so she would at least become more knowledgeable in the process—but now began to more clearly see that it was keeping her stuck in her depression.

External Control Strategies

The distinction between internal and external strategies is somewhat arbitrary—with the latter referring to more overt patterns of behavior—but I believe it nonetheless is useful to ensure that few forms of experiential avoidance are overlooked. Among external control strategies, the use of substances for emotional regulation ("self-medication") is perhaps the most widespread as reflected by the high rates of comorbidity noted between depression and substance abuse and dependency more generally and those between mood- and alcohol-related disorders in particular (Regier et al., 1990).

The ingestion of additional substances whether in the form of over-the-counter medications, prescription, or "recreational drugs" (such as marijuana, methamphetamine, cocaine, etc.) may serve the same experiential-avoidant function and should not be overlooked. Accordingly, specifically ask all of your depressed clients about the degree to which they ingest substances to regulate their dysphoric mood (for example, "Do you ever drink or take anything to help yourself feel better?"). Knowing the specific substances involved in most instances is less critical than identifying the particular affective states, thoughts, memories, and other private events from which the client is seeking escape, again, so that you can address alternative ways of reacting to them within therapy.

A second common form of external control involves the engagement in frequent bursts of intensive activities such as eating, shopping, gambling, and/or sexual activities that have been collectively regarded by some as "addictive behaviors" (for example, see Nakken, 1996). While I personally question the usefulness of applying the term "addiction" to such behaviors, I do believe it is important to evaluate their potential to serve an experiential-avoidant/mood-regulating function. Asking a question like "Are there any particular things that you do when you're feeling depressed to help yourself feel better?" is a way of initially probing for the use of external control strategies in the form of overt patterns of compulsive-like behaviors.

Situation-Specific Control Strategies

Depression is commonly viewed as a fairly stable psychological condition that is "carried around" by clients and accordingly is thought to be much less reactive to situational factors than other more transient emotional states such as anxiety. Nonetheless, despite variations due to individual differences, fluctuations in dysphoric mood and related thoughts, bodily sensations, and the like also appear to be context specific (Penner, Shiffman, Paty, & Fritzsche, 1994), which suggests that the avoidance of such situations could serve as another type of emotional control. To get at this, you might ask your clients, "Are there things you're unlikely to do or places you're unlikely to go to because they leave you feeling even more depressed?" Obviously some avoided activities and situations will have more of a detrimental impact in leading a valued life than others. No longer going to the movies, either by oneself or with friends, because the client did this with a departed spouse may be rather inconsequential. Choosing to severely limit contact with all friends because one is painfully reminded of the loss may not be. Compiling a list of avoided activities and/or situations may be useful in helping subsequently to guide exposure-type homework assignments.

In-Session Control Strategies

Behavior therapists are certainly not the first group of mental health professionals to recognize that a number of behaviors exhibited by clients in interaction with their therapists also may serve an experiential-avoidant function (Waterhouse & Strupp, 1984). This phenomenon is certainly acknowledged within ACT (see Hayes et al., 1999, pp. 130–132), but has been emphasized even more explicitly within functional analytic psychotherapy (FAP; Kohlenberg & Tsai, 1987, 1991). As suggested in chapter 1, FAP can also be regarded as part of the third generation of behavior therapy and is quite compatible with ACT. In effect, FAP can be readily combined and integrated with ACT, leading to the dictum "If you are doing ACT and not doing FAP, you are not doing ACT." (I believe I first heard this from Kelly Wilson but, unfortunately, don't recall the exact date or circumstance to offer an appropriate citation.) Consult the work of Kohlenberg and Tsai for a more detailed presentation and depiction of FAP than I offer here.

One of the assumptions of FAP is that clinically relevant behaviors on the part of clients that occur outside of therapy are quite likely to appear in therapy as well, although perhaps not in the same form. As applied to emotional control, this suggests that you will probably have an opportunity to observe some behaviors that serve an experiential avoidant/escape function in your interactions with clients. Clients, for example, may try to avoid thinking or talking about certain issues that are especially emotionally painful. They may do so in various verbal as well as nonverbal ways. The former may include changing the topic of conversation, offering a tangential response to a question, falling silent or, alternatively, talking a great deal but about largely irrelevant issues. Common nonverbal forms of in-session emotional control can include turning away and avoiding eye contact. Suggestions on how to respond therapeutically to such client behaviors will be offered in chapter 6.

Valuing

In my view and experience, I find it particularly useful to regard the assessment of valuing within ACT as an ongoing process. This is not because valuing itself changes within the typical time span of therapy, but because, as alluded to in the previous chapter, clients may often offer what they think you want to hear as their values if directly questioned about them. For this reason, it seems prudent to assess for valuing repeatedly through different means, both direct and indirect, and look for convergence. Here we will discuss indirect means for initially assessing values. More direct ways of further identifying and clarifying client values will be offered in chapter 7.

Goal Setting

Perhaps in large measure because the chapter on valuing (chapter 8) appears more than two-thirds of the way through the Hayes et al. (1999) book, it's understandable to think that valuing should be assessed later rather than sooner within therapy. However, I recommend that you do at least a preliminary assessment of valuing quite early on; a good time is when you discuss with your clients their goals for therapy. Values and goals are not one and the same, but discussing goals with your clients can help you get an initial reading on their values as well. Values serve as a critical reference point around which other core processes related to ACT can be oriented—for instance, defusion is only therapeutically appropriate within the context of valuing—and identifying and clarifying values earlier rather than later helps direct both assessment and treatment. Moreover, making the values of your clients explicit dignifies the considerable psychological pain and suffering they will likely experience both inside and outside of therapy if they are to successfully move their lives in a direction they value.

Client values are not the only values that are important in ACT; your values are important as well. When you ask, usually in the initial session with new clients, what their goals are for therapy, be sure to listen carefully to determine whether the overall goals are appropriate and not contrary to your own values. Perhaps more importantly, knowing your clients' goals will also help you better understand how they frame their depression. In my experience, it's much more likely that the goals articulated by your clients will relate more to being successful at experiential control (for example, "I want to be happy," "I want to get rid of this depression, "I want to feel better about myself," etc.) than to leading a more meaningful and valued life. While such goals are inappropriate therapeutic objectives within ACT, a discussion of them, nevertheless, provides a rich opportunity for indirectly evaluating valuing and further acquainting your clients with ACT.

An Illustrative Dialogue

The following is a typical conversation that might occur with a client at this point in the overall assessment:

Therapist: You said your goal in coming to therapy is to feel less depressed. I understand this is very important to you, and I wonder if you could help me better understand why that is. If you no longer had to struggle with depression the way you've been struggling, how would your life be different?

Client: Everything would just be a whole lot better if I felt better.

Therapist: Can I ask you to be a bit more specific? Imagine that the time, effort, and energy you have been spending in trying to feel better was now given back to you so you could now spend it differently and in whatever way you wanted to. How would you spend it? What would you do?

Client: I guess maybe I'd be more likely to spend more time with friends and do more things with my wife and kids. When I'm depressed, I get real grouchy around other people and would just rather be off by myself.

Therapist: It sounds like your relationships with other people—your friends and family—are very important to you. Would you want spending more time and doing more things with people who are important to you in your life to be one of our goals here?

Client: Sure, but I don't see how that can happen as long as I feel this way.

Therapist: I can see how that's how it seems to you. Right now though, let me ask you as best you can to imagine a different world. Suppose you were given the following choices. Option A is that you would feel better and no longer have any more depression in your life, but at the cost of also no longer having any more contact with your friends, your wife, or your children—you would never see them again. Option B is that you could spend as much time as you would like with your friends and family, but your level of depression might not change. Maybe it would and maybe it wouldn't. Which would you choose?

Client: I'd like to have my depression go away for good and still be able to see my friends and family.

Therapist:	I understand that's what you would like. Suppose just for a moment here that's not possible, and the only two options are the ones I've described. Which would you choose?
Client:	To still see my friends and family.
Therapist:	What if what we do here is about that—to see if we can find a way for you to spend more time with your friends and your family?

In these types of dialogues with clients, I prefer to not use phrases like "If you were no longer depressed ..." to avoid implying that emotional control is the goal of therapy. At the same time, framing it in this way, at least early on, is probably not that critical as there will be numerous other opportunities to emphasize that this—that is, the elimination of depression per se—is not the goal of ACT. At this point, you and your client may initially agree that spending more time with friends and family is one of the outcome goals of ACT. However, you are less likely to come to consensus on what the *process goals* are—that is, how the outcome goal itself will be attained. At this particular time, that issue is not crucial because it can be dealt with as therapy unfolds. In particular, it is quite likely that the client will keep returning to the process goal of wanting to "feel better" until the control agenda is abandoned through more work with defusion, acceptance, and engendering creative hopelessness.

Framing the client's predicament as a hypothetical choice serves at least two purposes. First, it helps clarify valuing by providing an initial evaluation of what clients are willing to suffer for. In this sense, the hypothetical question is derived from the overarching one of "What in life is so important to you that you would be willing to experience depression to get it?" Second, the choice enhances psychological flexibility by inducing alternative behavior, even if only momentarily and in imagination.

A legitimate concern that the client may be merely making the socially desirable choice (option B) would be heightened if the dialogue just presented were the only means used to assess valuing. For example, your assessment of suicidality provides a way for you to indirectly evaluate the relative strength of the value entailed within option B by ascertaining how much it is overshadowed by option A. After all, in contemplating suicide, clients often place the elimination of their suffering (option A) over everything else in their lives. Further assessment would obviously be warranted if a client opted for option B but was also imminently suicidal.

Relationship to Suffering

As noted in chapter 2, where you find suffering with your clients, you will also find their values (Wilson, 2005). This suggests a powerful and additional indirect way of assessing valuing. Suffering and valuing are inseparable and are merely two sides of the same experiential coin; we don't experience emotional pain about something that means nothing to us. Quite often, clients in offering their life story and explaining why they are seeking therapy at this time will have already identified major sources and areas of suffering within their lives. If necessary, ask some further questions as you seek to identify what values are being compromised and possibly even violated. Questions like "What's the worst thing about being depressed?" or "Why is being depressed so bad for you?" or "How has being depressed changed your life?" when presented tactfully may help illuminate valuing underlying client suffering.

It may also be useful to ask more specific yet similar questions about significant life events, such as a failed business venture cited by the client. What core value(s) are behind the suffering initiated by such an event? Was it that the client's sense of autonomy and self-determination was damaged when she had to go to work for someone else as a consequence? Did she feel that she was a bad mother and had let her children down in not being able to adequately provide for them financially? Was it a combination of the two, or was another core value of critical relevance? Asking a question like "What was it about your business failing that was so upsetting to you?' is one way of addressing such issues. If necessary, another means is to ask the client to close her eyes and, after becoming centered, relive what her thoughts, feelings, bodily sensations, and the like were when she had to acknowledge that the business had indeed failed. You can also use the same process in asking the client to recollect what it was like to engage in related actions, such as looking for another job and telling her children why she was doing so.

Committed Action

Your initial assessment of valuing sets the stage for conducting a preliminary evaluation of how tightly the clients' activities, or lack thereof, are linked to their apparent values. In doing so, consider not only activities that clients may not be engaging in that would be value directed, but also those in which they are involved, even possibly to the point of excess, that are not value congruent.

Behavioral Deficits

Clients who are weighed down by depression are not leading vital and value-infused lives. At the level of overt behavior, you will see this most obviously manifested by what clients are not doing. By this point in the initial assessment, having heard the client's life story and goals for therapy, you probably will have compiled a good deal of information about this issue. For example, with the client who indicated a goal of wanting to spend more time with family and friends, ask what specific activities he used to participate in with them (for instance, "What specific things would you do with your friends or family before you became depressed?" and "What things would you like to be able to do with them now?").

I believe it is important, for a more thorough initial evaluation, to ask similar questions about other client activities that may be less clearly linked to values but which also have been reduced in frequency or even discontinued altogether because of depression (for example, "What things are you not doing now that you used to do?"). Notice that the suggested question is not specific to pleasurable activities, although you could also ask about that (that is, "What things are you not doing now that you used to enjoy doing?").

This is because not all valued activities, such as work, are necessarily enjoyable and not all enjoyable activities are valued.

While it is by no means a fail-safe assumption, it seems reasonable to view your clients' predepression lives as having been generally more value directed than their current existence. To the extent that this is the case, at least some aspects of their depression ("behavioral deficits") are probably tied to having discontinued valued activities. We will discuss some additional assessment you can conduct to determine this, along with ways of clarifying barriers to the engagement in committed action, at greater length in chapter 7. At this point in the process, your goal is to identify behavioral deficits as likely candidates for discontinued value-related activities.

Behavioral Excesses

In all probability, by now you will have already identified certain client actions that have increased in frequency, intensity, and/or duration with the onset and continuation of depression, particularly during your initial assessment of emotional control strategies. Nonetheless, in order to complete a more comprehensive initial assessment, specifically ask about other behavioral excesses (for example, "Are there other things that you are doing more of now that you are depressed?"). Evaluate any activities identified by the client in relationship to the initial value assessment. It's possible that some behavioral excesses not previously identified, such as sleeping more, may be seen as being relatively "value neutral" and as neither in the service of or violation of core values of the client. Others though, such as thinking about having an extramarital affair, may be both incompatible with the value of being a loving spouse and constitute another form of experiential escape and avoidance (that is, "Maybe it would make me feel better for at least a little while"). If necessary, ask about the specific relationship between a given activity and an apparent value of the client (for example, "How does sleeping more relate to you wanting to spend more time with your friends and family? Does it move you closer to that or further away?").

Fusion

Your assessment of fusion within ACT, like that of valuing, is an ongoing process. It is useful to think of fusion within the context of valuing. Whatever fused verbal material—whether in the form of automatic thoughts, reason giving, or storytelling—stands in the way of engaging in committed value-directed actions ultimately becomes targeted for defusion. From this perspective, one of the purposes of the initial assessment leading to a preliminary case conceptualization and formulation within ACT is the identification of either single or networks of relational frames for defusion. I've already offered in this chapter and in the previous one a considerable number of suggestions for detecting fused material, and more will be provided in chapter 6. Therefore, I would like to make only a few additional comments about the assessment of defusion at different levels of languaging.

Automatic Thoughts

If necessary, questioning your clients about specific thoughts that occur when they feel particularly depressed can be used to supplement alternative strategies for their identification. You can do this by listening to what your clients say spontaneously and/or by catching the emotional concomitants of "hot cognitions" (that is, automatic thoughts that accompany strong feelings). For example, merely asking the question "When you feel especially depressed, what do you think about?" is perhaps the most direct additional way of identifying other fused automatic thoughts. Alternatively, ask your depressed clients to recollect some recent painful moment and notice what they are thinking (for instance, "Close your eyes and bring yourself back to when you were speaking to your wife and telling her that you didn't want to go out to dinner with her. Notice how that feels and tell me what thoughts you are having").

Reason Giving

As suggested earlier, you can readily identify many of the reasons clients offer for their depression by simply actively listening to their life stories. To clear up any ambiguity, however, verify your summarization of what you heard with your client: "Let me see if I understand what you've told me so far. As you see it, your depression was primarily caused by X, Y, and Z. Do I have that right? Have I missed anything? Are there any other reasons for your depression?"

Storytelling

Use a similar strategy of summarization and request for client clarification to also verify your initial assessment of fusion with the life story, which you garnered by simply listening to it. In doing so, pay particular attention to indications that your client may be caught up in "being right" and/or "playing the martyr." Such types of fusion can be especially challenging therapeutically. (More on this will be presented in chapter 10.) If necessary, verify your assessment by saying something like "Correct me if I'm wrong, but it sounds to me as if you firmly believe that you wouldn't have become depressed if your family had treated you better." Such a statement may also validate your client's experience and thereby strengthen your therapeutic relationship.

Three Senses of "Self"

The final area to evaluate during an initial assessment is your client's senses of self. Grounded in the associated core processes of mindfulness and self as context, ACT differentiates three major senses of self: self as process, self as concept, and self as context (Hayes et al., 1999, pp. 181–187). Let's look at each of these now.

Self as Process

Self as process refers to our capacity to be continuously aware of our ongoing stream of psychological reactions and experiences. All too often, however, we are not mindfully aware of them in the sense of Kabat-Zinn's (1995, p. 4) definition of *mindfulness*—that is, "paying attention in a particular way: on purpose, in the present moment, nonjudgmentally." Experiential avoidance and fusion compromise the self as process. The degree of compromise directly correlates with levels of experiential avoidance and fusion. Therefore, your assessment of these two processes already provides at least some evaluation of how much your client is likely to be living in the past or future rather than in the present moment. For a fuller evaluation, consider and evaluate the levels of rumination (living in the past) and worrying (living in the future) displayed by your clients as well as spontaneous comments they make about either the past or future instead of the here and now.

Although it is usually not needed, you can directly ask clients about how much they are preoccupied with the the past or future (for example, "How much do you find yourself thinking about either the past or the future? When you do so, can you tell me what you specifically think about?"). In more dramatic instances, the preoccupation may become apparent in your interactions with clients who seem to be distracted and are "off somewhere else."

Self as Concept

Self as concept as it is used in ACT refers to interconnected thoughts that we have about ourselves. From an RFT perspective, each of us constructs a relational network that helps define who we are and tells our life story.

Most depressed clients will make frequent and spontaneous negative self-evaluations (such as "I'm so stupid" or "I can't believe what an idiot I am"). Should this not occur, ask your clients about what they think about themselves (for example, "How would you describe yourself?"). It is often instructive to specifically probe not only for negative aspects of the conceptualized self (that is, "What is it about yourself that you dislike the most?") but positive ones as well (for instance, "What is it about yourself that you like the most?") to determine if the latter are even part of the picture. A client who responds with "I don't know," "I can't think of anything," or even more tellingly with "Nothing," is presumably reflecting a very tight level of fusion with a damaged conceptualized self.

You can also evaluate the degree to which fusion with a damaged conceptualized self has contributed to psychological inflexibility by slightly modifying some of the questions suggested earlier in the context of therapeutic goal setting (for example, ask, "If you felt better *about yourself*, how would your life be different?"). A relatively long and detailed answer linking the conceptualized self with *behavioral passivity*, that is, the absence of commited, value-directed activity (such as "I'd explore a career change" or "I'd seriously consider getting married again"), suggests the need for considerable defusion work in this area if the client is to become unstuck and move forward in life.

Self as Context

During the process of self-awareness, there is yet another aspect of the self that is aware of what we are aware of. This perspective from which self-awareness is possible—what is commonly referred to in ACT as the "observer" or "observing self" (Hayes et al., 1999, p. 184)—constitutes *self as context*.

Of all the core processes related to ACT, that involving the self as context has proved to be the most elusive to assess. This should not be surprising given its relatively ephemeral nature and lack of form. Unfortunately, I can offer no questions for you to ask your clients to evaluate the degree to which they are in contact with a transcendent sense of self. Asking "How spiritual are you?" comes to mind, but it seems quite likely that many clients would offer the obviously socially desirable answer in response. More formal means of assessment are also not presently an option. While self-report inventories have been developed for assessing the other processes within the hexaflex, efforts to empirically investigate the relationship between self as context and psychological flexibility through the use of a paper-and-pencil measure of spirituality and the AAQ, respectively, have not been promising (McDaniel & Zettle, 2006).

By default, it appears that the best way to currently assess the sense of self that is contentless is to do so indirectly through an evaluation of fusion with the conceptualized self. To the extent that rigid attachment to the conceptualized self precludes contact with a transcendent sense of self, the more fusion that is present with the self as concept, the more likely that the process involving self as context has been compromised.

Summary

View the assessment of ACT-related core processes in your work with depressed clients as an ongoing, dynamic process. In this chapter, we have considered suggestions about undertaking a preliminary assessment to obtain sufficient information to formulate an initial, individualized, ACT-consistent case conceptualization for each of your clients. This can then be used to guide the early stages of treatment. Much of this assessment consists of interviewing that occurs during the first sessions with clients and thus involves interacting with your clients in such a way that you simultaneously establish and foster a therapeutic relationship with them. A number of the assessment questions suggested in this chapter are summarized in table 1 by the processes they are designed to assess.

TABLE 1
ASSESSMENT OF ACT-RELATED CORE PROCESSES: SUGGESTED QUESTIONS

Process	*Questions*
Experiential Avoidance	"What types of professional help have you previously sought to help yourself feel better?"
Suicidality	"Can you tell me about your experiences with thinking about or trying to kill yourself?"
	"What were you trying to accomplish by trying to kill yourself?"
Internal Control Strategies	"How much do you try to put depressive thoughts and feelings out of your mind by trying to think of other things?"
External Control Strategies	"How much do you drink or take other substances to help yourself feel better?"
	"Are there any other particular things you do when you're feeling depressed to help you feel better?"
Situationally Specific Control Strategies	"Are there things you're unlikely to do or places you are unlikely to go because they leave you feeling even more depressed?"
Fusion	
Automatic Thoughts	(In response to client crying) "What are you thinking about right now?"
	"When you are feeling especially depressed, what do you think about?"
Reason Giving	"As you see it, what has caused your depression?"
Storytelling	"Can you tell me about your experiences with depression over the course of your life?"

Self as Process/Mindfulness	"How much do you find yourself thinking about either the past or the future?"
Self as Concept	"How would you describe yourself?"
	"What do you dislike the most about yourself?"
	"What do you like the most about yourself?"
	"If you felt better about yourself, how would your life be different?"
Valuing	"What are your goals in coming to therapy?
	"If you no longer struggled with depression, how would your life be different?"
	"What's the worst thing for you about being depressed?"
	"How has being depressed changed your life?"
	"What was it about [specific life event] that was so depressing to you?"
Committed Action	
Behavioral Deficits	"What things are you not doing now that you used to do before becoming depressed?"
Behavioral Excesses	"What things are you doing more of now that you are depressed?"

It is certainly also possible to undertake a more formal assessment of most of the core processes through the administration of various paper-and-pencil measures. A number of these inventories are listed in table 2. I don't recommend that these instruments be used as the only form of assessment, but instead that they supplement your assessment made through interviewing your clients. Their other obvious use is as process measures in research investigating the mechanisms of change within ACT (see Zettle & Hayes, 1986). Several of the inventories (such as the AAQ and RFD) have already been mentioned, and their potential use will be discussed at greater length, along with several that have not yet been cited, in upcoming chapters when we consider further the interrelationship between assessment and treatment issues within ACT.

My own preference clinically, apart from research considerations, is to administer most of these inventories selectively as part of an ongoing process of assessment on an as-needed basis. They can be helpful when ongoing treatment becomes bogged down. An alternative strategy, which will be discussed in greater detail in chapter 9, is to administer them collectively as part of a pretreatment assessment battery. Whether you administer these inventories on an as-needed basis or as a pretreatment assessment battery, use them to formulate a case conceptualization and an associated individualized plan of treatment. Further research is needed to determine which option—as needed or pretreatment—is more effective as shown by more favorable treatment outcomes.

TABLE 2
ASSESSMENT OF ACT-RELATED CORE PROCESSES: FORMAL MEASURES

Process	*Measure*
Psychological Flexibility	Acceptance and Action Questionnaire (AAQ; Hayes, Strosahl, Wilson et al., 2004)
Experiential Avoidance	
Thought Suppression	White Bear Suppression Inventory (WBSI; Wegner & Zanakos, 1994)
Rumination	Response Styles Questionnaire (RSQ; Nolen-Hoeksema & Morrow, 1991)
Fusion	
Thoughts	Automatic Thoughts Questionnaire (ATQ; Hollon & Kendall, 1980)
Reason Giving	Reasons for Depression Questionnaire (RFD; Addis et al., 1995)
Self as Process/Mindfulness	Kentucky Inventory of Mindfulness Skills (KIMS; Baer, Smith, & Allen, 2004)
Self as Concept	Rosenberg Self-Esteem Scale (RES; Rosenberg, 1965)
Valuing	Personal Values Questionnaire (PVQ; Blackledge & Ciarrochi, 2005)
	Valued Living Questionnaire (VLQ; Wilson & Groom, 2002)

CHAPTER 5

Case Formulation and Conceptualization

Not surprisingly, the two overarching questions within ACT for you to address in conceptualizing cases of depression are (1) What needs to be *accepted* in order to fulfill (2) a *commitment* to what? Stated somewhat differently, the values to which your clients' identified therapeutic goals may be linked and the psychological experiences and events that may function as barriers to committed action that moves your clients in the direction of those goals and related values must be clarified on a case-by-case basis. For example, it is certainly possible that the focus of significant defusion and acceptance work (such as negative self-evaluations and a life story filled with regret) may be quite similar for two clients even though their core values differ. Conversely, two other clients may be similar, if not identical, in their valuing but be blocked in moving forward in their lives by different types of fused material and different forms of experiential avoidance.

In large measure, this chapter acts as a bridge between the initial assessment of core processes discussed in the previous chapter and the beginning of active therapeutic interventions that we will cover in the next few chapters. More specifically, your formulation and conceptualization of each case of depression can be linked both back to your preliminary evaluation of the key core processes and forward to your development of an initial treatment plan.

Guidelines for Information Processing

Guidelines for processing initial assessment information that we will discuss in this chapter largely follow suggestions offered by Hayes, Strosahl, Luoma, et al. (2004). For this reason, you may find it useful to read and use their chapter in conjunction with this one. A bit more structured way to guide your thinking about the information garnered through the preliminary assessment is by organizing it according to an ACT Initial Case Conceptualization Form (see appendix A) developed by Jason Lillis and Jason Luoma (2005). It is being offered here in a slightly modified format with their kind permission and my gratitude.

I should acknowledge that I am not aware of any existing research that has evaluated the potential treatment utility associated with use of the case-conceptualization form. Nevertheless, I highly recommend that you use the form for at least three or four of your depressed clients in order to see if it is useful for you. In particular, compare your own experience and level of success in applying ACT in your work with depressed clients when the form is used versus cases in which it is not. To assist with your use of (and possible experimentation with) the form, the organization of this chapter closely parallels it.

Presenting Problem Analysis

Your first major task in case conceptualization is to reformulate your client's presenting problem and therapeutic goals from an ACT perspective. Because this book focuses on working with clients with depression, perhaps I should say a little more on this. In particular, I want to reemphasize that depression often is accompanied by other diagnosable forms of human suffering, particularly anxiety disorders and substance abuse/dependency (Brown, Campbell, Lehman, Grisham, & Mancill, 2001; Regier et al., 1990). For this reason, explicitly ask your clients if they have any additional problems, issues, or concerns apart from depression that they would also like to address in therapy.

Comorbidity Issues

While we will discuss the general issue of comorbidity more extensively in chapter 10, some consideration of it here also seems appropriate. If a copresenting problem (such as panic disorder, for example) is identified, the key question to consider is how it may be functionally related to the client's depression. In doing so, you may first have to assess the apparent secondary problem in order to determine its functions. One likely possibility is that the panic attacks in this case serve much of the same function(s) as the depression and are supported by similar ACT-related core processes (such as fusion, experiential avoidance, and the like) In such instances, as suggested in chapter 1, ACT as a transdiagnostic approach can proceed by, in effect, simultaneously treating both problems by targeting core functional processes that have been evaluated as central to both.

Another possibility, although presumably less probable from the perspective of ACT, is that the comorbid condition does not share some of the same ACT-related processes as depression, but is still functionally related to it. For instance, in our example here, it is quite likely that the panic attacks will serve as an experiential barrier for committed action, particularly if they have generated a fair amount of associated agoraphobic avoidant behavior. Although a common recommendation in such instances is to treat anxiety first and then depression, this treatment strategy generally lacks empirical support, and what little does exist comes from research on second-generation cognitive behavioral interventions (Joormann, Kosfelder, & Schulte, 2005). At this point, with few exceptions (Batten & Hayes, 2005; Petersen, 2007), ACT's ability to concurrently and successfully alleviate coexisting forms of human suffering has not been evaluated systematically. I am aware of no work, for example, that has specifically examined the treatment of comorbid depressive and anxiety disorders. In the absence of clear, empirically derived guidelines to the contrary, I believe that beginning ACT with the primary presenting complaint of depression and being prepared to address any co-occurring problems as they emerge is perhaps as useful as any other suggestion that could be offered.

Based upon the ACT model of human suffering, a third and even less likely possible relationship between depression and co-occurring problems is that the two are functionally unrelated. Although this seems quite improbable in the case of comorbid panic attacks and depression, it may be more plausible when the other presenting problem constitutes an alternative form of anxiety disorder, such as a specific phobia, or is diagnosable within another family of disorders entirely, such as a sexual dysfunction. Regardless of the specific nature of the other presenting problem, my previous recommendation of going forward and initiating ACT with a primary focus on depression seems justifiable provided you follow it flexibly and are open to changing strategies as necessary.

Therapeutic Process Goals vs. Outcome Goals

One of the challenges faced by new practitioners of ACT is in making and maintaining the distinction between process goals and outcome goals. *Outcome goals* refer to the ultimate desired outcome of therapy, such as leading a valued life, whereas *process goals* refer to presumably what has to occur for such outcomes to be attained. Many other therapeutic approaches and traditions, including cognitive behavioral approaches that emphasize first-order change, tend to regard the reduction of clients' presenting complaints as the appropriate goal of treatment. As mentioned in the previous chapter, however, what depressed clients typically identify as their objectives in seeking therapy (for example, "I want to feel better about myself" or "I'm tired of being depressed"), at best constitute ostensible process rather than outcome goals from the perspective of ACT. Because the ultimate objective is not mere symptomatic relief but instead to enable and empower clients to lead more full and meaningful lives, ACT case formulation usually requires a reframing and reconceptualization of their initial therapeutic goals. For example, if the client's stated goal is to "feel better," your task becomes one of identifying what life opportunities might subsequently open up to the client if this were to occur and how they would, in turn, relate to key values. Thus, the initial client goal of depression reduction, for instance, may be reformulated into one of "reducing experiential control efforts and reinvesting time and energy into pursuing value-directed activities." The particular ways of controlling unwanted psychological events and the valued activities that are compromised as a result will, of course, vary from client to client. For instance, one client may be unable to move on to a more rewarding career until he recaptures his self-confidence, whereas another cannot envision a better future for herself and so remains stuck in an unfulfilled marriage.

The process goals that must be attained to realize the reformulated outcome goal at this point in the case conceptualization—for example, would it be more useful to start with defusion and acceptance work first or focus on valuing?—may still be somewhat unclear. What should not be unclear, however, is that apparent process goals of the client, such as "feeling better about myself," are not appropriate process goals within ACT. Completing the rest of the case-conceptualization form should be useful to you in clarifying the relevant process goals and thereby help in the formulation of an initial treatment plan.

Related Questions

The following is a list of somewhat overlapping questions to ask of yourself in reformulating your client's presenting problem of depression in an ACT-coherent manner:

- What are the client's goals for therapy?

- Are the client's stated goals part of an emotional control agenda?

- Are the client's stated goals process goals or outcome goals?

- If they are process goals, how can they be reformulated into appropriate outcome goals?

- Are the outcome goals that emerge from a reformulation of the client's stated therapeutic goals (for instance, being a loving parent) ones that can be potentially attained by committed action (such as the client moving his/her feet in a valued direction)?

Identification of Avoided Content

The second step in case conceptualization involves inventorying the various types of psychological experiences and material your client seeks to escape from and/or avoid. While clients differ in their overall ability to tolerate psychological distress, most will avoid each of the specific psychological experiences listed on the case-conceptualization form (thoughts, emotions, memories, etc.), at least to some degree. Thus, your task here is not so much to determine whether or not certain types of experiences are avoided or not, as it is to ascertain your clients' overall level of distress tolerance and the relative degree to which they typically avoid some forms of psychological events over others. Defusion exercises and acceptance-promotion interventions are generally recommended in targeting a wide array of avoided psychological experiences, although the particular forms their application takes will vary somewhat depending upon the specific nature of the avoided content. For example, the Milk, Milk, Milk Exercise (Hayes et al., 1999, pp. 154–156) is a defusion technique that is more appropriate for troublesome thoughts than it is for emotional experiences. For unwanted feelings that are difficult to label, something like the Physicalizing Exercise (pp. 170–171) would likely be more useful.

Related Questions

In completing this section of the case-conceptualization form, questions to ask yourself include the following:

- What is the overall level of the client's ability to tolerate psychological distress?

- What key thoughts is the client reluctant to experience?

- What are the central emotions, feelings, mood states, and the like from which the client most often seeks experiential escape or avoidance?

- What memories is the client unwilling to recall?

- What other psychological experiences (such as bodily sensations, dreams, images, etc.) does the client try to avoid?

- What types of psychological experiences is the client generally most likely to avoid?

- What types of psychological experiences is the client generally least likely to avoid?

Analysis of Experiential Control Strategies

This facet of case conceptualization is designed to clarify your clients' preferred method(s) of experiential control. The most commonly used strategies may vary considerably from client to client but usually not a great deal over time for each particular client. Control strategies that a given client has relied upon in the past are likely to be continued at least during the early phases of ACT, not because they have been effective in the long run, but primarily because they reflect the psychological inflexibility and rigidity that characterizes depression. Knowing each client's preferred escape/avoidance strategies will thus alert you to what to be on the lookout for during your work with them.

Additionally, knowing a client's most commonly used experiential control strategies can be helpful in considering what alternative ways of responding to unwanted psychological material may be most useful to promote as part of the overall treatment plan. For example, incorporating a series of graduated in vivo exposure exercises (that is, those that approximate a real-life environment such as dealing with a stressful interpersonal relationship) at some point may be appropriate for clients who primarily resort to situation-specific avoidance. They may, however, be less useful for others who rely more heavily on internal control strategies.

Related Questions

In analyzing the experiential control strategies used by your clients, questions to ask yourself include the following:

- Does the client have a history of suicidality?

- If so, have the suicide-related behaviors served as a form of experiential escape?

- What type of internal control strategies does the client typically use to avoid unwanted experiences?

- What type of external control strategies does the client habitually use to avoid unwanted experiences?

- What type of situation-specific control strategies does the client commonly use to avoid unwanted experiences?

- What types of in-session control strategies have you observed thus far in your interactions with the client?

- What is/are the preferred type(s) of experiential control strategies used by the client?

Motivational Analysis

All clients are faced with the fundamental dilemma of choosing whether to stay where they are psychologically or to commit themselves to do whatever is necessary to become unstuck. Both actual as well as potential costs and benefits surround each option. These can create ambivalence, psychologically paralyze clients, and prevent behavioral change. Part of your task is to initially tip the balance point at least enough in favor of change to shift momentum in that direction.

Motivational Interviewing

Those of you familiar with motivational interviewing (MI; Miller & Rollnick, 2002) will undoubtedly recognize some similarity between the type of cost-benefit analysis being suggested here and what is referred to within MI as "decisional balance" (p. 15). While ACT would frame the issue as one of clients making a choice rather than a decision, the apparent strategic similarities between ACT and MI in undertaking a motivational analysis seemingly overshadow any obvious technical and stylistic differences. This is especially so as MI has increasingly recognized the importance of values identification and clarification within the context of its overall agenda of preparing clients for behavioral change (even though ACT and MI differ from each other in how values are construed). For example, there arc no mentions of values or their identification and clarification within the index of the first edition of Miller and Rollnick's (1991) MI book, whereas the second edition (Miller & Rollnick, 2002) includes an entire chapter on the issue (Wagner & Sanchez, 2002).

It is obviously beyond the scope of this book to provide even an adequate overview of the technical dimensions of MI. The primary purpose in mentioning it here is to encourage those of you who have experience with MI to feel free to integrate it with the suggestions offered in this book for conducting a preliminary assessment and case formulation. Those of you who are unfamiliar with MI might find it useful to better acquaint yourselves with it, although I don't mean to suggest that training in or extensive experience with MI is necessary for the successful practice of ACT. Nevertheless, MI seems quite compatible with ACT principles (Wilson & Byrd, 2004) and as such can be a useful adjunct at this stage in your work with depressed clients.

Costs and Benefits of the Status Quo

While the costs associated with remaining depressed will usually be more readily apparent to both you and your clients than the possible benefits, both need to be explicitly evaluated as part of a comprehensive motivational analysis.

Costs of Depression

Most clients are already acutely aware of the acute pain of depression—what Hayes and Smith (2005) have referred to as the "pain of presence" (p. 15)—and are seeking therapy for the express purpose of attaining relief from it. Consequently, it is generally not necessary for them to make contact with such costs as part of the motivational analysis.

Unworkability of the control agenda. Another set of costs, however, from which your clients may be relatively disconnected are those surrounding the futility of their efforts to escape from their depression. Impressing upon your clients the unworkability of their experiential control strategies, of course, is integral to engendering an optimal level of creative hopelessness. Your primary goal at this juncture, however, is not to induce creative hopelessness. Instead, evaluate the degree to which your clients experience the costs of continuing to pursue an unworkable control agenda in order to help guide your induction of creative hopelessness later on.

The costs associated with unsuccessful efforts to minimize depression can take several forms—including those involving time, effort, energy, and financial expenses—and all should be considered. Your evaluation in most instances can be based upon information you've derived through conversations with your clients during the preliminary assessment about what they have already tried in coping with their depression. However, discuss these issues further at any point on an as-needed basis.

Pain of absence. A third set of costs associated with depression involves the loss of treasured activities and life events. This loss results from the depression itself and/or the time, effort, and energy that was expended in trying to control it. Such costs have been referred to by Hayes and Smith (2005, p. 15) as the "pain of absence" and can be evaluated most directly by considering how much of valued living your clients have already lost to depression and their futile efforts to escape from it. An assessment of this sort obviously requires at least a preliminary appraisal of your clients' values. It will likely stay fluid because the identification and clarification of valuing often remains a moving target. Accordingly, don't view your analysis of the pain of absence as complete at this point. It is, nonetheless, useful for at least two reasons. First, as with the costs accruing from the unworkability of the control agenda, evaluating the costs associated with what has been lost to depression may be useful in determining an optimal level of creative hopelessness. Second, serious consideration of how much of their lives your clients have lost to their struggles with depression can be a profoundly sobering experience for you and your clients and one that solidifies an empathetic bond with them.

Costs to daily living. Thus far most of the costs associated with depression that have been considered as part of the motivational analysis have been accumulated over its duration. However, as long as your clients' struggles with depression go on, the "cost meter" continues to run and is also likely to include the toll it takes on the quality of their daily living. Consequently, also consider what your clients continue to lose on a moment-to-moment, day-in-day-out basis to depression and their struggles with it. For example, as discussed previously, a depressed client may decline social invitations and instead spend that time in rumination.

Benefits of Depression

Apart from environmental factors (to be covered in the next section of the case-conceptualization form) that may support its continuation, one of the largest "benefits" that your clients may derive from remaining stuck in depression is "being right." As discussed in chapter 2, this is most likely to occur when there is a high level of fusion with a life story in which the client has been victimized and traumatized by others. As long as they continue to be depressed, clients in such a position at least have the consolation of being right. In such cases, as suggested previously, a treatment plan that includes considerable defusion work surrounding the life story and the conceptualized self as well as highlighting for clients the continued costs of being right is called for.

As suggested in chapter 2, another potential payoff may be when the depression itself enables clients to avoid facing even more threatening psychological experiences, such as fears of failure and rejection. This possible consequence is not incompatible with the benefit of being right. Both are likely to occur when clients have experienced a history of loss and disappointment coupled with a fused investment in the life story about such events.

Costs and Benefits of Therapeutic Change

In considering the relative costs and benefits to your clients of therapeutic change, maintain the distinction discussed earlier between appropriate process and outcome goals in ACT. Thus "the change" under consideration here is not the commonly expressed therapeutic goal of the client to "feel better," but that of living a more vital, engaged, and meaningful life.

Costs of Changing

Costs can be construed as both losing something desirable as well as encountering something that is unwanted. In this regard, we have already considered some of the costs of change associated with the former (for instance, giving up being right). At this point in the motivational analysis, reconsider what unwanted and (at least up until now) largely avoided psychological experiences your clients would likely encounter in moving their lives in a valued direction. For example, clients may experience considerable self-doubt and uncomfortable levels of fear, shame, embarrassment, regret, and other unwanted emotions as they begin to take the first steps necessary to lead their lives differently. A successful ACT-treatment plan in such circumstances most likely will deal with such potential experiential barriers to committed action through interventions that promote defusion, mindfulness, and acceptance.

Benefits of Changing

The obvious benefit of change for clients from the perspective of ACT is the opportunity to lead a more invigorating life. Unfortunately many depressed clients, particularly the chronically depressed, are so far removed from such an existence that this possibility no longer exerts much pull. Moreover, as suggested previously, some clients may have experienced so much painful disappointment in their lives that they actively avoid even thinking about what they once wanted from life. In order to evaluate the degree to which your clients are in psychological contact with the potential benefits of committed action, further clarification and discussion with your clients about valuing can be useful in two respects.

First, for the purpose of completing the motivational analysis, part of your task is to gauge the distance that exists between the depressed lives your clients have been living and what a fully engaged life would look like for each one of them. Think about how their current depression-related behaviors and the possible changes they could make to them relate to their core values. As indicated earlier, it is perhaps not coincidental that accomplishing this through a conversation with your clients is also integral to MI (Miller & Rollnick, 2002, p. 83), suggesting that speaking in particular ways with your clients about their values can also serve to increase their desire for behavioral change.

Second, from the perspective of RFT, talking with clients about their values can function as a *motivative augmental* (Barnes-Holmes, O'Hora, Roche, Hayes, Bissett, & Lyddy, 2001, pp. 109–110), that is, it increases the capacity of certain events and experiences to function as reinforcers. Stated more colloquially, sometimes the more you talk about something you want, the more you want that something. This may be especially so if you once had that "something you want." For instance, a hypothetical conversation that illustrates this process with a depressed client who appears to value being an active, caring parent might unfold like the following:

Therapist:	Have there been times in the past when you've spent time with your kids, maybe you've been doing something with them, and you had this sense of really being close and caring with them?
Client:	Sure, before I became depressed but not much since.
Therapist:	Tell me more about what that was like and what you were doing with your kids at the time.
Client:	Oh, I can remember just teaching and introducing them to new things that would excite them, like taking them to the zoo and how excited they were to see an elephant for the first time.
Therapist:	How much would you like to have more times like that with your kids? It may or may not be possible. I suppose the only way to find out would be to do what would be necessary for it to be possible. Is that possibility something that would be worth the two of us working together for?
Client:	I'd like that.

A type of *discrepancy analysis* can also be woven into the conversation in discussing the gap that exists between the client's current state of affairs (for instance, "How close are you now to spending the kind of time we've been talking about with your kids?") and the client's desired life (for example, "What could you do to make it more likely for that to happen?").

Related Questions

Questions to consider in completing the motivational analysis include the following:

- What has the client already tried that has not worked in controlling depression?

- How much time did the client invest in such efforts?

- How much energy did the client put into such efforts?

- How much did such efforts cost the client financially?

- What has the client already lost and sacrificed during the struggle with depression?

- How does the client's struggle with depression impact the quality of life on an ongoing and daily basis?

- How much is the client invested in being right about the depressive life story?

- How much is the client invested in a depressed conceptualized self?

- Are there other more intimidating psychological issues (like fear of intimacy, abandonment, failure, etc.) that the client would have to face if no longer depressed?

- What would the client be giving up if no longer depressed?

- Who would be "wronged" by the client improving?

- What experiential barriers for the client stand in the way of committed action?

- What are the client's values?

- How much would the client's life have to change for the client to move in the direction of these values?

- Overall, how much is the client in psychological contact with what depression has already cost and continues to cost?

- Overall, how much is the client in psychological contact with the benefits of giving up the experiential control agenda in favor of commitment to value-directed living?

- How much more work may be necessary in engendering a state of creative hopelessness until the client abandons the control agenda?

Analysis of Environmental Barriers

Unfortunately another set of barriers to psychological change and increased flexibility (apart from those already discussed that are experiential in nature) also often exists in the external world of depressed clients. From the functional contextualistic perspective that serves as the philosophical foundation of ACT, all psychological events, including depression, are seen as resulting from the interaction between organisms and a context that can be defined both historically and situationally (Hayes, Strosahl, Bunting et al., 2004). Thoroughly understanding the function(s) of depression thus requires a consideration of not only the pathways that have historically given rise to depression but also of the current situational factors that may help maintain its continuation. In doing so, evaluate external contingencies that reinforce staying depressed separately from those that punish getting better.

Reinforcement for Staying Depressed

Contingencies that support the continuation of depression can be both financial and social in nature.

Financial Contingencies

Perhaps the most obvious financial reason for remaining depressed occurs with clients who receive disability payments. Staying depressed in effect continues a source of financial support, whereas getting better will likely terminate it. In such instances, reviewing and eventually pursuing alternative sources of acquiring income (such as returning to work, going back to school, applying for vocational-rehabilitation services, etc.) may have to be integrated into a comprehensive treatment plan.

Social Contingencies

Depressive behavior may be inadvertently supported by socially mediated positive and negative reinforcement. Regarding the former, your clients may receive more attention and sympathy from family members and/or friends when displaying depressive behaviors (such as withdrawing socially, speaking of suicide, etc.) than when acting in more psychologically flexible and healthy ways. In addition, depression may be negatively reinforced by others when they excuse the client from certain undesirable duties and responsibilities. In extreme cases, it may be necessary, with the client's permission, to request that key family members and/or friends of the client attend a session where such issues are addressed.

Punishment for Getting Better

It seems useful to also distinguish between financial and social contingencies that weaken client behavior incompatible with depression. Interpersonal circumstances and those involving money can often work together to effectively dissuade clients from getting better. However, they can also operate independently of each other and, for this reason, should be considered separately for each of your clients.

Financial Contingencies

Apart from the possibility that some clients may likely lose disability payments, other financial contingencies may effectively punish other clients for behaving in more psychologically healthy ways. For example, physically moving to a different part of town might be therapeutic for a client but be prohibitive because of the cost. Alternatively, clients who make good money in otherwise stultifying jobs may be discouraged from actively looking for other work that pays less but which is more value congruent.

Social Contingencies

Sometimes, unfortunately, other central individuals in a client's life may have such an investment in the client not getting better that any movement in that direction is effectively sabotaged. For example, perhaps a power differential between the client and their spouse can only be maintained as long as the depressed client remains in the "one down" position.

Another set of social contingencies that may actively work against therapeutic change may have been unintentionally established by clients who have broadly shared their life story with others, particularly when it is fairly traumatic in nature. Under such circumstances, clients who show improvement may be potentially subjected to some critical questioning and comments by others (for example, "You must not have been mistreated as badly as you said you were if you're no longer depressed") as they begin to step out of the depressive social role they have inadvertently created for themselves. Staying depressed and not getting better may be one way of not only "being right" but also of saving face within such a context and thereby avoiding social scrutiny.

Related Questions

The following are suggested questions to consider in completing your analysis of environmental barriers to therapeutic change:

- What financial factors may be keeping the client stuck in depression?

- Is the client receiving a psychiatric disability for depression?

- If so, what other means does the client have of financial support?

- What financial costs and losses might the client incur in getting better?

- What social factors may be keeping the client stuck in depression?

- What social costs and losses might the client incur in getting better?

- How widely has the client shared his/her life story about why he/she is depressed?

- How much "face" would the client lose by getting better?

Factors Contributing to Psychological Inflexibility

Because we discussed rather extensively in chapter 3 the different forms that psychological inflexibility can assume little further elaboration is warranted here. The issue to be addressed in this portion of the case formulation and conceptualization is not a mere listing of the different types of psychological inflexibility displayed by a given client, but an appraisal of their relative strength both individually and collectively. Most, if not all, of your depressed clients, for example, will engage in some degree of reason giving and of trying to understand and figure out their depression through rumination. They quite likely, however, will differ from each other in the most predominant form that psychological inflexibility takes and also in their overall levels of psychological rigidity. Having a reading on both of these issues should be useful to you in formulating a unique treatment plan for each client.

Related Questions

Questions to think about in completing this section of the case-conceptualization form include the following:

- What forms of psychological inflexibility does the client display?

- What are the most dominant or preferred forms of psychological inflexibility displayed by the client?

- Overall, how rigid is the client in following rules, particularly "shoulds, oughts, and musts"?

- How perfectionistic is the client?

- How much does the client value intellectually based knowing (that is, logic and reasoning) over that which is experientially based?

Targeting of Core Processes

In the course of undertaking an assessment and case conceptualization of each of your depressed clients, you have by now accumulated enough information and analysis to identify the core processes that will be targeted as part of each client's initial treatment plan. In doing so, you may find it more useful to group the six processes of the hexaflex (and the related antagonistic processes contributing to psychological inflexibility) into the following three pairs rather than considering them separately:

- Processes involving defusion and acceptance

- Processes involving commitment and behavior change

- Common processes involving contact with the present moment and self as context.

I suggested these same pairings in chapter 3. I will also use them to organize the next three chapters, which will cover targeted interventions specific to each pairing.

Although the case-conceptualization form instructs you to identify both the core processes and related ACT interventions to be emphasized in treatment, focus on the former should take precedence over the latter at this point. Once you have clarified the pair of core processes that is apparently dominant for each client, you may find it useful to jump ahead to the chapter on related interventions in order to more specifically identify the particular strategies and techniques most appropriate for each client's overall treatment plan.

While most of your clients will display a dominant pair of core processes, it is certainly possible that you may encounter others for whom all three pairs of processes appear to be, and in fact may be, at equal strength. This is not as problematic as it might first seem as it suggests that you can usefully start anywhere with such cases. Nor is it that problematic if your appraisal of the core processes is off and you therefore begin ACT by targeting the "wrong" pair of processes. As alluded to previously, the hexaflex and the pairing of processes within it serve a heuristic function, and accordingly you literally can't get it wrong. Moreover, also as noted earlier, core processes pull for each other such that treatment that initially focuses on what is a weaker pair of processes is likely to be pulled in the direction of whatever processes are relatively stronger. As long as you are flexible enough to go with this pull, ACT is essentially self-correcting. While the efficiency of your treatment may be compromised somewhat, its overall efficacy is less likely to be negatively impacted.

Related Questions

Issues to be addressed in identifying the core processes for each client include the following:

- What is the relative strength of processes that interfere with defusion and acceptance for this client?

- What is the relative strength of processes that are antagonistic to commitment and behavior change for this client?

- What is the relative strength of processes that are incompatible with mindfulness and self as context for this client?

- Of the three pairs of core processes, which is the dominant one for this client?

- Of the three pairs of core processes, which is the weakest one for this client?

Identification of Client Strengths

Clients, like all of us, have relative strengths as well as weaknesses. An appropriate and necessary focus on weaknesses should not preclude your thorough consideration of strengths as you formulate a comprehensive treatment plan. Simply because clients may be exhibiting extreme difficulties at the moment in coping with emotional distress does not mean that they have not had success in doing so in the past. Two clients who may be functionally equivalent in the processes that contribute to their depression may warrant different treatment plans because of the personal assets and strengths that they also bring to therapy.

Perhaps the most important issue to consider in assessing potential strengths of your clients is the degree to which they have been able to cope reasonably well with previous life difficulties and challenges, including previous actual or potential episodes of depression. Common precipitating events for depression include some type of personal loss, especially that of a loved one. What deaths has the client had to deal with in which the bereavement process was relatively uncomplicated, and how did the client successfully cope with such losses? Also, to identify some of the client's effective coping skills and capacity for psychological flexibility, consider how the client has reasonably managed other types of losses, such as those involving employment, personal property, and failed romantic relationships. In short, review circumstances in which your clients could have easily become depressed, but did not, in order to identify their unique coping skills and abilities.

I mentioned earlier the high rates of comorbidity between depression and substance abuse/dependency. This likely means that not only will a number of your depressed clients have co-occurring problems in this area, but also that some may have already successfully resolved them. If so, encouraging your clients to share with you how they were able to attain and maintain their sobriety may highlight personal strengths that can be used as assets in treatment. Moreover, because of the obvious similarities between some aspects of 12-step programs in general and of Alcoholics Anonymous (AA) in particular, on the one hand (Wilson & Byrd, 2004), and the emphasis upon acceptance within ACT on the other (Wulfert, 1994), you may find it especially useful to know if the client's previous experiences with such interventions were successful.

A final area to explore to uncover client strengths and sources of psychological flexibility involves the attainment of difficult goals. Clients may be more open and receptive to talking about how they have managed successful events in life than about how they have coped with personal loss and disappointments. Ask your clients to identify what goal they have attained in their life for which they had to work the hardest. Such a conversation may not only reveal particular strategies that the client used in continuing to persist in the face of adversity, but also the core values to which the goal in question may have been linked. For example, a recent client of mine was able to relate the level of commitment and acceptance necessary for him to successfully complete a marathon as a younger man to the challenge he now faced in struggling with depression.

Related Questions

A list of questions to answer in analyzing the unique personal strengths of each client include the following:

- With what personal losses has the client successfully coped?

- What did the client do to cope successfully?

- Has the client ever successfully overcome an addictive behavior (such as use of alcohol, tobacco, other substances, etc.), and if so, how did he/she do it?

- Does the client have any favorable experiences with 12-step programs like AA?

- Does the client have any previous training or experiences in meditation practices or yoga?

- Does the client have any familiarity or experiences with religious practices, such as Buddhist or Christian meditation, that are ACT compatible?

- What difficult goals in life has the client attained, and how did he/she do so?

- What core value(s) relate to hard-fought goals that the client has attained in life?

- What other personal assets does the client bring to therapy?

Formulation of the Treatment Plan

The final section of the case-conceptualization form asks you to formulate an initial ACT treatment plan. Use whatever pair of core processes you have identified as being dominant to guide the initiation of treatment. Suggestions on specific interventions and techniques that can be used to target each of the paired core processes are offered in the next three chapters. I wrote these chapters to stand alone, so you do not need to read and apply them sequentially. Rather, use your case conceptualization to determine which of the three chapters to consult first. For example, I recommend that you initiate treatment under the guidance of chapter 8 with a client whose depression appears to be most closely linked to excessive rumination and fusion with a damaged conceptualized self. Conversely, chapter 6 may be a more appropriate starting point for clients who display more diverse forms of experiential avoidance and fusion.

Strategic vs. Technical Dimensions of ACT

Despite the emphasis on the technical aspects or procedures of ACT within the next three chapters, ACT in a broad sense is still more usefully thought of as an overarching strategic and even paradigmatic (see chapter 11) approach, rather than merely as a set of procedures. This is true for several reasons. Perhaps most importantly, holding ACT as an approach appropriately places more emphasis on its overall agenda of increasing psychological flexibility rather than on determining how to use the tools in its toolbox. For example, appreciating the function of a hammer by knowing when and why to use it seems more useful than knowing how to forcefully strike objects with it.

Maintaining ACT's strategic focus on increasing valued living through strengthening psychological flexibility is also likely to result in a more skillful, creative, and flexible use of the tools that are employed. Finally, the toolbox of ACT contains interventions and techniques that have been uniquely developed as well as those that have been appropriated and adapted from other psychotherapeutic approaches and traditions, but it still has room for more. New ACT-consistent techniques and procedures are constantly being developed as it becomes more widely disseminated and practiced. It seems more likely that you also may be able to make a contribution to ACT's ever-expanding toolbox if ACT is viewed from a more strategic and functional perspective rather than one that is technical in its focus.

Summary

The purpose of this chapter was to guide you through the process of conducting a case conceptualization in order to formulate a tailored treatment plan for each of your depressed clients. In closing, an issue that appropriately supercedes where to begin with ACT merits some mention. The preliminary treatment plan may suggest an appropriate initial therapeutic focus, but it may be less useful as ACT unfolds. View the preliminary treatment plan as a suggested starting point for therapy rather than a road map for its entire duration. Unexpected twists and turns often occur over the course of therapy, and you are therefore encouraged to hold the initial treatment plan lightly and be open to making adjustments to it. Especially as ACT unfolds and perhaps moves in unanticipated ways, your actions as a therapist are apt to be more helpful and responsive to your clients if they are more flexibly under the control of the behavior of your clients rather than that which comes from rigidly following an original, but by now suspect, treatment plan. There may be no wrong treatment plans, but certainly some are more useful than others, and it makes no sense to follow a plan that is no longer working. In short, all of us—clients and therapists—are in the same boat, and paying attention to what works as a way of supporting psychological flexibility therefore applies to us all.

CHAPTER 6

Interventions for Promoting Defusion and Acceptance

This chapter specifically focuses on interventions and techniques that help teach your clients alternative ways of responding to depressing thoughts, feelings, and related private events that have been the focus of an experiential control agenda. Interventions that promote defusion from troublesome thoughts and acceptance of unwanted emotions serve this purpose.

Nature of Defusion and Acceptance

If you are a newcomer to ACT and even if you're not, you may tend to think of many of the key concepts and processes—such as creative hopelessness, willingness, and acceptance, which we will discuss in this chapter—as feelings or emotional states. We may attribute part of this to how we become entangled by our own languaging when nouns (such as "acceptance") are used rather than gerunds (like "accepting") in speaking about behavior (Zettle, 1994). Recall that ACT is first and foremost a behavior therapy. Accordingly, it is useful to view defusion, willingness, and acceptance as behaviors that can be shaped and acquired just like other skills. Indeed, to hold them as private events and feeling states is to at least implicitly endorse an agenda that is antithetical to ACT. Deliberately attempting to either eliminate what are construed as unwanted feeling states (for example, unwillingness) or induce their ostensible positive counterparts (willingness) is still emotional control and therefore likely to be counterproductive in the long run. Moreover, willingness as an emotional state cannot be freely chosen, whereas *willingness* as the behavior of being open to nondefensively experience whatever psychological events show up can be.

Acquisition of Defusion and Acceptance

In principle, two broad strategies are available for you to use in helping your clients acquire defusion and acceptance skills. Some new skills are most optimally acquired and subsequently strengthened through direct, experiential learning, whereas others may be learned more readily, albeit indirectly, through instructional control, that is, through your teaching your client the skills by providing them with a set of rules or guidelines to follow. Behavior that is contingency-shaped, or acquired through experiential learning, however, has been found to differ from that which is rule-governed, or learned by following a set of instructions, in several important respects (Skinner, 1969). In contrast to responding that has been directly shaped, a number of studies, for example, have rather consistently found that following instructions leads to behavior that doesn't readily change even if it is no longer effective in producing a desired outcome (Catania, Matthews, & Shimoff, 1982; Hayes, Brownstein, Zettle, Rosenfarb, & Korn, 1986; Shimoff, Catania, & Matthews, 1981). For example, on a given task, pressing a button slowly may initially produce more points than responding quickly. Some subjects may have been given the rule "The best way to earn points is to respond slowly," whereas others are left on their own to discover that responding slowly works better. If the way to earn points on the task is now suddenly and without warning changed to require rapid button pressing, the second group of subjects finds it easier to switch to a faster rate of responding; subjects who were given the instruction to respond slowly are more likely to continue to do so. The greater degree of rigidity and lack of psychological flexibility seen more generally in rule-governed behavior suggests that responding under instructional control often constitutes pliance (Hayes, Zettle, & Rosenfarb, 1989), or loosely speaking, doing what you are told simply because you are told to do it. Stated somewhat differently, the behavior in question is more often under the control of tightly following an instruction instead of doing what works. This obviously is not problematic when the two sources of control coincide (for example, wearing heavy clothing as you've been advised to do *and* it's winter), but it is problematic when the context changes and the two are now in opposition (you're wearing heavy clothing as you've been advised to do *and* it's now summer).

The subtitle of the Hayes et al. (1999) book, *An Experiential Approach to Behavior Change*, underscores that ACT favors a *direct shaping process*, or learning by consequences rather than learning by rule following, with clients initially acquiring and further honing their skills in defusion and acceptance. This is not to say, as we will see, that the use of instructions, suggestions, and other forms of verbal behavior by you as therapist are outright prohibited in establishing defusion and acceptance. However, it does imply that you should keep such strategies to a minimum and use them cautiously to increase psychological flexibility and avoid pliance. To discourage clients from responding to language literally, metaphors are preferred over more direct forms of verbal behavior. This is because metaphors, while certainly verbal, do not present rules that can be literally followed. However, they can functionally guide behavior change and skill acquisition if the same processes being referenced in the metaphor apply to the skill being taught. For example, let's say you want to learn to swim. Sitting in a classroom listening to a teacher describe strokes, kicks, and breathing is entirely different than being in the water, feeling your body and limbs move through the water in particular ways, getting water in your nose when you breathe incorrectly, and so on. The experience of being and moving in the water—the experiential learning—will help you learn (and retain) how to swim much more quickly than being told what to do. You might use this metaphor in pointing out to your clients that learning how to be more accepting is like learning how to swim.

Learning defusion and acceptance skills are more like learning to ride a bicycle than learning to assemble one. Written or verbal instructions may be very useful if you have to assemble the bicycle. However, if you want to learn to ride that bicycle, written or verbal instructions—other, perhaps, than someone telling you how to get on it—will not be much help. Instead, you simply have to give it a try—learning to balance, pedal, and steer by trial and error. Put another way, experiencing the natural consequences of attempting to balance, pedal, and steer is more critical to both skill acquisition and being able to flexibly apply such skills than being told how to do it.

Behavioral Deficits vs. Excesses

From a behavioral perspective, a lack of defusion and acceptance may be viewed as skill deficits. However, it's important to remember that these may not be "zero rate" behaviors, that is, behaviors that clients do not possess at all, as they may already exist at some level of strength for a number of clients. As I suggested in the last chapter, clients who have a history of having coped successfully with previous personal losses and life challenges may already have weak forms of defusion and acceptance as part of their behavioral repertoire. In such instances, your task may be more one of further strengthening and shaping such skills than it is in having your clients acquiring them from scratch. In a related approach, you seek to weaken ways of responding—that is, you seek to weaken fusion and experiential avoidance, which are incompatible with defusion and acceptance. Inducing a necessary level of creative hopelessness so clients will abandon their control agenda exemplifies this approach of weakening behavioral excesses.

The Difference Between Defusion and Acceptance

Although defusion and acceptance may be grouped together as similar and functionally related behavioral processes, I offer separate interventions and techniques for the promotion of each in this chapter because of distinctions between the two. The most helpful differentiation between defusion and acceptance is revealed by the different types of unwanted private events each targets. The targets of defusion are the client's automatic thoughts, reasons, life story, and problematic by-products of relational framing, such as attachment to a damaged conceptualized self.

(Parenthetically, a bit of clarification may be in order: What is being discussed here as "defusion" was more often referred to as "deliteralization" by Hayes et al. (1999, p. 150) to underscore its purpose of weakening the negative impact exerted by the literal meaning of language. More recently, the term "deliteralization" has been replaced with that of "cognitive defusion" (Strosahl et al., 2004). For our purposes, defusion, as noted above, seeks to alter the way clients respond to automatic thoughts, reasons, their life story, and other troublesome by-products of relational framing, thereby rendering the use of the adjective "cognitive" in describing defusion redundant.)

By contrast, the targets of acceptance are primarily the client's feelings, bodily sensations, memories, and the like. I'm certainly not suggesting that languaging plays no role in contributing to how these other private events function. They are, after all, typically evaluated as "bad," "awful," "intolerable," or otherwise framed in ways that lead to client efforts to experientially control them. It is also possible to speak meaningfully of accepting a depressing thought (like "I'm stupid"), although this is usually following some defusion work targeting the same thought. Defused thoughts are more likely to be accepted, whereas fused thoughts continue to be avoided, suppressed, or controlled in other ways.

Promoting Defusion

As discussed in chapter 1, fusion occurs when clients buy into their negative self-evaluations, reason giving for depression, life story, and other self-talk to such a degree that no other ways of responding to such verbal by-products are possible. Stated somewhat differently, fusion involves holding cognitive content as "literally true" so tightly that alternative ways of responding to it are precluded. By contrast, defusion as broadly construed involves inducing and promoting alternative ways of responding to fused material, such as specific negative automatic thoughts or the client's life story. In doing so, other psychological functions associated with languaging, such as the mere sounds or cadence of self-talk when it is expressed aloud in different ways, can emerge and influence client behavior, thereby expanding their repertoire and enhancing psychological flexibility.

Your Mind Is Not Your Friend Exercise

While most of the defusion techniques we will cover in this chapter can be usefully organized according to the complexity of the verbal constructions they target, the intervention we will first discuss—Your Mind Is Not Your Friend Exercise—can be regarded as a more global defusion exercise that cuts across different levels of dysfunctional self-talk. Your objective in using it is twofold: (1) to enable your clients to begin to see and respond to the overall process that leads to their self-critical thinking and other negative languaging, and (2) by doing so, give them an alternative—that is, observing and responding to the process instead of "buying into" and fusing with the negative material. Observing the process of relational framing by, for example, noticing that you are engaging in negative self-evaluation, is quite different from merely responding to the evaluation itself. Looking at thoughts is different from looking at the world from (or through) thoughts.

I recommend using this intervention—Your Mind Is Not Your Friend—as a prelude to the introduction of more focused defusion techniques that target specific types of cognitive content (such as automatic thoughts, reasons for depression, and the life story). It was first introduced by Hayes et al. (1999, p. 151) and is presented below in a modified form to be more responsive to the experience of clients struggling with depression. It should be noted that here I'm using the term "mind" metaphorically for "relational framing" and not to imply any sort of mentalistic explanation for human suffering.

The initial purpose of this intervention is not for your clients to completely disparage or reject whatever their mind has to say, but to encourage them to begin to hold its output more lightly and with a healthy degree of skepticism. In short, it is a type of discrimination training. The ultimate goal of the intervention is to help clients successfully differentiate between thinking that is useful and that which is not. Present the intervention by saying something like the following:

> *Let's talk a little bit about how our minds work and whether or not they are always our friends. What I mean by our minds is that incessant chatter that goes on in our heads, how we constantly talk to ourselves. Our minds seem to be especially good at spotting problems and figuring out how to fix them. In fact, maybe none of us would even be here today if our ancestors' minds weren't there to help them figure out how to survive. Luckily most of us no longer have to worry about where our next meal is coming from and how to get it without being killed ourselves in the process. That's the good news.*
>
> *The bad news is that our minds continue to do what they evolved to do even if it means looking for, finding, and trying to figure out how to solve problems that may not be there to begin with. For example, sometimes our minds are so used to worrying about things that they worry if we don't have something to worry about. So, our minds then create something else to worry about. At other times, our minds seem to stubbornly try to solve problems that simply can't be solved, such as why we can't be perfect in everything we do. Another thing our minds are very good at is playing the "blame game" in assigning fault for problems they detect, for instance, when they conclude that we must be stupid or incompetent if we forget something. How often does your mind blame and criticize you for problems it's identified? What I'd like you to consider is that when this happens, your mind is simply doing—and doing it very well—what all minds do. There's nothing wrong with your mind, and so our challenge here is not in fixing it. You can't live without your mind, but it's also not your friend. So our challenge is one of learning how to live a more meaningful and full life with your mind.*

For purposes of convenience, I've presented the intervention here as a monologue. In actual practice, you'll find it more useful if you do it interactively by inviting client comments and answers to related questions (such as "How much does this sound like how your mind works?").

Related Techniques

At this point, it may also be useful, if they can be worked into the flow of the conversation, to introduce a few related techniques. If not, they can be introduced at other opportune times.

The Mind in the Third Person Technique. Point out that there are four "people" present in the therapy room—you, your mind, the client, and the client's mind (Hayes et al., 1999, p. 97–98). Clients can even be encouraged to name their mind (for example, "Ol' Grumpy") and, at other points in therapy, engage in conversations with it as they would a third person.

Thank Your Mind for That Technique. One of the verbal interactions you can prompt your clients to engage in with their minds is to acknowledge its troublesome input (Strosahl et al., 2004, p. 41). Doing so reemphasizes to clients that their minds are functioning fine and that the agenda of trying to get their minds to act differently is fruitless. A more useful reaction is for clients to simply recognize and even compliment their mind for doing what it does so well. At first, you may have to initiate this process by pointing out specific instances of fusion:

> So, your mind tells you that you're too stupid to go back to school. Can you thank your mind for that? Can you go ahead and actually say that out loud to your mind right now?

With further experience in observing the process of relational framing and self-talk, clients can be asked more generally the question of "What is your mind telling you about this?"

Defusing Automatic Thoughts

ACT has by now accumulated too many tools for defusion of automatic thoughts to cover all of them in this section. Accordingly, our primary focus will be on ways of defusing negative self-evaluations. These automatic thoughts are most troublesome with depressed clients. See Strosahl et al. (2004, table 2.3) for a more exhaustive list of defusion techniques and interventions for automatic thoughts.

Milk, Milk, Milk Exercise

A procedure originally described by Titchener (1926, p. 425) and subsequently adapted by Hayes et al. (1999, p. 154–155) as the Milk, Milk, Milk Exercise for use in ACT is designed to strip words of their *derived stimulus functions*, or psychological properties they share with the objects or stimuli to which they refer. Ask your client to follow after you in rapidly repeating a word that elicits a number of sensory associations. Once those derived functions are removed, the only remaining stimulus properties should be those directly available; in short, the sound of the word but not its meaning. The exercise is known by the word commonly used in conducting it, but others can be employed as well. To illustrate this point, the following example will use "lemon" in place of "milk":

Therapist: If you're willing to do so, I'd like us to do a little exercise together. Say the word "lemon."

Client: Lemon.

Therapist:	What came to mind when you said that?
Client:	A yellow, oblong-shaped fruit. Fairly small, not too big.
Therapist:	So you could almost see it. What else?
Client:	I don't know.
Therapist:	How about smell?
Client:	Yeah, it smells like a lemon—lemony.
Therapist:	What else?
Client:	Well, the taste of a lemon—you know, kinda sour.
Therapist:	So notice what happened when you said the word "lemon." It's as if a lemon was actually here—you could see it, smell it, and taste it. There's no lemon actually here, but it was here psychologically. Now comes the silly part of this exercise. I want you, along with me, to say the word "lemon" over and over again as fast as we can. Let's just do it and see what happens.
Therapist:	[Rapidly repeats the word "lemon" with the client for at least 30 seconds.] What happened?
Client:	It just sounds like some silly blabber, like nonsense.
Therapist:	What happened to the sour-tasting, lemony-smelling, yellow, oblong fruit that was just here a little while ago?
Client:	It's gone.
Therapist:	Let's try the same thing with a different word. Several times now I've noticed that you call yourself stupid.
Client:	Well, I am. I'm just trying to be honest with myself.
Therapist:	Are you ready? Let's go. ["Stupid" is rapidly repeated aloud with the client.]

There is really no need to spend a great deal of time processing the exercise afterward, although repeating it as needed is useful whenever you catch the client using negative self-references (for instance, "loser, loser, loser ...").

Revocalization Exercises

A series of related exercises can be used to further defuse negative self-talk by altering the typical manner in which it is expressed. The overall strategy is to induce your clients into vocalizing frequent self-evaluations in atypical ways. For example, your client can say "I can't do anything right" in a low voice in which each syllable is drawn-out

("IIIIII caaaaa nnnnnntt …"), in the voice of a cartoon character (like Donald Duck, for example), in a song (as in a musical or opera), or even in another language (for instance, "No puedo hacer nada bien" for clients not fluent in Spanish). These alternative ways of speaking lessen the sting and pull of damaging negative self-talk by minimizing its negative associations, or derived stimulus functions.

Thoughts on Cards Exercise

For the last revocalization option (that is, clients reciting negative automatic thoughts in another "language"), you may need to have the translation written on an index card for the client to read. The same technique can be used with thoughts that are not translated into another language. In contrast to hearing their thoughts come out of their mouths, having clients read their thoughts written out on paper can evoke a sufficiently different response, which can constitute yet another means of defusion. The thoughts to be written down, one per card, can be gathered in therapy, or alternatively be completed as a type of self-monitoring homework assignment. Either way, have your clients record their thoughts. Merely writing them down is yet another way to induce a different response or reaction. The deck of completed cards can subsequently be used in several ways. If needed, instruct your clients to periodically go through the deck, slowly looking at each card as a type of exposure exercise. For example, ask your clients to read the cards aloud at least two or three times during the day. Doing so can serve as another defusion procedure as it requires your clients to respond to their depressing thoughts in a different way. A more common use is to have your clients carry cards with them when they engage in committed actions. This is especially helpful if any of the cards contain thoughts that would otherwise function as barriers to such behavior. For instance, clients who have negative thoughts about looking for a more fulfilling job, such as "I'll never find anything better" and "Even if I were lucky enough to find something, I'd end up blowing the interview," may typically try to suppress or dismiss such thoughts. Instead, instruct them to acknowledge such thoughts and deliberately opt to take them along when job hunting.

Taking Inventory Exercise

Another defusion intervention for automatic thoughts, which you can often use in conjunction with the Thoughts on Cards Exercise above, is to ask your clients to simply list all of their private events at a particular moment in time, such as immediately following some depressing event (see appendix B for a form that can be used for this purpose). The exercise can be conducted as homework as well as in session. Ask your clients to not merely list each specific automatic thought, emotion, bodily sensation, memory, or other private events that they may be experiencing at that moment, but also to preface each by identifying its particular category (for example, "I'm having the thought that I'm worthless," "I'm having a feeling of sadness," or "I'm having a weighed-down sensation in my shoulders"). This exercise is analogous to what someone might do in taking inventory of a storeroom. The exercise provides the opportunity for your clients to treat their own reactions as physical objects apart from themselves.

Self-Evaluation vs. Self-Description Exercise

Implicit within all of the interventions and exercises discussed thus far for defusing automatic thoughts is a type of discrimination training in which clients learn to distinguish between self-evaluations and self-descriptions. When fusion with a negative self-evaluation occurs, the client responds to such self-talk as if it is a literal self-description. Depressed clients who are thinking "I'm no good" usually are not able to see that it is merely a thought they are having. Furthermore, they cannot see that their thought is a momentary evaluation rather than a static self-description. Instead, they respond to their thought of "no-goodness" as inherent, that is, part of their very being.

To sharpen the distinction between self-evaluations and self-descriptions, you can provide a more explicit form of discrimination training. Start out with physical objects as examples and then extend the training to self-talk. What follows is adapted from the Bad Cup Metaphor offered by Hayes et al. (1999, p. 169):

Therapist: You may remember that we've talked before about how your mind is not your friend. Let's talk a bit about a specific way that this occurs. Our minds are very good about evaluating things around them, even evaluating ourselves as good or bad, weak or strong, and so on. Our minds churn out so many evaluations that we often have trouble telling the difference between what's an evaluation of something and what's a description. For example, suppose I say that this chair here is a "good" chair. Is that an evaluation or a description?

Client: An evaluation, I guess.

Therapist: What if I said this chair is made of wood. Evaluation or description?

Client: Description.

Therapist: What if you disagreed because you thought the chair was made of metal instead of wood. Is there any way to determine which description is the correct one?

Client: I suppose we could tear the chair apart to see what it's made of or cut off a little piece of it and have it analyzed in a lab somewhere.

Therapist: Okay. So the two descriptions about the chair both say something about the very nature of the chair—what it's made of—but both can't be right. Now, what if I say the chair is "good" and you say the chair is "bad." Is there any way to determine which one of the evaluations is the correct one?

Client: It sounds like a difference of opinion.

Therapist: The "woodness" or "metalness" of the chair resides in the chair—it *is* the chair. But where does the "goodness" of "badness" of the chair reside? Is it in the chair?

Client: I guess it must be in the evaluation of the chair.

Therapist:	When your mind tells you "I'm stupid," is that an evaluation or a description?
Client:	An evaluation.
Therapist:	When your mind tells you you're in your forties and married with two kids, is that an evaluation or a description?
Client:	A description.
Therapist:	When your mind tells you "I'm stupid," where does the stupidity lie?
Client:	I want to say with me, but I can see that's not really true.
Therapist:	It may be more a matter of what's useful rather than what's "true." In any case, your mind doesn't like to be contradicted. Can you thank your mind for insisting that the thought you have that "I'm stupid" is really a description *and* at the same time recognize that it's an evaluation? Try saying this on for size: "I'm having the evaluation that I'm stupid."
Client:	I'm having the evaluation that I'm stupid.
Therapist:	Now, say "I'm stupid."
Client:	I'm stupid.
Therapist:	How do the two compare?
Client:	Saying it like an evaluation doesn't seem as heavy. I don't feel quite as weighed down by it.
Therapist:	It's more useful to say it that way.

Once this exercise is completed, you can offer additional discrimination training as opportunities present themselves in session. For example, when clients spontaneously make a negative self-evaluation, gently prompt them to explicitly frame it as such (that is, "I'm having the evaluation that …").

Defusing Reason Giving

Several of the interventions and exercises just discussed for defusion of automatic thoughts can also be used to weaken reason giving for depression. For instance, ask your clients to revocalize specific reasons and/or also inventory them (for instance, "I'm having the thought that one of my reasons for being depressed is …"). More recently, I've also developed an exercise specifically for defusion of reason giving. It is useful with clients who are heavily invested in the causes to which they attribute their depression.

Reasons for Depression Exercise

This exercise has an accompanying form (see appendix C), which makes it possible for you to use it either in session or as a homework assignment (see session 3, chapter 9). I use it more often in session so I can give the instructions orally and can complete a copy of the form along with the client. The exercise consists of the following steps:

1. An initial exhaustive listing of all of the reasons offered by clients for their depression

2. A listing of additional "good reasons" that could be offered for depression, but which may not be of personal relevance to the client (like termination from a job for a client who has never been fired)

3. Rating the "goodness" of each of the reasons generated in the two previous steps

4. A fairly extensive listing of "bad reasons" for being depressed

5. Rating the "badness" of these reasons

Any difficulties clients encounter are most likely to occur in completing step 4. If necessary, suggest a range of possibly bad reasons for depression for the client's consideration. These can vary from the semiserious (such as their favorite football team lost the Super Bowl) to the facetious and more humorous (they didn't win the Publishers Clearing House Sweepstakes, for example). It's possible that some of your clients may experience the exercise as invalidating, although I can't recall a single case at the moment where that has occurred in my use of it. Should this happen, view it as a further reflection of the level of fusion with reason giving (such that, in the most extreme instance, any questioning about reasons may be reacted to as a personal attack). This means you will need not only to engage in more defusion work but also in promoting the contextual self.

The various steps of the exercise are designed to induce the client to contemplate a vast and varied array of reasons that could (or could not) be offered for depression. This underscores the arbitrary relationship that commonly exists between languaging about depression and depression itself. When successful, the mere completion of the exercise itself typically has this effect and simply asking the client for their reactions to it usually suffices. If the exercise doesn't seem to have its intended impact, rather than engage in a prolonged processing of it, ask the client to consider questions like the following:

- Is your mind acting as your friend when it comes up with reasons for why you are depressed?

- Are the reasons that you offer for being depressed useful?

- Are the reasons you offer for being depressed more likely to keep you stuck or help you become unstuck?

- Do the reasons that you offer for being depressed have to change for you to become unstuck?

- How useful and necessary is it for you to be sure of the reasons why you're depressed?

Flat Tire Metaphor

Another defusion intervention that you can use to complement the exercise just discussed seeks to further underscore the costs of reason giving on living a valued life. First, identify some activity or event that is valued by your client, such as attending their child's musical recital or a critical meeting at their work, before presenting the following metaphor:

Therapist: Suppose that right after our session today you have to hurry across town to catch your daughter's piano recital. But when you leave here and get out to your car, you discover you have a flat tire. What would you do?

Client: Well, I guess I could call a cab, but that would probably take too long. I could call my motor club, but that would probably take too long too. I guess since I'm in a hurry, I'd just have to go ahead and change it myself as best I can. I'm not that good at changing flats, but I've done it before, and it would probably be the quickest.

Therapist: Wouldn't you want to know why the tire was flat?

Client: Maybe later, the next day or so. But not right now.

Therapist: Why not?

Client: Because changing the tire is much more important than trying to figure out the reason why it's flat. Why it's flat doesn't really matter.

Therapist: What if the depression you've been struggling with is like that flat tire?

Defusing Storytelling

The primary intervention for promoting defusion with your clients' life stories is a slight adaptation of one presented more broadly for use in ACT by Hayes and Smith (2005, pp. 91–92). Ask your clients initially to write down the story of their depression, being sure to incorporate all major life events and circumstances that they see as contributing to their suffering and struggles with depression. It is useful to assign this as homework. (For a form designed for this purpose, see appendix D.) Once the form is completed, review it with the client and collaboratively underline personal facts embedded within the story, such as particular life events (marriage, birth of children, changes in employment, deaths, etc.) and place those events on a timeline to highlight their temporal relationship with each other. Then, for homework, ask your clients to write another life story incorporating the same facts but one that does not end in depression. (Appendix D also contains a form that can be used for this purpose.)

Clients may protest the second writing assignment, claiming that the first story was true and anything beyond it would be a lie. This suggests a very high level of fusion with their life story. If this occurs, I have found it useful not to argue the point with clients, but to gently, though persistently, push for an alternative narrative. For example, "Imagine that you are a creative writer and you have been given these facts about your character. Would you be willing to go ahead and write a story that has a different ending?" Quite interestingly, a client who insisted that her initial story was "just the way it was and there is no other way," returned with a second narrative that unearthed new facts. In the first version, her depression was triggered by a divorce for which she was responsible. In the second, new facts were revealed about infidelities and secret financial dealings by her husband that were now instrumental in the divorce.

You may find it necessary to consider even more than one rewrite with clients who display extreme identification with the initial life story. The client just described wrote three alternative versions, with the last two weaving in historical facts that occurred around the same time as the breakup of her marriage (such as the death of John F. Kennedy Jr. and the results of the 2000 election) until she experienced sufficient defusion. She still retained a slight preference for the original life story, but its grip on her had been loosened sufficiently enough to move forward with other aspects of therapy. Her smiling in response to my comment of "It sounds like you still want to insist 'This is my story, and I'm sticking with it!'" reflected this.

Promoting Acceptance

As suggested earlier in this chapter, I believe it's useful to view acceptance as a behavioral deficit to be strengthened and its apparent opposite, experiential avoidance, as a behavioral excess to be weakened. A common behavior-modification strategy recommended in most books in the area (see Martin & Pear, 2007) is to always simultaneously strengthen new responding that is incompatible with any behavioral excesses that are being weakened. To do otherwise is to potentially fail the "dead-man test" by focusing exclusively on the elimination of behavioral deficits as the therapeutic objective. As originally introduced by Ogden Lindsley in 1965, the dead-man test poses the following simple but critical question: "Can a dead man do what you're wanting your client to do?" (Malott, Whaley, & Malott, 1991, p. 10). If you're asking your client to stop running away from unpleasant feelings, not be depressed, and so on, the answer to the question would be "yes," because a dead man doesn't run from unpleasant feelings and is not (we assume!) depressed. If the answer is "yes," the focus of therapy is misplaced as it is not focused on behaviors that may need to be strengthened to move the client's life in a valued direction. Similarly, it's helpful to focus more on what acceptance skills would be most useful to promote with your clients rather than on merely eliminating emotional control efforts. To simply abandon the control agenda, as important as that is, is not synonymous with attaining acceptance. Weakening experiential escape/avoidance seems necessary for acceptance to occur, as doing so creates conditions under which acceptance is now possible. It is not possible to embrace unwanted feelings while also trying to push them away. However, merely stopping the act of pushing away feelings of helplessness, for example, does not automatically induce acceptance of them. Acceptance as an alternative way of responding and relating to unwanted private events by "receiving what is offered" (Hayes et al., 1999, p. 77) must be promoted and fostered in its own right.

Weakening Experiential Control

The most common strategy within ACT for weakening the agenda of emotional control involves the induction of creative hopelessness. As discussed in chapter 4, I recommend that you consider titrating the level of creative hopelessness, that is, adjust the "dose" of intervention necessary to induce an optimal level of creative hopelessness as appropriate for each individual client. I feel this is particularly important with clients for whom suicidality has functioned as a form of experiential escape. One way of controlling the dose of creative hopelessness your clients receive is by selectively choosing which related interventions and techniques to present. For example, the Person in the Hole Metaphor ("Man in the Hole" in Hayes, 1987, pp. 346–347; Hayes et al., 1999, pp. 101–102) seems to lend itself most readily to a more rigorous assault against the control agenda, as you can exhaustively review and emphasize the futility of each form of experiential escape/avoidance employed by the client. It can, however, in some instances constitute "overkill." This metaphor is, therefore, recommended with clients for whom suicidality is not a concern as well as with those who have not responded favorably to alternative ways of weakening experiential control.

Because of space limitations, the application of the Person in the Hole Metaphor with depressed clients will not be presented here, but it will be presented in chapter 9. Here, instead, we will cover other techniques (such as the Tug-of-War with a Monster Metaphor and Quicksand Metaphor) that can be more readily used in inducing a titrated level of creative hopelessness. See Hayes et al. (1999) for the generic version of the "in the hole" metaphor and Eifert and Forsyth (2005, pp. 136–138) for an example of adapting it for use with clients struggling with anxiety.

Tug-of-War with a Monster Metaphor

This particular metaphor (Hayes, 1987, p. 366; Hayes et al., 1999, p. 109) is useful not only for inducing an optimal level of creative hopelessness with your clients but also, with some slight modification, for underscoring some of the costs associated with the continued pursuit of their control agenda. As discussed in the previous chapter, one such set of costs involves what clients miss out on in life (that is, the pain of absence) while unsuccessfully struggling to control their depression. Provided at least one potential area of valued living has been identified (in the example which follows, that of being a caring parent), the metaphor can be presented in the following manner:

Therapist: It sounds as if your struggles with depression have been like being engaged in a prolonged tug-of-war with a monster. You've been pulling really hard on your end of the rope, and the depression monster is pulling on the other end. In between you and the monster is a bottomless pit, so if you pull really, really hard, maybe you can drag the depression monster over to its edge, and with one final tug, pull it into the pit and be done with it forever. Meanwhile, as this is going on, you can hear your kids in the background asking you to come play with them, to take them to the park or to the zoo. You want to spend time with them, but you also have this tug-of-war you're involved in and you very much want to win that too. Maybe you even call out to your kids and ask them to just wait until you get rid of the depression monster. But now imagine as you pull on that rope that you, rather than the monster, are being pulled ever so slowly toward the bottomless pit. So maybe you dig in your heels, brace yourself, and pull even harder. But it doesn't work—you find yourself still being pulled closer and closer to that pit. What are your options?

Client: I'd call out for someone to come help me pull on my end of the rope.

Therapist: Has that worked for you so far? Further, imagine this battle is just between you and the depression monster.

Client: I guess I'd have to pull even harder.

Therapist: Imagine that you're pulling as hard as you can and it's not making any difference. Is there anything else you could do?

Client: Let go of the rope?

Therapist: What would happen if you just dropped the rope?

Client: The depression would still be there.

Therapist: It might. I guess the only way to find out would be to drop the rope. The one thing that would be certain is that at least you wouldn't be struggling with it and your hands and feet would be freed up to do other things. What might you do?

Client: I guess I could take my kids to the park instead.

Of the two metaphors to induce creative hopelessness that we will discuss here, this one involving the tug-of-war is more readily adaptable to weaken suicidality as a form of experiential control. To the extent that suicidal behavior is simply one of the ways that your clients have attempted to manage their depression, inducing a level of creative hopelessness sufficient for the control agenda to be abandoned should significantly reduce any suicidal risk. Weakening of the control agenda is especially critical with clients who have a history of resorting to suicide as a form of experiential escape. Slightly modify the metaphor in the following way to provide a dose of creative hopelessness sufficient to accomplish this, while at the same time not increasing suicidality:

From what you've told me, it sounds as if there have been times in your life when you've found yourself being pulled by the depression monster closer to the edge of the pit. So maybe you've pulled even harder—as hard as you can possibly pull on the rope. But it didn't work, and you got pulled closer and closer to the edge of that pit. At those times, killing yourself may have seemed like the only way to get out of the struggle and to avoid being pulled down into the pit. Is there anything else you could do in that situation besides keep pulling and risk getting dragged into the pit or killing yourself to prevent that from happening? Could you drop the rope?

In terms of the metaphor, it will be useful for both you and your clients to view the dropping of the rope as more than a one-time event. Your clients will find themselves reverting back to the control agenda and the depression monster may even goad them into repeatedly picking up the rope and resuming the struggle. What is most important is to recognize when the struggle has been taken up again (that is, "Are you back into the tug-of-war?") and that it is not a therapeutic setback. As many times as the rope is picked up, it can be dropped, and each occasion provides another trial in the discrimination training that may be necessary for your clients to experience the difference between living a life of attempting to control depression versus one of pursuing valued activities. Each temporary dropping of the rope moves your client closer to the goal of acceptance being extended over a more prolonged period of time.

Quicksand Metaphor

This metaphor (Hayes & Smith, 2005, pp. 3–4) is another that you can use to discourage experiential control, but it also has the advantage of more explicitly shaping willingness and acceptance as alternative responses to depression. For this reason, it is perhaps a better choice than the Tug-of-War with a Monster Metaphor in segueing into work on the promotion of acceptance. The following dialogue is illustrative:

Therapist: I don't imagine you have any personal experience with quicksand.

Client: No.

Therapist: Have you ever seen depictions of people caught in quicksand in the movies or on TV shows?

Client: Sure.

Therapist: What happens when people who find themselves in quicksand struggle to get out?

Client: They just seem to sink in even deeper.

Therapist: That's right. The more they try to get out of the quicksand, the worse things get. What do you think would be the best thing to do instead?

Client: Don't struggle?

Therapist: Even more than that. The best thing they can do is be in full contact with the quicksand, by leaning back, and floating on it—like floating on your back on water. What I'd like you to consider is the possibility that your depression is like quicksand. Could it be that struggling with it only sucks you deeper into it and that another option is to allow yourself to come into full contact with it?

Client: But I'd be afraid it would just swallow me up.

Therapist: It seems really scary to you. That's a very understandable fear and one that we will need to address. Specifically, we'll need to consider different ways you might respond to this fear other than struggling with it.

The client in this exchange has identified fear as a potential barrier to acceptance, suggesting the need to promote his willingness to experience more fully the fear that the "depression quicksand" will swallow him whole if he stops struggling against it. This must happen if his control agenda is to be sufficiently abandoned.

Chinese Finger Cuffs Exercise

Some of your clients may be more responsive to experiential exercises than metaphors. An exercise that is adapted from a metaphor originally developed by Hayes et al. (1999, p.105) presents a Chinese finger cuff to your client. The finger cuff is a woven tube of straw into which the index fingers are inserted, one on each end. Following the suggestion of Eifert and Forsyth (2005, pp. 147–149), it seems preferable to engage in the exercise along with your clients. Once both of you have the cuffs on, say something like the following:

Therapist: Let's see if we can get out of these now. What happens when you try to pull your fingers out?

Client: It doesn't work. The cuffs pull more tightly on my fingers.

Therapist: Maybe you're not pulling hard enough. Let's both of us pull really hard. What happened?

Client: It just made them even tighter.

Therapist: What else can we do? What happens if you push your fingers further into the cuffs toward each other?

Client: It's not as tight. At least I can more my fingers now a little.

Therapist: You now have some wiggle room. What if your depression is like that? What I'd like you to consider is this: Based upon your experience, how well has your life worked when you've tried to pull away from depression?

Client: Well, I guess it hasn't worked all that well or I wouldn't be here.

Therapist: Are you willing to consider and try out another way of responding to your depression—one that may give you a little more wiggle room, like pushing your fingers in rather than trying to pull them out of these cuffs?

Clients may respond by noting that nothing has been addressed about how to get out of the cuffs. Should this arise, ask them to consider the possibility that the agenda of getting out of the cuffs may be more part of the problem rather than the solution:

> *Your mind's not going to like what I'm about to say. See if you can notice that and not get caught up in believing or not believing what I say. Rather, look to your experience in struggling with depression. We don't know what your life would look like and how it might work if you were not trying to pull your fingers out of the cuffs—if you were not focused on trying to lead your life without thoughts, feelings, and other experiences you don't like. But how has it worked when that is what you have been doing? Are you ready to at least be open to trying something that may be quite different from what you have been doing? If you don't like the way it works, you can always go back to trying to pull your fingers out of the cuffs.*

Your clients are not free to move, even if just momentarily, while they are pulling on the rope or trying to extract their fingers from the cuffs. The goal of these initial metaphors and exercise is to provide wiggle room. The next step is to prepare your clients for unwanted psychological experiences that they may encounter as they begin to relate differently to their depression and begin to move forward.

Promoting Willingness

As emphasized previously, think of willingness as a behavior that can be actively chosen rather than as a feeling or emotional state that is simply experienced or not. In making and maintaining this distinction, it is critical not to equate "willing" with "wanting." Neither you nor your clients *want* to feel vulnerable, apprehensive, or unsure of the outcome associated with pursuing ACT. The critical question to ask your clients is this: "Are you willing to experience that which you do not want, if doing so is necessary to become unstuck from depression and to begin moving your life in a direction that you value?" The critical question for you is this: "Are you willing to experience whatever you encounter in participating in this process with them?"

All of us often seek to strike a type of bargain with unwanted psychological experiences by agreeing to be willing to temporarily encounter them if they will then permanently go away and leave us alone. This, at best, illustrates tolerance rather than willingness and, as part of a larger experiential control strategy, is counterproductive in the long run. Being "willing," if that "willingness" is dependent upon the elimination of depression, is an experiential control strategy and therefore is incompatible with psychological flexibility, the goal of ACT. The willingness you seek to engender is one in which your clients actively embrace depression and are open to it, regardless of the outcome. Your clients will be asked if they are willing to experience what they have been working very hard to escape and avoid. This is not done for its own sake, to somehow strengthen their character or, most assuredly, to remove their depression, but as needed for them to be able to lead more meaningful and purposeful lives.

Clean vs. Dirty Pain Exercise

To underscore the difference between willing and wanting and to further clarify the objective of willingness, some work on the distinction between clean and dirty pain will be useful for most of your clients at this point. As discussed in chapter 2, "clean pain" refers to healthy and normal psychological experiences, such as dysphoria, that may nevertheless be unwanted and consequently be the target of experiential control efforts. "Dirty pain," by contrast, constitutes the psychological consequences of unsuccessfully pursuing the agenda of attempting to control "clean pain" (that is, dysphoria escalating into clinical depression).

Carrying Your Depression Exercise. A common metaphor within ACT for distinguishing between the two types of pain is that of the Two Scales (Hayes et al., 1999, pp. 133–134). Even though the metaphor as originally developed is specific to struggling with anxiety, it is readily adaptable for use with depressed clients. Because of this as well as the length of the metaphor, it is not presented here, but it will be presented in chapter 9. However, the experiential exercise below complements the Two Scales Metaphor. To conduct the exercise, you will need a fairly heavy and preferably unattractive object (like a large book, metal trash can, etc.) as a prop.

Therapist: Think of this trash can as the various thoughts and feelings you don't like that you experience as part of your depression. Now suppose—as much as your mind doesn't like to think about it this way—that you simply can't put the can down and walk away from it. If you don't have that as a choice—that is, you must hold the can and take it with you wherever you go—the only choice you have is how to carry it. (Hand the trash can to the client). Let's check out your options here. You obviously don't like feeling depressed, and this is a pretty ugly trash can. So maybe it's best, if you have to carry it, to keep it as far away from you as possible. If you would, stand up, hold the trash can as far away from you as possible, and walk around the room here for a while (or down the hallway, if necessary). How is that for you?

Client: It's too heavy, and my arm is starting to hurt.

Therapist: Okay, this time hold the can to your chest as if you are cradling a baby and walk around. How is that?

Client: A lot easier.

Therapist: Suppose the depression you've been struggling with is like this trash can in that you have a choice in how you carry it. Which do you choose—to hold it closer or at arm's length?

Client: Closer.

Therapist: Now notice that even when you hold it closer, it may still be unpleasant. This discomfort is what we mean by clean pain—the sadness, disappointments, and regrets in life we all experience from time to time merely because we are actively alive. Compare this clean pain with how uncomfortable it was to hold the can as far away from you as possible. This is what we mean by dirty pain—the additional suffering that gets heaped on top of the clean pain that we're not willing to accept. A question we will come back to many times is whether you are willing to receive the clean pain that comes from leading a full and engaged life. I'm not asking you if you want to carry the trash can, but if you are willing to do so. Let me make it very clear that saying "yes" will not make the clean pain go away—you will still have people you love in your life who will die on you, and you will not always be successful in meeting your goals. You can, however, minimize the dirty pain by how you choose to carry the sadness and disappointment that quite naturally come from leading a full life. The choice is yours. This is what is meant by willingness.

As suggested earlier, willingness, like any behavior, can be shaped. From this perspective, your goal is to support longer periods of time and more varied situations in which willingness and acceptance occur instead of experiential control. I'd like to conclude this chapter with a discussion of two final exercises that can be used for this purpose. Although both will be presented as techniques for specifically promoting the acceptance of unwanted feelings and emotions, they can also be extended to automatic thoughts and other types of troublesome private events.

Physicalizing Exercise

Appropriated from the Gestalt therapeutic tradition, this exercise encourages your clients to respond to their depressed feelings and related emotions as they would physical objects outside of themselves (Hayes, 1987, pp. 366–367). Like defusion techniques, this exercise also induces clients to respond differently to unwanted private events, but this time the specific focus is feelings rather than thoughts. Asking your clients to relate to their own depression as they would some external object is designed to put some greater psychological distance between them and the unwanted emotions with which they have been struggling.

To complement the exercise as originally presented by Hayes et al. (1999, pp. 170–171) and to illustrate the process of placing some distance between your clients and their depression, use a physical prop, such as a newspaper (Zettle, 2004, pp. 90–91), as follows:

Sometimes it may be useful to back up from things that are right in our face in order to more clearly see them for what they really are. Take this newspaper, for example. [Place a page of it so close to the client's eyes that it becomes an indistinguishable blur.] Can you read this? [Move it away from the client's eyes to normal reading distance.] How about now? The same thing can happen with feelings we don't like that get in our face. We can become so entangled in them and caught up in them that we lose perspective on them. If you're willing to do so, let's see what happens if we, at least for a short while, set your depression out in front of you to where you can get a better and different look at it. Please close your eyes and imagine taking your depression and setting it on the floor here a few feet in front of you. Let me know when you have it out there. Now, let me ask you a few questions about your feeling of depression. If it had a size, how big would it be?

Ask additional descriptive questions about the "object's" color, weight, density, texture, temperature, and so on. Have your client answer out loud. After the first round of inquiry, repeat some of the initial questions to see if the related physical attributes have changed in any way. For instance, ask, "Is size of the depression different?" If they have not done so, ask your client to identify a reaction to the depression (such as frustration, hopelessness, etc.), which is then subjected to the same process. After doing so, repeat the same original sequence of questions about the feeling of depression.

In my experience, the response of clients to this exercise tends to be all or nothing. For example, one client initially described her depression as a dark, dense, and mountainlike structure with jagged peaks and spikes that made it impossible to scale. After several presentations of the exercise over successive sessions, however, her depression was transformed into a misty fog that she was able to walk through. For clients who are not initially responsive to the exercise, don't press the issue, but simply acknowledge and validate whatever reactions are reported. Other techniques and exercises can be considered (see Strosahl et al., 2004, table 2.2), in addition to that which will be discussed next, as well as the possible re-presentation of the exercise at some later point in therapy.

Sitting with Feelings Exercise

This last exercise is somewhat deceptive. While it seems rather simple, it is one that many of your depressed clients will find quite challenging. Your clients may have various ways—ranging from rumination, distraction, and other forms of experiential avoidance to hopeless resignation—in which they have habitually responded to unwanted feelings. What is unlikely to be familiar to them is essentially doing nothing with unwanted feelings apart from sitting quietly with them. You can give this exercise as a homework assignment, but you'll find it is most useful to initially conduct it in session when particular feelings that typically pull your client into the control struggle emerge. In such instances, ask your clients to stop talking, close their eyes, and "just notice" whatever they are experiencing at that particular moment. Ask clients who are already familiar with taking inventory to engage in a covert form of it by silently listing not only central emotions but also related thoughts, memories, and bodily sensations, including the urge to do something else with what they are experiencing other than just notice it.

It seems as if right now you're being pulled into a struggle with some feelings you don't want to have. If you would, please stop talking, close your eyes, and as best you can, follow my voice. First, just take a moment to become centered by noticing how your body feels against the chair you're sitting in. Now shift your focus to your feeling of being overwhelmed. Can you take a few moments and be open to just notice what that is like. Notice what it feels like. Also notice any thoughts you might have or physical sensations. Notice any urge or pull you might experience to make the feeling go away. See if you can leave your hands off it and just sit with the feeling for a while.

As with the other defusion and acceptance skills discussed in this chapter, that of sitting with uncomfortable feelings is one that can be shaped and honed over time and with practice. Toward this end, initially conduct the exercise over fairly short periods of time in session (for example, one to two minutes) and then gradually increase its duration before extending it to homework assignments. From the perspective of more traditional behavior therapy, the exercise could be construed as a type of exposure or habituation procedure. From that of ACT, however, its purpose is not for the depressed feelings to somehow become extinguished or go away. Rather, the exercise is another means you can use with your clients to discourage experiential control and actively strengthen willingness and acceptance as alternative ways of responding to unwanted emotions. Additionally, the exercise resembles other techniques and procedures within ACT that are more in the service of promoting mindfulness and, consequently, can also, if necessary, serve as a prelude to more focused work in this area.

Summary

This chapter has selectively highlighted a number of techniques, metaphors, and exercises designed to increase the psychological flexibility of your clients by changing the way they have typically responded to depressing self-talk, feelings, and other related and unwanted private events. Interventions for promoting defusion and acceptance are apt to be especially useful initially with clients who are immobilized by the negative thoughts and associated feelings of hopelessness, helplessness, and of being overwhelmed that accompany depression. One of your first objectives with clients who are bogged down and stuck in depression is to induce them to drop the rope and disengage in the tug-of-war long enough for other actions to become possible. What these other activities might involve is an issue that we will take up in the next chapter.

Some of your other depressed clients may be more active overall but in the pursuit of goals that are not congruent with their values. In such instances, the key thoughts and feelings to be targeted by defusion and acceptance interventions are less likely to be ones that have kept your clients immobilized while they engaged in a futile struggle to escape from them. Rather, focus your defusion- and acceptance-promoting efforts on whatever psychological experiences your clients have been actively avoiding, and which, as a consequence, have also served as barriers to value-directed behavior.

CHAPTER 7

Interventions for Promoting Commitment and Behavior Change

If chapter 6 can be viewed as having addressed the acceptance side of ACT, this chapter concerns its commitment half. Because any committed action that you seek to begin with your clients should be consistent with their values to have an optimal therapeutic effect, it's important for you to help your clients further assess, identify, and clarify their values before promoting overt behavioral change. Typically following an assessment of values, you will also need to specify goals for your clients that are linked to their values as well as clarify and minimize barriers to committed action before they can begin to move toward their goals. Especially with clients who have been chronically depressed, any change in long-standing action patterns has the potential to increase psychological flexibility. The success of behavioral activation as a stand-alone treatment for depression (Dimidjian et al., 2006) underscores the impact of helping clients to break out of their behavioral ruts. However, as I pointed out previously, ACT goes beyond behavioral activation as it seeks to maximize the therapeutic benefits of any behavioral change by explicitly linking committed action to core values of your clients.

Valuing and Pathways to Depression

As I suggested in chapter 2, clarifying your clients' values may not only help guide their subsequent goal setting and movement toward their goals, but doing so also may shed light on the varying pathways that have lead to their depression. This will help you tailor your treatment plan and therapeutic approach more closely to your clients' needs. Because of this, I'd like to briefly review the three differing ways that valuing may be implicated in depression—pursuit of value-incongruent goals, failure to attain value-congruent goals, and failure to pursue value-congruent goals—that were initially discussed in chapter 2.

Pursuit of Value-Incongruent Goals

From most outward appearances, some of your clients may appear to "have it all" (including a successful career, stable marriage, healthy children, etc.), yet they still struggle with depression. They may have been quite successful at setting and attaining goals throughout their lives, but they experience their accomplishments as hollow because those activities and accomplishments were disconnected from their core values. In an absolute sense, such clients remain active and do not display behavioral passivity. However, a disconnect is present between their activities and their values. Your primary task in such cases is not one of overcoming the behavioral passivity and/or inactivity of your clients, but one of rechanneling their energy and behavior in a valued direction. As I suggested previously, a major challenge you face in accomplishing this task is creating a therapeutic climate in which your clients can clarify their values by moving toward what they desire rather than moving away from what they want to avoid. Clients who suffer from "success depression" most likely have been pursuing values that are not really their own. It's crucial that any values they identify be their own. In particular, be alert to values that may be strongly influenced by social desirability, political correctness, what they think you want them to say, or similar factors. For these reasons, you may find that more indirect means of assessing and identifying values are preferable. In particular, you'll need to take steps to minimize your clients' attempts to offer values designed to please or appease others (including you), which is a form of pliance. Some of these methods have been suggested previously in chapter 4, and I will talk more about them a little later in this chapter.

Failure to Attain Value-Congruent Goals

You will also undoubtedly encounter clients whose pathway to depression grows out of their experiences of being blocked and frustrated as they have attempted to reach goals that reflect their values. Unlike clients dealing with success depression, you may not need to dig to find these clients' values. You will, nonetheless, find it useful to confirm their values. The key problem is not that these clients lack clarity about their values nor that they lack motivation to initiate committed action. Instead, their efforts to pursue goals that they value have been blocked. Sometimes these blocks are external rather than psychological in nature (for instance, a client who values education cannot further hers because she lacks financial resources). Approach obstacles of this sort in a fairly direct, problem-solving manner. At the same time, be on the lookout for underlying psychological blocks or barriers (for example, she is reluctant to ask for a raise that would help pay for her education because she fears being turned down). You can target blocks or barriers such as this with ACT. As I suggested in the previous chapter, address psychological barriers to the attainment of value-consistent goals through interventions that promote defusion and acceptance.

Failure to Pursue Value-Congruent Goals

The final way that valuing can be implicated in your clients' depression is through their failure to even seek goals congruent with their core values. In extreme cases, through various traumatic life events, clients may have been so thwarted in successfully attaining valued goals that they give up all hope or aspirations of ever doing so. If you ask these clients directly about their values, they may claim that they have no values. This form of experiential avoidance prevents further disappointment and psychological pain. Unlike clients who are blocked in attaining valued goals, such clients are unmotivated to even minimally engage in their pursuit, and direct attempts to assess and identify related values are nonproductive. Don't accept at face value a statement by a depressed client that they no longer hold any values. Rather, view it as experiential avoidance. These clients still have values, although you will most likely need to use indirect means to find them.

Direct Means of Value Assessment and Identification

Three instruments—the Values Narrative Form, Values Assessment Rating Form, and the Goals, Actions, Barriers Form—are available in the Hayes et al. (1999, pp. 226–227) book for conducting a formal assessment of your clients' values. In addition, as mentioned in chapter 4 and as listed in table 2 (see chapter 4), at least two paper-and-pencil inventories have been developed more recently that can also be used in the evaluation of your clients' values. At this point in the development of the Personal Values Questionnaire (PVQ; Blackledge & Ciarrochi, 2003) and Valued Living Questionnaire (VLQ; Wilson & Groom, 2002), there appear to be few compelling reasons to favor the exclusive use of one over the other. Moreover, because they assess somewhat different dimensions of valuing, you can use them together in a complementary fashion, particularly with clients who have been frustrated in their pursuit of valued goals. The PVQ and VLQ can also be administered to clients who may be chasing value-incongruent goals and those who claim to have few or no values, although as I already suggested, primarily using indirect means of assessment is likely to be more useful in such instances.

The PVQ and VLQ are presented in appendix E and appendix F, respectively. Both instruments assess the same nine life domains (family relationships, friendships/social relationships, marital/intimate relationships, work/career, education, recreation, spirituality, community/citizenship, and health), with the VLQ also evaluating parenting values. Both also ask the client to rate the importance of each value domain and provide an assessment of the degree to which the client's actions have been consistent with each set of values, although they differ from each other in the time frame under consideration. The PVQ asks clients to provide consistency ratings for the last month, whereas the VLQ specifies a week. While both instruments can thus be used to guide treatment by identifying life domains in which the greatest discrepancies exist between valuing and committed action, the VLQ is somewhat more useful in tracking this measure over the course of therapy.

If you opt to use only one of the instruments, the possible advantage of the PVQ over the VLQ is that it asks clients to specify values in each of the nine domains it assesses and it also attempts to identify the sources of motivational control over valuing. For example, clients are asked to indicate the degree to which what they value in each of the domains is "because somebody else wants me to ..." versus "because doing these things makes my life better, more meaningful, and/or more vital." Such ratings are unlikely by themselves to be valid indicators of the degree to which client valuing is intrinsically or extrinsically motivated as they are merely yet more forms of verbal behavior and thus may also constitute pliance (that is, your clients may rank the "right" reason for holding a given value higher than the actual reason). The primary benefit of including such items is in opening a dialogue with your clients to clarify if what they are telling you about their values is based upon their own choice or because they think they "should" have that value for one reason or another.

Values Clarification

To verify that what your clients reveal about valuing is not unduly influenced by what they think their parents, society/culture, and/or you want them to say, ask a series of follow-up questions once key values have been identified, especially if more direct means have been used to do so. Throughout the entire process of values assessment, identification, and clarification, but perhaps especially at this juncture, it is important to minimize reinforcing your client's verbal behavior. Accordingly, avoid as much as possible any comments such as "good," "OK," or even "I see," as well as any nonverbal reactions that could be taken as signs of approval or disapproval of what your clients have to say about their values.

Parental Control

The undue influence that parental control can exert over the values that your clients present as their own can take two forms: pliance and counterpliance. With pliance, clients may passively espouse the same values as their parents because it is what's expected of them. By contrast in the case of counterpliance, clients actively rebel against the values of their parents.

Pliance

The most obvious of the two is pliance, in which your clients' values mirror those of their parents or parental figures. This is not to suggest that your clients cannot truly have "ownership" of the same values as their parents, but you will need to determine this through further clarification rather than merely assume it to be the case. To do so, ask questions like these:

You say you value being a loving parent to your children. What if your own parents were to never know that about you? Would it still be that important to you? What if it were the case that the more loving and caring you are toward your own children, the more your own parents see you as not loving and caring for your children? What would you do?

Although the questions you ask reflect hypothetical contexts, they may be useful in clarifying not only if the value being presented by your client is their own, but also if it really is a value instead of functioning as a goal for some other value. For instance, in the example just cited, the client's dedication to being a loving parent may be more important in maintaining status in the eyes of others than it is for its own sake. Although we will have more to say on this point a bit later, *goals* are means to an end, whereas *values* are ends in themselves. Repeatedly ask the question, "What is this [the value] in the service of?" to discriminate between goals and values.

Counterpliance

Pliance, more generally, can also take the form of counterpliance, in which a listener does just the opposite of what the speaker is seeking (Zettle & Hayes, 1982). For example, pliant children do not put beans up their nose when a parent implores, "Whatever you do, don't put beans up your nose!", whereas counterpliant children do. As applied to clarifying the valuing of your clients, you may find that some hold certain values primarily because they are at least in apparent opposition to those of their parents or other authority figures. Although this perhaps occurs most often with younger clients surrounding political and religious affiliations, attitudes, and beliefs, at least consider the possibility that valuing may function as a type of rebellious behavior for all clients. With a few twists, ask the same type of questions used to identify pliance to accomplish this (for example, "What if your parents converted to your religion?").

Social/Cultural Control

Social and cultural influences can be even more powerful and pervasive than those of parents in creating pliant and counterpliant values. Probably the most common manifestation of this process is when clients cite socially desirable values that are highly appraised and approved of within a given cultural context. Again, I'm not suggesting that you should dismiss values such as "contributing to my community." Indeed, from a behavioral perspective, functional communities and societies are those that induce their members to act in ways that contribute to the survival of such social organizations. Nevertheless, pending further clarification, initially view client values that are highly acclaimed within a particular social-cultural backdrop with a healthy degree of skepticism.

Ask a set of key hypothetical questions centered around societal/community knowledge of and possible recognition of value-consistent client actions (for instance, "If you were able to make a large financial donation to your community, would you prefer to make it anonymously or not?").

Also, take a closer look at the measures of value-action discrepancy provided by the PVQ and VLQ and ask related questions. It is certainly possible, for instance, that clients may "truthfully" indicate a wide gap between how important they value citizenship to be and their level of related behaviors because of possible psychological barriers to committed action. Further clarify the nature of any wide discrepancies by directly asking your clients about it (for example, "You rated reducing illiteracy in your community as an important value and yet you've been doing very little to help with it lately. Can you explain that?"). Target barriers that are identified in the process with defusion and/or acceptance interventions. If you find that your efforts are unsuccessful, it suggests that the value in question is not owned by the client, but is instead likely being cited for socially desirable reasons. Should clients indicate a high level of activity consistent with a suspected value, ask about the specifics of such behavior (for instance, "What all have you done in the last month to help reduce illiteracy in your community?").

Therapist Control

Because the assessment, identification, and clarification of client valuing occurs within the therapeutic relationship, you are likely to be the most immediate source of undue influence over what your clients present as their values. Pose hypothetical questions to gauge your power as a controlling variable. For example, ask your clients if what they have identified as their values would change if you did not know what these values were or if you disagreed with them (for example, "What if I said to you that I thought your working to reduce illiteracy in your community was a waste of time?").

Indirect Means of Value Assessment and Identification

We've already considered at least two indirect ways—following suffering and setting therapeutic goals—to identify client values in chapter 4. For this reason, we will only briefly revisit them here and instead provide a more extended discussion of a few alternative methods.

Follow Suffering

As lyrically stated by Donovan (Leitch, 1973), "Life's joys and misery walk hand in hand and keep each other company." Uncovering the values associated with suffering may be particularly useful with clients who claim that they no longer hold any personal dreams. For example, being actively involved in a nurturing relationship may be a central value for a client who has been traumatized by interpersonal rejection. Values can be found where suffering exists, and the suffering of clients who claim to be devoid of values has likely continued at intense levels over prolonged periods of time. Paradoxically, values not only contribute to suffering through their violation, but also place certain limits on it. In this regard, ask your clients, "What has prevented your struggles with depression from getting even bigger?" Use a response—for instance, one that indicates concerns about how friends and family members might be adversely impacted—to reflectively acknowledge likely client core values (for instance, "It sounds like you care a lot about other people").

Through Therapeutic Goal Setting

With some persistence on your part, you can also often follow objectives that your clients specify as therapeutic goals back to underlying values. As I mentioned previously, many of your clients will initially cite emotional release or control (such as "I am tired of feeling depressed" or "I want to feel better about myself") as their goal in entering therapy. Asking the question "What would that be in the service of?" or "What would that do for you?" may lead to related goals and/or values that can be differentiated from each other by repeating the same inquiries. For example, "feeling better" may be in the service of a client spending more time with his family, but repeat the question to determine if increased "family time" is itself merely another goal or if it's a value.

Revisiting Childhood Wishes

Even clients who present themselves as having been beaten down by life so severely and repeatedly that they hold no values, or who claim, alternatively, that they don't know what they value anymore, likely entertained hopes, dreams, and aspirations for themselves at some point in time. Indeed, from the perspective that ACT takes on the relationship between suffering and valuing, such traumatization must have occurred against the backdrop of the clients' values being violated. For some clients, you may have to go as far back as childhood to identify a time period that preceded the onset of traumatizing life events.

As I suggested earlier, when your clients assert that they can't articulate any values, view that as experiential avoidance. It's likely that they make this assertion to avoid contact with the psychological pain coming from the discrepancy between what they want their life to be and what it is really like. Even revisiting the long-abandoned dreams of childhood may be painful, and for this reason, seek the permission of your client before proceeding.

I'd like to ask you to think about some things that may be unpleasant and even painful for you to think about. I wouldn't ask you to go there if I didn't believe that it would be helpful in the long run to do it. Are you willing to go there with me?

You may also find it useful to do some defusion, acceptance, and mindfulness work in preparing your client for responding to any unwanted thoughts and/or feelings that might emerge before inquiring about previous valuing.

You say you no longer have any values and have given up wishes and dreams you once had for yourself. Can you tell me what those wishes and dreams were? Can you remember a time—maybe going even as far back as childhood if necessary—when you looked out at the world and had some hopes and dreams of where you fit into it? What was that like, and what did you want your life to look like at this point in time?

Ideally clients will identify goals that relate to values that still resonate and are applicable today. For example, a client may mention that she wanted to be a teacher as a little girl but never became one. If necessary, repeatedly ask "What would that be in the service of?" to uncover a value that is still viable (for example, helping others learn) and that can be used to help guide committed action (such as being a volunteer tutor). Even if specific values that are still vibrant are not identified, you may find the exercise useful in reconnecting your clients with valuing as a more generalized process that adds vitality and meaning to their lives.

Whose Life Do You Admire?

Most of us either have known or know of others whose lives we admire. Sometimes our heroes and heroines are more personal and come from the ranks of family, friends, and even mere acquaintances. Other times they are individuals of national or international stature. Clients who may be reluctant to talk about what they want their own lives to stand for may be more open to reflecting on what they have admired about the lives of others. Initially ask your clients to identify such individuals and then talk about what values the lives of their personal heroes and heroines represent and embody (for example, "What is it about Martin Luther King Jr. that you admire so much? What did his life stand for?").

With some further discussion and processing, you will usually be able to identify at least one core value in the lives of the heroes and heroines that is also held by the client. In the example above of Dr. Martin Luther King Jr., it might be King's commitment to civil rights and justice or the "courage of his convictions" and personal integrity with which he continued to persist in the face of adversity. Once a shared core value has been identified, both you and your client can use it as a marker around which goals and related actions can then be formulated.

What Do You Want Your Life to Stand For? Exercise

This exercise, which comes from the Hayes et al. (1999, pp. 215–217) book, is probably the most common means for indirectly assessing and identifying client values. As originally presented, clients were asked to imagine that they had died and were attending their own funeral. With at least some of your depressed clients, you may wish to lessen the intensity and morbid nature of the exercise by modifying it so that death per se is not involved. For example, à la the TV show *Lost* (Abrams, Lindelof, Cuse, Bender, Pinkner, & Burke, 2006), ask clients to imagine that they have been missing for some period of time; that family and friends have assumed that they have, in fact, died; and that they have returned just in time, unbeknownst to others present, to attend their own funeral. (Parenthetically, it should be noted that this twist on the exercise was suggested in a posting on the ACT Listserv. Unfortunately, I don't recall the identity of the poster to appropriately cite him or her.) Offer something like the following:

> *If you're willing to do so, I'd like you to participate in an exercise with me that may help us clarify what you'd like your life to be about. Please close your eyes and just take a few moments to get focused. Now I'd like you to imagine that your friends and family mistakenly think that you have died. Perhaps you survived a plane crash like the characters in the TV show* Lost, *and are returning home just in time to attend your own funeral. Imagine that you go to it and perhaps are in the back or are in disguise so that no one who will be offering the eulogies knows that you're there. What would you like these people to remember you for? What would you like to be remembered for in the eyes of your wife or husband? What would you want her or him to say about you?*

Also ask similar questions about other key figures in the client's life such as other family members (parents, siblings, and children) and close friends. Afterward, devote at least a few minutes to summarizing what core values emerge from the exercise.

Epitaph Exercise

A final way of indirectly identifying values asks clients to essentially write their own epitaphs. You can use it either in conjunction with the previous exercise (Hayes et al., 1999, pp. 217–218) or by itself (Eifert & Forsyth, 2005, pp. 154–155):

> *Imagine that the funeral now continues at the site of your grave where what are taken to be your remains will be buried. There at the head of the grave is your tombstone. What do you want to see written on it? If it could be anything, what would you want others to remember your life has having been about?*

Indirect Means for Assessing and Identifying Client Values: A Summary

We have reviewed a number of indirect means for assessing and identifying client values. I don't recommend that all of these exercises and techniques be administered with each of your clients. Some may prove more useful than others, and it is possible after trying each of them a number of times, that you will settle on one or two for which you have a personal preference. More important than which specific indirect assessment procedures you follow is your integration of them with each other as well as with more direct measures of valuing, such as the PVQ and VLQ. This integration will enable you to formulate a picture of your clients' key values that can direct the next stage of the therapeutic process—goal setting—which will ultimately lead to committed action.

Values Conflicts

Before discussing goal setting, I'd like to say a few words about the possibility of values conflicts. One challenge you may encounter in conducting values work in ACT is to not become sidetracked by what you and/or your clients may mistakenly believe to be conflicts among their values. Recall that values are not things, but rather are more usefully regarded as "verbally construed global desired life consequences" (Hayes et al., 1999, p. 206), that is, they reflect, in words, what the client most desires in life. From this perspective, conflicts at the level of values are not possible.

The very term "conflict" suggests a battle to be determined between antagonistic forces or entities, such that one will have to surrender or be vanquished by the other for the conflict to be resolved. However, values are not mutually exclusive, and valuing in one life domain does not need to change or be compromised for that in another to flourish and remain viable. For example, there is no inherent incompatibility or conflict between the value of "being a caring parent" and "being a devoted employee." Both can coexist.

By this, I'm not suggesting that valuing cannot and does not change or that conflicts do not exist that are associated with values. Such conflicts, though, involve goal-related activities rather than the values themselves, and, most importantly, the values of your clients do not need to change to resolve them. For example, "taking my children to the zoo" and "working overtime" may be actions congruent with the values of "being a caring parent" and "being a dedicated employee," respectively. A conflict may be created if the boss asks the client to work additional hours when plans had already been made to spend that time with her children at the zoo. The two activities cannot occur simultaneously, and so one must be chosen over the other. The value related to the action that is not chosen, though, is not mitigated in the process. Taking the children to the zoo instead of working overtime does not mean the client is any less of a "dedicated employee," and working overtime does not diminish the client's commitment to "being a caring parent." The children can be taken to the zoo another time or the client can engage in other activities (like perhaps doing something special with them when she gets home from work) that are in the service of being a caring parent. Similarly, she can find additional ways, other than working overtime, that she can live her value of being a dedicated employee.

If a client presents a purported "values conflict," particularly if done with a considerable sense of urgency, it's likely to be yet another manifestation of experiential avoidance. Such a "conflict" ostensibly must be resolved for clients to move their lives in a valued direction, and as long as it is not, they can avoid the responsibility of doing so. (In this case, the term "responsibility" is being used not to imply blame, but to accentuate the ability to respond differently to one's own values, that is, being "response-able.") Even conflicts that are appropriately held by your clients at the level of goal-directed actions can be quite uncomfortable, and your clients may, therefore, understandably present themselves as under considerable pressure to resolve them. For example, caring for an ailing parent may take time away from shared activities with friends. Particularly with your clients who typically escape such discomfort by quickly selecting one option over the other (that is, terminating the tension of the conflict is more important than how it is accomplished), you may find it therapeutically beneficial to help them approach the conflict in an alternative and mindful way. For example, your clients could be asked to pause and just notice whatever thoughts, feelings, bodily sensations, and other private events emerge as they sit with the conflict. Such reactions can then also become the focus of related defusion and acceptance work.

Goal Setting

Within the perspective of ACT, goals of necessity are related to values, but they can and must be distinguished from them. As I suggested earlier, asking your clients "What is that in the service of?" is perhaps the most useful way of distinguishing between goals and values. Goals are a means to an end and, therefore, are in the service of values, whereas values are ends in themselves and, consequently, are in the service of themselves.

Also, to keep them separate, think of goals as outcomes and values as related processes. Goals as outcomes have a definitive quality about them as they are either attained or not attained, whereas values do not as they are ongoing and have no endpoint. For example, obtaining a college degree is an outcome that may be one of many goals (learning a foreign language might be another) in the service of valuing education. Earning a degree has finality to it; being "well educated" does not, as there is always more to be learned. The behaviors of continuously setting and pursuing goals, even if not achieved, engage us in an ongoing and valued process, leading to the saying in ACT that "outcome is the process through which process becomes outcome" (Hayes et al., 1999, p. 219). Even if clients who value education never receive a degree, the courses that they took toward earning it still served to better educate them. The outcome was not realized, but the clients were still true to their values. If the clients pursue enough education-related goals, the process of becoming better educated will have been realized.

Compass Metaphor

A final way of discriminating between goals and values that may prove useful to both you and your clients is to liken the latter to points on a compass that help provide direction in life (Hayes et al., 1999, p. 209). Present the following metaphor to your clients to illustrate this:

> Our values are like points on a compass. If you were lost and had a compass, you could use it to see if you were, in fact, moving in the direction you wanted to be. For example, suppose you valued moving south. You could use the compass to first make sure that you were facing south and then pick out a landmark, like a mountain peak on the southern horizon, as a goal to move toward. As long as you kept the peak in sight, you wouldn't even need the compass itself to know if you

were moving in a southerly direction. Now what happens when you actually reach that mountain peak? Are you now south? Or is there now more south still ahead of you for you to move toward? What if moving south is like being a caring parent [or some other identified client value]? There are many ways in which you can be a caring parent—different goals you could set that move you in that direction—but does it ever end?

Does there ever come a time where you can check being a caring parent off of your things-to-do-in-life list, or is it continuous? If that is a central part of what you want your life to be about, can't it continue to be just that as long as you are alive? Even if you outlive all your children, can you still honor that value?

Graduated Goal Setting

Similar to the use of graded task assignment within cognitive therapy (Beck et al., 1979), approach goal setting in a graduated and sequential fashion. Identify a number of short-term as well as long-term goals that are related to each of your clients' key values. If necessary, break down a larger, more long-term goal, such as earning a college degree, into a series of small steps, depending upon how much distance exists between where your clients are at the moment and where they would be if the goal in question were obtained. At the most elementary level, the first goal in "heading south" is to simply place one foot in front of the other and is an appropriate starting point for clients who are showing no valued movement.

A good rule of thumb is to link goals to client values that can be accomplished within the time period between sessions (that is, a week in most instances). For clients who have been immobilized, break down this time period even further into a succession of daily goals. A useful question to ask and, if necessary, to answer in collaboration with your clients is something like "What is the first thing that you would need to do to earn a college degree?" Follow up the answer by considering when the first goal could be met and what additional steps can be reasonably accomplished before the next session (for example, "When could you find out if you can apply to college electronically and, once you find that out, what would be the next step?"). A Goals-Action Form that can be used to denote goals, associated actions, and other pertinent information, as well as to help structure related homework assignments is provided in appendix G. It is adapted from a similar form designed by Hayes et al. (1999) that is included in their book (p. 227).

Define goals, regardless of whether they are short-term or long-term, so it's easy to determine if they are met or not. For example, the goals of "checking into college" or "being nicer to people" are too vague. They can be more usefully redefined as "obtaining an admission application" and "asking at least four other people about their well-being each day." If possible, have your clients set their specific goals, but your collaborative input may be necessary to ensure that they are tightly related to key values, are clearly defined, and, where appropriate, constitute an appropriate link within a larger sequence of steps culminating in a valued long-term objective. When one goal within a longer chain has been achieved, shift focus to the next step (for instance, once the application is obtained, it must be completed and then turned in and so on).

Prioritizing Values

Because goals are related to values, a logical question that arises in setting goals is this: which values should take precedent over others? As a consequence of the values assessment, identification, and clarification process, both you and your clients by now should have some sense of the relative importance of the differing life domains and the degree to which they have been engaging in value-consistent actions within each. Using the PVQ and VLQ provides this information in a more direct fashion, but even exclusive reliance on indirect ways of assessing values will likely yield it as well.

If ambiguity still remains between you and your clients over which valued domain in which to initiate goal setting, ask your clients to choose. In such instances, verify the appropriateness of the choice. By default, I suggest starting with the most important life domain that shows that greatest deficit of value-related behavior. If you have clients who defer this choice, collaborate with them in making the choice of where to start rather than deciding for them. In any case, regard any movement by your clients in a valued direction as therapeutic. Solving the potential conundrum of where to start is less important than simply getting off square one.

Once sufficient progress has been made and momentum built up in one valued domain, initiate goal setting and related committed actions in others. Because valuing is a process, one cannot be completed before another is started. Moreover, because value-related goals may be long-term (like earning a college degree), it is unrealistic to defer activity in other domains until that long-term objective is achieved. For example, a client who, in addition to being well-educated, values being a caring parent can also be active in that domain and does not need to put such valued activities on hold until he obtains a college degree. Values per se do not conflict with each other, and they can be lived concurrently rather than sequentially.

Committed Action

The third and final step in the process of inducing value-directed behavior is committed action, that is, having your clients seriously engage in activities necessary for the attainment of their goals. Depending upon where a particular goal falls in relation to a larger valued objective and its specific nature, the committed action and the goal it seeks to achieve may be virtually inseparable (visiting a friend, for instance). Other goals may have a wide array of related actions that might lead to their achievement. In this case, the distinction between a particular goal and the actions necessary to attain it become more meaningful. For example, obtaining a college admission application as the initial step in the long process of earning an undergraduate degree can be accomplished in a myriad of ways (that is, the application might be accessed online, picked up in person, or requested by telephone, regular mail, or e-mail). Just as multiple goals can be in the service of the same value, a given goal may potentially be reached through a number of specific actions.

For homework assignments, you can list goals on the Goals-Action Form along with a list of specific behaviors your clients should do to reach each goal. If necessary, ask your clients the following question in relation to each goal: "What will you specifically do to obtain this goal?" Please note that any behaviors listed in the Related Action column should be necessary to attain the goal in question, but they may not be sufficient. The primary focus in any such homework assignment is on the client's commitment to engage in the related behavior rather than on achievement of the goal itself. That is, the client's commitment is to the process of engaging in the goal-directed behavior, which is directly under his or her control, and not to the outcome, which is not. For example, earning more money may be a goal in the service of being a caring parent, and asking for a raise may be necessary to obtain one. The mere act of making the request, however, does not guarantee that it will be granted. A related action that is ineffective may be repeated, or other means of attaining the goal may be tried (such as looking for other jobs that pay more).

Nature of Commitment

Commitment involves not only saying we will do something but, more importantly, doing it. Sometimes we accomplish a goal in our first attempt; other times we must try and try again before we successfully attain a goal. I've sometimes found it useful to remind clients of a quote by Mark Twain that speaks to this issue:

> *Giving up smoking is the easiest thing in the world. I know because I've done it thousands of times* (Mark Twain quotes, n.d.).

Increasing Psychological Flexibility

Many of your clients may habitually engage in one or two unsuccessful attempts to attain a goal and then abandon any further efforts. Unlike Mark Twain, they've not given up smoking a thousand times, but have instead simply given it up once or twice. Then they give up on giving it up anymore. This is often the case with clients who claim to no longer hold any values. The disappointment of goal-seeking failure can be effectively avoided if there are purportedly no valued goals to pursue. Your challenge with such clients is to weaken their old, entrenched approach to committed action and support more flexible ways of responding. In this case, persevering in the face of disappointment, initial failure, and other experiential barriers that would otherwise undermine keeping a commitment to valued living represents such an increase in psychological flexibility. I'll say more shortly on ways you can address both environmental and psychological barriers to committed action, but before doing so, I want to flesh out some further issues in promoting committed action.

Setting goals in a graduated fashion with your clients maximizes the likelihood that they will be successful in their initial efforts to attain them. Sometimes, however, they will fail to even attempt the action agreed upon as a homework assignment. This provides you with an especially rich therapeutic opportunity to assist your clients in breaking out of their old, rigid, and dysfunctional ways of responding to commitments. In particular, make a distinction between the client's typical manner of approaching commitments—for instance, saying he'll do something, not doing it, feeling guilty and like a failure, avoiding saying he'll do it again, giving up, feeling even more like a failure—and an alternative way of responding. Undertake some defusion, acceptance, and mindfulness work to address the feelings of failure and guilt that apparently function as psychological barriers to committed action. More importantly, ask the client if he is willing to make a recommitment as a way of shaping and supporting an alternative behavioral chain (specifically, feeling guilty and like a failure, saying he'll do something again, do it). Commitments are like falling off a horse: one is well advised to get back on them as quickly as possible.

Reframing Success

As I pointed out previously, some valued goals are inseparable from the behaviors necessary to achieve them (like stopping smoking), whereas others are not. For the former type of goals, mere engagement in the related action leads to their successful attainment. Your central challenge, in this case, is to support your clients in changing their behavior. You face a different challenge when goals and related actions are not one in the same, as clients may become discouraged and give up if their repeated efforts to attain a given goal are unsuccessful. Values can be enacted in multiple ways, and one option, of course, is to simply select an alternative goal related to the same value that may be more achievable (for instance, seeking a better-paying job or adding a second part-time job may be more effective in increasing income than repeatedly asking for a raise). Another option is to reframe what constitutes success in order to place more emphasis on the process of pursuing valued goals than in their attainment. For example, in many instances, you can refer to one of the client's heroes/heroines, or at least some noteworthy figure who the client would agree has led an admirable life.

Therapist:	You said you admired Dr. Martin Luther King Jr. As you see it, what was his life about?
Client:	Standing up for minorities in this country; to see that they received the same civil rights and were treated just like everybody else.
Therapist:	And did he accomplish that? Because of Dr. King, for example, are blacks in this country treated the same as whites?
Client:	No, not yet entirely.
Therapist:	So you must think that Dr. King's life was a failure. He never achieved his goal.
Client:	No, but he made progress even though there's more work to do.
Therapist:	So I guess you might think about success in at least two different ways. One way to define success is through achieving certain goals—like ensuring civil rights for minorities. Another way to think about success is to see it as following your dreams, values, and vision, even if you never get there—like Dr. King's "I Have a Dream" speech. Which way of thinking about success seems more useful to you?
Client:	The second way you just described.
Therapist:	Could you apply that same way of thinking about success to the values and goals that matter to you in your life?

Trying vs. Doing Exercise

Do not unilaterally assign behavioral homework involving goal-directed actions. However, once you and your clients have collaboratively identified a particular goal and related action to record on the Goals-Action Form for homework, directly ask them about their willingness to honor their commitment (for instance, "Between now and our next session, are you willing to ask your boss for a raise?"). A fairly common client response of "I'll try" undermines committed action and, therefore, warrants a response on your part. One response is to rephrase the question: "I'm not asking if you will *try* to ask your ＞ boss for a raise. I'm asking if you *will* ask your boss for a raise." Present this experiential exercise to further underscore the distinction. After placing an object such as a pen within easy reach of the client, say something like the following:

> *Please try to pick up the pen lying on the table there next to you. (Most clients will pick it up.) No, I didn't say to pick up the pen. I said to try to pick up the pen. Please, again, try to pick up the pen. (At this point, clients typically either pick up the pen again or move their hand close to it, hovering over it, as if their hand were paralyzed.) No, I didn't say move your hand toward the pen and then stop. I said try to pick up the pen. Can you do it, or is it simply the case that you either choose to pick up the pen or choose not to? What if trying to ask your boss for that raise we've talked about is like trying to pick up the pen?*

On this point, you can also remind your clients of what that underappreciated ACT therapist Yoda has remarked:

> *No! Try not. Do. Or do not. There is no try.* (Yoda Quotes, n.d.)

Just as "there's no crying in baseball" (Marshall, 1992), there's no trying in ACT.

Partial vs. Full Commitments

Another way that your clients may seek to avoid commitment failure is to only do things halfway. While you will likely find it useful, as discussed, to structure your clients' goals in a graduated manner, the same does not apply to the specific actions necessary to attain each individual goal. Committed actions are like jumping and must be framed in an all-or-nothing fashion. The client can either chose to ask for the raise or not, but there is no in-between.

Jump Exercise. Use a variation on the Jump Exercise presented by Hayes et al. (1999, pp. 240–241) to support this dimension of committed activities:

> *What if keeping a commitment is like jumping? You can jump off lots of things, but you can't do it partway from any of them. You can choose what you jump off of. Sometimes it can be something that's very close to the ground, like this book. (Take a book, stand on it, and then jump off.) Other times it can be jumping out of something that's thousands of feet up in the air, like skydiving out of an airplane. Now suppose you went skydiving, but when you got up in the plane and it was time to jump out, you felt scared and so decided you only wanted to*

jump a little. Is that a choice you can make? You can choose what you jump off of—whether it's a book or a plane—and you can choose whether to jump or not jump, but can you choose to jump a little? What if keeping a commitment is like that?

As a follow-up, if necessary, liken the use of graduated goal setting to varying heights that objects that are jumped off of extend above the ground.

We can start off with jumping off objects close to the ground, like this book. That's like getting that application so you can apply to school. But you've said you have your sights set on the higher goal of getting your college degree. That may be more like jumping out of that plane. Obviously, that's a bigger jump and something to work up to. Can jumping off the book be a step in that direction?

To Whom Is the Commitment Made?

Now let's discuss a final challenge you may encounter when you encourage your clients to act on their goals. This challenge arises when you and/or your client confuse the object of their commitment, that is, to whom the commitment is being made. Be clear—to yourself and to your clients—that their commitments are made to themselves and not to you as their therapist. Because commitments are to actions necessary for the attainment of the clients' value-directed goals, taking steps, as discussed previously, to identify values that are truly owned by your clients should minimize such confusion. If necessary, explicitly reemphasize this point, for example, by saying something like, "What matters here is what matters to you. Any commitments you make and keep are for you and not for me. My job is to help you more fully lead the type of life you want for yourself."

Clients are less likely to incorporate committed action into their lives outside of therapy if they take action more for your approval than for their own benefit. Nevertheless, inducing your clients to state their intended actions aloud in the interpersonal context of therapy is likely to increase the likelihood that they will do what they commit themselves to do (Zettle & Hayes, 1983). However, as long as your clients' committed actions are appropriately linked to an articulation of their values that is not unduly influenced by your presence, I recommend that you insist that your clients clearly and explicitly indicate the committed actions they intend to take.

It is quite likely that a number of your clients' key values will speak to their relationships to family members (such as being a caring parent) and friends (being a dependable friend, for example). Accordingly, committed actions in the service of such values may also benefit significant individuals in your clients' lives apart from them. However, view commitments in this context as still being made by your clients to themselves rather than to family and friends. An exception would be when the purpose of a committed action is to gain something in return from others (for example, when being a caring son to elderly parents is enacted for the purpose of gaining their approval). Ask the client in this instance if he would continue to act in a caring way toward his parents even if they continued to spurn such efforts. This will help clarify to whom the commitment is made.

Barriers to Committed Action

As I suggested in chapter 5, barriers to committed action, more specifically, and to psychological flexibility, more broadly, can consist of both environmental and psychological obstacles. While our primary emphasis in this section will be on the management of experiential barriers to committed action, attention should also be paid to apparent environmental barriers.

Environmental Barriers

Because psychological barriers may masquerade as environmental ones, closely scrutinize any external circumstances that your clients cite as having prevented committed action. For example, if your clients tell you that they were unable to complete the homework assignment of obtaining a college admission application because their computer was down, it's likely this is experiential avoidance. They could have gotten an application in other ways (such as a phone call), or they could have asked to use a friend's computer. Regarding the latter option, it's possible they considered this but rejected the idea because of fears of being turned down or being seen as a pest. In such instances, use the suggestions that follow for responding more generally to psychological barriers to committed action. Alternatively, approach environmental barriers that appear to be legitimate with problem-solving strategies such as brainstorming (Osborn, 1953).

Experiential Barriers

Space is included on the Goals-Action Form for your clients to note any psychological barriers that they had to overcome in engaging in goal-directed behavior or that prevented its completion. Use information about any experiential barriers that were surmounted by your clients in completing homework to guide proactive efforts to minimize the same or similar obstacles to other subsequent forms of committed action. For example, the same fears of failure, concerns about embarrassment, and self-conscious discomfort that a client successfully overcame in completing one assignment may be likely to reappear when other actions are attempted. Once they have been identified, you and your clients can work together to minimize such experiential obstacles by using interventions that promote defusion, acceptance, and mindfulness.

Passengers on the Bus Metaphor

Psychological reactions experienced by your clients that effectively stand in the way of their completion of committed actions are obviously even more problematic and warrant even more focused work in weakening fusion and experiential avoidance. You can often identify such obstacles ahead of time with a bit of troubleshooting. Ask your clients, "What sort of thoughts, feelings, or other reactions can you see coming up for you when it comes time for you to complete the homework we've talked about? What might stand in the way of you doing it?" At other times, experiential barriers to committed action may not be as readily foreseen, but only emerge and become identified by clients completing the appropriate space on the Goals-Action Form when a homework assignment is not completed.

What is commonly referred to in ACT as the Passengers on the Bus Metaphor is a defusion intervention (Hayes et al., 1999, pp. 157–158) that seems to be particularly useful in addressing private events that undermine committed action. Say something like the following:

> *Suppose the thoughts and feelings that seem to stand in the way of you pursuing goals that you value are like the rowdy, uncooperative, and ill-mannered passengers on a bus you are driving. There may also be pleasant passengers on the bus too, but let's talk about how you respond to the unpleasant ones, because they seem to be the ones who give you the hardest time. Now notice that, as the driver of the bus, you get to choose where the bus is going and how to get there. But if you steer the bus in the direction you want to go in, this may not sit at all well with some of the passengers.*
>
> *You said you value being well-educated. Let's imagine that, as you're driving along in the bus, you come to a fork in the road with a sign that points left to "being well-educated" and points right to "doing something else." As you begin to turn to the left, the passengers start to raise holy hell. They begin berating, questioning, and criticizing you: "Why are we going this way? You don't know what you're doing! You're not smart enough! You'll get us all lost! This is a waste of time!" and so on. Let's look at your options here. One choice is to simply keep going in the direction of being well-educated, but the passengers may become even more demanding and obnoxious. If that's part of the package—to go in the direction you want to go in—are you willing to have those passengers go along for the ride?*
>
> *Another option would be to stop the bus and try to bargain with the passengers. For example, you might try to persuade them to get off the bus. But there are more of them than you, and what if they defiantly say, "We ain't gettin' off and you can't make us!"? I suppose you can try and strike another type of deal with them by telling them that no one is going anywhere until they shut up and start behaving themselves. Notice, though, who now has the power to determine whether or not you get to go where you want to go. What if they never shut up? Are you willing to spend the rest of your life stuck along the side of life's highway?*
>
> *I suppose a final option is to turn right— in the direction the passengers insist upon—instead of left in the direction that you value. Doing so would probably placate the passengers for at least the time being. But what would you be giving up in the process? Would what you might gain—some short respite from thoughts and feelings you don't like—be worth the cost of heading off in a direction that gets you further away from, rather than closer to, what matters most to you in life? The choice is yours. How are you going to respond to the passengers on your bus?*

While most clients respond to the metaphor by reaffirming their commitment to moving their lives forward in a valued direction, you should, nevertheless, be prepared for responding to clients who may opt not to do so. Most importantly, it is useful not to see this as a therapeutic failure, provided it represents a client choice that is being made freely rather than a decision being dictated by the bus passengers, and it is held as a choice that can be changed. Under such circumstances, as suggested by Hayes et al. (1999, p. 260), respond in a way that validates the client's experience and respects the difficult choice being made by saying something like this:

> *If I were you—if I were driving the bus with the passengers you have aboard—I can see how the choice you're faced with at this point in your life would be a very difficult one to make. Under the circumstances, I could also see myself opting not to go forward right now.*

Summary

In this chapter, we have focused upon some of the central interventions within ACT that you can use to further the commitment of your clients to pursue their valued goals. Other related techniques, metaphors, and exercises—such as the distinction between choosing and deciding that was just alluded to—will be covered in chapter 9. As was the case also with defusion- and acceptance-promoting interventions, don't regard the use of techniques and procedures that specifically support value-consistent behavior as a one-time event, regardless of the particular point in the larger therapeutic process at which they are introduced. Even when the promotion of valued action is a major focus within the early stages of ACT, you will likely need to reapply related interventions on an as-needed basis.

In particular, I recommend that you and your clients collaboratively view any major changes in their overt behavior over the course of therapy (like changes in employment, living arrangements, intimate relationships, and so on) through the lens of their personal values. Such behavioral changes should include those, as discussed in this chapter, that may be strategically instigated as an integral part of a comprehensive treatment plan for each of your clients as well as actions that are spontaneously initiated by them. In both sets of circumstances, consider the same essential question in evaluating such changes in client behavior: does the behavior in question move the client closer to or further away from what he or she values most? Any substantial actual or contemplated change in the overt behavior of your clients that is not in the service of leading a valued life suggests that you and your client need to conduct further work in values clarification, goal setting, and the promotion of committed, goal-related behavior

CHAPTER 8

Interventions for Promoting Contact with the Present Moment and Self as Context

This chapter discusses ways in which you can support your clients in mindful living while further developing a transcendent sense of self. As I suggested previously, working with your clients to promote contact with the present moment and self as context addresses two core processes that contribute equally to both the acceptance and commitment facets of ACT. However, in addition to facilitating the other two sets of paired core processes already discussed—those dealing with defusion and acceptance, on the one hand, and commitment and behavior change, on the other—interventions that support living in the present moment can also have more focused and strategic applications. In particular, use the shaping and promoting of mindfulness as an especially effective strategy with clients who engage in a great deal of rumination (see Broderick, 2005).

Increasing Contact with the Present Moment

Insofar as rumination, with its preoccupation with a regretted past and dreaded future, is incompatible with living in the here and now, any efforts to strengthen contact with the present moment should simultaneously weaken dwelling in either the verbally constructed past or future. Consequently, and in accordance with the "dead man's test" (see chapter 6), your task is promoting the present-moment awareness of your clients rather than merely weakening their ruminative behavior. The mere absence of rumination is not the same as being nonjudgmentally aware of the ongoing stream of experience, although being mindful precludes fixation on the past and/or future.

The Relationship of Mindfulness to Defusion and Acceptance

At least for the purposes of this chapter, we will use the terms "contacting the present moment" and "mindfulness" synonymously, with *mindfulness* defined as "paying attention in a particular way: on purpose, in the present moment, nonjudgmentally" (Kabat-Zinn, 1994, p. 4). A number of your clients may have heard of the term "mindfulness," but most, in all likelihood, will not have practiced related forms of meditation or other exercises that promote contact with the present moment to an appreciable degree. To the extent that mindfulness thereby constitutes an alternative way that your clients can learn to respond to troublesome thoughts, feelings, bodily sensations, images, memories, and the like, techniques that promote it also serve a defusing function. Likewise, a number of the defusion interventions discussed in chapter 6, especially Thoughts on Cards and Taking Inventory, can also promote present-moment awareness.

As suggested by Kabat-Zinn (1994), mindfulness is not merely being deliberately aware of whatever psychological events are unfolding in the here and now, but it also involves relating to such experiences in a nonevaluative manner. Thus, a type of synergistic and reciprocal relationship also exists between interventions that support acceptance as discussed in chapter 6 and those that foster mindfulness. For example, having your clients "just notice" whatever emotional reactions and related private events emerge during the acceptance procedure of the Sitting with Feelings Exercise can also promote the nonjudgmental awareness of such experiences. This is especially likely to the degree that your clients are able to merely acknowledge the presence of any evaluative-type thoughts that occur surrounding the feelings targeted for acceptance (for example, "I notice that I have the thought that depression is awful") without being lured into a struggle with them. Moreover, your clients are more likely to maintain the distinction between evaluations and descriptions, as applied to the conceptualized self (see chapter 6) as well as other objects and entities, if both are responded to mindfully.

Considerations in Promoting Mindfulness

Like defusion and willingness, mindfulness is a skilled behavior that can be shaped and acquired. As in any shaping process, in determining where to start, you will find it helpful to know if the desired response already exists within your client's repertoire, even if only in a weak, rudimentary form. As I noted in chapter 5 in assessing client strengths, those who already have experience with formal meditative practices and/or yoga (Kabat-Zinn, 1990, chap. 6), particularly if it was positive in nature, will be at a different starting point than clients without such a history. For clients of the former group, your task in increasing present awareness is largely one of further strengthening, shaping, and extending mindfulness skills that already presumably exist at some level. For clients in the latter group with no similar history, you will start from scratch, and those clients are more likely to respond, at least initially, to mindfulness exercises with some degree of caution and skepticism.

Regardless of your starting point in promoting mindfulness with a given client, the desired, terminal response is nonjudgmental awareness of psychological events that up until now have been experientially controlled. You have successfully accomplished the goal of your clients mindfully living in the present when they are able to dispassionately just notice unwanted thoughts, feelings, and other private events from which they have previously sought escape. Being able to respond to troublesome psychological experiences in an accepting manner, as will be seen, also contributes specifically to the development of a transcendent sense of self and more generally to the psychological flexibility required to lead a full and valued life.

Types of Mindfulness Interventions

Although various types and forms of meditation are some of the more common means for increasing present-moment awareness (Kabat-Zinn, 1990, 1994, 2005), interventions that you may use to promote mindfulness are by no means limited to these. As I already suggested, you can also use a number of exercises and techniques that foster defusion and willingness, such as Taking Inventory and Sitting with Feelings (see chapter 6), to shape mindfulness. Our primary focus within this chapter will be on a progression of exercises and techniques, including both formal meditative and nonmeditative procedures, that have been more explicitly identified and developed to promote mindfulness.

While there are a few standard techniques within ACT that have been developed to strengthen present-moment awareness, such as the Leaves on a Stream (Strosahl et al., 2004, p. 44) and Soldiers in the Parade exercises (Hayes, 1987, p. 367; Hayes et al., 1999, pp. 158–162), I recommend, especially early in the process of developing mindfulness with your clients, that you supplement them with some forms of meditation or other related interventions that lead up to them. As of this writing, a wide variety of mindfulness-based approaches (Baer, 2003, 2006) and possible forms of meditation exist; you can choose any one these to promote contact with the present moment. For example, the current Wikipedia entry for "meditation" lists fourteen different types (Meditation, n.d.).

Selection Guidelines

Unfortunately, you'll find it difficult to select one type of meditation over others on empirical grounds alone as the existing research that has directly compared different meditation approaches with each other (Fling, Thomas, & Gallaher, 1981; Valentine & Sweet, 1999; Yuille & Sereda, 1980) has been among nonclinical populations. For both conceptual and methodological reasons (Caspi & Burleson, 2005), there are no substantive published findings that I am aware of as of this writing that have compared the impact of different types of meditation upon clinically relevant behavior (Delmonte & Vincent, 1985; Perez-De-Albeniz & Holmes, 2000). In the absence of extensive comparative empirical findings to use as a guideline, the various meditation exercises and related techniques for enhancing present moment awareness that I suggest in this chapter come from those that have been developed and demonstrated to be efficacious by Jon Kabat-Zinn and his colleagues (Kabat-Zinn, Lipworth, & Burney, 1985; Kabat-Zinn et al., 1992; Miller, Fletcher, & Kabat-Zinn, 1995). Such various forms of "mindfulness meditation" not only serve as the basis for mindfulness-based cognitive therapy (MBCT; Segal et al., 2002)—and, therefore, have received additional empirical support from favorable investigations of this approach—but have also been incorporated into other presentations of ACT (see for example Eifert & Forsyth, 2005; Hayes & Smith, 2005).

As I noted previously, ACT places relatively less emphasis on mindfulness-enhancing techniques than does MBCT, and I encourage you to consult the book on this approach by Segal et al. (2002) as well as those by Kabat-Zinn (1990, 1994, 2005) for additional procedures and exercises that can be used with your clients in promoting mindfulness meditation. The best mindfulness approach is one that works, and these additional techniques that are not highlighted here may be useful alternatives with clients who fail to respond to those techniques that we will look at here. Additionally, you can also use other mindfulness procedures to supplement those that will be presented here.

The Roles of Shaping and Fading

As I suggested earlier, mindfulness as a skill can be gradually molded and strengthened by using the same gradual change procedures of shaping and fading that are applicable in modifying other forms of operant behavior (Martin & Pear, 2007). Shaping can be used in the initial acquisition of mindfulness as well as in supporting its occurrence over longer periods of time. *Shaping* involves the gradual change of a response while the stimulus remains about the same, whereas *fading* entails the gradual change of a stimulus while the response stays unchanged (Martin & Pear). Use fading in gradually shifting the focus (the "stimulus" in this case) of nonjudgmental awareness (the "response" in this case) of your clients from the initial sensory experiences provided by external sources of stimulation to troublesome thoughts, feelings, and other private events.

Related Errors

Generally two types of errors are common in both shaping and fading—either going too slow, so that clients become stuck at an earlier step in the process and have to be unstuck from it before the next is established, or going too fast, so that earlier steps are lost in the process and attainment of the terminal goal is unnecessarily delayed. Of the two errors, the first appears to be rather inconsequential in promoting mindfulness as it is unlikely that your clients can "overdose" or become fixated on transitory forms of it. For example, spending too much time in training and practicing mindfulness of the breath is unlikely to hinder shifting the focus of their attention to unwanted thoughts and feelings. Mindfulness training as a fading process often starts by focusing externally rather than internally. Breathing mindfully is a step in the progressive transition from focusing on external stimulation (like listening to music) to private events. It's unlikely though that you have to worry about spending too much time on mindfulness of the breath before moving on to private events. In other types of fading, however, going too slow in this way, would cause the behavior to become fixated or stuck at an earlier stage in the training. This is commonly seen in what is known as "prompt dependence." Perhaps you wish to have a child stand up by simply making a hand gesture. To accomplish this, you may first also have to use a verbal command with the goal of fading out the command and fading in the gesture. If too much training occurs with the verbal command (going too slow), the behavior may become dependent upon it, making it that much more difficult to shift control to the hand gesture. This same phenomenon seems unlikely to be a concern with mindfulness training.

Of greater concern is going too fast in expecting your clients to be mindful of difficult private events before their level of skills is up to the task. Consequently, a useful rule of thumb is to be patient and err on the side of going too slow rather than too fast in working with your clients on their mindfulness skills. Once your clients are able to be nonjudgmentally present with unwanted thoughts and feelings, their mindfulness skills are likely to be strong enough to apply to a wide array of psychological experiences.

Presenting the Rationale for Mindfulness Interventions

One challenge you are likely to encounter in training your clients to openly contact the present moment (and in further honing this skill through related homework assignments) is that your clients may try to use mindfulness interventions as a form of experiential control. Although it may be easier to simply strengthen the mindfulness skills of clients who already have some previous experience with different types of meditation, it may be more of a challenge in working with such clients to see that they are used in an ACT-consistent manner. Meditation, yoga, and related practices are often either explicitly, or at least implicitly, offered as ways of reducing stress, regulating moods, or otherwise controlling private events. Even if such experiences were not presented in this manner to your clients, there is a high probability they were at least seen and sought out by your clients as a means of experiential control.

The concern I underline here is certainly greater with clients who have previously used meditation and similar experiences as a way of controlling unwanted private events, but it also exists with clients who lack such a history. Such clients may see mindfulness meditation as another shovel to be used in digging their way out of the experiential-control hole in which they are hopelessly trapped or as an alternative way of winning the tug-of-war with the depression monster.

Offer a rationale similar to that which follows to all of your clients upon introducing mindfulness interventions, and be prepared to repeat it as necessary. Because reference is made in the rationale to the Tug-of-War with a Monster Metaphor, you will also need to present it to clients who may be unfamiliar with it.

> *If you are willing to do so, I'd like to begin having you try out some different exercises that may help you explore and develop a different way of responding and relating to thoughts and feelings you've been struggling with. These exercises are commonly referred to as mindfulness exercises. Many of them we can first have you try out here and then have you practice them further as part of homework. Let me make it very clear what these exercises are designed to do and what they are not designed to do. They are not designed to make your depressing thoughts and feelings go away. They may or may not go away as your mindfulness skills become stronger, but that is not their purpose. The exercises are not designed to teach you a new and better way of pulling on the rope in order to win your tug-of-war with the depression monster. The purpose of the exercises is not to slay the depression monster—it may well still be there—but to see if it's possible for you to develop a new way of responding and relating to it. This new way does not involve your picking up the rope, but instead your walking away from the depression monster and focusing on what you can do to have your life be what you want it to be.*

This rationale is designed to not only discourage the use of mindfulness exercises as an experiential control strategy, but also to simultaneously serve an augmenting function by emphasizing, from an ACT-perspective, the natural reinforcing consequences of increased present-moment awareness. Loosely speaking, this way of introducing mindfulness should reduce the likelihood that your clients will evaluate their experience with it on how well it reduces unwanted thoughts and feelings and instead make it more probable that their appraisal of it will be based upon how mindfulness training liberates themselves from struggling with troublesome private events. Be prepared, at least early on, to arbitrarily reinforce the client behavior of practicing mindfulness exercises through praise and other words of encouragement. Ultimately, however, mindfulness must be maintained by its natural consequences.

One potential natural consequence that supports mindfulness comes from the negative reinforcement associated with the reduction of unwanted private events, that is, depressing thoughts and feelings occur less often. Notice that the rationale above explicitly refers to this possible outcome but in order to deemphasize it. Specifically telling clients that the purpose of mindfulness training is not to get rid of unpleasant thoughts and feelings is designed to make it less likely that they will use such consequences in evaluating its worth to them. Instead, the long-term objective of liberating your clients to lead more valued lives will become the positive reinforcer for their practice of mindfulness. From this perspective, the purpose of the rationale is to orient and sensitize your clients in their exploration of mindfulness techniques to its later, vitalizing consequences and away from the short-term consequence of experiential escape.

Presenting Mindfulness Interventions Progressively

Consistent with a fading strategy (that is, in which the stimulus is gradually changed while the response remains unchanged), present your clients with a progressive sequence of exercises and techniques for promoting mindfulness. The terminal goal of the training is for your clients to be able to be nonjudgmentally attentive to depressing private events that they previously would have ruminated about or responded to with other forms of experiential control. Specifically, I suggest a series of in-session mindfulness exercises in which the focus of directed awareness is progressively shifted from (1) the sensations of tasting, chewing, and swallowing food to (2) the stimulation associated with engaging in routine, daily activities to (3) sensations related to breathing, and finally to (4) unwanted thoughts, feelings, and other private events.

Step 1: The Raisin Exercise

This initial exercise was first discussed by Kabat-Zinn (1990, pp. 27–29) as a way of introducing mindfulness meditation to clients attending his stress clinic. It has since been adapted for use in both MBCT (Segal et al., 2002, pp. 103–104) and ACT (Hayes & Smith, 2005, pp. 110–111). I recommend this exercise as a starting point for mindfulness work with your clients who lack any previous experience with meditation and related practices. You may wish to bypass it at your discretion for your clients with such a history, although there do not appear to be any drawbacks with including it.

Although it is commonly referred to as the Raisin Exercise, you can use any small edibles such as popcorn, jelly beans, or oyster crackers. In any case, it is preferable that you use edibles that your clients are familiar with to heighten the difference between how they typically eat mindlessly and how they deliberately and mindfully eat within the exercise.

The instructions that follow are purposefully designed to slow down how your clients routinely interact with the edible in question (raisins in this example) in order to allow for enhanced directed attention toward it. As such, present the instructions slowly with a ten to fifteen-second pause between specific directives.

> *I'd like you to imagine that you have never before in your life seen the objects that are now before you. It's as if you are seeing them for the first time—as if they are completely new and foreign to you. Take one of them and place it in the palm of your hand. Look at it very closely. Notice the sense of curiosity you have as you slowly study it. Look at the way the light shines and reflects off it so that some parts of it are lighter in color and other parts are darker. Examine the wrinkles and contours of it—how it bulges out in some places and dips in in others.*

Take one of your fingers of your other hand and slowly rub over it, noticing its texture. Explore what it feels like and notice how your finger knows exactly what to do.

Notice where the object rests in the palm of your hand. Focus on where the object touches your hand and what that feels like. Notice the weight of the object as you feel it contacting your skin.

Now slowly pick up the object. Feel it between your fingers.

Slowly bring the object up toward your nose. Now smell the object. Place it to one side of your nose and then the other as you slowly and deeply inhale, while carefully noticing its smell.

Now slowly move the object to your mouth. Notice how your mouth and hand know exactly what to do. Gently open your mouth and place it inside, noticing how it feels. Slowly run your tongue over the surface of the object. Notice what it feels like. Carefully notice what it tastes like.

Now very slowly and gently bite into the object, noticing any change in its taste. Slowly chew the object. Feel it making contact with your teeth and the saliva in your mouth changing its consistency.

Finally, when you are ready, see if you can slowly and deliberately swallow it and notice it settling into your stomach.

Afterward, solicit your clients' reactions about their experience and validate them in an open-ended manner without subjecting their comments to further analysis. Conclude the exercise by reemphasizing that it was designed to enable clients to become more aware of what goes on both inside and outside of them as it occurs, and that mindfulness, like any skill, can be strengthened with further practice.

Related Exercises and Homework Assignments

Because your clients can't "fail" the Raisin Exercise, it is appropriate that you assign related exercises for homework following it. Clients can use the Mindfulness Exercise Diary (see appendix H) to list the specific activities or exercises they do, how long they were practiced, and how they reacted to them. I recommend that your clients complete at least one mindfulness assignment similar to the Raisin Exercise each day before the next session and that they return their completed diary for review with you at that time.

The easiest way to structure the exercise is to have your clients select at least one food item or beverage each day that they will consume in a mindful manner. Simple edibles, such as a carrot or potato chips, or drinks (like water or milk) will suffice, although more stimulating items are preferable. Hayes and Smith (2005, pp. 111–112), for example, recommend mindfully brewing and drinking a cup of tea. Mindfully preparing and eating a bowl of vegetable soup is another flavorful suggestion. Although the total time required to complete any exercise may be fairly brief (perhaps as short as five to ten minutes), impress upon your clients the importance of doing so slowly, while paying close attention to their related experiences at the time.

Other fairly stimulating experiences can be used in place of mindful eating and drinking. Hayes and Smith (2005, pp. 113–114) also suggest carefully listening to classical music. Focused listening to other types of music may also work as long as it's possible to shift attention among the various instruments and/or vocals within it. Carefully and deliberately studying the different brush strokes and changes in color, tone, and hue within a painting may also serve as a similar type of mindfulness exercise.

Step 2: Performing Daily Activities Mindfully

You can usually introduce the second step in the progression of mindfulness exercises at the next session following the Raisin Exercise, provided your clients have completed their homework. If not, conduct another in-session exercise using another edible or beverage before proceeding. As with the previous step, provide an in-session exercise to your client to illustrate how mindfulness can be extended to performing everyday activities. In doing so, select an activity that is more active and effortful than eating or drinking and which can be easily performed at normal speed.

Walking Exercise

Walking provides a good example (see Kabat-Zinn, 1990, chap. 7) of an activity that you can engage in with your clients either outdoors or, if necessary, depending upon the weather and other circumstances, within the therapy room itself.

Introduce and conduct the exercise by saying something like the following:

I think we are ready to extend some of the mindfulness exercises you've been practicing this past week to other activities that we all engage in every day. Let's take walking, for example. If you're willing to do so, I'd like for the two of us to go on a little walk together. Unlike the exercise that we did in our last session and the ones you practiced for homework this past week, there's no need for you to walk slower than you normally do. Please walk at your usual pace. However, as best as you are able to, I would like you to walk mindfully. By that, I mean I would like you to closely attend to the experience of walking itself. Let's start to walk. Focus your attention on the sensations in your feet and legs. Notice how your legs and feet know just how to move without you watching and looking down at them or telling them how to move. As they move, be aware of one foot coming down and making contact with the ground [or floor] as the other comes up. Notice the slight pressure you feel in the heel of your foot coming down. At the same time, be aware of the slight pressure in the toes and front of your other foot as it begins to lift. Also, notice the movement in your legs as they move back and forth. Be aware of how your entire body feels as it moves. Focus your gaze in front of you and not at your feet. If you find your mind and attention start to wander, notice that and gently bring it back to focusing upon your feet.

The exercise does not need to be long (five to ten minutes should suffice) and it may not be necessary to continue the instructions throughout its entire duration. Afterward, provide some reflective discussion similar to that recommended following the Raisin Exercise.

Related Exercises and Homework Assignments

In preparation for homework, collaborate with your clients to identify other daily activities—such as showering/bathing, teeth brushing, dressing/undressing, or even chores (for instance, washing dishes, cleaning, and so on)—that they can engage in mindfully as another way of increasing their moment-to-moment awareness (see Kabat-Zinn, 1990, chap. 9; Segal et al., 2002, p. 123). List such exercises in the Mindfulness Exercise Diary and ask your clients to add any others as they are completed. Instruct your clients to perform at least one routine activity mindfully each day before the next session. They should also record any related comments and reactions they have to these mindful activities in the Mindfulness Exercise Diary. If possible, have your clients select a different activity each day. However, variety is less important than doing whatever activity they do each day mindfully.

Step 3: Breathing Mindfully Exercise

This next step extends the mindfulness exercises to a more formal meditative practice of teaching your clients how to focus attention on their own breathing (see Hayes & Smith, 2005, p. 118; Kabat-Zinn, 1990, chap. 3; Segal et al., 2002, pp. 150–151). This particular point in the progression of mindfulness experiences is critical for several reasons. The focus of moment-to-moment awareness is shifted to internal stimulation associated with the natural, ongoing, and rhythmic respiration of the body and away from that provided by external stimulation (edibles and outside objects and activities). Because breathing, the new focus of attention, is done continuously, your clients can always return to it as an anchoring point to help them refocus and center when their minds wander.

As with the introduction of the mindfulness exercises in the previous two steps, first have your clients practice breathing mindfully in session by saying something like the following (with each unspecified pause lasting for fifteen to thirty seconds):

We are now ready to extend the mindfulness exercises to focusing attention on our breathing. Breathing is something we do continually and naturally, and usually with very little thought. If you're willing to do so, I'd like you to close your eyes and follow my voice as I talk you through the exercise. First, take a moment to settle into a comfortable sitting position. Position your back so that it is slightly away from the back of the chair and your feet so that they are flat on the floor. Your legs should be uncrossed, and your arms and hands may be positioned on the armrest of the chair. Take a moment and notice the parts of your body that are making contact with the chair. Notice where you feel your buttocks and legs pressing against the chair, where your arms and hands touch the chair, and where your feet touch the floor. Imagine being able to go inside your body and, with a crayon, being able to color in the parts of your body making contact with the chair and the floor. [Pause for up to a minute.] Now bring your attention and awareness to your breath. Notice your breath entering your nostrils as you effortlessly inhale. See if you can be aware of your breath at the very moment it enters your nostrils. [Pause.] Notice the changing sensations in your chest and abdomen as you breathe in. Bring your attention to how your chest gently moves upward and inward as the breath enters your body. [Pause.]

See if you can follow your breath all the way down into your body. [Pause.] Notice where the breath stops. Focus your awareness on the exact point where it stops and then begins the process of moving out of your body. See if you can follow the breath from that point to the exact moment where it leaves your nostrils as you exhale. [Pause.] Focus your awareness on the changing sensations in your chest and abdomen as you exhale—as your chest gently falls back into a comfortable resting position to await the next breath. See if it's possible to notice the time between each breath that is exhaled and the next one that is inhaled. Bring your attention to the cusp—that moment just before the next inhalation occurs. [Pause.]

If your mind begins to wander at any point, see if you can notice that and gently bring your attention back to your breath.

This initial in-session exercise does not need to exceed five to ten minutes as this is generally long enough for your clients to experience the difference between focusing their attention on their breathing and having it be disrupted by automatic thoughts, feelings, or other sources of distraction. Afterward, probe for moments where you clients became distracted, if they have not spontaneously mentioned them. Use this opportunity to share your own experiences with the exercise and assure your clients that it is one that nearly everyone finds challenging, especially at first, but it is one at which they cannot fail. On this point, emphasize that every time your clients find that their attention wanders, it is another opportunity for them to notice that, recognize what may have distracted them, and gently return their awareness to their breathing.

Related Exercises and Homework Assignments

Perhaps even more so than with the exercises associated with the first two steps in the mindfulness progression, stress with your clients that breathing mindfully is a skill that they can hone further with additional practice. During the week following its introduction, ask your clients to practice the exercise at least twice daily for increasingly longer periods of time. I suggest your clients begin with five minutes of mindful breathing on the first day. Each following day, they should try to extend their mindful breathing by two to three minutes. By their next session, the goal is to practice mindful breathing for at least fifteen minutes, twice daily. Remind your clients to complete the Mindfulness Exercise Diary each time so that both of you can track this shaping process.

Because many of your clients will find breathing mindfully more challenging than the exercises in the first two steps, provide them with a bit more instruction and structure to guide their practice of it for homework. You may use the handout in appendix I for this purpose. You may also want to make a tape or CD that talks your clients through the exercise. Audiotapes/CDs for practicing other forms of mindfulness meditation are available through Kabat-Zinn (1990). While the handout and/or tape are useful in guiding initial practice sessions, I recommend that you fade them out as your clients become more proficient in the breathing exercise to reduce any dependency upon them. The goal is for your clients to eventually breathe mindfully and flexibly in a variety of contexts in which contacting the present moment is useful. It's important that they be able to do that without being dependent on a handout, CD, or audiotape.

Step 4: Thinking and Feeling Mindfully

The final step in shaping and strengthening your clients' skills in present-moment awareness entails fading out focus on the breath and fading in their attention on thoughts, feelings, and other related private events. During their mindful-breathing homework, your clients will have already experienced thoughts distracting them. It's highly likely that many of these intrusive thoughts and related feelings were unwanted and of a depressive nature. The goal of this final step in mindfulness training—to explicitly shift your clients' nonjudgmental attention to unwanted private events—is thus not that big a leap.

Your major challenge at this point is ensuring that exercises designed to promote moment-to-moment contact with your clients' ongoing stream of thoughts and feelings do not revert to rumination. This can occur when your clients, perhaps mindfully at first, notice a passing thought (for example, about a previous romantic interest), but then become fused or caught up in other thoughts and feelings associated with it (such as how they bungled it, can never do anything right, feel like a failure, and so on). To minimize this, impress upon your clients that one thought is likely to lead to a stream of related thoughts and feelings and that their task is to just notice the entire process, especially reactive evaluative thoughts (such as "that's a bad memory," "I'm stupid," and so on). All unwanted private events are simply more grist for the mindfulness mill, and, with sufficient practice, the goal of your clients being able to pay attention nonjudgmentally to even private events as troublesome as negative self-evaluations is attainable.

Despite your best efforts, however, your clients undoubtedly will find themselves being carried away at times by certain troublesome thoughts. Your objective is not to completely eliminate nor prevent such occurrences, but to enable your clients to dispassionately recognize evaluative and fused thoughts for what they are as they occur. This will help your clients disentangle themselves from those negative thoughts. As with the breathing exercise, don't view having your clients' attention captured by fused thoughts as failures but as rich opportunities for them to further sharpen their mindfulness skills by directing their awareness back to the ongoing flow of consciousness.

As I mentioned earlier in this chapter, several exercises have been developed within ACT that you can introduce at this point in mindfulness training, including Soldiers in the Parade (Hayes et al., 1999, pp. 158–162) and Leaves on a Stream (Strosahl et al., 2004, p. 44). A third is the Watching the Mind-Train Exercise (Hayes & Smith, 2005, pp. 66–68). All three share the common element of asking your clients to simply step back and just notice from a nonjudgmental perspective whatever psychological experiences unfold in the present moment.

Gazing at the Clouds Exercise

Another related exercise that has been favored by some of my depressed clients is Gazing at the Clouds. It was first suggested by Linehan (1993b, p. 67) and will be used here for purposes of illustration. You may wish to experiment with all four exercises—

Gazing at the Clouds plus those mentioned in the previous paragraph—and/or describe each to your clients and allow them to choose which one to initially practice in session as well as for homework.

> *We are now ready to extend our work in mindfulness to a most difficult area—that of our own thoughts, feelings, memories, and so on. We often find many of our thoughts and emotions bothersome. It's challenging to simply observe them without being lured into wrestling with them. If you're willing to do so, I'd like to introduce you to a new exercise that may provide another way for you to respond to thoughts and feelings that you don't like.*
>
> *Please close your eyes and take a moment to become centered. Notice where you feel your body making contact with the chair. [Pause 10 to 15 seconds.]*
>
> *Take a moment now to focus your attention on your breath as you've been practicing for this past week. [Pause 15 to 30 seconds.]*
>
> *Now I'd like you to shift your attention to following the sound of my voice. Imagine it's a warm spring day and you are comfortably lying on your back in a meadow watching clouds as they lazily drift across the sky. Imagine as you lie there that each thought that you have is being carried by its own cloud as it slowly moves across the sky. See each thought you have—as you have it—slowly and effortlessly floating by in the sky on its own cloud. Just as one cloud drifts by, another comes along to carry the next thought.*
>
> *Just lie back and watch your thoughts drift by. If you find yourself distracted at any point—if you find yourself no longer lying in the meadow but in the clouds themselves or elsewhere—see if you can back up a bit and notice what you were doing before that happened. Then take a moment to recenter by focusing on your breath, and when you are ready, return to the meadow and watch your thoughts drift by on the clouds. One by one—just lay back and observe the flow of your thoughts. At some point, you may have the thought that this exercise is stupid or that you don't like some of the thoughts that are coming up. If so, see if it's possible to take those thoughts and have them drift by on their own clouds.*

End the exercise after five to ten minutes and follow it with a review of your client's reactions to and experience with the exercise. If necessary, reemphasize that it is impossible for your client to fail the exercise while soliciting from the client instances in which the exercise broke down. Use such moments not only to sharpen for your client the discrimination between responding to thoughts in a mindful versus fused fashion, but also to identify particularly troublesome private events that, if necessary, may be addressed with related defusion and acceptance work.

Related Exercises and Homework Assignments

Homework assignments at this step parallel those associated with breathing mindfully. They are designed to help your clients attend to ongoing thoughts in the present moment for longer periods of time as well as to facilitate fading the focus of awareness away from less bothersome thoughts, memories, and so on and toward more troublesome private events. Provide a handout (see appendix J) and/or CD or audiotape to help guide your clients through the homework. Ask that they follow a schedule in which one of the exercises is initially practiced for at least five minutes, twice a day. Also ask your clients to use the Mindfulness Exercise Form to document how they've done with increasing the exercises by two to three minutes each day. The goal, again, is that the exercises will be practiced for at least fifteen minutes, twice daily, by their next session.

Many, and perhaps even most, of the automatic thoughts and related private events that your clients will be mindfully attending to in completing the homework exercises will be ones from which they have previously sought experiential escape and avoidance. In reviewing the homework experiences of your clients, determine explicitly the degree to which this was the case. Doing so will help you complete the fading process by strategically shifting the focus of attending mindfully to such specific psychological experiences. At this point, encourage your clients as part of their ongoing homework to selectively engage in whichever specific exercise among the four—Soldiers in the Parade, Leaves on the Stream, Watching the Mind-Train, or Gazing at the Clouds—seems most helpful whenever they find themselves struggling with thoughts, feelings, and other private events. Just as importantly, prompt your clients to also use their mindfulness skills at critical moments in session when they become overwhelmed and/or bogged down by depressive thoughts and feelings.

Progression of Mindfulness Exercises: A Summary

The progression of mindfulness exercises that I have just suggested would unfold over four weekly therapy sessions. However, hold this one-month time frame lightly and feel free to compress or expand it depending upon the particular needs of your clients. For example, you can combine steps 1 and 2 as well as steps 3 and 4 to present the sequence of mindfulness training over a two-week time period for your clients who may already have some meditation skills; you may even skip the first two or three steps altogether. For clients who are especially prone to rumination, you may find it necessary to progress through the steps at a more slow and deliberate pace than that suggested here. In either case, the timetable that you follow should not be determined arbitrarily but by the response of your clients to the exercises.

Promoting Self as Context

Because they complement each other, you can present specific interventions for increasing present-moment awareness before, after, or concurrently with exercises and techniques within ACT that are designed to foster a transcendent sense of self. However, there may be some advantage in working first with your clients on mindfulness training as many of the exercises also indirectly promote self as context. This is because all mindfulness exercises, regardless of their specific attentional focus, provide your clients with the opportunity to repeatedly see their experiences from the same perspective, which never varies. For example, point out to your clients that there was a part of them (specifically, "the observer you") present to notice their thoughts floating by as leaves on a stream and that the exercises that they will be invited to participate in next are designed to enhance and sharpen this experiential vantage point.

> *You've now had considerable practice in just noticing in a nonjudgmental way your moment-to-moment experiences. Notice also that for you to be able to do this, you must have a part of you that is able to stand back enough from your ongoing thoughts and feelings to observe them as they occur. So, while you have thoughts and feelings, there must be a part of you that is not merely your thoughts and feelings. If you are willing to do so, I'd like to shift our work a bit here to see if it might be possible to find a place where you can firmly stand above and apart from thoughts and feelings and other experiences you may have been wrestling with. Like the mindfulness exercises, what we do next is not designed to somehow destroy the depression monster. Rather, the purpose is to see if we can find a space in which you can position yourself in relationship to the depression monster in such a way that your leading a full and meaningful life is not compromised by tugging on the rope. Are you willing to explore this with me?*

The Relationship of Self as Context to Valuing and Committed Action

It is useful clinically, although not from a scientific perspective, to regard the values held by your clients and their pursuit of related goals as freely chosen actions. From the perspective of ACT, however, a free choice is only possible from the position of an invariant sense of self, that is, a sense of self that remains constant. The alternative is to have potential life-altering actions decided upon and determined by thoughts, feelings, and other "passengers on the bus" rather than being freely chosen by self as context as the "bus driver."

While interventions that promote a transcendent sense of self obviously also contribute to the promotion of defusion and acceptance, the role they play in supporting committed action and behavior change may be more apparent but are still worth emphasizing. When used successfully, procedures within ACT that support the self as context help free your clients from the oppressive weight of thoughts and feelings with which they struggle. An array of interventions have been developed that can be used for this purpose (see Strosahl et al., 2004, table 2.5). Because of space limitations, only two—the Chessboard Metaphor and the Observer Exercise—will be detailed here. Others will be discussed at appropriate points in the next chapter.

The Chessboard Metaphor

This intervention was first presented by Hayes (1987, pp. 359–360) and is modified slightly here to be more responsive to the experiences of clients who suffer from depression. The purpose of the metaphor and others closely related to it, such as Furniture in the House (Strosahl et al., 2004, p. 46), is to help your clients draw a distinction between consciousness as a continuous process or perspective, and the content of consciousness. The metaphor itself does not need much set up and can be presented by saying something like the following:

> I don't know if you've ever played much chess, but even if you haven't, you're probably familiar enough with it to know that a chess match is like a war that gets fought out between different armies of colored pieces. The goal of the white pieces is to get rid of the black pieces, and that of the black pieces is to vanquish the white pieces. For a moment, I'd like you to imagine a chessboard that is infinitely large and extends forever in all directions. On the chessboard are hundreds, if not thousands, of both black and white pieces—many more than participate in a normal game of chess. The white pieces hang out and band together to go off and do battle with the black pieces that, in turn, team up with each other against the white pieces.
>
> Think of your thoughts, feelings, memories, and beliefs as pieces on the chessboard. You may like and be fond of some of your thoughts and memories. Like white pieces that band together, you may, for example, have pleasant thoughts and feelings about certain memories that you've accumulated. But there are also lots of black pieces on the board. Think of them as depressing thoughts like "my life is a hopeless mess" and negative feelings about yourself—for example, that you're stupid or unlovable—that you wish weren't even there. Notice, as we said, that the way chess is played is for the white pieces and black pieces to do battle with each other—to fight each other to the death. In fact, it may seem that they can't possibly coexist. One white piece says you're okay, but over here is an opposing black piece that says you're not okay. So the way the game is normally played is that one of them has to win out over the other. Now, check and see—you don't need to answer me aloud, but please be honest with yourself—if it isn't the case that you've quite understandably had a stake in who wins this struggle.
>
> It's as if it becomes so important that the white pieces win that you, me, and really all of us get lured into going down to board level to organize the white pieces against the black. It's like we jump on the back of the white knight to organize and lead the other white pieces off into battle against the black army of self-doubt, feelings of worthlessness, and depression.
>
> Now I'd like you to take a moment to consider what happens when this occurs. Do the black pieces, when you're down there on the board, seem bigger and more intimidating or less so? Are they even more dangerous and threatening because they are now as big as you are?
>
> Also, remember that the board goes on forever. As much as you are trying as hard as you possibly can, will you ever kick the black pieces you don't like off the board? Or will they still be there regardless of what you do, just maybe at a different place on the board? Have you ever rid yourself of a bad memory you no longer wanted to think about? I'm not asking you to believe what I'm saying, but I am asking you to consider what your experience with depression tells you about what we're talking about here. To what degree have your struggles with depression been like fighting a war that you haven't been able to win?

At about this point, transition what has primarily been a monologue by you into a dialogue that reflects on a sense of self as perspective.

Therapist: We said in this metaphor that your thoughts and feelings are like the pieces on the chessboard. Who are you?

Client: The pieces?

Therapist: How can the pieces be both your thoughts and feelings *and* you? You have thoughts and feelings like you also have a car, but is the car *you*? So who are you in this example?

Client: The player?

Therapist: Well, we talked about how you've tried to be the player and what happens when you try to move the pieces around. Suppose you can be something else besides the player. What does that leave?

Client: The board?

Therapist: Is it more useful to see yourself as the board than as the player? Notice that without a board, the pieces can't function as pieces. The board holds the pieces and provides the context in which the pieces can be pieces. This may seem like a strange question, but do your thoughts exist without you? Are they off somewhere else when you're not thinking them?

Client: I don't think so.

Therapist: I suppose we may not know for sure, but it doesn't seem useful to think that they are. Notice that if you are the board, you can watch the war unfold among the pieces without being part of it. But if you lead your life as the player, that's not possible. You can't merely watch the war—you are part of it, and it's as if your very life depends on which side wins. We said that you as the board can hold the pieces without having a stake in which ones win, as it makes no difference to the board. I'd also like you to consider one other thing that the board can do, and that is to move forward—to choose to go in any direction you as the board choose to go, taking all of the pieces, both the white ones and the black pieces, along for the ride.

Although this metaphor is being presented here as one that primarily promotes self as context, I hope it's apparent that it also simultaneously supports defusion (by likening thoughts to external objects) and committed action (by emphasizing the ability of the board to move in a chosen direction). Accordingly, it potentially impacts both the acceptance and commitment facets of ACT at one time. You don't need to process the metaphor immediately after you present it. However, you may find it useful to frequently refer back to it at other points in therapy, especially critical moments when your clients appear to be stuck and overwhelmed (for example, "Are you responding to the pieces that are on your chessboard right now as the board or as the player?").

The Observer Exercise

This intervention normally follows the presentation of the Chessboard Metaphor. You can certainly reverse their order, but the Observer Exercise is considerably longer than the Chessboard Metaphor, and it tends to elicit more intense and powerful emotional reactions on the part of clients. For these reasons, I recommend that you use the Chessboard Metaphor as a lead-in or warm-up for the Observer Exercise.

This procedure is traceable back to an "exercise in dis-identification," originally developed as part of psychosynthesis by Assagioli (1965, pp. 116–119). It was first adapted for use within ACT by Hayes (1987, pp. 360–361) and subsequently expanded somewhat (Hayes et al., 1999, pp. 193–195). Like the Chessboard Metaphor, the version presented here has been modified slightly to be more responsive to the experience of clients who struggle with depression. In particular, I've found it useful within the exercise to ask clients to recall a specific time during their lives (perhaps going back to childhood, if necessary) when they were not bothered by depression. Doing so not only underscores the continuity of self as context as well as its ability to transcend depression, but it also enables clients to grasp that the same "self" that was present then is still here now.

It is, of course, possible that some of your clients may report that they cannot recall any point during their lifetime when they were not depressed. In such instances, still ask them to recall earlier life events without emphasizing the corresponding absence of depression at those times. At this point, you are likely to have this needed information from a previous telling of your client's life story. If not, ask your clients to clarify the chronology of their experience with depression before presenting the exercise.

What follows illustrates how the exercise could be presented to an adult female client who reports being fairly continuously depressed since adolescence but having had a childhood free of depression. Because some clients may mistake the exercise for hypnosis, explicitly address this issue at the outset and obtain their permission to participate in it before proceeding.

> If you're willing to do so, I'd like to have you participate in an exercise that may be helpful in clarifying the difference we talked about between you as the chessboard and your thoughts and feelings as the chess pieces. It's not designed to create or put any more new pieces on the chessboard, but rather to see if it's possible to find a place where it may be a bit easier for you as the board to see all of the pieces that you have accumulated. During the exercise, I will ask you to close your eyes and to follow my voice as I ask you to imagine and reflect upon some of your experiences in life. However, the exercise is not hypnosis and you are free to discontinue it at anytime. Do you have any questions at this point?
>
> If you're willing to participate in the exercise, please close your eyes and get comfortable in the chair. Sit with your back straight, away from the back of the chair, with your legs uncrossed, feet flat on the floor, and your arms and hands resting on the chair. Take a moment to become centered by noticing where you can feel your body making contact with the chair. Now, become aware of your breath as you gently inhale and then exhale. [Pause 15 to 30 seconds.]
>
> Take a moment now to focus on my voice. If you notice that your mind begins to wander at any time during the exercise, just gently bring yourself back

to the sound of my voice. Take a few moments to focus your attention on yourself in this room. In your mind's eye, picture this room, picture your chair in relation to the rest of this room, and picture yourself sitting in the chair. Notice how you are sitting in the chair. Take a few moments to go inside and get in touch with the parts of your body that are making contact with the chair. Imagine being able to take a crayon and color in the points on your body where you feel it pressing against the chair. Notice any other bodily sensations. [Pause 10 to 15 seconds.]

Also, take a moment to notice any thoughts you are having. Just acknowledge them as they move on. Now notice any emotions you are having and just watch them for a few seconds. [Pause 10 to 15 seconds.]

Now I want you to see if you can notice something else—that as you noticed how your body is feeling and you observed your thoughts and feelings, a part of you noticed them. You noticed how your body feels, what you're thinking, and how you are feeling emotionally. Let's call this part of you that does this noticing the "observer you." In some deep sense, this observer you is the you that you call "you." You have been you your whole life. The same you that is here right now behind your eyes noticing what I'm saying is the same you that has been you as long as you have been you. I'm not asking you to believe what I'm saying but to simply see how what I'm saying squares with your own experience of being you.

Let's explore this a bit further. I want you to remember something that happened last year around this same time. You don't have to tell me aloud what it is, but when you have something in mind, please raise the index finger of your right hand. [Pause until the client raises right index finger.] Very good. Now I'd like you to keep your eyes closed, but look around at what was going on then. Notice where you were and who else may have been there. Remember what you were thinking and feeling. Notice the sights and sounds around you. And as you do that, see if you can notice that you were there then—the part of you that we are calling the observer you. You are here now and you were there then. See whether it's possible—even if just for a fleeting moment—to notice the essential continuity between the you that was present last year and the you that is here today. To experience that you have been you your whole life—that no matter how much your life has changed over the years, that the you that you call you, has not changed.

Let's move on to another time in your life. Now I'd like you to remember something that happened when you were a teenager. Again, please raise your finger when you have something in mind. [Pause until the client raises finger.] Good. Take a few moments to recall what was happening then—what was going on, where you were, what you were doing, and who else may have been there. Notice all the sights and sounds around you. See if you can be aware of what you were thinking and feeling at that time. And as you recall what the world looked like as you saw it then, see if you can notice that the same teenager who was behind your eyes looking out at the world then is the same person who is here in this room right now. You were there as a teenager and you are here now. You have been you your whole life. See if it's possible not to believe this but to experience this.

Let's move next to an earlier time in your life—a time when you've told me you did not feel depressed and weighed down by the worries and concerns you have had as an adult. I'd like you to remember a more carefree time when you were a child, say age seven or eight, when life may have seemed quite different to you. I'd like you to remember a pleasant, happy event you can recall as child of that age—maybe a birthday party or holiday celebration, for example. Take a few moments and once again, please raise your finger when you have something. [Pause until the client raises finger.] *Notice where you were, what you were doing, and who else was there. Remember all the sights and sounds around you and what you as that child were thinking and feeling at the time. And as you notice all of this, see if you can also notice—even if just for a few seconds—that that same carefree child that was there then is still here now. You have been you your entire life. Take a moment, check your experience, and see if it isn't the case that the same person aware of what you're aware of is here now and was there then.*

Everywhere you've been in life and at every time during your life, you've been there noticing. This is what we mean by the "observer you." From this perspective, let's look at some other areas of living and aspects of your experiences in life. Let's start with your body. Notice how your body is constantly changing. Sometimes it's tired, and at other times it's full of energy. Sometimes it's sick, and sometimes it's healthy; sometimes it's weak, and at other times it's strong. Take a moment and consider all of the changes your body has undergone. As a baby and child, your body was much smaller than it is now. Your body has grown taller, and over the years it may have both gained and lost some of its weight. You may have even had surgeries or operations where parts of your body have been removed or have had objects placed in it to repair it. Your bodily sensations come and go. Cells within your body die and are quickly and continuously replaced by other cells so that the very body you have right now is not even the same body you had when we began this exercise. So what this must mean, if the you that you call you—the observer you—has not changed, but your body has, is that although you have a body—as a matter of belief and not experience—you do not experience yourself to be just your body. Take a few moments to notice your body, and as you do so, every so often notice that you are the one doing the noticing. [Pause.]

Let's move next to another aspect of your life—your roles. Notice how many different roles you've had in your life. As a child, you were someone else's playmate and friend. When you went to school, you were in the role of student. Notice how many roles you have now and how they are constantly changing. Sometimes you are in the role of a wife, a mother, a daughter, a sister, a cousin, an aunt, or a grandmother [other "relative roles" that are relevant can also be cited]. *Sometimes you are in the role of a leader and other times in the role of a follower. You are always in some type of role or another—even right now you are in the role of a therapy client. Yet across all these different roles, notice that you are there and that part of you does not change. So, if the roles you play are constantly changing but the observer you does not change, it must mean that while you have roles, you don't experience yourself to be your roles. Again, don't*

husb
father
son
brother
cousin
uncle

believe this but simply see how what is being said speaks to your experience of you. See if you can become aware of the difference between what you are looking at and the you that is doing the looking.

Now let's move on to another area—your emotions. Notice how your emotions are constantly changing. Sometimes you are calm, and at other times tense. Sometimes you are angry and other times relaxed. Sometimes you feel love and at other times hate. Notice whatever emotions you are experiencing right now. Think about how your emotions have changed over the course of your lifetime—how things that frightened you as a child may no longer bother you, or others that were of no concern for you as a child now worry you a great deal. Notice how things that you once liked may no longer interest you, or how what you like now may be things that you once cared very little about. About the only thing you can count on with certainty about your emotions is that they will change—that as one feeling comes and goes, another will rise up to take its place. Yet notice that, while your emotions ebb and flow, you do not change. The same you that was frightened of the dark as a child is the same you that has different fears as an adult. So it must be that though you have emotions, you don't merely experience yourself as being your emotions. The same feeling is not constant—it doesn't last, but the part of you that you call you does last. You have been you your whole life and have been there to experience every feeling and emotion you have ever had. Take a few moments to notice what you are feeling right now, and as you do, notice who is noticing. [Pause for 15 to 30 seconds.]

Let's move on finally to probably the most difficult area of your experience—your own thoughts. Thoughts are especially tricky because they so easily lure us into arguing with them. When that happens, we are pulled out of our role of the observer you and into the world of belief or disbelief. If that happens to you as we go through this, see if you can catch it and gently come back to the sound of my voice. Notice how your thoughts are constantly changing—how what you are thinking right now as I speak may not be what you were thinking just a moment ago. Thoughts pop up, almost automatically, as if out of nowhere. Sometimes they may seem to make sense and other times to make no sense at all. Look at how your thoughts have changed just during the time you have been here today. Consider how much your thoughts have changed over your lifetime. As a child you had beliefs—like in Santa Claus and the Easter Bunny—that you no longer have. And you have thoughts and beliefs now that were completely unknown to you as a child. Some things that you were once ignorant of may now be something you know a great deal about. Sometimes you may think of something one way and very quickly find yourself thinking about it another way. Notice all of the thoughts you have about yourself. Sometimes you have been proud of yourself and at other times very critical of yourself. Yet through all of this, see if you can notice that the you that has experienced all of these different thoughts has not changed. The you that has thoughts today is the same you that had thoughts last year and as a child. So it must be the case that although your thoughts are constantly changing and in motion, the you that knows what you think has not changed. You have thoughts but are not your thoughts. Again, don't believe this. It's not a matter of belief. See if you can *experience it; just notice it, even if just for a brief moment before you become caught up in another wave of thoughts. Even when this happens, see if you can catch a glimpse of that part of you that is able to stand above the fray and simply watch it unfold. Take a few moments to watch your thoughts, and as you notice them, notice that you are noticing them.* [Pause 15 to 30 seconds.]

So, as a matter of experience and not of belief, you are not just your body or your roles or your emotions or your thoughts. All of these things are the content of your life, the pieces on the chessboard. You are the context, the board, in which all of these things unfold. See if you can notice from this space that a great deal of what you have been struggling with—depression, your own thoughts and feelings about yourself, regrets, and bad memories—all of these pieces, are not you anyway. No matter how the war that goes on down on the chessboard turns out, you as you will still be here as you always have been. See if you can use this realization to free yourself up a bit from the struggle you've been entangled in, to stand apart enough from the battle you've been fighting, and to find a place where you can drop the rope and keep it out of your hands long enough to begin to move your life in the direction you value. [Pause 10 to 15 seconds.] *Picture yourself again in this room.* [Pause 10 to 15 seconds.] *Picture the room and where the chair you're sitting in is in relation to the rest of the room.* [Pause 10 to 15 seconds.]

And when you are ready to come back into the room, you may do so by opening your eyes.

It is not necessary, nor do I recommend, that you spend a great deal of time afterward processing the exercise or debriefing your clients about it. Do, however, provide an opportunity immediately following the exercise to validate whatever reactions your clients may have had to it. Not all of your clients will get the exercise, but many who do will have a discernible and powerful emotional reaction as evidenced by crying, for example. In my experience, the overall reaction of clients to the exercise generally has been uplifting and calming. I can recall only one instance in which a client had a clearly negative reaction to the exercise, and this occurred in a group setting where it was difficult to monitor the moment-to-moment response of each of its members. As with the Chessboard Metaphor, once the exercise has been presented, you can make further references to it, particularly in promoting committed action (by, for instance, saying, "What does that part of you, that we've called the observer you, choose to do?").

Summary

In this chapter, I've presented some of the major interventions within ACT for you to use with your clients in promoting contact with the present moment and self as context. As with techniques covered in the previous two chapters—those that strengthen defusion and acceptance (chapter 6) and those that support commitment and behavior change (chapter 7)—interventions within ACT that foster mindfulness and increased awareness of self as perspective can be strategically applied at any point during treatment, depending upon the individualized case conceptualization and unique needs of your clients. You can initiate mindfulness exercises, in particular, at any point, and they can be expanded upon and/or reintroduced, as necessary, over the entire course of therapy.

Interventions such as the Chessboard Metaphor and Observer Exercise that have been specifically developed and adapted for use within ACT for promoting a transcendent sense of self, unfortunately, usually do not as readily lend themselves to the same degree of flexible application. For example, a given mindfulness exercise, such as mindful breathing, may be practiced continually and/or be initiated on an as-needed basis. It's unlikely that you would want to similarly repeat the Chessboard Metaphor and Observer Exercise with your clients. However, other related techniques serve the same purpose within ACT (such as the Get Off Your "Buts" Intervention and the Furniture in the House Metaphor) and can be used to supplement those presented in this chapter. Some of these will be discussed at appropriate points within the next chapter.

CHAPTER 9

Putting It All Together: A Sample Twelve-Session Protocol

Thus far we have considered interventions within ACT that have been organized according to a case-conceptualization approach and around paired, related processes (such as defusion and acceptance, commitment and behavior change, and mindfulness and self as context) that they are designed to promote. As I noted in chapter 1, this is one way, but certainly not the only way, of conducting ACT with your clients who struggle with depression.

This chapter describes, in a series of session-by-session guidelines, an alternate approach in which you present ACT in a more structured manner. Interventions that of necessity have already been presented in the last three chapters may be mentioned here, but they will not be reiterated in any more detail. Rather, our more extensive focus in this chapter will be on additional interventions, such as another defusion technique or way of undermining experiential control, not previously covered. Similar to the format followed by Eifert and Forsyth (2005) in their book on ACT for anxiety disorders, each session begins by reviewing and outlining the goals for that session. This is followed by a discussion of guidelines for attaining each goal as well as suggestions on how much time to spend on each.

As I mentioned in chapter 1, I am aware of no research to suggest that the more flexible, case-conceptualization approach to ACT with depressed clients that has been highlighted thus far is any more or less efficacious than the more sequential approach that will be detailed in this chapter. Consequently, experiment with each approach to determine your personal preference and to discover for yourself whether one is more useful than the other. While the case-conceptualization approach has the obvious advantage of being able to be applied more flexibly, more closely following a protocol in conducting ACT with your depressed clients may be more attractive for several reasons. For one, because the protocol takes a one-size-fits-all type of approach, you can follow it in much the same way with all clients with depression. Moreover, such a package approach ensures that each client will be exposed to interventions within ACT that comprehensively address all of the processes represented within the hexaflex. Accordingly, this minimizes the possibility that some key processes might somehow be overlooked in pursuing a more prescriptive and case-oriented approach.

A final point in favor of conducting ACT according to a protocol is that a similar approach has been used in research comparing ACT to other interventions. For example, session-by-session manuals were developed and followed to ensure the integrity of ACT in the two studies (Zettle & Hayes, 1986; Zettle & Rains, 1989) that have evaluated its relative efficacy against cognitive therapy in treatment of depression. In particular, the protocol of twelve weekly, hour-long sessions of ACT that will be presented here roughly parallels those followed in these two projects. As a consequence, using this chapter to guide your application of ACT will ensure that doing so most closely approximates the manual-based approach to it that has been shown to compare favorably to cognitive therapy.

Pretreatment Issues

The protocol presented in this chapter is focused solely on a session-by-session application of ACT as an active treatment. For this reason, you will need to obtain informed consent for treatment from your clients and complete any formalized, pretreatment assessment that you may wish to conduct before beginning session 1. Doing both is most readily accomplished by scheduling a pretreatment session prior to the first of the twelve treatment sessions.

Informed Consent

Despite the increased visibility that ACT has received fairly recently within publications that reach a lay readership (see M. Beck, 2002, 2006; Cloud, 2006), it is unlikely that many of your depressed clients will have ever even heard of ACT. Of those who may have at least heard of it, most will not contact you to explicitly request that they receive ACT as a treatment for depression. Accordingly, one of your responsibilities before initiating ACT proper will be to obtain the informed consent of your clients to participate in treatment. It seems appropriate to provide both verbal and written depictions of ACT to your clients in doing so.

A useful place to start the process of informed consent is to simply ask your clients if they have ever heard of ACT, and if so, what their understanding of it is. Assuming that they have not contacted you to request ACT and/or know very little about it, tell clients something like the following:

A number of different psychological approaches have been shown to have promise in helping people cope with depression, including what are known as cognitive therapy, interpersonal therapy, and different types of behavior therapy. Unfortunately no one way of dealing with depression has been shown to work for everyone. Because of this, we're left with choosing a particular approach and trying it for a long enough period of time to see if it's working. If it doesn't appear to be working, we can try other options.

The particular approach that I would suggest in our work together is a fairly new type of behavior therapy for depression known as acceptance and commitment therapy, or ACT. If you're agreeable to consenting to this approach, I will give you a handout you can take with you that describes ACT in greater detail, but at this point let me clarify a bit more about it. It's called acceptance and commitment therapy because, as I think you'll see, it focuses on helping you more clearly see what about your struggles with depression can be changed through commitment and what unfortunately cannot and may have to be dealt with through acceptance. In particular, in dealing with depression, ACT takes the approach that it is most useful to commit ourselves to actively doing what we can to have the kind of life we value and to learn how to accept experiences that we may not like but can't change or control.

A good deal of our time together here will not just be spent on talking about how to apply ACT but on having you learn by doing it. For example, we can have you try out and practice some of what makes up ACT during our sessions. Another valuable way to practice ACT is through homework assignments. For this reason, I will be asking you each week between our sessions to complete a homework assignment.

Because it is a relatively new approach, ACT has not been as thoroughly evaluated as some other approaches in dealing with depression, such as cognitive therapy. However, research that has directly compared ACT and cognitive therapy in helping people with depression has found them to be equally effective. While I certainly can't guarantee that ACT, or any other approach for that matter, will work for sure in your particular case, I also don't have any reason to suspect that it won't.

What I would ask you to consent to is a trial of ACT in which we would meet for an hour each week for twelve weeks. This should give us a long enough period of time to see if ACT works for you. If it doesn't, we can certainly explore some other options. You should be aware that you have the option at any point to ask that we discontinue ACT and consider another approach. We can also switch to another approach if it becomes obvious before the end of the twelve sessions that ACT is not working.

After answering any questions, finalize the formal granting of informed consent by asking your client to sign an appropriate document. A handout that closely follows the verbal depiction of ACT presented above is provided in appendix K. You can offer a copy of the handout to your clients to take with them. I also recommend that a copy of the handout be attached to the signed consent form to document the information offered to your clients about ACT. Additionally, you may wish to further familiarize your clients about ACT by providing them with a copy of one of Martha Beck's (2002, 2006) articles to read for homework prior to their first therapy session.

Pretreatment Assessment

You have several pretreatment assessment options to consider, ranging from the administration of no instruments to that of asking your clients to complete a battery of different measures. Because of this, you may find it informative to experiment a bit with these options to find out which ones are most useful for you and your clients.

Assessing Depression

At the very minimum, I recommend that you formally assess the level of depression for each of your clients prior to their first treatment session by administering the Beck Depression Inventory-II (BDI-II; Beck, Steer, & Brown, 1996) or a similar self-report measure. If you also administer the BDI-II prior to each session, you will have a pretreatment, baseline level of depression against which any changes that occur throughout the course of treatment can be evaluated. While the primary goal of ACT is to increase psychological flexibility and not eliminate depression, weekly reductions in client self-reports of depression, nevertheless, can be seen as providing some useful feedback on therapeutic progress for several reasons.

First, any increases in BDI scores are likely to reflect your client's overall level of emotional distress and suffering, and elevations, if not short-lived, are likely to be associated with disengagement from and even dropping out of therapy. Second, to the extent that what the BDI assesses primarily reflects the dirty pain of clinical depression and not merely the clean pain of dysphoria, reductions in its scores are to be expected. Moreover, research that has found ACT to compare favorably to cognitive therapy (Zettle & Hayes, 1986; Zettle & Rains, 1989) has relied upon BDI scores as one, albeit not the only, index of treatment outcome. Although the ultimate goal of ACT is not merely symptomatic relief, reductions in levels of depression should also not be dismissed as inconsequential, especially given the weight that feeling better understandably receives from clients.

A third and final advantage of administering the BDI weekly is that it affords you an efficient and convenient way of not only monitoring changes in the overall level of depression being reported by your clients but also, more specifically, of tracking any increases in suicidality. In particular, an increase in client ratings in response to item 9 may reflect a return to suicidal behaviors as a form of experiential control and the need to address this issue in therapy.

An Assessment Battery

You may also wish to administer at pretreatment some or all of the measures discussed in chapter 4 and listed there in table 2. Should you choose not to administer a full battery of these instruments, I recommend that you opt for one of the values questionnaires. While issues involving valuing are explicitly addressed in some of the later sessions of the protocol, the administration of either PVQ or VLQ at pretreatment can provide you with a useful early point of reference. Knowing what your clients value, as revealed in the questionnaire(s), provides important information around which much of your further thinking about therapeutic issues and activities can be oriented and anchored. For example, as we will see, your work promoting defusion and acceptance that is begun early in the twelve-session protocol will be most productive when informed by an initial reading of your clients' values. All unwanted private events do not warrant the same therapeutic focus. Rather, give priority to the defusion and acceptance of thoughts and feelings that function as experiential barriers for value-directed activities.

Session 1

The goals of the first session are as follows:

- To further acclimate your clients to ACT

- To identify therapeutic goals that are ACT-consistent and linked to client values

- To begin undermining the experiential control agenda

Outline

1. Further Introduction to ACT (5 min.)

2. Verification of Presenting Problem (5 min.)

3. Obtaining Client's Life Story (10 min.)

4. Identification of Therapeutic Goals and Relationship to Values (10 min.)

5. Initial Induction of Creative Hopelessness (20 min.)

   - Person in the Hole Metaphor

6. Assignment of Homework (10 min.)

Agenda

1. Further Introduction to ACT

Allocate a few minutes at the start of the session to address any further questions or comments clients have about ACT that may have been generated by their reading the "What Is Acceptance and Commitment Therapy?" handout (see appendix K) or either of the M. Beck (2002, 2006) articles that may have been assigned as homework. In particular, regarding the articles, ask specific follow-up questions about anything they may have read that seemed to be especially relevant to their own experiences with depression. Assure your clients that any specific interventions described in either article, such as the Soldiers in the Parade Exercise (2002), that they express interest in will be introduced at the appropriate time by saying something like the following:

> I'm glad you found the article interesting and are excited about trying out some of the exercises that it described. We will get to them, but I think it might be helpful to first do some work leading up to them.

Part of the work that is alluded to here, of course, is first engendering creative hopelessness. This reduces the likelihood that any specific technique, like a mindfulness exercise, will be used as another way of pursuing the experiential control agenda.

2. Verification of Presenting Problem

Spend a few minutes, if necessary, to verify that the presenting problem as the client sees it is one of depression.

3. Obtaining Client's Life Story

As discussed in chapter 4, ask your clients to provide you with an account of their experiences with depression. Pay particular attention to client references to how they attempted to manage their depression and, if necessary, directly ask for such details. Refer back to whatever previous attempts your clients have made to control depression and, in particular, the futility of such efforts, in inducing an optimal level of creative hopelessness later in this session.

4. Identification of Therapeutic Goals and Relationship to Values

A critical part of acclimating your clients to ACT involves, reframing in an ACT-consistent manner, whatever therapeutic goals they initially identify. Recall that in chapter 5 we discussed how initial client goals that are in the service of experiential control, such as "feeling happy again" or "improving my self-esteem," and are, therefore, ACT inconsistent, can still be linked to valued living. If either of the values questionnaires were administered pretreatment, make direct reference to the findings to assist in this process. For example, for a client who indicated on his completed PVQ that "being a caring parent" was his most important value, say something like the following:

> In looking over the questionnaire you completed last week, I noticed you indicated that being a good, caring parent to your children was very important to you. If you had to choose between feeling better about yourself or being a more caring parent to your kids, which would it be? Which is more important to you? Can the two of us agree that what our work here will be about is this?

It is certainly possible that your clients may opt to change the focus or priority of their therapeutic goals over the course of treatment. This should not be problematic as long as there is an agreement and at least an informal contract between you and your clients that whatever therapeutic goals are identified initially, as well as perhaps subsequently, are ACT consistent and congruent with their values.

5. Initial Induction of Creative Hopelessness

Work on weakening experiential control and promoting acceptance can be begin as early as the second half of this initial session. In listening to the client's life story, you should have already generated a list of strategies and techniques that he or she has typically used in trying to escape from depression. Your objective at this point in the session is to induce an optimal level of creative hopelessness by emphasizing the futility of such efforts.

Person in the Hole. As discussed in chapter 6, use techniques such as the Tug-of-War with a Monster and Quicksand metaphors as well as the Chinese Finger Cuffs Exercise to provide a more titrated dose of creative hopelessness with clients who have a history of engaging in suicidal behavior as a form of experiential control. For clients without such a history, present the Person in the Hole Metaphor. This technique (previously known as "Man in the Hole") was first described by Hayes (1987, pp. 346–348), later further developed by him and his colleagues (Hayes et al., 1999, pp.101–104), and has been modified slightly here to be more responsive to the experience of depressed clients.

Therapist: You told me earlier about how long you've been bothered by depression, that sometimes it seems to go away for at least a little while, but that it always seems to come back again. So the depression has never really gone away for good, and now it looks as if it's back again or you wouldn't be here. You also talked about some of the things you've tried either on your own—like reading some self-help books about depression and trying different diets—or through the help of other people, such as friends and mental health professionals, to rid yourself of depression. What other things have you tried?

Client: Well, trying to figure out why I just can't seem to shake depression. Maybe if I could just figure out why I feel this way, I could make myself feel better.

Therapist: How much time and effort have you spent trying to figure it out?

Client: Oh, I don't know, I haven't ever really stopped to count it all up, but I'm sure it's a lot.

Therapist: Isn't there something about all of this that strikes you as a little odd? Look at all the time, money, and effort you've put into trying to feel better— reading books, trying different diets, asking friends for advice, trying to figure out why you feel the way you do, taking antidepressants, trying different kinds of therapy. Yet none of this has worked for you—at least in the long-term—or you wouldn't be here. Why is that?

Client:	I don't know. I've thought maybe I just have bad depression genes.
Therapist:	That's an interesting thought, but it doesn't seem that thinking about your depression in that way has been any more helpful than anything else you've tried. Let me ask you to consider another way of looking at your struggles with depression by likening it to having fallen into a hole that you can't seem to get out of. In fact, I've heard a number of people, like yourself, say that their depression is like falling into a deep, dark hole. How does that seem to compare to your experience?
Client:	Yeah, I know how that feels and can relate to it.
Therapist:	So let's imagine that your depression is like falling into a hole you can't seem to get out of. Suppose that these are the circumstances that have lead up to you falling into the hole: You've been blindfolded, given a small backpack of tools to carry, and given the mission of making your way across a vast field. However, because you're blindfolded, you can't see that the field is full of holes so that no matter how you walk across the field, you are bound to fall into one of them sooner or later. And sure enough, you fall into one of the holes. You immediately try to pull yourself out of the depression hole, but it's too deep. What do you do?
Client:	I could call for help.
Therapist:	Haven't you already done that—haven't you called out to your friends to help lift you out of the hole of depression? Did it work? If it did, why are you here? What else could you do?
Client:	I don't know.
Therapist:	I suppose you could try to figure out why you fell into the hole. For example, that if you would have turned left instead of right, you wouldn't be in this hole.
Client:	That's right.
Therapist:	But how has that worked for you? You told me just a few minutes ago about how much time and effort you've put into trying to figure out why you're depressed. How has that worked for you? If it's worked so well, why are you here? Plus, also notice I said the field is full of holes. So, while it may literally be true that if you had turned left instead of right, you wouldn't be in this hole, it just means you would be in another hole. What else could you do? Recall that you have a backpack of tools with you.
Client:	Maybe I could use the tools to get out.
Therapist:	Suppose you open the backpack and that all the tools that are in there are shovels. Some of them are bigger than others and some are made of

different materials—some are wooden, others made of metal—but all of the tools are shovels. Now what?

Client: I could still use them.

Therapist: Are shovels for creating holes or for getting out of them? The more you dig, are you getting closer to getting out of the hole or simply digging yourself in deeper?

Client: I guess you're right. I'd just get in deeper.

Therapist: Here's what I'd like you to consider—not whether I'm right or wrong about this, but what your experience tells you about how well all that you've tried to use to dig yourself out of your depression has worked for you. Don't believe what I say, but what your experience says. Over the years that you've been struggling with depression, has it gotten bigger or smaller? The more you dig, does the hole get bigger or smaller? What if everything you've tried in order to rid yourself of depression has been digging? Could it be that you're even coming to see me in order to find a better shovel?

     Maybe you think I've got a better shovel than the ones you've been using. I don't, but even if I did, it wouldn't help you get out of the hole. Shovels are for making holes, not getting out of them. What if it's the case, that there is simply no way to dig yourself out of the hole? What if I suggested you weren't digging hard enough, would that help? What if I said you didn't want to get out of the hole bad enough, would that help? What if I said you weren't holding the shovel properly, would that help? What if I said it was you own darn fault you were in the hole in the first place, would that help get you out? What if all of this doesn't help any more than anything and everything you've already tried, because they are simply different ways of digging? What if it's the case that the ways in which you've been trying to control your depression haven't worked and never will? Don't believe me—look at your own experience. Maybe that deep, dark feeling you've had from time to time that there is no way out is telling you something.

Client: I don't know what else to do. I want to get out of the hole so badly.

Therapist: I fully believe this. You do want to get out of the hole of depression, and if you knew anything else to do, you would have done it. You've done everything you know how to do, but what if all the things you've been doing are just different ways of digging? What if there is a way out of the hole, and you haven't used it for at least two reasons? First, you have been working so hard at digging that there has been no opportunity for doing anything else. Doing something else is not possible as long as the shovel remains in your hands. The agenda of digging is too strong. So, the first step is to drop the shovel. Simply doing that won't get you out of the hole, but it will stop the hole from becoming bigger. What if there is a way out of the hole, but the second reason you haven't used it is because you haven't known what it is? Also, what if the way out of the hole is something you are capable of doing? It hasn't been done, not because you are unable to do it—you are not responsible for being in the hole, but you are for getting yourself out of it in the sense of being *response-able*—but because, as you say, you don't know what is. If you knew what it was, you would have done it. What if what we do here is not to see if we can discover other ways to dig, but is instead about exploring what else you can do?

Client: Sounds good to me.

Therapist: Okay, but we first have to work on you giving up on digging. I'm afraid if I did hand you a ladder right now, you'd drop the shovel *and* try to dig with the ladder. If you're willing to do so, I'd like to suggest a homework assignment that may be useful to both of us in recognizing all the different ways digging can occur for you.

There is no need to process or engage in a lengthy discussion of the metaphor afterward. Any reactions by your clients to the metaphor, such as wanting to engage in an argumentative debate about it or even comments about how it seems to be logical or make sense, are likely to be further forms of experiential control. At the very least, make note of this. Any response on your part should serve to "loop" client comments and reactions back to the metaphor by saying something like this:

> *It seems as if it's important to you* [to be right about this, have this make sense, for it to be logical, or whatever]. *What I'd like you to consider is the possibility that this too may be more digging.*

6. Assignment of Homework

The homework assignment following this first session is a self-monitoring exercise designed to expand the client's awareness of the pervasiveness of the experiential control agenda. Provide your clients with the Mood Regulation Diary, a form that has been designed for this purpose (see appendix L). Instruct the client to make note of the different ways that they attempt to regulate their mood and emotions. Refer back to whatever metaphor or exercise—Chinese Finger Cuffs, Person in the Hole, Quicksand, or Tug-of-War with a Monster—was primarily used in inducing creative hopelessness to clarify the purpose of the assignment.

> *We've just talked some about different ways that you* [dig or tug on the rope]. *But there may be other ways as well. In order to* [drop the shovel or rope], *it's useful to be more aware of the different ways in which* [digging or pulling on the rope] *can occur. That's the purpose of this assignment. Please make note of any instances between now and our next session of what you find yourself doing when you notice a shift in your mood that you don't like or in how you may be feeling. Include not only activities you may do at those times, like watching TV to distract yourself, but also what you might think or daydream about.*

Session 2

This session has three goals:

- To increase client awareness of the pervasiveness of emotional control as well as its normalcy

- To further emphasize the futility and associated costs of such control efforts

- To introduce willingness and acceptance as alternatives to experiential control

Outline

1. Review Homework (5 min.)

2. The Pervasiveness and Normalcy of Experiential Control (10 min.)

3. The Futility and Costs of Experiential Control (20 min.)

    - Chocolate Cake Exercise

    - Polygraph Metaphor

    - Falling in Love Metaphor

4. Willingness as an Alternative to Experiential Control (20 min.)

    - Two Scales Metaphor

    - Carrying Your Depression Exercise

5. Assignment of Homework (5 min.)

Agenda

1. Review Homework

Start off this session by reviewing with your clients what additional forms of experiential control they may have noticed during the week by looking over their Mood Regulation Diary. Increasing client awareness of the pervasiveness of emotional control is more important than the completion of the diary per se, and, if it was not filled out, still ask you clients what additional ways of digging or pulling on the rope they may have noticed themselves using. As illustrated in chapter 4 with the client who identified reading as a preferred and long-standing experiential control strategy, it is not unusual for clients to uncover methods of mood regulation to which they had previously been oblivious. Ask your clients to consider two basic questions about whatever is identified:

(1) Has it worked in the long-run? (2) If so, at what costs? The client mentioned above responded that reading had worked quite well in regulating her mood, but it did so at the cost of interpersonal isolation.

At this point, your clients may raise a question about whether a particular practice or activity is a form of experiential control. For example, a client returned to his second session questioning whether his use of antidepressants was another type of digging, despite it not being explicitly mentioned in the metaphor. In such instances, raise the same two questions as posed above as long as there is no pressure to answer the client's question(s) immediately.

2. The Pervasiveness and Normalcy of Experiential Control

For your clients to sufficiently abandon the control agenda and be open to willingness as an alternative, they need to see the different forms that their control agenda can take. Clients, in effect, can't be expected to drop the shovel if they don't recognize the many subtle ways in which digging can occur. While it is also useful to sensitize them to the costs of pursuing the control agenda, suggesting that doing so is somehow abnormal does not appear to be helpful. Thus, your task at this point in the session is to emphasize to your clients both the pervasiveness and the dysfunctionality of experiential control, as well as its normalcy, by saying something like the following:

We've now had a chance to look at some of the different ways that you try to regulate your mood and control how you feel emotionally. We can compare it to digging [or tugging on a rope], *but for right now let's just refer to it as emotional control—the tendency we all have to deliberately run away from unpleasant feelings and thoughts and to run toward ones we like.*

We all make conscious, deliberate efforts and create plans that we follow in order to control things we don't like. Let's take a broader look at how those work. For example, suppose you didn't like the way the furniture and other furnishings in this room are arranged. Could you do anything about it? If I offered you a thousand dollars to rearrange the furniture in this room, could you do it? What if instead of furniture, what you try to rearrange is how you think and feel about something? For instance, what if you take your thoughts and feelings about [mention some personal event from the client's life story, linked to depression] *and try to arrange them so they're no longer depressing to you?*

How well does that work? Could you rearrange them for a thousand dollars? Here's what I'd like you to consider—the possibility that the control agenda that works so well in the world outside of ourselves, like the world of furniture, doesn't work when we try to apply it to the world inside of ourselves, to the world of our own thoughts and feelings. What if it's the case that the operative rule about the outside world is "if you don't like something, just change it," but the operative rule about our own thoughts and feelings is "if you're not willing to have them, you've got them"?

I'm not asking you to believe me—maybe it seems to you that it shouldn't be this way, and that it's not fair—but instead what does your own experience tell you about the way it is?

168   ACT for Depression

At about this point, shift to an emphasis on the normalcy of the control agenda. Doing so helps minimize client self-blame and, perhaps more importantly, also validates your client's struggles and suffering and helps build an empathetic bond between the two of you. Point out that all of us engage in experiential control for several reasons: (1) effective external control generalizes to emotional control, (2) others may have suggested it should work for us ("just cheer up!"), (3) it often appears to work for others, and (4) it may even work for us in the short-term. Further normalize experiential control by referring back to the Person in the Hole Metaphor.

> So it's no wonder you've been digging, and, as you say, you haven't known what else to do. Quite likely most, if not all of us—including myself—have done and would do exactly as you have done. We all have our own holes. The only advantage I have so I can help you with yours is one of perspective—that is, whatever hole I may be in is not the same hole as the one you're in.

3. The Futility and Costs of Experiential Control

You may find, however, some danger in normalizing experiential control. Some of your clients may see this as minimizing its costs or even as providing some immunity from blame and/or the consequences of not acting in a "response-able" manner. Address this by further emphasizing both the futility and dysfunctionality of the experiential control agenda through a series of related exercises and metaphors.

Chocolate Cake Exercise. To illustrate the futility of thought suppression, ask your clients to deliberately "not think" of a particular object. The original exercise presented by Hayes et al. (1999, pp. 124–125) used chocolate cake (and thus the origin of its name), although other objects can be used. Hayes and Smith (2005, pp. 24–25), for example, used a yellow jeep in their version of the exercise, and I personally prefer jelly donuts in presenting it.

> If you're willing to do so, I'd like to have you participate in a little exercise with me. Whatever you do right now, don't think of jelly donuts! You can think of anything as long as it's not a jelly donut. You know the kind of jelly donuts that are soft and sweet smelling so that when put them into your mouth and bite into them, the jelly squirts out into your mouth and is all sticky and sweet-tasting. Don't think about them! You can think of anything else, but whatever you do, don't think about jelly donuts.

Afterward, underscore the similarity between the exercise and spontaneous attempts by your clients to suppress unwanted thoughts.

> Instead of jelly donuts, suppose it's important that you don't think about how you may have messed up your life. And so you tell yourself not to think about mistakes you may have made. How well has that worked for you?

Polygraph Metaphor. Extend the futility of the experiential control agenda to efforts to avoid unwanted emotions by presenting the Polygraph Metaphor (Hayes et al., 1999, pp. 123–124).

Therapist: Let's see how trying to control not what you think but how you feel works. Imagine a situation in which it becomes very important that you not feel anxious. Suppose I have you hooked up to the world's most sensitive polygraph and in such a way that both of us can see its findings as the pen moves across the paper. Your task is very simple—just remain relaxed. To impress upon you how critical it is for you not to become anxious and to help motivate you not to be anxious, I also have a loaded .44 that I tell you I will use to shoot you if you become anxious. How well would you do on the task?

Client: You might as well just shoot me right now and get it over with.

Therapist: So you couldn't stay relaxed under those circumstances. Could anyone?

Client: Certainly no one I know.

Therapist: So anyone in that situation—you, me, the average guy on the street— couldn't stay relaxed. Anxiety itself has now become something to be anxious about, and if you're not willing to have it, you've got it. So you're now anxious about being anxious. Let's see how this might work with depression. You've told me when you're depressed, you've tried to cheer yourself up. How has that worked?

Client: Not very well.

Therapist: What's more depressing than trying not to feel depressed and failing? Now suppose instead of not feeling anxious, your task is one of not moving the furniture in this room and I told you I would shoot you if you did? What would happen?

Client: I could do that.

Falling in Love Metaphor. Because experiential control in depression can also take the form of clients deliberately trying to induce certain desirable emotional states, such as "feeling happy" or "good about myself," offer the following metaphor as well:

Therapist: Sometimes the way we try to control emotions we don't like is to create and hold on to their opposites. So, for example, instead of trying to avoid feeling unhappy and depressed, we try to find and capture happiness. Let's take a closer look at how this works. Suppose I have a million dollars, and I tell you that what you need to do to earn it is quite simple. We will leave the office here, and all you have to do is fall madly in love with the first stranger you see, regardless of their gender, age, or physical appearance. Could you do it?

Client: I could sure tell you that I have.

Therapist:	But could you do it? Suppose I had some fancy machine I could hook you up to that would tell us if you were madly in love with the first person you meet. What would we find?
Client:	That I was just saying I was madly in love with them.
Therapist:	So doesn't it seem to be the case that deliberately trying to create certain emotions doesn't work any better than trying to get rid of certain feelings? Don't take my word for it. Look at your own experience. Now notice what would happen if I said, "Okay, you don't have to actually fall madly in love with the first stranger you see, but you have to run up to them and profess your passionate love for them." Could you do that? Would you do that?
Client:	For a million bucks, sure.
Therapist:	So you can't control how you feel, but you can control how you move your mouth and feet.

4. Willingness as an Alternative to Experiential Control

At about this point, introduce acceptance and willingness as alternative ways of responding to unwanted thoughts and feelings. This is also a good time to further underscore the costs of emotional control by introducing an experiential exercise discussed in chapter 6 for distinguishing between clean and dirty pain.

Two Scales Metaphor. This metaphor was originally presented by Hayes (1987, pp. 352–353) and subsequently further developed by Hayes et al. (1999, pp. 133–134) as a means of suggesting to clients an alternative to the experiential control agenda. It is modified here slightly to be more specific to depression.

> *Imagine that we have before us a piece of electronic equipment—like an amplifier for a stereo system—only this particular piece of equipment is like a depression amplifier.*
>
> *How much depression comes out of your speakers will depend upon where you set the knobs on the equipment. Suppose one of the knobs is labeled "Depression" and ranges from 1 to 10. What brought you in to therapy is that there is too much depression coming out of your speakers, and so it makes perfectly good sense to try to adjust the depression knob. Maybe it's been at a 10, and you want to lower it to a 1 or 2.*
>
> *And so you've grabbed hold of the depression knob, and you've been trying as hard as you can to change its setting. But it hasn't worked, or you wouldn't be here. Furthermore, it will never work, and I don't have some new technique of resetting the knob to change the volume of the depression coming out of your speakers. Now suppose there is another knob on the amplifier and another option.*

This other knob is smaller, so it's easy to overlook. We've been working our way up until now to shifting our attention to it. This other knob is labeled "Willingness." It also ranges from 1 to 10, and as it turns out, it is really the more important of the two. This is because, unlike the depression knob, you can freely choose its setting. It takes no effort to change it from a lower setting to a higher setting, but here's the difference that it makes. Right now your willingness knob has been set low, let's say at a 1. Willingness refers to how open you are to experiencing your own thoughts, feelings, memories, bodily sensations, impulses, and the like when you experience them, without trying to control or run away from them. What happens when willingness is set low is that any background sadness, disappointment, or negative thoughts that just emerge from leading a full and valued life—what we call in ACT clean pain—get amplified into the loud noise of depression, or what we call dirty pain. If you're not willing to have it, you've got it, and you end up being depressed about being depressed. Consider what might happen if the willingness knob is set at a 10. Now any unwanted sounds coming out of the speakers will not be artificially amplified. Notice I didn't say all of the unwanted sounds would be lowered to the level you want or that they would go away entirely. They may still sound like depression to you from time to time. The point is that those sounds are now free to move rather than being locked in at a high level when all of the focus is on lowering the depression knob. If the willingness knob is set at a higher level, sometimes the unwanted sounds will decrease in volume and sometimes they will increase. You can't control their volume—all you can control is where you set the willingness knob. Are you open at this point to explore how your life might be different if we shift focus to changing the willingness knob instead of the depression knob?

Carrying Your Depression Exercise. Immediately following this metaphor, present the Carrying Your Depression Exercise detailed in chapter 6. This exercise further underscores the costs of experiential control by clarifying the distinction between clean and dirty pain. Recall that this exercise uses a physical prop (such as a heavy, metal trash can) to illustrate to clients the difference in carrying their depression in an accepting versus avoidant manner.

5. Assignment of Homework

Also discussed in chapter 6 was the Thoughts on Cards Exercise. For homework, provide your clients with a deck of index cards on which they are asked to write down (one per card) unwanted, depressing thoughts that they encounter during the week. Instruct your clients to note on the back of each card any ways they attempted to control the thought or emotions related to it. Model the assignment by selecting a negative automatic thought expressed by the client in session. Use the completed cards to begin some defusion exercises at the beginning of the next session.

Session 3

The goals of this session are as follows:

- To identify private events to target for defusion and acceptance work

- To begin to refocus the attention of clients on the process of languaging instead of its contents

- To introduce some initial defusion and acceptance interventions

Outline

1. Review Homework (5 min.)

2. Your Mind Is Not Your Friend Exercise (10 min.)

   - The Mind in the Third Person Technique

   - Thank Your Mind for That Technique

3. Defusing Automatic Thoughts (20 min.)

   - Milk, Milk, Milk Exercise

   - Revocalization Exercises

   - Taking Inventory Exercise

4. Accepting Unwanted Emotions (20 min.)

   - Physicalizing Exercise

   - Sitting with Feelings Exercise

5. Assignment of Homework (5 min.)

   - Taking Inventory Exercise

   - Reasons for Depression Exercise

Agenda

1. Review Homework

Begin this session by reviewing the Thoughts on Cards Exercise. Ask your clients, if necessary, to restate descriptions of cognitive activity, such as "thought about my last job," as specific instances of self-talk ("How could I have been so stupid to screw it up like I did?" for example). Also, identify any unwanted emotions related to each thought and assess the degree to which each thought elicits experiential control (and if so, the forms that it takes) and/or functions as a barrier to valued behavior. On this latter point, if necessary, clarify the extent to which private events stand in the way of values identified during session 1 or through the pretreatment administration of one of the values questionnaires (for example, "To what degree does this thought stand in the way of you spending more time with your children?"). This portion of the session identifies problematic private events that can be used as targets for later defusion and acceptance techniques.

2. Your Mind Is Not Your Friend Exercise

Before beginning some defusion and acceptance work, underscore the pervasiveness and normalcy of negative self-talk and other forms of relational framing by presenting the segment and exercise entitled Your Mind Is Not Your Friend described in chapter 6. Point out that our minds are like the monster that goads us into pulling on the rope and that the challenge you may assist your clients with is one of learning how to drop the rope and how to respond to our mind when it baits us to pick it up again. Also, emphasize the pain of absence costs incurred when the experiential control agenda precludes committed action.

> *Another way in which your mind is not your friend is that it sidetracks you from what you value in life. So instead of spending quality time with your children, you spend your time arguing with your mind, pulling on the rope, or trying to solve unsolvable problems that your mind has identified. Are you open to exploring some things you can do, not to shut your mind up—that's not possible—but to respond differently to what it tells you so that you, rather than your mind, can be more in control of your life?*

The Mind in the Third Person Technique. At about this point, suggest (as discussed in chapter 6), referring to the mind in the third person as one way of minimizing its negative influences.

Thank Your Mind for That Technique. You may recall that this particular defusion-promoting technique was also covered in chapter 6. It is more useful to present it in response to negative automatic thoughts as they occur in session by your clients, but you can also offer it here as a lead in to some of the more intensive defusion work that comes next.

3. Defusing Automatic Thoughts

It is preferable to target depressing automatic thoughts of your clients that spontaneously occur in session in presenting the first defusion interventions. If this is not possible, the default plan is to use the depressing automatic thoughts identified through the Thoughts on Cards homework assignment. In such instances, preface the exercises that will be introduced by saying something like the following:

We've talked about how trying to control thoughts that our mind tells us we don't like just gets us tangled up in them. I'd like to spend the next few minutes introducing you to some other ways that you might respond to thoughts that usually lead you to pick up the rope and start tugging. We can have you try them out here as well as for part of your homework.

Milk, Milk, Milk Exercise. As discussed in chapter 6, either introduce this exercise on its own or spontaneously in response to negative self-evaluations by your clients. For example, ask a client who remarks "I'm stupid" to rapidly repeat the keyword "stupid" along with you.

Revocalization Exercises. These exercises, also presented in chapter 6, similarly can be introduced by using in-session automatic thoughts or ones identified through homework.

Taking Inventory Exercise. Look for a shift in the mood or affect of your clients as an opportune time to introduce this defusion exercise that was described in chapter 6. Alternatively, ask your clients to recall a recent incident that they found particularly depressing, preferably one that also interfered with value-congruent behavior. For example, ask a client who opted to have a drink or two to feel better rather than taking her children to the park as promised, to list her thoughts, feelings, and other private events as she recreates her experience of the incident. If you find yourself somewhat pressed for time in this session, cover this specific defusion technique before the others because it will constitute part of this week's homework assignment.

4. Accepting Unwanted Emotions

The defusion techniques just covered are primarily designed to target troublesome automatic thoughts. At this point, also introduce some interventions for promoting the acceptance of related emotions that have also been the focus of experiential control efforts. As with the defusion procedures, work with troublesome emotions that emerge within the session, although they may also be induced, if necessary, by asking your clients to recall a depressing life event.

Physicalizing Exercise. Of the two acceptance interventions that may be introduced in this session, this one seems to lend itself a bit more readily to working with induced emotions. Refer back to chapter 6 where this exercise was first described for guidelines on its presentation.

Sitting with Feelings Exercise. This intervention, also covered in chapter 6, is preferable in conducting acceptance work with "hot emotions" that may spontaneously be elicited in session by the discussion of certain topics or issues. Introduce this exercise following any discernible shift in your client's mood or affect as evidenced by changes in body language, facial expression, or crying. On that point, you need not present the defusion and acceptance exercises and techniques to be introduced during this session in the order suggested here. Rather, present them flexibly by looking for the most opportune times to introduce them.

5. Assignment of Homework

There are two assignments for homework during the week before the next session.

Taking Inventory Exercise. Present the client with sufficient copies of the Taking Inventory form (see appendix B), which was discussed in chapter 6, to complete for homework. In particular, instruct your clients to fill it out regarding incidents that tend to get them stuck in their depression and/or interfere with their pursuit of valued goals and activities.

Reasons for Depression Exercise. This second homework assignment is designed to transition defusion work in the next session to reason giving for depression. Provide your client with a copy of the Reasons for Depression Exercise (see appendix C) along with the following rationale:

> *As we talked about earlier today, our minds constantly chatter away about one thing or the other. Among the other things our minds do is to come up with reasons or explanations for problems that it identifies. Because of this, it is quite likely that your mind has identified some reasons for your depression. If you're willing to do so, I'd like you take this form and complete it as part of your homework for this week.*
>
> *Please don't be overly concerned about doing it right. If you find that thought gets in the way of completing the form, thank your mind for that thought, and go ahead and fill it out as best you can. Its purpose is to help you more clearly see what reasons your mind may have come up with for your depression by stepping back and noticing them. Please bring the completed form with you next week so we can spend some time at the start of the session going over it.*

Session 4

The two goals of this session are as follows:

- To extend defusion work to self-evaluations and reason giving

- To introduce mindfulness

Outline

1. Review Homework (5 min.)

2. Distinguishing Self-Evaluations from Descriptions (15 min.)

3. Defusing Reason Giving (15 min.)

   - Why, Why, Why? Exercise

- Flat Tire Metaphor

- Get Off Your "Buts" Intervention

4. The Raisin Exercise (15 min.)

5. Assignment of Homework (10 min.)

- Mindfulness Exercise

- Writing Your Life Story Exercise

Agenda

1. Review Homework

The first half of this session can be viewed as an extension of the homework assignments from the last. Consequently, at the beginning of this session, take a few minutes to see if both assignments—Taking Inventory Exercise and Reasons for Depression Exercise—were completed and acknowledge any client reactions or difficulties they may have encountered. Of the two, the Reasons for Depression Exercise is likely to be more challenging to clients. Because of this, have two more blank forms (see appendix C) available in case it is necessary to later complete the exercise in session.

2. Distinguishing Self-Evaluations from Descriptions

Identify some of your client's common negative self-evaluations to be used as examples in clarifying the difference between evaluative and descriptive talk. Use the completed Taking Inventory assignment for this purpose and/or the Thoughts on Cards Exercise. First, present the adaptation of the Bad Cup Metaphor as discussed in chapter 6 for distinguishing between the evaluation and the description of objects. Then, also as covered in chapter 6, extend this distinction to the client's own self-evaluations. Afterward, prompt your clients whenever appropriate to explicitly frame any negative self-referential talk as evaluations (such as "I'm having an evaluation of myself that ...").

3. Defusing Reason Giving

As I mentioned above, your first objective relating to the goal of defusing reason giving is to obtain from your client the completed Reasons for Depression Exercise. If it was not filled out for homework, regardless of your client's explanation, guide your client through its completion in session. Next, use the guidelines suggested in chapter 6 for processing it. In doing so, be sure to emphasize the functionality of reason giving as a process, rather than whether any particular reason is justified, reasonable, logical, or makes sense. For example, refer back to whatever metaphors you used to induce creative hopelessness.

Is all this talk coming from your mind helping you get unstuck from depression or keeping you stuck? Could it be just another way of digging or tugging on the rope? How useful is it for you to buy into the reasons that your mind has come up with for why you are depressed?

Why, Why, Why? Exercise. Present the following brief exercise to further underscore the arbitrariness of reason giving (see Strosahl et al., 2004, table 2.3; Zettle & Hayes, 2002, p. 47):

Therapist: If you're willing to do so, I'd like you to participate in a little exercise with me that may help us better see how reason giving works. Suppose I have two dishes of ice cream here, one vanilla and the other chocolate. Which do you choose?

Client: Chocolate

Therapist: Why?

Client: Because I like it more than vanilla.

Therapist: Why?

Client: Because it tastes better.

Therapist: Why?

Client: I don't know; it just does.

Therapist: Why?

Client: I don't know what else to say.

Therapist: So what does it suggest if your mind can come up will all sorts of reasons why you prefer chocolate ice cream over vanilla, but, as we've just seen, when it comes right down to it, your mind can't explain it? If what your mind has to say about something as simple as preferring one flavor of ice cream over another is just more talk and chatter, what about something as complex as what it has to say about why you are depressed?

Flat Tire Metaphor. Next, present this metaphor as described in chapter 6 to emphasize how ruminative reason giving interferes with valued living. Introduce it by saying something like "Let's take a look next at how trying to figure out why you're depressed may affect how you want to live your life."

Get Off Your "Buts" Intervention. This segment of the session complements the Flat Tire Metaphor by examining other ways that the process of reason giving contributes to a lack of committed action (see Hayes et al., 1999, pp. 166–168). Reasons offered by depressed clients for not pursuing valued goals typically involve private events (for example, "I want to look for another job, but I lack self-confidence"). This particular intervention promotes defusion from such excuse giving. Also, as I suggested at the end of the last chapter, it can also serve to promote your clients' contextual self because of the emphasis it places on perspective taking in responding to seemingly incompatible private events.

> *We've talked about how your mind offers reasons for why you do certain things, such as selecting one flavor of ice cream over another. Let's consider another way that our minds may not be our friends when it involves coming up with reasons for not doing things that we say are important to us.* [If possible, offer an example here that is personally relevant to your client, preferably something you heard in session.] *Does this sound familiar—"I'd really like to spend more time with my kids, but I just don't seem to have the energy"? This is the way our minds talk. It's the way your mind talks and it's the way mine talks. There's nothing wrong with your mind here—it's doing its job very well. It's just that taking what your mind has to say about excuses seriously may back you into a corner.*
>
> *The word "but" is literally a contraction of two words—"be" and "out"* [Hayes et al., 1999, p. 167]. *So what your mind is suggesting when it says something like "I'd like to ask the boss for a raise, but I'm afraid of being turned down" is that you have two experiences—wanting the raise and being fearful about asking for it—that somehow can't coexist. When you buy into what your mind is telling you about this, the fear of being turned down has to "be out" for the asking of the raise to occur. If the fear was not there, you would ask for the raise. And it is, so somehow it must be gotten rid of before you feel you can ask for the raise. What happens though when you try to get rid of feelings you don't like?*
>
> *If you're not willing to have it, you've got it. So listening to your mind here means you don't get the raise and you now have another monster—the fear monster—to have a tug-of-war with.*
>
> *Let's take a look here at how you—not your mind, but you—can change what gets said and what might happen when you get off your "buts." Here's a little convention that we can follow here and I'd also urge you to practice for homework outside of our sessions. See if you can catch yourself when a "but" occurs and replace it with the word "and." So instead of "I want to ask the boss for a raise but I'm afraid of being turned down" say "I want to ask the boss for a raise and I'm afraid of being turned down."*

Afterward, playfully apply the lesson of the intervention to what both you and your clients say in the remaining sessions. Point out in a somewhat bemused but (or is it "and"?!) consistent manner when you hear "buts" from your client, and also encourage your client to gently correct you in a similar way.

4. The Raisin Exercise

If you are going to follow the sequence of mindfulness exercises outlined in the previous chapter over the course of four weeks, present the initial one now. Follow the guidelines provided in chapter 8 in presenting a version of the Raisin Exercise and the rationale for mindfulness exercises more generally. Point out to your clients that the two of you have been exploring some different ways of responding and reacting to thoughts and feelings that help keep them stuck in depression or moving forward in life, and that mindfulness is simply another way of doing so.

5. Assignment of Homework

Assign two forms of homework to your clients to be completed before the next session.

Mindfulness Exercise. Provide your clients with a copy of the Mindfulness Exercise Diary (see appendix H) and follow guidelines offered in the previous chapter in asking them to complete one exercise daily prior to the next session.

Writing Your Life Story Exercise. Also, ask your clients for homework to write an initial version of their life story. Provide them with a copy of the appropriate form (see appendix D) in accordance with suggestions about this exercise offered in chapter 6.

Session 5

The goals of this session are fourfold:

- To extend defusion work to the life story

- To expand the mindfulness exercises to the performance of daily activities

- To begin the promotion of self as context

- To further clarify client values

Outline

1. Review Homework (10 min.)

    - Writing Your Life Story Exercise

    - Mindfulness Exercise

2. Performing Daily Activities Mindfully (15 min.)

3. Chessboard Metaphor (10 min.)

4. Indirect Values Assessment (15 min.)

    - Follow Suffering

- ■ Through Therapeutic Goal Setting

- ■ Revisit Childhood Wishes

- ■ Whose Life Do You Admire?

- ■ What Do You Want Your Life to Stand For?

- ■ Epitaph Exercise

5. Assignment of Homework (10 min.)

- ■ Mindfulness Exercise

- ■ Rewriting Your Life Story Exercise

Agenda

1. Review Homework

Because of the way the rest of the session is sequenced, review the two homework assignments in the order in which they are discussed below.

Writing Your Life Story Exercise. First, determine if your client has completed the assignment. If not, reassign it for next week, or preferably, if possible, ask your client to complete it after the session, before leaving. If the assignment has been completed, collaborate with the client as suggested in chapter 6 in underlining personal facts contained within the story. Inform the client that one of the assignments for next week, that will be clarified further at the end of the session, will to be rewrite the life story using the facts that have been underlined but with an ending that doesn't result in depression.

Mindfulness Exercise. Review the client's Mindfulness Exercise Diary to initially determine how often he or she ate or drank mindfully throughout the week. If the client did not practice the exercise at least three times, re-present the Raisin Exercise using a different edible during the segment of this session that follows. Do this before moving on to the next step in the progression of mindfulness exercises. If the client has completed the assignment, review whatever reactions he or she may have had with an open and nonevaluative attitude.

2. Performing Daily Activities Mindfully

Introduce the second step in the progression of mindfulness training with the Walking Exercise described in chapter 8. Provide some time afterward to solicit and validate your client's reaction to the exercise.

3. Chessboard Metaphor

By this point in the protocol, your client will have already practiced several defusion, acceptance, and mindfulness exercises and techniques that indirectly promote a transcendent sense of self. Now make the focus on self as context more explicit by presenting the Chessboard Metaphor according to the guidelines offered in the previous chapter. Preface your presentation of it by saying something like the following:

> So far we've had you explore several different ways that you can react differently to thoughts and feelings that tend to pull you into a struggle with them. This may be a good spot to step back a bit to perhaps get some further perspective on the relationship between you and the thoughts and feelings you've been struggling with.

Time permitting, you may wish to supplement the Chessboard Metaphor with another dealing with Furniture in the House (Strosahl et al., 2004, table 2.5) that further highlights the distinction between self as context and the content of psychological experience. Say something like the following:

> Another way to think about the relationship between the you that has thoughts and feelings that pull you into a struggle and those same thoughts and feelings is to see them as being like pieces of furniture within a house. Suppose you built a multimillion dollar house but filled it with furniture you found at the dump or at thrift shops. Would such furniture in any way reduce the value of the house? Or suppose you built a house out of old cardboard boxes and then went to the finest furniture store to furnish it. Would the expensive furniture somehow change the nature or value of the cardboard box house in any way? What if you are like the house and your thoughts and feelings are like the pieces of furniture? You may like some of the furniture, and other pieces you may not like. But the furniture is not the house, and you are not your thoughts and feelings. The house merely provides the context in which the chairs, couch, and tables, and so on can be furniture, and the furniture neither adds nor takes anything away from the value of the house.

4. Indirect Values Assessment

Although some initial values work already occurred in the first session, I recommend that you do some further assessment of client valuing now to ensure that the overall treatment plan is on track and congruent with your client's values. All of the indirect means detailed in chapter 7 that can be used to accomplish this are summarized below. You don't have to use all of the procedures. Feel free to pick and choose from among them.

Follow suffering. If necessary, reclarify why depression is so depressing to your clients by discussing valued goals that have been compromised in the process: "What have you missed out on in life as a consequence of your struggles with depression?"

Through therapeutic goal setting. Verify that the therapeutic goals identified in session 1 have not shifted and, if they have, that any new goals are ACT consistent and linked to client values.

Revisit childhood wishes. As I pointed out in chapter 7, accessing values by asking your clients to recontact childhood hopes and dreams is especially recommended with those who claim that they have no values and have given up on whatever goals they once had for themselves in life.

Whose life do you admire? Identify your client's personal heroes and heroines and what values were embodied by their lives.

What do you want your life to stand for? Ask your clients to talk about what they would like to be remembered for and/or what they would want friends and family to say in eulogizing them.

Epitaph Exercise. Ask your clients to indicate what they would like their gravestone to say about them.

5. Assignment of Homework

Mindfulness Exercise. As I suggested in the previous chapter, provide a new Mindfulness Exercise Diary (see appendix H) on which daily activities that the client plans on performing mindfully can be listed. Recommend that at least one activity be engaged in mindfully each day.

Rewriting Your Life Story Exercise. Provide your clients with the appropriate form (see appendix D) on which to rewrite their life story. Instruct them to take the facts that were underlined in their initial life story and incorporate all of those facts into a new version that has a nondepressing ending.

Session 6

The three goals of this session are as follows:

- To complete defusion from the life story

- To extend the progression of mindfulness training to breathing

- To further promote a transcendent sense of self

Outline

1. Review Homework (15 min.)

- Rewriting Your Life Story Exercise

- Mindfulness Exercise

2. Breathing Mindfully Exercise (15 min.)

3. The Observer Exercise (20 min.)

4. Assignment of Homework (10 min.)

- Mindfulness Exercise

- Values Questionnaire

Agenda

1. Review Homework

Of the two homework assignments for this week, review rewriting of the life story first so that your discussion of the second assignment can provide a lead-in to the next mindfulness exercise.

Rewriting Your Life Story. With your clients, review the rewritten life story to verify that the same facts contained in the initial version now result in a different outcome. As discussed in chapter 6, it is also acceptable if your clients discover new facts in the process of completing the assignment and incorporate them into the rewrite. Remember that the objective of the exercise is to loosen up the grip with which clients often hold their life stories and not to convince them of the preferability of another version, which they then grasp just as tightly. Your task is to promote other possibilities, not alternative realities.

Mindfulness Exercise. Go over the Mindfulness Exercise Diary with your clients to determine if they mindfully performed at least one routine activity each day since their last session. Use the same guideline suggested earlier to decide if your client is ready to progress to the next step in the sequence of mindfulness exercises. If your clients have not performed the exercise at least three times, mindfully guide them through another routine activity—such as stretching, putting a coat on and taking it off, or walking up stairs—in session instead of moving on to the breath exercise.

2. Breathing Mindfully Exercise

Follow the guidelines from the previous chapter in introducing your client to this exercise. Allow at least five minutes after the exercise to review client reactions to it and to give them a bit of a break before moving on to the Observer Exercise, which is next.

3. The Observer Exercise

As suggested in the last chapter, preface this exercise by referring back to the Chessboard Metaphor from last session. The promotion of mindfulness and self as context can occur simultaneously and synergistically. Introducing the Observer Exercise here thus serves as a bridge linking together your work to date on mindfulness and the final step in the progression involving thoughts and feelings to be addressed in the next session. Follow guidelines offered in the previous chapter in presenting the exercise to your clients.

4. Assignment of Homework

There are two homework assignments for next week, which can be discussed in any order.

Mindfulness Exercise. Provide your clients with another Mindfulness Exercise Diary (see appendix H) as well as the associated handout (see appendix I), CD, or audiotape to help guide them through the Breathing Mindfully Exercise. Ask your clients to practice the exercise at least twice daily, and slowly increase the duration of the exercise from five minutes at the start of the week to fifteen minutes by its end.

Values questionnaire. Also ask your client to complete one of the values questionnaires described previously—either the PVQ (see appendix E) or VLQ (see appendix F)—for homework, if neither was administered at pretreatment.

Session 7

The goals of this session are as follows:

- To complete the progression of mindfulness training by extending it to thoughts and feelings

- To further assess and clarify client values

- To identify value-congruent goals

- To initially instigate related committed action

Outline

1. Review Homework (5 min.)

2. Thinking and Feeling Mindfully (15 min.)

3. Direct Values Assessment (10 min.)

4. Goal Identification (10 min.)

5. Instigating Committed Action (15 min.)

   ■   Environmental Barriers

   ■   Experiential Barriers

6. Assignment of Homework (5 min.)

   ■   Mindfulness Exercise

   ■   Committed Action

Agenda

1. Review Homework

Review the Mindfulness Exercise Diary to assess how much your client practiced breathing mindfully since last session. If your client has not practiced the exercise at least once each day and/or by now is not doing so for at least ten minutes each time, re-present the breathing exercise in session and reassign it for homework before moving on to the last step in the mindfulness training. Also, briefly verify whether the values questionnaire was completed.

2. Thinking and Feeling Mindfully

Follow the suggestions offered in the last chapter for presenting one of the mindfulness exercises—Soldiers in the Parade, Leaves on a Stream, Watching the Mind-Train, or Gazing at the Clouds—to your client.

3. Direct Values Assessment

Collaboratively review the completed PVQ or VLQ with your clients to compile a prioritized list of their values. As discussed in chapter 7, be aware of unduly influencing your clients and evaluate the degree to which there is consensus with what your indirect assessment undertaken in session 5 has revealed about their values. Your objective is to identify an initial client value around which related goals can be discussed and set before moving on to goal identification.

4. Goal Identification

Follow suggestions offered in chapter 7 in working with your clients to develop a list of goals that are closely related to their foremost value. For example, "going on more frequent 'dates'" and "setting aside a time each day to listen to my wife tell me about her day" may be goals congruent with the value of "being a more caring spouse." Some of the goals may be more long-term and require several graduated steps to complete, whereas others can be accomplished on a daily basis. In any case, stay with the task long enough to identify a specific value-related goal that your client can potentially attain before the next session. Time permitting, also develop lists of goals surrounding other client values.

5. Instigating Committed Action

Determine a specific action for your client to take as part of homework to achieve the goal that has just been identified. For example, if the client's goal is to go on a "date" consisting of dinner and a movie with his wife, he may have to make reservations, select a movie, and plan a way of coordinating both activities. If necessary, repeatedly ask the question, "What will you have to do in order to accomplish this goal?" Once it has been answered satisfactorily, move on to a discussion with your client about barriers that might stand in the way of committed action by asking "What could/would prevent you from doing what you've said you will have to do to accomplish this goal?"

Environmental barriers. Identify and discuss with your client ways of surmounting external obstacles that might prevent goal-directed behavior. For example, adjustments might have to made in both where to dine and what movie to see if finances are a major limiting factor.

Experiential barriers. Ask your clients first to report whatever thoughts and feelings appear when they imagine engaging in the committed action itself or behaviors leading up to it (such as, making a dinner reservation). Next, ask your clients to indicate the degree to which such private events might stand in the way of the committed action and how they could apply some of the defusion and acceptance procedures they've learned. Refer back to the mindfulness exercise presented earlier in this session ("Is it possible to 'just notice' whatever thoughts and feelings occur to you?") and appeal to the client's transcendent sense of self ("Is it possible for the observer you—you as the chessboard—to choose to move and take along with you whatever thoughts and feelings would stand in the way of doing what you need to do to accomplish the goal?").

Finally, before finalizing homework, do a bit of troubleshooting in how your client might respond to additional experiential barriers that have not been addressed but which still might emerge by asking something like the following:

> You said you don't see any negative thoughts and feelings as we talk about it here that would stand it the way of you scheduling and going on the date with your wife. Suppose you have everything set up and as it gets closer to actually going on the date, you find that you have the thought that "I picked the wrong movie and restaurant" and you have the feeling that you don't have enough energy to be good company to your wife. What could you do?

6. Assignment of Homework

There are two homework assignments for your client to complete during the week before the next session.

Mindfulness Exercise. Provide your clients with another Mindfulness Exercise Diary (see appendix H) as well as a handout (see appendix J) and/or CD/audiotape to guide them in practicing mindfully thinking and feeling. Follow the guidelines offered in the last chapter by asking your clients to practice the exercise twice daily and to gradually increase its length up to fifteen minutes.

Committed action. Provide your clients with a copy of the Goals-Action Form (see appendix G). In the appropriate spaces on the form, record the goal identified earlier in the session and the related action that they have agreed to complete as part of homework. Finally, discuss with your clients how to make note of any barriers they encounter in completing the assignment.

Session 8

The four goals of this session are as follows:

- To determine the status of further mindfulness training

- To clarify the nature of commitment

- To further address ways of managing barriers to committed action

- To further promote committed action through related homework

Outline

1. Review Homework (10 min.)

    - Mindfulness Exercise

    - Committed Action

2. The Nature of Commitment (20 min.)

    - Trying vs. Doing Exercise

    - Partial vs. Full Commitments

3. Managing Barriers to Commitment (20 min.)

    - Passengers on the Bus Metaphor

    - Choosing vs. Deciding

    - The Swamp Metaphor

4. Assignment of Homework (10 min.)

    - Mindfulness Exercise

    - Committed Action

Agenda

1. Review Homework

Take a few minutes at the beginning of the session to see if both homework assignments from last session were completed, and, if not, what may have prevented this. Your approach to this session will need to be different for clients who successfully completed both assignments compared to those who failed to complete one or both of them. Having this information at the start of the session will help you structure the rest of it.

Mindfulness Exercise. Review the Mindfulness Exercise Diary to determine if your clients practiced thinking mindfully. If they have not practiced the exercise at least once a day for at least ten minutes each time, allocate some time in this session from the second and third agenda items to present one of the exercises (such as Soldiers in the Parade or Leaves on the Stream).

Committed action. Go over the Goals-Action Form to discern whether your clients engaged in the goal-directed behavior agreed upon for homework. Make note of any environmental and/or experiential barriers that may have prevented the completion of the assignment to ensure that they are addressed later in the session as well as those that your clients were able to surmount in executing the goal-directed behavior.

2. The Nature of Commitment

Further clarify the nature of committed action in order to promote persistent goal-seeking behavior. In one sense, this may be easier if your client did not successfully complete the homework assignment as this experience can be used to illustrate some of the critical dimensions of commitment. If your client did complete the assignment, view this agenda item as being more preventative in nature.

Trying vs. Doing Exercise. If your clients failed to complete the assignment, it is quite likely that they will explain that they nevertheless tried to do so. This is an opportune time to underscore the difference between *keeping* a commitment versus *trying* to keep a commitment by presenting the exercise described in chapter 7 in which clients are instructed to try to pick up a pen or similar object.

Partial vs. full commitments. It is not uncommon for clients to report that they did not complete the entire assignment that had been agreed upon, but that they did accomplish part of it. For example, a client with the assignment of going on a date with his wife may come back and state that they did not go out to dinner and a movie, but they did watch a DVD together at home. While this is preferable to doing nothing as it is still congruent with the value of being a caring spouse, it nonetheless also constitutes a failed commitment and should be addressed as such.

Present the Jump Exercise detailed in chapter 7, which likens committed action to jumping. In terms of this exercise, point out that the client did "jump" but in effect did so from a lowered height, suggesting that the initial step of committed action was too large to take. Use this acknowledgment later in collaborating with your client in determining

an appropriate homework assignment for next week. It is preferable to keep the commitment to jump from a height set at a more modest level than to set it at a more ambitious
level only to have the client then lower it when the time for jumping arrives.

3. Managing Barriers to Commitment

As with the previous agenda item, addressing this one is also more timely if your
clients encountered unwanted thoughts and feelings that functioned as obstacles to committed action. Even if this is not the case, still discuss with your clients how to respond to
possible experiential barriers because sooner or later they will face this challenge.

Passengers on the Bus Metaphor. Present this metaphor, which was described in
chapter 7, to underscore the continued presence of private events that can block value-
directed behavior. Emphasize how the passengers are most likely to protest and cause a
commotion at precisely those times when the client is about to turn down a valued road.
As long as values are not being actively pursued, the passengers (such as self-doubt and
fear of failure) may be relatively dormant and docile, but this "calm" costs the client who,
because of the passengers, is not leading a meaningful and invigorating life.

Choosing vs. deciding. The Why, Why, Why? Exercise was presented in session 4 as a
way of defusing reason giving. Present a variation on it at this point to weaken the power
of reason giving to undermine committed action by directing this exercise to the choosing
of values.

Therapist:	For much of last session and a good part of today's session, we've been looking at goals that are related to your values and what actions you can then take to meet those goals. But where do your values come from, and why do you have *this* value rather than *that* value? For example, we've identified being a caring parent as one of your top values. Why do you value that?
Client:	I don't think anyone should have kids if they aren't going to be responsible enough to take proper care of them.
Therapist:	Why is that?
Client:	Because if they don't, the kids may not grow up right and will suffer as a consequence.
Therapist:	Maybe that's so, but suppose I said it didn't matter to me if children grew up right. Why is that important to you, why do you value being a caring parent?
Client:	I guess maybe it goes back to how I was raised.
Therapist:	Could you have been raised differently and still value being a caring parent to your children? Is it possible for someone to be raised as you were and not share your parenting values?
Client:	I guess so.

Therapist:	Remember the two dishes of ice cream—which do you choose and why?
Client:	Yeah.
Therapist:	What if choosing your values is like that? I'm not asking this to suggest that your values and a dish of ice cream are somehow equally important, but to ask you to consider if both aren't freely chosen in the same way. You can offer me reasons for the flavor of ice cream you prefer just like you just did when I asked you why you care so much about being a good parent. But are you choosing chocolate ice cream over vanilla because of reasons or with reasons? Are you choosing to be a caring parent versus an uncaring parent because of reasons or with reasons?
Client:	When you put it that way—with reasons I guess.
Therapist:	Is there anything I could say—reasons I could offer you to convince you to be an uncaring parent—that would cause you to change your choice?
Client:	No, nothing.
Therapist:	Doesn't that suggest that reasons—whatever your mind might say about why it's important for you to be a caring parent—are just so much babble? Could it be that the reasons all of us offer for what we do, including what values we place above others, are like little stories that we tell to justify our choices? In that sense, you choose your values with reasons but not because of reasons. What I'd like you to consider is what it might mean to also view seeking goals that are linked to your values, such as taking your kids to the zoo, in the same way. What if instead of you choosing where the bus is going and where to turn, the passengers get to decide? Is it possible to have a whole list of reasons why to turn left but to choose to turn right instead, for no reason other than it moves your life in a valued direction? Will the making and keeping of commitments be choices that you make—with and not because of reasons—or decisions that are made because of reasons? If they are decisions, what happens to your commitment if the reasons for making them change? So from here on out, even though it might seem silly to you, I'd suggest that we use the term "choice" to refer to selections that are made by that part of you that you call you, the observer you, and that we use the term "decision" to refer to selections that are instead made by your mind, the passengers on the bus, or the chess pieces.

Afterward when your client encounters experiential barriers both in and out of session surrounding committed action, repeatedly refer back to the same fundamental question: "Is doing or not doing X something that you are choosing or something that the passengers on the bus are deciding for you?"

The Swamp Metaphor. So far, most of the emphasis within this session on managing barriers has been on thoughts and feelings that may prevent the initiation of committed action. Sometimes the greater challenge clients face is not in starting goal-directed behavior but in sticking with it. Because unwanted and unanticipated private events may also emerge in the course of committed action, it's also necessary that you work with your clients on how to respond to such circumstances. Present the Swamp Metaphor as described by Hayes et al. (1999, p. 248) to encourage client perseverance in the face of adversity.

> *Your values can be used to provide direction in your life, like the points on a compass. Suppose you choose to go west. So to orient yourself in that direction, you pick out a spot on the western horizon, let's say a mountain peak, to walk toward. You begin walking in that direction, and, at first, it's quite pleasant and easy. But soon you come upon a swamp that stands between you and the mountain peak and stretches out as far as you can see. The only way to keep going west and get to that mountain peak is to go through the swamp. So suppose you choose to start through the swamp, and you only take a few steps before you find out that it's smelly and so muddy that it takes a lot more effort than you thought it would just to pull your feet through all the muck. Now you have another choice—do you keep going or give up on going west? If you choose to continue, are you willing to go through the swamp if that's what it takes to get to the mountain peak? Suppose you say, "But I didn't head in this direction to get all bogged down in a smelly, muddy swamp!" That's right. You headed in that direction to go west, and you are in the swamp simply because it stands in between you and where you're going. The purpose in going through the swamp is not to become muddy and smelly but to go west. Are you willing, for the moment anyway, to get all bogged down in a smelly, muddy swamp because of what you value?*

As with the previous intervention, remind your clients of it when they encounter unforeseen obstacles in pursuing valued goals. For example, "Sounds like you've run into a swamp you hadn't planned on. Are you willing to do what needs to be done to get through it to get to where you want to go?"

4. Assignment of Homework

Homework for this week includes the continuation of mindfulness training and committed action.

Mindfulness Exercise. Reassign the final exercise in the progression of mindfulness training to your clients who did not complete last week's assignment. Provide them with another copy of the Mindfulness Exercise Dairy (see appendix H) to record their progress and, if necessary, a copy of the related handout (see appendix J) and/or CD/audiotape. Encourage the continuation of the mindfulness exercises for those clients who have completed the training sequence.

Committed action. Also, reassign the same goal-directed homework from last session for clients who failed to complete this assignment. In collaboration with your clients, select another form of committed action for homework for those who did complete the assignment. The behavior in question could be either related to last week's assignment as the next step in a graduated progression of valued action or be unrelated and associated with another prominent value.

Record the goal and related action on the Goals-Action Form (see appendix G) and also discuss how your clients can manage any experiential barriers that they anticipate encountering. Remind them of defusion, acceptance, and mindfulness procedures and techniques that they have been exposed to and could use in responding to unwanted thoughts and feelings that they may experience either leading up to or during the assigned activity. Finally, engage in some troubleshooting by asking your clients how they would respond to certain unforeseen troublesome experiences or reactions.

Sessions 9–11

The common primary goal of these three sessions is as follows:

■ To promote the continuation of value-directed activities

At this point in therapy, you will typically focus more on supporting your clients in persevering when they face unwanted thoughts and feelings that would otherwise undermine their commitments than on how to overcome behavioral inertia in getting started in the first place. Accordingly the secondary goals of these three sessions are as follows:

■ To increase willingness to experience unwanted thoughts and feelings surrounding persistent committed action

■ To clarify the distinction between the process and outcomes of committed action

■ To further promote mindfulness

Outline

1. Review Homework (10 min.)

    ■ Mindfulness Exercises

    ■ Committed Action

2. Managing Success (20 min.)

3. Managing Failure (20 min.)

    ■ The Gardening Metaphor

    ■ The Magic Pill Metaphor

4. Assignment of Homework (10 min.)

    ■ Mindfulness Exercises

    ■ Committed Action

Agenda

1. Review Homework

Because you will be asking your clients to continue the mindfulness exercises through the last session and will also be assigning additional goal-directed activities following sessions 9 through 11, it is critical that you review the completion of homework at the beginning of each session.

Mindfulness Exercises. Monitor whether your clients continue to practice the mindfulness exercises by reviewing their Mindfulness Exercise Diary (see appendix H) before each session. Be prepared to re-present any of the individual exercises in session if necessary.

Committed action. At the beginning of each session, determine if your clients have completed that week's behavioral homework assignment. Review the completed Goals-Action Form (see appendix G) to identify whatever experiential barriers your clients encountered that either prevented the completion of the assignments or, alternatively, that they successfully overcame. Collaboratively work with your clients in discussing other ways they could respond to unwanted private events that stand in the way of committed action. At this point in therapy, first ask clients what they could do rather than instructing them in specific defusion and acceptance techniques they might use, for example. If necessary, suggest and even re-present certain interventions, such as the revocalization of thoughts and physicalizing of feelings.

2. Managing Success

By now, many of your clients' value-directed activities will be successful in that the related goals being sought will be attained. Such successes, however, are not without a hidden danger. One challenge you may now encounter comes from goal attainment being corrupted by the experiential control agenda. Your clients may, in effect, fall back into using the attainment of goals as yet another form of digging. That is, clients may place more emphasis on whether obtaining external goals successfully eliminates certain unwanted private events (such as feeling like a failure) and/or induces desired states of mind (such as being happy) than on how goal seeking fits into a larger pattern of valued living. Checking to see if meeting a particular goal had the intended impact on unwanted thoughts, for example, paradoxically has the effect of inducing them and thereby turns successful goal-directed behavior into perceived failures. Looking to see if my self-doubts have gone away because I have accomplished a difficult goal is guaranteed to spoil that experience by reenergizing the same old demons. If we're not willing to have it, we've got it.

A metaphor that speaks to this issue is an adaptation of the Joe the Bum Metaphor as originally proposed by Hayes et al. (1999, p. 240). Present it by saying something like the following:

Therapist: Imagine that after working very hard for a number of years and saving up enough money, you've finally been able to buy your dream house.

To celebrate, you host a housewarming party to which everyone in the neighborhood is invited. In fact, to get the word out to everyone, you post invitations on the bulletin board of the local grocery store and on a sign near the street leading to your house. Sure enough, the day of the party arrives and you're having a wonderful time greeting and talking to all of your guests. As you greet one of your guests, she asks if Joe the bum is here at the party. You ask her to explain, and she tells you that she saw Joe the bum who sleeps in the trash dumpster behind the grocery store looking at your invitation posted on the bulletin board there. Because the invitation said everyone was welcome, she says she wouldn't be surprised if he showed up, but she hopes that he wouldn't. Has the party now changed for you in any way?

Client: I guess I would want to look around and make sure Joe the bum somehow didn't slip into the party without my noticing him.

Therapist: Do you see what's happened? Your place in the party has changed from welcoming and enjoying the company of all of your guests to one of making sure one of them—namely Joe the bum—isn't there. How much time is that going to take away from mingling with the guests that you want to have there? Suppose you look around for several minutes and finally find him, standing near the punch bowl, all dirty looking and foul smelling. Now what would you do?

Client: I could give him a sandwich or two and politely ask him to leave.

Therapist: Suppose he says he doesn't want to, that your sign invited the entire neighborhood, that he's part of the neighborhood, and so he's staying.

Client: Maybe I could offer him some money to leave.

Therapist: So now you're going to bribe him—see if you can't cut a deal with him. Meanwhile what's happened to your party? Isn't it now all about getting rid of one unwanted guest rather than enjoying the company of everyone else who's there? Suppose he still won't leave; what could you do?

Client: I suppose I could somehow tolerate him by trying to act like he's not really there. Maybe if I act like it's not a big deal, he'll just go away and leave us alone.

Therapist: Maybe he will or maybe he won't. It sounds though like you're still trying to get rid of him but just using a different strategy to do it. If you're only willing to have him be there in order for him to leave, are you really willing to have him be at the party? Can you fool yourself this way? Does Joe need to leave the party? Could you welcome him, just as you would any other guest, even though you wish he were not there? Let's imagine a slightly different situation. After your guest tells you about Joe the bum, you go throughout the entire house looking to see if he's already there and you don't find him. How would you feel?

Client: Relieved.

Therapist: How long would that last though? Joe the bum hasn't arrived yet, but you worry that he might be on his way. So maybe you periodically look out the window or step out onto the porch to see if you can see him coming to try to head him off. Now what's happened to your party? Hasn't your agenda become one of trying to make sure that Joe the bum doesn't show up to spoil the party? Here's what I'd like you to consider—whether continually checking to see if Joe the bum is on his way has already spoiled it. He doesn't even have to show up. Could you instead enjoy the guests that are present and welcome Joe the bum if and when he arrives? What if the guests at the party are like thoughts and feelings that show up for you when you reach certain goals that you've set for yourself. You may find some of the guests like the young, well-educated couple down the block quite attractive. Others, like self-doubt and feelings of insecurity, are like Joe the bum.You don't want them to be there, but they regularly show up anyway. No matter how successful you are in attaining goals you set for yourself, will it prevent the unwanted guests from showing up? If not, are you willing to have them and welcome them as you would any guest even though you don't want them to show up?

Once this metaphor has been presented, refer back to it, particularly when your clients reflect a lack of willingness to experience certain psychological events by asking, "Are you willing to welcome the bums to the party?"

3. Managing Failure

Another challenge you will likely face occurs when clients engage in committed action but fail to attain related goals. For example, a client may not be able to land a more engaging and fulfilling job despite multiple job applications and interviews. Clients may become discouraged and disheartened, and, most importantly, give up as a result. Your task then becomes one of promoting persistence and perseverance in the face of repeated setbacks. In doing so, remind yourself that such experiences are not failures from an ACT perspective even though they are likely to be seen as such by your clients.

A useful strategy to take in such circumstances is to reframe what constitutes success by emphasizing with your clients the distinction between the process and outcomes of committed action. The outcomes of committed action refer to the goals being sought and can, therefore, usually be easily judged as a success or failure. For example, did the client receive the raise that was asked for, the better job that was being sought, and so on? The process of committed action, by contrast, refers to actually engaging in the goal-directed behavior, such as asking for the raise and going on the job interview. Your client can always freely choose to engage in the process of value-directed, committed action even though doing so may not always result in goal attainment.

There are several metaphors within ACT that you can present to your clients to orient them to the process of committed action by distinguishing it from goal attainment, two of which will be described here. See chapters 8 and 9 by Hayes et al. (1999) and table 2.7 by Strosahl et al. (2004) for additional related exercises and interventions.

The Gardening Metaphor. This particular metaphor, first presented by Hayes et al. (1999, p. 220), promotes perseverance in committed action in the face of private events that would otherwise undermine such behavior. I have modified it slightly to be more responsive to the experiences of depressed clients.

> *Imagine that you want to plant a vegetable garden. You look at several possible spots, and after comparing them and mulling over your options, you finally select the one that you think is the best. So you go ahead and plant your seeds, water them, and sit back and wait for them to grow. But nothing comes up, and you start to feel impatient. You also begin to wonder if you planted the seeds right or have been watering them properly. Maybe you've watered them too much or not enough. You begin to think that maybe you even selected the wrong spot to begin with. Maybe the seeds would already be producing vegetables by now if you'd planted them in one of the other spots. So you dig up the seeds and replant them in another spot. And you wait, but you still don't have any vegetables. You begin to question whether you are capable of growing any vegetables or maybe the second spot you selected still isn't the best plot. So you pull up the seeds again and replant them in another spot. And you wait. But by now the growing season is just about over, and just about the time that the seeds are now sprouting up out of the ground, the first killing frost comes and you end up with no vegetables at all.*
>
> *What if your values are like the spot where you plant your seeds and the goal-related homework we've been focusing on these last few sessions is like planting the seeds?*
>
> *The goals themselves are like the vegetables that grow from the seeds. Some vegetables may take longer to grow than others, and not all seeds that are planted will germinate, so there are some inherent uncertainties in growing a garden. But what does seem certain is that you won't have any vegetables at all unless seeds are planted and that the seeds need to be given time to grow into vegetables. Once you choose where to plant them, they need to stay put. You will have no vegetables if the seeds are constantly being dug up and replanted.*
>
> *How important is it to you to have the possibility of having a garden?*
>
> *Are you willing to plant your seeds even though you may have doubts that the spot you've selected is the best one? And are you willing to water and nurture those seeds even though you may have the thought that they will never grow?*

The Magic Pill Metaphor. This next metaphor is a type of thought experiment that further pulls apart the relationship that normally exists between the process and outcome of valued action. Clients are asked to choose between a guaranteed outcome inversely related to process, or commitment to a process with no assured outcome. For example, say something like the following in presenting the metaphor to a client whose primary value is being a caring parent:

Suppose I offer you some magic pills. If you take these pills and have your children swallow them, I guarantee that they will always see you as a loving, caring parent for the rest of their lives provided you do one other thing. The other thing you must do for the pills to work is to be as mean and uncaring toward your children as possible. In fact, the way these pills work is that the more hateful and mean you are toward your children, the more they will see you as loving and caring. The pills are one option—option A. Option B is that you can forego the magic pills and commit yourself to relating to your kids in a kind and caring way with no guarantee that they will see you as a loving parent. In fact, despite how kind and caring you are toward them, they may never see you that way. Maybe they will and maybe they won't. Which do you chose, option A or option B?

For other values, it may be the client who takes the pills. For example, would a client who values being well-educated take a pill that would provide her with vast knowledge but whose effects would wear off if she ever read another book of nonfiction? I have never had a client opt to take the magic pills, although the possibility can't be ruled out that what clients choose reflects more what they think you or I as the therapist want to hear than their values.

4. Assignment of Homework

At the end of each of these three sessions, assign continued mindfulness practice and forms of value-directed activities for homework.

Mindfulness Exercises. Only the self as context can be expected to meaningfully make and keep commitments. For this reason, I recommend that your clients continue their practice of mindfulness exercises not only to directly foster a transcendent sense of self but also to indirectly promote committed action. Encourage your clients to continue to practice the mindfulness exercises they were taught, particularly those involving thoughts and feelings, on a daily basis. Provide them with copies of the Mindfulness Exercise Diary (see appendix H) and related handouts (see appendix I and appendix J) and/or CD/audiotapes to support them in doing so.

Committed action. Have your client select at least one goal-related activity for homework at the end of each session. Record the goal and related activity on the Goals-Action Form (see appendix G). Collaboratively discuss with your clients any environmental and/or experiential barriers they anticipate in completing the assignment and how they might manage such obstacles.

Session 12

The goals of this last session are threefold:

- To process the reactions of you and your client to treatment termination

- To review ACT-consistent strategies and techniques

- To promote the posttermination maintenance of therapeutic gains

Outline

1. Review Homework (5 min.)

2. Process Reactions to Termination (10 min.)

3. Summarize Barriers to Willingness (15 min.)

    - *F*usion with Your Thoughts

    - *E*valuation of Experiences

    - *A*voidance of Your Experiences

    - *R*eason Giving for Your Behavior

4. Summarize Guidelines for Valued Living (10 min.)

    - *A*ccept Your Reactions and Be Present

    - *C*hoose a Valued Direction

    - *T*ake Action

5. Discuss Life After Therapy (20 min.)

Agenda

1. Review Homework

Briefly review and discuss your clients' homework from last session. Encourage them to continue the mindfulness exercises and the setting and seeking of value-directed goals following the termination of therapy.

2. Process Reactions to Termination

Ask your clients to share with you whatever reactions they have to the ending of therapy while you listen attentively and nonjudgmentally. Be prepared to offer your own reactions à la inventorying, such as "I have a feeling of sadness" or "I have the thought that depression may continue to be a struggle for you." Your task is not to reassure your clients about any doubts or misgivings they may have about the end of treatment nor (with one exception) to restructure any associated negative thoughts they may experience, but rather to help normalize such reactions through acknowledgment and validation. For example, you might say something like the following:

> *Remember that your mind is not your friend. Now is a time for your mind to do what all minds do, which is to create all sorts of chatter and negative thoughts about this being our last session together—thoughts like maybe your depression will come back and you'll be overwhelmed by it, and so on. What is your mind telling you right now?*

The one type of negative thought that is appropriate to restructure is any that would preclude the client's return to therapy should it become necessary, such as "You won't see me anymore after today if I need to come back."

3. Summarize Barriers to Willingness

Ask your clients if there are any issues, exercises, or techniques that were discussed and/or presented in the previous sessions that they would like to review. Use the FEAR acronym (Hayes et al., 1999, p. 246) as a convenient way of summarizing the work that the two of you have done to increase willingness and reduce experiential avoidance. The acronym summarizes the key processes that limit psychological flexibility from the perspective of ACT or, stated differently, the ways we end up back digging and tugging on the rope. On one side of an index card—you will use the other side for the ACT acronym (see below)—print "FEAR." Below the acronym, print the processes: Fusion with your thoughts, Evaluation of experiences, Avoidance of your experiences, Reason giving for your behavior. Summarize the processes and related interventions denoted by each of the letters of the FEAR acronym.

Fusion with your thoughts. If necessary, point out that "fusion" refers to "buying into your thoughts and treating them as facts rather than as mind chatter." Ask clients about different ways they could respond to fused thoughts that get them stuck. If needed, remind them of the Milk, Milk, Milk Exercise, the Revocalization Exercises, and other defusion exercises and techniques.

Evaluation of experiences. Ask you clients to summarize why evaluations of thoughts and feelings, especially those that are self-referential, may be problematic. Be prepared to review the distinction between evaluations and descriptions with your clients as well as means of defusing evaluations by, for example, explicitly recognizing them as such (as in "I have an evaluation that …").

Avoidance of your experiences. Again, first ask your clients about their understanding about this part of the acronym and be prepared to provide clarification with examples from their experiences with depression as needed. For instance, asking something like "What have you possibly missed out on in life in order to avoid bad feelings like sadness and guilt?" calls attention to the pain of absence and other costs of experiential avoidance.

Reason giving for your behavior. Finally, ask your clients why or how reason giving may be problematic. If necessary, remind them of the Passengers on the Bus Metaphor as well as the Reasons for Depression and Why? Why? Why? exercises.

4. Summarize Guidelines for Valued Living

Use the other side of the index card to print the ACT acronym (Hayes et al, 1999, p. 246) and its corresponding processes: Accept your reactions and be present, Choose a valued direction, Take action. Point out to your clients that together you just reviewed ways of getting stuck in depression—the FEAR acronym and related processes—and now it's time to summarize general strategies for getting unstuck. Do so by reviewing processes and related courses of action associated with each letter of the ACT acronym. (After your review of the FEAR and ACT acronyms and related processes, give the card to your clients to take with them. Encourage them to carry it in their wallet or purse where it can be quickly referenced as needed.)

Accept your reactions and be present. First, ask your clients what this means to them and, more importantly, how they could enact the rule. If necessary, remind your clients of and review with them various exercises and interventions that they have either participated in or learned over the course of therapy that promote acceptance and willingness. These include but are not limited to the various mindfulness exercises as well as the Sitting with Feelings, Taking Inventory, and Physicalizing (of feelings) exercises.

Choose a valued direction. Review this part of the acronym by asking your clients for their understanding of the difference between deciding upon a valued direction versus choosing one. If needed, revisit the Swamp and Passengers on the Bus metaphors.

Take action. This final step in the acronym is largely self-explanatory and thus requires little review or elaboration. Nevertheless, you and your clients may find it useful to reconsider the Trying vs. Doing Exercise as well as Yoda's related advice: "No! Try not. Do. Or do not. There is no try" ("Yoda Quotes," n.d.). In addition, the Swamp and Passengers on the Bus metaphors may also be revisited.

5. Discuss Life After Therapy

The remaining segment of the last session is an opportune time to visit with your clients about how they can continue to apply what they have learned in therapy. A metaphor that I have found useful to share with clients is to liken the end of therapy to graduation from college or high school. It marks the end of a formal period of education but also the beginning of a new one in which what has been learned can be applied and further developed. There is a reason why graduation ceremonies are called commencements as they do signal a beginning. In some sense, the same applies to therapy. In short, encourage your clients to see the end of therapy also as a new beginning.

On a somewhat more practical note, also discuss with your clients any upcoming circumstances that they anticipate will present serious challenges to them. In particular, do some troubleshooting to help your clients prepare for difficult life events that they know will be occurring in the near future. Help them review how they can manage their psychological reactions to events such as a family reunion, the anniversary of a loved one's death, or a move because of a change in employment.

Summary

In this chapter, I've presented a twelve-session protocol for applying ACT in your work with depressed clients. You may wish to use this as an alternative to the case-conceptualization approach outlined in the previous chapters. Other protocols could be designed that differ both in content and length from what I've offered here. As I mentioned earlier, the protocol contains twelve sessions to correspond to those that were followed in comparing ACT to cognitive therapy in treatment of depression (Zettle & Hayes, 1986; Zettle & Rains, 1989). Because research has not yet determined the most efficacious length of treatment for various levels of depression, the length of this protocol could not be selected on an empirical basis. A protocol with fewer sessions (perhaps as few as six or eight) or more (as many as sixteen to twenty), for example, might ultimately be shown to be more efficacious and/or cost-effective than one that contains twelve, especially depending upon the severity of depression being treated. For all of these reasons, by all means use the protocol in this chapter but do so flexibly.

CHAPTER 10

Additional Issues and Concerns

In this chapter, we will consider a number of issues and concerns that you are likely to encounter in applying ACT in your work with depressed clients. Many of these issues and concerns were mentioned or discussed briefly in other chapters and are not necessarily unique to ACT with depression. However, they are common and problematic enough in taking this therapeutic approach with this particular client population to warrant a more detailed elaboration of them here. These concerns include management of challenging client behavior, comorbidity and other concurrent treatment issues, and ethical considerations.

Managing Challenging Client Behavior

Some client behaviors, such as suicidality, present a challenge to any efforts to successfully treat depression. Others, like homework noncompliance, may be more of an issue within cognitive behavioral therapy more generally than within other psychotherapeutic approaches to depression that place less emphasis on between-session assignments (Ronan & Kazantzis, 2006). Finally, there are certain client behaviors—for instance, withholding forgiveness and playing the martyr role—that present somewhat unique challenges to ACT because of the importance it places upon defusion from client verbal constructions, such as storytelling, that can severely limit psychological flexibility.

In the sections that follow, I will offer and discuss specific guidelines and considerations in managing each of these types of challenging client behavior. Before doing so, however, I want to emphasize that all forms of problematic client behavior can be dealt with by staying within the ACT model. Think of any client actions or inactions that might compromise the therapeutic impact of ACT as simply more grist for the ACT mill. Therefore, I do not recommend a strategic approach that goes outside of ACT for managing challenging client behavior.

Suicidal Behavior

Suicidality is hardly limited to clients suffering from depression (Chiles & Strosahl, 2005). Regardless, it co-occurs often enough with depression (Maris et al., 1992) that all of your depressed clients should be assessed for suicidal risk. While most of the emphasis in managing suicidality has understandably been on preventing suicidal completions, merely thinking about suicide represents the most common form of suicidal behavior (Chiles & Strosahl). Accordingly, our focus within this chapter will not be limited to the prevention of suicide attempts but will also consider how ACT can address client suicidal behavior as more broadly defined.

Much of what follows in this section is hardly new. A good deal of what I have to offer is culled and summarized from the work of Kirk Strosahl, including a chapter about ACT with multiproblem clients (2004) and an excellent book that provides more extensive guidelines for the assessment and treatment of suicidal behavior from an ACT perspective (Chiles & Strosahl, 2005). I strongly recommend both, particularly the book, to those of you who wish to receive a more comprehensive treatment of this topic.

Assessment of Suicidal Behavior

Two fundamental assessment questions need to be answered for each client with a presenting problem of depression: (1) Is this particular client at risk for suicide, and if so, (2) does the suicidal behavior appear be serving an experiential-avoidant function?

Assessment of suicidal risk. The process of determining the likelihood that a given client will attempt suicide, unfortunately, is an inexact science. Most often, mental health professionals weigh an array of historical and current variables regardless of the therapeutic approach being considered or their own theoretical orientation. For example, a family history of suicidal behavior as well as a personal history of previous attempts are commonly regarded as risk factors (Meichenbaum, 2005). Other historical information to consider is the degree to which previous attempts used potentially lethal means and were well planned.

Also, extend the assessment of the "plan-availability-lethality" triangle (Chiles & Strosahl, 2005, p. 75)—that is, does the client have a lethal plan and the means to carry it out?—to any present thoughts of suicide. In addition to an open-ended interview, you may also wish to use somewhat more formal means of assessment in evaluating other current risk factors for suicide that are not unique to ACT. For example, clients can be administered the Beck Hopelessness Scale (Beck, Weissman, Lester, & Trexler, 1974), which, independently of levels of depression (Beck et al., 1975), has been shown to be predictive of suicidality (Brown et al., 2000). In addition, you can follow the Scale for

Suicide Ideation (Beck & Kovacs, 1979) in conducting a semistructured client interview that assesses other psychological variables, such as the wish to die and the desire to make an active attempt, that represent further risk factors for suicidality.

Assessment of suicidality as experiential escape. Suicidality, like any behavior, can be determined by multiple factors, and clients who are at risk for suicide may be thinking of killing themselves for differing reasons. Your task thus becomes one of evaluating the extent to which at-risk clients use suicidal behavior to avoid or escape from unpleasant thoughts and feelings, including the dirty pain of depression itself. In particular, for depressed clients who have been unsuccessful in minimizing their emotional suffering, thinking about, planning, and attempting suicide becomes a way of solving what to them has been an intractable problem. As Chiles and Strosahl (2005) point out, the allure of suicide is likely to be especially powerful for clients who additionally exhibit a low ability, more generally, to tolerate psychological distress and lack other means of coping with it.

Consider multiple sources of converging information to determine whether a given client's suicidal behavior is for the purpose of experiential escape and avoidance. A good deal of this information will emerge from listening to the life story of your clients and within the context of completing your assessment of their overall suicidal risk. For example, ask clients, as I suggested previously, what they hoped to accomplish by any previous suicide attempts. The best predictor of future suicidal behavior is past suicidal behavior, especially when both serve the same experiential-avoidant function.

As with the initial assessment of suicidal risk, consider both historical and current variables in determining whether present suicidal behavior may be used by your clients to run away from unpleasant private events. Chiles and Strosahl (2005), in particular, have suggested assessing five key factors (table 4-1, p. 75) in addressing this issue: (1) evaluation of suicidal behavior as a way of solving problems, (2) level of psychological pain tolerance, (3) level of hopelessness, (4) perceived inescapability, and (5) reasons for living. Your consideration of these same current factors can also subsequently help guide your management of client suicidal behavior and, therefore, will be enumerated here as a list of questions to be asked and answered:

1. How effective does the client see suicide as a problem-solving strategy? What problems, such as termination of emotional suffering, might committing suicide solve? How effective, from the client's perspective, would suicide be in solving these problems?

2. If the client's situation did not improve, how well could he or she continue to tolerate it?

3. What changes, if any, does the client see occurring in the future? If there are expected changes, are they for the better or for the worse?

4. How effective have efforts by the client been in remedying the current situation? Have such efforts even seemed to make things worse?

5. What reasons does the client have for continuing to live? How important are these reasons?

While you can evaluate these five factors by simply asking your clients the questions listed above, you can also approach two of them (factors 3 and 5) by administering related paper-and-pencil instruments. As I suggested previously, the Beck Hopelessness Scale (Beck et al., 1974) can be used to quantify the client's level of pessimism about the future (factor 3). The first four of the five factors listed above from Chiles and Strosahl (2005) collectively reflect what could be regarded as reasons why a client may be contemplating suicide. The last, however, focuses on client motives that support continued living and can thereby act as a counterweight against suicidality. Your client's desire to continue living can be further evaluated by the administration of the Reasons for Living Inventory (RFL; Linehan, Goodstein, Nielsen, & Chiles, 1983).

Either ask your clients to complete the RFL on their own or, alternatively, do so by interviewing them. Regardless of how it is administered, there are several advantages to using the RFL. First, because more reasons for living have been shown to be inversely related to suicidality (Ivanoff, Jang, Smyth, & Linehan, 1994), the RFL can be used to complement your assessment of suicidal risk. Among its forty-eight items, the RFL asks clients to rate the degree to which concerns about children specifically ("I want to watch my children as they grow") and family more broadly ("I have a responsibility and commitment to my family") may serve as deterrents to suicide. From the perspective of ACT, such items may also reflect important core values of the client. Accordingly, administering the RFL can also provide you with useful additional information about valuing that may help direct your management of your client's suicidal behavior. Clients may kill themselves because of their relationships with family members, but they may also choose to live because of them.

Management of Suicidal Behavior

Your first objective in managing suicidal behavior is to simply buy yourself some time. What's critical is not the mere passage of time, but what you and your suicidal clients do with whatever time you are granted by their postponement of any attempts to kill themselves. In particular, use this grace period to (1) increase the client's tolerance of psychological distress, (2) promote valuing and reasons for living as deterrents to suicide, and (3) to develop and implement alternative problem-solving skills.

Increasing emotional pain tolerance. From the perspective of ACT, the more suicidal clients try to run away from unwanted thoughts and feelings, the more such unwanted experiences become exacerbated and locked in place. When other emotional control efforts inevitably fail at least in the long run, clients are even more likely to hold little hope for an improved future and to see suicide as a way of terminating what seems to be increasing and unending psychological pain. Your task in such circumstances is to encourage your clients to at least temporarily disengage from the experiential control struggle long enough (for example, by dropping the rope) to provide the opportunity for you to engage in some defusion and acceptance work with them.

Sometimes environmental changes alone, such as leaving an abusive relationship, can have a major impact on the client's level of psychological distress. If this is not possible, the long-term goal of ACT is not to increase client tolerance of unwanted psychological experiences but to promote their acceptance. When dealing with clients who may be acutely suicidal, however, supporting an immediate increased tolerance of emotional pain is a necessary initial goal in the larger process of promoting experiential acceptance and willingness. Use the array of techniques and interventions discussed at previous points in this book, especially chapter 6, for promoting defusion and acceptance of whatever thoughts and feelings contribute to their acute distress. For example, present the Your Mind Is Not Your Friend Exercise to provide clients with a different, yet validating, perspective on suicidal thoughts, that is, that such thoughts are quite understandable when we are faced with what seems to be inescapable and unending emotional suffering, and that such thoughts do not need to be acted upon. Once clients have acknowledged that suicide provides a way out their psychological pain, ask them if they are willing to give the two of you enough time to explore other means of problem solving. Reframing the therapeutic agenda in this way removes emphasis on suicidality per se as the problem and appropriately shifts it to one of how suicidal behavior fits into the broader context of problem solving (Chiles & Strosahl, 2005, p. 104).

Promoting valuing. Your objective in promoting valuing is to dignify the amount of suffering your suicidal clients have already endured and are likely to continue to experience at least in the near future until their ability to tolerate emotional pain has been successfully strengthened. As Nietzsche observed, "He who has a *why* to live for can bear with almost any *how*" (as cited by Frankl, 1965, p. 76, emphasis in Frankl). From this perspective, you can address the "how" part of living by increasing client tolerance of psychological distress and developing problem skills and strategies other than suicide. Identify and emphasize your clients' reasons for living to address the "why" part of living.

As I suggested earlier, you can use a number of methods, such as administration of the RFL or one of the values questionnaires as well as indirect ways of assessing client values (such as following the suffering), to identify reasons why suicidal clients would choose life over death. Often it is more clear what suicidal clients are willing to die for—namely, relief from their emotional suffering—than what it is they are willing to live for. Part of your job is to highlight client values, such as "watching my grandchildren grow up," that can serve as a deterrent to suicide.

From an RFT perspective, your challenge is to formulate a rule for your suicidal clients to follow (like, "If I don't kill myself, I can watch my grandkids grow up") that augments both the short- and long-term consequences of continued living. The immediate consequences of opting to live may well be increased psychological distress and the potentially reinforcing consequences of this choice (that is, "watching the grandchildren grow up") are long delayed. You are thus faced with the task of finding a way to talk with your clients about their suicidal behavior in such a way that the aversiveness of the immediate consequences of choosing to live (possible continued distress) are minimized and the capacity of its delayed consequences to function as reinforcers (seeing the grandkids growing up) are maximized. Say something like the following to clarify the choice that is before the client and the stakes involved:

> *You are faced with a choice here. One option is to kill yourself; the other is to continue living. We know that the option of killing yourself has certain consequences. One sure outcome is that you will no longer feel depressed. Another certain outcome is that you also won't get to see your grandchildren grow up. If you choose to live, the consequences are a bit less certain. Choosing to live gives*

you the opportunity and possibility of being able to see your grandkids grow. Think of what that would be like for you—to be part of their lives, to watch them grow from being children and then teenagers to adults. You may even live long enough to watch their children, your great-grandchildren, grow up. What would it mean to you to hold your first great-grandchild? All of this is possible if you choose to live; none of it is possible if you choose to kill yourself. Choosing to live also gives you the opportunity and the possibility for us to work together to develop some other ways of dealing with the problems that have brought you to the point that suicide seems to be the only way out.

Is watching your grandchildren grow up important enough to you that you are willing to choose to live, even though there is no guarantee that the emotional pain you are experiencing right now will go away? We wouldn't be able to know whether it would or it wouldn't until we have had some more time to work together. I'd like to see us have the opportunity to find out, but we won't have that if you kill yourself. You are faced with a choice here. Which do you choose— to live or to die?

If a client still opts for suicide, search for other values that could serve as a deterrent by, if necessary, asking "We've identified what you are willing to die for. What are you willing to live for?"

Developing alternative problem-solving skills. You will likely find it useful in thinking about the problems from which your clients may be seeking relief through suicidality to draw a distinction between those that are exclusively experiential in nature, such as guilt over a past transgression, and those that are currently unfolding in the external environment, such as living in poverty or in an abusive relationship. While clients are most likely to see suicide as a solution to psychological or emotional problems, they may also regard it as way of escaping from oppressive and stressful environments. From the perspective of ACT, the external world is potentially more controllable than the inner, psychological world. For this reason, look for opportunities, no matter how modest, for your suicidal clients to effect change in their present external circumstances that may be contributing to their overall level of emotional suffering. Use defusion- and acceptance-promoting techniques and methods for strengthening the ability of your clients to manage and cope with unwanted psychological states, and active problem-solving strategies for addressing their external circumstances.

As Chiles and Strosahl (2005) have argued, selecting a readily doable client action for homework that represents a "small success" is preferable to a more ambitious task that has less likelihood of being completed and, even if completed, a low probability of effectively solving the problem at hand. For example, you are likely to find that brainstorming with your clients about things they could do to obtain temporary respite from a stressful living situation, such as going for a walk, may be more useful in the short-term than suddenly moving out. I'm not suggesting, in this example, that finding another place to live be excluded as a possible solution but that doing so will often take more time and effort to enact. Indeed, moving out might constitute a more permanent solution and may even be a necessary short-term remedy should the client's physical well-being be in jeopardy. Be sure, however, that the reach of your clients does not exceed their grasp. If necessary, ask the following question as suggested by Chiles and Strosahl: "If we could select a small task that, if you accomplished it, would tell you that things were just a little bit better, what would that be?" (p. 106).

Homework Noncompliance

Between-session assignments have long been an integral component of behavior and cognitive behavioral therapy more generally (Kazantzis, Deane, Ronan, & L'Abate, 2005) and of these approaches, in particular, in their treatment of depression (Garland & Scott, 2005; Gaynor, Lawrence, & Nelson-Gray, 2006; Thase & Callan, 2006). ACT as another form of behavior therapy is no exception. While assignments following each session are part of the treatment protocol offered in chapter 9, the overall emphasis that ACT places on homework seems not to be overly heavy but comparable to the role it plays within other cognitive behavioral approaches in treating depression.

A potential challenge within any therapeutic approach that emphasizes homework is ensuring that such assignments are adequately completed by clients. The importance of homework compliance is increased to the extent that there is empirical evidence supporting its role within therapy. On this point, correlational research fairly consistently has found that homework compliance is associated with significantly better outcomes, within cognitive behavioral therapy, of depression (Thase & Calan, 2006). However, experimental research that has examined the effect of homework assignments as an independent variable upon various outcome measures as dependent variables has been more mixed. While researchers found that homework assignments had no impact upon group self-control therapy (Kornblith, Rehm, O'Hara, & Lamparski, 1983) or group cognitive therapy for depression (Neimeyer & Feixas, 1990), Zettle and Hayes (1987) reported greater general improvement by depressed clients within individual cognitive therapy who were assigned behavioral homework.

Unfortunately there has not been enough comparable research within ACT for depression to draw any even tentative, empirically based conclusions about how homework assignments as a treatment component affect therapeutic outcome. For this reason, I will offer guidelines for the management of homework noncompliance that are based upon the strategic roles that homework assignments play in addressing the three sets of core-related processes within ACT that contribute to increased psychological flexibility. From this vantage point, between-session activities that help promote commitment and behavior change carry considerably more weight than those that support the other two sets of related processes (defusion and acceptance, on the one hand, and mindfulness and self as context, on the other). Accordingly, if you must choose which homework noncompliance battles to fight, opt for those that involve committed action. Give next priority to assignments that promote mindfulness and the least to homework that involves defusion and acceptance.

As discussed at length in chapter 7, homework assignments that help promote commitment to living a valued life typically involve a series of related actions for clients to engage in between sessions. ACT without a change in valued living is not ACT, and homework noncompliance in this aspect of ACT thus severely compromises its overall integrity. Client failure to complete homework assignments that promote defusion and acceptance (such as taking inventory) and contacting the present moment (such as the practice of mindfulness exercises) are less critical because these activities, if necessary, can be repeatedly provided within session. Defusion and acceptance interventions, in particular, lend themselves a bit more readily to this approach—thus, the basis for my recommendation above to place the lowest priority upon the completion of defusion- and acceptance-related homework assignments. While there may also be occasions for clients to engage in committed action in session in their interactions with you, such opportunities are more rare. Thus, most of your clients will need to make substantive changes in their out-of-session behavior if they are to move their lives in a valued direction.

Like any other behavioral deficit, the failure of clients to complete value-directed homework assignments may occur for multiple reasons that are not mutually exclusive. Part of your challenge will be to first determine the function(s) of homework noncompliance for each of your clients in which it occurs. Then use your resulting assessment and conceptualization to guide your management of the problem. In the subsections that follow, I will discuss a number of factors that may contribute to client noncompliance with homework assignments designed to promote committed action. I'll also discuss related suggestions for addressing these factors.

Disconnection from Values

Your clients understandably are likely to lack motivation in completing behavioral assignments that are not congruent with their values. Therefore double-check to verify that any assignments that were not completed are in the service of client values, even though you may have already spent quite a bit of time in identifying and clarifying them. If necessary, use some additional direct and indirect means to further assess client values. It's possible that pseudovalues had been initially identified either because clients were saying what they believed you wanted to hear or because their true values simply were not detected by the forms of assessment used.

Too Much Change

Small changes in behavior are easier to make than larger ones. The initial assessment of client values that you and your clients are using to guide the formulation of homework assignments for them may be on target, but the degree of behavioral change being sought is too large. Both you and your clients may be somewhat overly ambitious. ACT, like life itself, is not a race, and it is preferable to go too slow and take a bit longer to effectively move your clients' lives in a valued direction than to go too fast and fail. Use a graduated task approach as discussed in chapter 7 to select a more modest assignment that your clients are more likely to complete and that can be used as an initial step in shaping a broader pattern of committed action.

Counterpliance

All of us at one time or another have likely resisted doing something that was in our best interests simply because it was suggested by someone else. Similarly the failure of clients to complete homework may also constitute a form of counterpliance even if the assignments are clearly value directed. Just as there is a danger that some clients may keep commitments for you rather than themselves, there is also a risk that they may break them because of you. This is most likely to occur with clients with a history of being subjected to authoritarian control. If necessary, revisit the client's life story and/or specifically ask about previous incidents of rebellious behavior in response to being told what to do to rule this out as a contributing factor.

From your perspective, you are not ordering your clients to complete homework, but they may nevertheless respond to whatever you say about their assignments as an opportunity to reassert their autonomy by doing the opposite. If this is the case, the more insistent you become that the assignments be completed, the more resolute they are likely to become in resisting. In such instances, back off and, if necessary, make it clear that you have no personal investment in whether they complete the homework or not. Also, some motivational interviewing (Miller & Rollnick, 2002) should help further minimize any possible power struggle over homework assignments between you and your clients. For example, saying something like "On the one hand, you want to do what's important to you, but on the other, it may seem like you don't have much choice in the matter if I'm bossing you around" may reaffirm your clients' autonomy while also acknowledging their point of view.

Client homework noncompliance that serves a counterpliant function provides you not only with a challenge but also with an opportunity to meaningfully address a clinically rich issue. Quite likely, clients who display rebellious behavior toward you are also apt to relate to other important authority figures in their lives, such as bosses and parents, in a similar self-defeating way. As suggested in chapter 4, functional analytic psychotherapy, or FAP (Kohlenberg & Tsai, 1987, 1991), can be readily integrated with ACT in addressing such clinically relevant behavior that occurs in session. In doing so, ask your clients whether the same pattern of behavior that seems to be unfolding in the context of homework assignments within therapy also occurs in their relationships with others outside of therapy, and, if so, how such tendencies may impact their overall level of valued living.

Fear of Failure

Homework noncompliance as counterpliant behavior can be construed as also serving an experiential-avoidant function. More specifically, clients may refuse to complete assignments to avoid a loss of self-respect and related damage to the conceptual self that accompanies what that they see as kowtowing to others. In short, clients may prefer being defiant and being their own person to feeling subservient and allowing others to push them around.

A more common psychological experience that clients can avoid by not completing their homework is that which comes from trying and failing. Clients may be so motivated to avoid coming into contact with feelings of failure that assignments are not even attempted. In effect, their operative motto is that it is better to do nothing than to do something and have it be unsuccessful. You can address this issue in several ways in an ACT-consistent manner.

One strategy is to do some intensive defusion and acceptance work around the feelings of failure and associated thoughts and emotions. A related approach is to dignify the experience of failure by reemphasizing the values that are directing the homework assignment in question by, for example, saying something like the following:

Anything that's worth doing, is worth doing poorly (de Posada, 2003). *If a goal is worth attaining, is it worth trying for it and falling short? Is the goal we are talking about valuable enough to you that you are willing to try for it and fail?*

Finally, as suggested in the last chapter, you can also heighten the distinction between trying and doing in reframing what constitutes the successful completion of a behavioral homework assignment. That is, success is defined by doing the assignment. Trying is not doing (remember Yoda), and success is not determined by whether or not the specific goal being sought through the assignment was attained or not.

Other Barriers to Commitment

A fear of failure as just discussed can be regarded as an experiential barrier to clients even attempting behavioral homework assignments. Other barriers, both experiential and environmental, may also contribute to homework noncompliance, but by impacting the completion of assignments that are attempted. For example, clients may encounter unexpected external obstacles (such as finances being depleted by a car suddenly needing repairs) as well as experiential ones (such as a loss of self-confidence and a flood of self-doubt) that emerge during the process of completing a homework assignment and, as a result, cut it short. Encourage clients to record any barriers they encounter that preclude the completion of homework on the Goals-Action Form (see appendix G) so that they can be further addressed in your sessions.

An occasional occurrence of homework being started but not completed is not problematic as you can use it to further hone your clients' skills in managing and overcoming barriers to committed action. Much more problematic is a prolonged pattern of attempted but uncompleted homework assignments. Under such circumstances, pull back and do some more defusion and acceptance work to address experiential barriers. You may also find it useful to reverify client values before assigning any further homework.

Choosing Not To

Finally, as discussed in chapter 7, there may be some assignments that you suggest to your clients that they simply choose not to do. Try to determine whether doing so on their part constitutes a free choice or whether it is being driven by experiential avoidance or some of the other factors just discussed. If it appears to be a free choice, respond in a way that respects and validates the difficult choice being made. Some behavioral homework assignments must be completed within ACT for it to be ACT but certainly not all.

Extreme Rigidity

Psychological flexibility and rigidity are most usefully thought of as endpoints on a continuum. From this perspective, most of your depressed clients will fall somewhere on the inflexible side of this continuum, but some will obviously demonstrate more extreme levels of rigidity than others. A metaphor may be useful here. Think of psychological rigidity as rust on a bolt. Some bolts are rusted more badly than others. If your task is to remove a nut from each of the bolts, it will be made more difficult by the amount of rust on the bolt. Quite a bit of work and effort is required to remove the nuts even from bolts that are only slightly rusted. Unfortunately, some clients are so extreme in their psychological rigidity that they are like the badly rusted bolts—even slightly nudging the nuts on them becomes a major challenge. Once they are loosened up, however, the amount of effort to remove the nuts the rest of the way may be no greater than what it is for the bolts with less rust.

The toughest nuts to loosen are those that become rusted in place through fusion with a life story in which the client has been unfairly treated by others and/or has committed some unpardonable act. Clients who hold their life story as the literal cause of their depression have no way out of it as long as the constructed narrative that links previous life events and emotional suffering remains unchanged. As discussed in chapter 6, ask clients who display this type of fusion to rewrite their life story as many times as may be necessary until they acknowledge that a different outcome is a least possible, even if it is not the most probable.

This approach will work well enough with most depressed clients. Unfortunately, though, you will likely encounter a few clients who still rigidly cling to their original life story despite multiple rewrites of it. A useful way to manage this challenge is to identify and weaken various barriers that may prevent defusion from the life story. Clients may be highly invested in the narrative they have constructed and may offer to account for their depression with a number of reasons that are often related to each other and are not mutually exclusive. The one such barrier that I addressed at the greatest length thus far is that of being right (see chapter 2 and chapter 5), and for this reason, I will not reiterate it here. Instead our focus will be on reducing extreme client rigidity through the management of forgiveness issues and weakening of the martyr role.

Forgiveness Issues

Clients may remain tightly fused with their life story because of a refusal to forgive either others or themselves. While we will discuss these two types of forgiveness separately in what follows, be aware that some of your clients may have issues with both.

Forgiving others. The withholding of forgiveness that could be granted to others occurs most often by clients who present a life story in which they have been victimized and traumatized by others, quite frequently by members of their own family or other people of significance in their lives. From an RFT perspective, having been mistreated by others and forgiving them for doing so are held in a frame of opposition. This is typically reflected by client comments such as "They don't deserve my forgiveness" and "Anyone who had to endure what I have would be depressed." As long as the possible forgiveness of the transgressor(s) remains related to the life story in this manner, the entire verbal system becomes solidified and no movement is possible. In effect, depression is an inevitable outcome of the way the client was mistreated (as told by the life story), and depression remains locked into place as long as the narrative about it remains unchanged.

The life story could be changed, but doing so would be tantamount to forgiving the transgressors. If the client did not have to suffer the way that he or she has at the hands of wrongdoers, they are let off the hook as if they have done nothing that would justify forgiveness. The client's choices are to righteously withhold the granting of forgiveness and continue to suffer emotionally or grant forgiveness and be released to the possibility of leading a more vitalized life.

Part of your challenge is to make this choice clear to your clients in a nonvalidating way. In talking with your clients about choosing forgiveness, be clear yourself on what it does and does not involve from the perspective of ACT. Because much of what I have to offer on these matters is derived from the treatment of forgiveness by Hayes et al. (1999, pp. 257–258) and Strosahl (2004, pp. 240–241), I encourage you to consult these sources for further details. Perhaps most importantly, forgiveness is not for the transgressors but for the benefit of the client. Clients' claims that those who may have done them wrong don't deserve to be forgiven obscures this issue in two respects. First of all, the more important questions are these: Does the client who can offer forgiveness *deserve* it? What would it do for them? What it might do for the offenders is inconsequential. Second, clients do not have to feel or believe that their transgressors deserve forgiveness for it to be offered. The irrelevance of their feelings and beliefs can be underscored by asking clients if they are willing to offer forgiveness even though they believe that those to whom it is being offered are undeserving.

Also, be clear that forgiveness is not a feeling or emotional state, but an active form of willingness that can be freely chosen. The offering of forgiveness will become hostage to any number of experiential barriers if it is held as a decision rather than a choice. For example, clients may claim that forgiveness can't be offered because they don't feel like forgiving or that they can't forget what others did to them. When forgiveness is held in this way, it becomes conditional on the elimination or induction of certain thoughts, feelings, or other passengers on the bus. Freely chosen forgiveness is unconditional, and clients can offer it even though the mistreatment they suffered at the hands of others is never forgotten.

Another common precondition that clients may establish for the offering of forgiveness is that it must first be requested by the transgressor. This obviously creates an insurmountable obstacle to forgiveness for wrongdoers who have died or whose whereabouts are unknown. Even transgressors with whom clients have continued contact may never seek their forgiveness because they believe they have done no wrong, would see asking for it as an admission that they had, or for any number of other reasons. The bottom line is that forgiveness cannot be conditional on it being requested. Accordingly, through the empty-chair technique and/or letter writing, clients can still offer forgiveness to those who could not possibly ask for it, such as those who are deceased. In the empty-chair technique, ask your clients to offer forgiveness to a transgressor who they imagine to be seated in front of them. In addition, you can instruct them to convey forgiveness in a written letter (which does not have to be sent). These means can also be used by clients to offer forgiveness to those who could request it but don't. Clients can also offer forgiveness to such individuals in speaking to them face to face, but doing so has both advantages and disadvantages. The plus side is that the offering of forgiveness is bolder and less ambiguous. The potential down side is that the offer may be rejected and lead to an argument between client and transgressor about whose version of their relationship is right.

Offering forgiveness to others is also like keeping a commitment. Accordingly, be wary of clients who say that they will *try* to forgive. If necessary, compare forgiving with jumping for your clients. Similar to choosing what height to jump from, clients can select what they are and are not willing to forgive. Once this has occurred, the next choice is to simply jump or not jump, to offer forgiveness or not. Finally, clients may sometimes claim that they would like to forgive someone who abused them in the past, but that they don't know how to do it. Again, liken forgiving to jumping. Trying to jump is not an option, nor is trying to offer forgiveness. The act of jumping requires no effort and occurs naturally when one allows gravity to simply do what it does. The same applies to forgiveness.

The following is an example of speaking to a client about forgiving a father who was abusive to him as a child:

> *I understand that you believe that you wouldn't be depressed today if your father had not treated you the way that he did. Unfortunately there is no way we can change what he did to you. Let's instead give some thought to something you could do right here, right now about what happened. What you have control over and can choose or not choose to offer is forgiveness to your father. In asking you to consider this option, let me make it clear that I'm not suggesting that how you say your father treated you was somehow okay. That's not the issue. The issue is the choice you have before you now and how it may affect your life. The offer of forgiveness I'm asking you to consider is not for your father—it's for you. So whether he deserves to be forgiven, whether you even offer it to him face to face, or whether you never forget what he did to you doesn't really matter here. The question is what offering forgiveness versus withholding it does for you. What if it's the case that withholding forgiveness helps keep you stuck in your depression and offering it might free you up to get on with your life? What if this is the choice you're facing? I say "might free you up" because I don't think either one of us would know for sure how different your life might be if you forgave your father. The only way to know would be to forgive him and find out. One thing though that I think we can say with some certainty is that withholding forgiveness has not helped you get free of your depression. I'm not asking you to try to forgive—there is no trying, only doing. Forgiving is like jumping—either you choose to jump or you don't. This is your choice. Do you choose to offer forgiveness and give yourself the possibility of being freed up to lead a more vital and meaningful life, or do you choose to continue to withhold it and stay stuck?*

I offer one final point: be aware that offering forgiveness may not be a single, terminal act. Rather like willingness and acceptance more generally, you may find that clients offer forgiveness only to later take it back as they re-fuse with the life story. For this reason, forgiveness may have to be reoffered multiple times.

Forgiving oneself. Clients who struggle with guilt over previous transgressions they have committed and/or who regret failed opportunities in the past are likely to benefit from offering forgiveness to themselves. In such circumstances, the transcendent sense of self as context is in a position to freely choose to offer forgiveness to the conceptual self. For this reason, be sure that you have adequately promoted self as context through interventions such as the Chessboard Metaphor and Observer Exercise with clients who are candidates for self-forgiveness. If necessary, mindfulness exercises can also be helpful in preparing clients to consider forgiving themselves. Such practices indirectly help the client contact the sense of self that is capable of offering self-forgiveness.

The same points discussed above for forgiving others—that it is freely chosen as an act of willingness, that trying is not an option, and so on—also apply to the act of clients forgiving themselves. The biggest obstacle to self-forgiveness is often the claim of clients that they somehow don't deserve to be forgiven for past mistakes of commission or omission. Be careful not be lured into taking a thought like "I don't deserve to be forgiven" literally by attempting to restructure it or persuade clients who verbalize it that it is "not true." It is much more productive to focus on the usefulness of "buying into" versus "not buying into" such a thought. Use a defusion strategy and emphasize that guilt-inducing thoughts are more mind chatter by saying something like the following:

> Recall that your mind is not your friend, and one of the things our minds are especially good at is playing the blame game. Put these two together and what do you get? On the one hand, you get a mind that is very good at blaming you for things you did in your life that you now feel ashamed or guilty about, and, on the other hand, you get a mind that's also good at blaming you for not doing other things that you now regret. We could try to convince your mind that it is wrong or mistaken and that the incidents it's blaming you for never even occurred. I suspect you may have already tried that—most of us do—and it hasn't worked, or you wouldn't be here. We could also acknowledge that the things your mind is blaming you for did happen but try to convince your mind that it should stop blaming you for them. Tell me if I'm wrong, but I suspect you've also tried this and it hasn't worked either, or you wouldn't be here. What if it's the case that there is simply no way to get your mind to shut up about what happened and to have it stop finding fault with you about it? Let's talk about what you can control and what choices you have. And by "you" here, I mean that part of you that is not your mind and is not your thoughts and feelings—that part of you that is the chessboard and not the pieces. What I'd like you to consider is that this part of you can choose to forgive yourself despite what your mind may have to say about it. In fact, your mind may get quite upset at the mere thought of forgiving yourself. But this is a choice you can make, and it's not something for your mind to decide. Suppose these are your options. You can choose to continue to withhold the forgiveness that you are capable of offering to yourself and stay stuck in your guilt, shame, and regret, or you can offer forgiveness to yourself and have the possibility of being freed up to lead a more vital and meaningful life.
>
> What if, despite what your mind may be telling you about how you don't deserve forgiveness, it is a gift you can freely give to yourself? Do you choose to give it or withhold it?

As with the act of forgiving others, be prepared to address claims that clients don't know how to forgive themselves. Use the empty-chair technique in which the client as the contextual self offers forgiveness to the conceptual self. Alternatively, clients may also write a letter of forgiveness to themselves much as they could to any other transgressor. Finally, also be ready to reinduce the act of self-forgiveness should clients again become mired in guilt, regret, and self-loathing.

Playing the Martyr Role

Another form of extreme rigidity that precludes increased psychological flexibility occurs when clients have an investment in continuing to play a martyr or victim role (see Hayes et al., 1999, pp. 252–254). Like the refusal to forgive others, it is most likely to unfold with clients who have a life story filled with traumatization and victimization. For this reason, playing the martyr or victim role is not incompatible with the withholding of forgiveness, although it does seem to have its own distinct flavor. In particular, the withholding of forgiveness appears to be a bit more passive in nature: "I have something you [the transgressor] want, but you don't deserve it, and so I'm not going to give it to you." Playing the martyr role has more of an active, vengeful, in-your-face color to it: "You deserve to have me hold up my suffering for you [the transgressor] and for all the world to see how badly I've been treated by you."

The term "role" is being used here not to trivialize this client behavior, but to indicate that it often is played out in an enduring and consistent manner. It's almost as if the client follows a set of rules or script in which he or she is the victim, and select individuals, or sometimes even life itself, are the villains. In fact, if taken to extremes, enacting the role can have tragic and fatal consequences. As suggested by Hayes et al. (1999), remaining depressed for some clients is the functional equivalent of a murder producing a dead body. Just as a corpse is incontrovertible evidence that a homicide has occurred, living a depressed life devoid of vitality and meaning can be presented by clients as proof that they have been subjected to a grievous injustice. In effect, to prove that a crime was committed against them, clients present themselves as the dead body (Hayes et al., p. 253). Unfortunately some clients take this literally rather than figuratively, and playing the martyr role can thus encompass another motive for suicidal behavior. In particular, committing suicide may be seen as the ultimate act of revenge against wrongdoers as exemplified by client comments such as "I'll show them; they'll be sorry when I'm gone."

Killing oneself to get back at others is not incompatible with using suicidality to terminate emotional suffering, and both motives should be assessed with any clients who report a history of suicidal behavior and/or current thoughts of harming themselves. You can usually identify which of your clients are playing the martyr role by merely listening to their life stories. If necessary, ask them about previous and current suicidality and whether they have ever thought of killing themselves as a way of getting even with those who may have done them wrong. At least in my experience, depressed clients with such a suicidal motive have not been reluctant to talk about it. Your challenge thus lies not in identifying which clients of yours may be playing the martyr role, as this is usually fairly obvious, but in undermining the type of fusion that supports it.

Although there is a risk of your clients feeling invalidated, the consequences of not dealing with the issue directly are too great to approach it in a roundabout manner. The following suggestions of what to say are adapted from those offered by Hayes et al. (1999, p. 253) to be somewhat more responsive to the experience of depressed clients:

> *I'd like to have us talk about an issue that you may not like my bringing up. And if you get angry at me for bringing it up, I'm willing to have you be pissed off at me. We can talk about that too, but I want you to know I'm wanting*

us to talk about what I'm bringing up not to make you angry or irritated, but because the stakes involved in not talking about it are simply too great. The issue is not whether others have treated you unfairly. They have. Rather, the issue is how important is it to you to convince those who have harmed you that you have suffered and continue to suffer as a result of their actions? The issue is also how important is it to you to have outsiders see you as someone who has been mistreated by others? And how important is it that these outsiders know who has victimized you? What if the only way you can accomplish all of these important things is to remain victimized by leading a life of depression? As long as you stay stuck in your depression, it becomes evidence for everyone to see of how badly others have mistreated you.

What if it doesn't have to be this way? You have a choice to make here. One option is to continue to have the kind of life you've been leading. You stay stuck in your depression, and doing so holds those who have mistreated you accountable for their actions. The other option is to get unstuck and move ahead in life. The disadvantage of this option is that by getting better, you'd be letting everyone who ever mistreated you off the hook. It wouldn't change the mistreatment, but you would no longer have to continue to suffer to prove that it had occurred. Which is more important to you—leading a valued life or making sure that those who mistreated you don't get away with it? You can't have both. Which do you choose?

If necessary, reassure your clients that you don't question the parts of their life story that detail their mistreatment by others, but only the necessity of having to lead a depressing life as a consequence. Also, be prepared to openly acknowledge and address any anger or hostility expressed toward you for initiating the conversation.

Concurrent Clinical Issues

There are several concurrent clinical issues that you may encounter that can compromise your ability to effectively apply ACT with depressed clients. The two that we will consider in this section arise from clients who present comorbid problems in addition to depression and/or are also receiving other forms of concurrent treatment.

Comorbidity Issues

The odds are that a sizeable percentage of the clients you work with who seek treatment for depression will also exhibit other diagnosable forms of human suffering, particularly anxiety disorders (Brown et al., 2001; Mineka et al., 1998) and/or substance abuse/dependency (Regier et al., 1990). At least screen for the presence of these other co-occurring patterns of behavior and explicitly ask if there are any other problems that the client wishes to address in therapy. Some clients may report coexisting problems but say that they are content with the services they are receiving for them from other health or mental health professionals. This presents a somewhat different challenge, which will be addressed in the section following this one, than the one you face in being the only clinician responsible for offering treatment for multiple client problems.

As I mentioned in chapter 5, up until now only a few studies (Batten & Hayes, 2005; Petersen, 2007) have evaluated the ability of ACT to successfully address concurrent diagnosable problems. While the findings have been promising, they provide an insufficient base from which to derive empirically supported guidelines about how to deal with comorbidity issues in practicing ACT. As I also mentioned in chapter 5, there is some evidence to suggest that it is preferable to treat anxiety before depression (Joorman et al., 2005), but the extent to which such findings from second-generation cognitive behavioral interventions can be generalized to ACT remains unclear.

If anything, the picture that emerges from examining the literature on the treatment of comorbid depression and substance abuse/dependency is even murkier. Because of both funding and training issues (McNeese & DiNitto, 2005), the treatment of clients with both sets of disorders has characteristically occurred in a disjointed manner, with clients typically receiving primary therapy for either depression or substance abuse and only minimal, and often delayed, services for the other problem (Kessler et al., 1996). There have been some efforts to offer more coordinated services to clients who present with both sets of problems (Cross-Drew, 2002), but again not enough research on the concurrent treatment of both (Mueser, Noordsy, Drake, & Fox, 2003) has been conducted to serve as an adequate base for any empirically derived therapeutic guidelines.

As I suggested in chapter 5 and in the absence of any other guidelines to follow, determine as best you can how any copresenting problem, such as generalized anxiety disorder or alcohol dependency, may be functionally related to your client's depression. For example, depressed clients with a diagnosable anxiety disorder have quite likely struggled in trying to run away from their dysphoric mood as well as worries and related emotions. Those who have become dependent upon alcohol may have used intoxication as a means of experiential escape, even though in all likelihood, as Merle Haggard (1966) pointed out, some nights "the bottle let [them] down." Some of the same techniques within ACT used in working with depression, such as those for the promotion of defusion and mindfulness, can easily be extended to include specific private events, like worries and "old memories" that come around, that are more characteristic of other forms of suffering. The particular psychological content that is being addressed may vary from disorder to disorder, but the same experiential-avoidant processes may be in operation. To the degree that this is the case, depression and other co-occurring problems can in effect by treated simultaneously by ACT.

In seems unlikely but nonetheless possible that some of your clients may present other problems, which, at least at first, appear to be functionally independent of their depression. In such circumstances, go ahead and target the depression and, if necessary, address the comorbid disorder afterward. Don't be surprised, however, to find that as you work on depression, the other disorder gets pulled into the process. This is not a problem as it merely suggests that your initial conceptualization that the two problems were functionally independent of each other was incorrect. When this occurs, shift to an integrated approach that addresses the common processes that simultaneously contribute to both.

Concurrent Treatment Issues

You are presented with a differing set of issues by clients who are currently receiving other forms of mental health services at the same time they are seeing you for treatment of their depression. This can occur in at least two ways. Clients may have no comorbid problems but may be receiving additional therapies for depression at the same time. Alternatively, clients may have additional diagnosable problems that are being simultaneously treated by other professionals. It's also possible that both types of concurrent treatment may be present. Under any of these circumstances, a key consideration is how these other treatments may relate to and potentially interact with ACT. It's possible that other types of treatment may complement ACT, but it's also possible that they may work at cross-purposes, thereby compromising the integrity and efficacy of ACT.

Treatment of Depression

Additional concurrent treatment for depression that your clients may be receiving can take several forms, including antidepressant medication and other types of psychotherapy.

Pharmacotherapy. Over the last twenty years, outpatient treatment of depression in this country has increasingly involved the use of antidepressant medication. In the decade from 1987 to 1997, the proportion of depressed clients treated with medication in the United States increased to 75 percent, whereas the percentage of those receiving psychotherapy decreased to 60 percent (Olfson et al., 2002). Not only are more and more depressed individuals being treated with antidepressants, but these medications are increasingly (over 87 percent) being prescribed by nonpsychiatric physicians such as family physicians, general practitioners, and, in the case of women, gynecologists (Olfson et al.).

Because of these trends, you will commonly encounter clients seeking treatment for depression who are already taking medication prescribed by their family physician. Obtain a two-way release from your clients permitting you and their physician to communicate with each other about a comprehensive treatment plan for them.

Unlike with some other cognitive behavioral approaches for treatment of depression (see Hollon, Thase, & Markowitz, 2002), there has been no research to date examining how the combination of pharmacotherapy and ACT compares to ACT alone. Moreover, the two studies comparing ACT to cognitive therapy for depression (Zettle & Hayes, 1986; Zettle & Rains, 1989) screened out participants taking antidepressants. By default then, you are left to make decisions about the advisability of combining ACT and antidepressants on a case-by-case basis. However, even if there was a reasonable body of research comparing ACT alone to ACT plus medication, you would still need to conceptualize how antidepressants fit into a comprehensive treatment plan for each client.

The more functional question to ask is thus not one of whether the combination of the two treatments is generally more efficacious than either alone, but whether it is useful for a given client to simultaneously be taking an antidepressant while being treated with ACT. In considering this question, also ask both yourself and your clients about why the medication is being taken. In short, what purposes does it serve and are they the same as the purposes that ACT serves? In my clinical experience with ACT for depression, the majority of clients who are already taking antidepressants when they present themselves for treatment are doing so for the purpose of mood regulation. However, most of these same clients on their own will also begin to question at least the long-term usefulness of pharmacotherapy as they become more familiar with ACT and begin to consider the futility of the emotional control agenda. This questioning can begin to occur as soon as the next session following the induction of creative hopelessness. As I mentioned previously, I have had clients, for example, return to the session after the presentation of the Person in the Hole Metaphor wondering whether their use of antidepressants was another form of digging. Discuss with your clients any thoughts they may have about discontinuing their medication, but emphasize that the choice to do so or not is theirs. In any event, ensure that any move by clients to discontinue or reduce their medication is discussed with and overseen by their prescribing physician by, if necessary, consulting with them about such plans.

A certain level of energy and vigor may be required by some clients to engage in the forms of committed action integral to living a full and valued life. For this reason, clients who experience insomnia, fatigue, and difficulty in concentrating as part of their depression may be more responsive to ACT by taking medication to minimize such symptoms. Antidepressant medication in such a context does not serve a primary experiential-avoidant function and is therefore less likely to work at cross-purposes with ACT. Rather, it may serve a more restorative function and increase the likelihood that value-directed activity occurs.

Thus far we have considered issues pertinent to clients who enter therapy already taking antidepressant medication. It is also possible that you may encounter clients who are currently not taking medication but may be candidates to do so. Because we have focused on the outpatient treatment of depression, you are likely to find yourself working with fewer such clients than would be the case at an inpatient facility. For this reason, I have never personally referred a client not already taking antidepressants for pharmacotherapy. However, I could imagine doing so with a client who was severely limited in their range of physical activity by the "vegetative signs" of depression (Ward, Bloom, & Friedel, 1979).

A more likely scenario is for your clients at some point in their course of therapy to raise the issue of seeking additional treatment in the form of pharmacotherapy. Temper your response by how many sessions have already occurred, how much progress the client has made to date, and the purpose of taking medication. In particular, encourage clients who raise the issue early in ACT to allow more time to gauge their overall response to it. Regardless of when it occurs, it seems inappropriate to support the pursuit of antidepressants if they are being sought in order "to feel happy" or in other ways serve an emotional control, mood-regulation function. By contrast and as suggested, it does not seem incompatible with ACT to support clients who are considering medication to help alleviate their insomnia, fatigue, and difficulties in concentrating, although other means of providing relief of these symptoms, such as behavioral interventions for insomnia (Smith et al., 2002), should also be considered. ACT itself could also be used to treat insomnia (see Hayes et al., 1999, p. 133), although there has been no published research that I am aware of examining its efficacy in doing so.

Other types of psychotherapy. If you are a psychologist, it is not unethical to accept a client for treatment with ACT who is also receiving psychotherapy for depression elsewhere (American Psychological Association, 2002). However, you are certainly not ethically obligated to accept such individuals as clients, and you are encouraged to give serious consideration to the potential implications of doing so. We will discuss some of the ethical issues involved in concurrent treatment more generally later in this chapter, and if you are not a psychologist, please consult the ethical code of your profession for more guidance on these matters.

Because ACT is a rather unique approach to the treatment of depression (see chapter 1), it is quite likely that any other concurrent psychotherapy would be working at cross-purposes with it. In particular, as discussed in chapter 1, ACT is a second-order approach, whereas many other psychotherapies seek first-order change by altering the form, frequency, or content of problematic psychological events rather than the functions they serve. From this perspective, ACT seeks to discourage experiential control, while many other psychotherapeutic approaches to depression at least implicitly, if not explicitly, seek to foster it. As a consequence, depressed clients being simultaneously treated with ACT and cognitive therapy, for example, would be receiving distinctly different messages about how to respond to their depressing thoughts. While it is possible to rationalize and reframe certain techniques and procedures that are an integral part of other psychological therapies for depression from an ACT-consistent perspective, doing so would likely seriously detract from the overall amount of time and energy available to apply ACT. For all of these reasons, I advise you not to attempt to work with clients who are simultaneously participating in other forms of psychotherapy for depression unless you have established that a conflict with the agenda and purposes of ACT is not present.

Similar concerns would also apply to a situation where one of your existing clients was planning on seeking additional psychological treatment for depression. Discuss your concerns with your client and, if necessary, initiate termination as long as you are assured that he or she will continue his or her treatment for depression with the other therapist.

Treatment of Comorbid Problems

As discussed previously, the most common co-occurring problems for which your depressed clients may be receiving other services are anxiety disorders and substance abuse/dependency. Concurrent treatment of these other problems can potentially compromise the efficacy of ACT for depression to the extent that they work at cross-purposes with it.

Anxiety disorders. From 1987 to 1999 in the United States, the proportion of outpatients receiving medication for treatment of anxiety disorders increased to 70 percent, while the proportion treated with psychotherapy fell below 50 percent (Olfson, Marcus, Wan, & Geissler, 2004). Clients of yours who are being treated by others for an anxiety disorder are thus mostly likely to be receiving pharmacotherapy. Unfortunately the treatment objectives of any medications used to reduce anxiety are typically incompatible with those of ACT and quite likely to convey mixed messages to clients about how to best manage their struggles with anxiety (Eifert & Forsyth, 2005, pp. 251–252).

Especially problematic are the use of benzodiazepines by depressed clients whom you are treating with ACT. Not only can the use of benzodiazepines, such as diazepam (Valium) and alprazolam (Xanax), result in both psychological and physiological dependence (*PDR Drug Guide for Mental Health Professionals*, 2002), but they also appear to attenuate the treatment efficacy of cognitive behavioral interventions for anxiety disorders (Sanderson & Wetzler, 1993; Wardle, 1990). This most likely occurs by anxiolytics interfering with the objective of exposure exercises within behavior therapy. Benzodiazepines minimize anxiety while exposure exercises are often designed to maximize it. ACT for depression does not include exposure exercises as such, but committed action in the world outside of therapy is an integral part of treatment. To the degree that behavioral homework may constitute a form of exposure to anxiety-eliciting stimuli and contexts, the efficacy of ACT might also be compromised by clients taking benzodiazepines while completing such assignments.

Concerns similar to those expressed earlier about clients who are receiving other forms of psychotherapy for depression also extend to instances in which anxiety disorders are being simultaneously treated by other psychotherapists. Clients are not likely to be well-served by receiving treatment approaches that pursue incompatible agendas and which convey conflicting messages to them. Although it is obviously a delicate matter, an ethical course of action is to discuss with potential clients the option of transferring the treatment of any comorbid problems to you. You may risk being accused of stealing another mental health professional's client, but your actions are also consistent with the ethical principles of beneficence and nonmaleficence (American Psychological Association, 2002, p. 1062). Alternatively, you may wish to decline to accept a client for treatment of depression with ACT who is receiving psychotherapy for an anxiety disorder from another therapist.

Substance abuse/dependency. The scenario you are most likely to encounter involving the concurrent treatment of a substance abuse/dependency disorder is of clients participating in AA for alcohol-related problems (Weisner, Greenfield, & Room, 1995). Concerns that such involvement might attenuate the efficacy of ACT are much less than those associated with the other concurrent treatment circumstances that we have considered thus far. As I mentioned previously, the emphasis that 12-step programs in general and AA in particular also place upon experiential acceptance is quite compatible with the agenda and objectives of ACT (Wilson & Byrd, 2004; Wulfert, 1994). I still advise you to monitor your clients' involvement with AA or similar programs. This is not so much to be on the lookout for sources of conflict to minimize between ACT and these approaches as it is to identify opportunities to integrate what your clients may have been exposed to and learned from AA with what you are presenting to them through ACT. If you can do this successfully, the impact of both approaches and the ability of your clients to live a more vital and valued life through the skillful management of their co-occurring struggles with depression and alcohol may be enhanced.

Ethical Considerations

A number of ethical considerations involved in treating depression with ACT have been mentioned previously in this and other chapters. In this last section, we will briefly revisit several of these issues dealing with informed consent, management of suicidality, and concurrent treatment that are pertinent to any psychological approach to the treatment of depression and reclarify how they more specifically apply to ACT. Because I am a licensed psychologist, I will refer to the "Ethical Principles of Psychologists and Code of Conduct" (American Psychological Association, 2002) for guidance in dealing with these matters. If you are not a psychologist, please consult the corresponding set of ethical guidelines for your mental health profession.

Informed Consent

You are ethically obligated to obtain informed client consent to therapy regardless of the nature of the intended treatment. However, your ethical responsibilities in obtaining informed consent for ACT may be somewhat more extensive than for some other treatment options, such as cognitive therapy, because of its overall relative empirical status. According to Standard 10.01 of the APA ethical code, psychologists must inform clients about "the developing nature" of any "treatment for which generally recognized techniques and procedures have not been established" (American Psychological Association, 2002, p. 1072). It is unclear whether ACT for depression does or does not constitute a "developing" treatment as the code does not specify how this term is to be defined or determined. Under such circumstances, a conservative approach, as embodied in the handout "What Is Acceptance and Commitment Therapy?" (see appendix K) that you can give to clients, will ensure that they are being fully informed about ACT before consenting to it. Although ACT has been shown to compare favorably to cognitive therapy of depression (Zettle & Hayes, 1986; Zettle & Rains, 1989), it clearly does not yet enjoy the same breadth and depth of empirical support as cognitive therapy, interpersonal therapy, and behavioral activation to warrant its recognition as another "well-established" treatment for depression at this point in time (Chambless et al., 1996, 1998; Task Force, 1995).

Psychologists are required as part of Standard 10.01 to also inform clients about "alternative treatments that may be available" and "potential risks involved" with the proposed treatment approach (American Psychological Association, 2002, p. 1072). You can also address both of these issues through the client handout "What Is Acceptance and Commitment Therapy?" (see appendix K). Specifically, cognitive, interpersonal, and behavior therapies are mentioned as alternative approaches to depression as well as the possible risk of not responding to ACT, although you may also want to cover these points about informed consent in conversing with your clients.

Management of Suicidality

The APA ethical code does not provide specific standards to guide the management of suicidal clients. However, at least two of the general principles upon which the ethical standards themselves are based appear to be relevant, and ethical issues inherent in how you choose to respond to depressed clients thinking of killing themselves are inescapable. On the one hand, according to Principle A: Beneficence and Nonmaleficence, the behavior of psychologists should benefit their clients and, at the very least, do no harm. However, according to Principle E: Respect for People's Rights and Dignity, psychologists are also expected ethically to honor the self-determination and confidentiality of clients.

An obvious conflict arises between these two aspirational principles if you are faced with the prospect of seeking involuntary hospitalization for suicidal clients. Pursuing this option may protect clients from self-harm but at the cost of violating their confidentiality and autonomy. Not doing so respects their self-determination but at the risk of serious self-harm, if not death.

Because the ethical code does not detail an unambiguous course of action for you to take in managing suicidal behavior, there is also room to temper your response with your own values and morals as well as your personal, philosophical, and religious beliefs about suicide. As Chiles and Strosahl (2005) point out, it is therefore essential that you periodically reevaluate and reclarify your own moral stance on suicide and nonfatal forms of self-harm, for example, to ensure whether the choice to hospitalize clients against their will is indeed to their benefit. Whose interests are best being served by such actions—yours or your client's? As Chiles and Strosahl also stress, the option of resorting to involuntary hospitalization to protect suicidal clients from themselves can be minimized by selecting an approach for reducing suicidality that is designed more to help clients than to reduce your own anxiety and fears. One such approach that is ACT consistent was outlined earlier in this chapter and is discussed in greater detail by Chiles and Strosahl in their book.

Concurrent Treatment

As pointed out earlier and according to Standard 10.04 of the ethical code, it is permissible for psychologists "to offer or provide services to those already receiving mental health services elsewhere" (American Psychological Association, 2002, p. 1073). Just because such behavior is allowed ethically, however, does not mean that it is justifiable ethically. In such matters, the critical question is not whether you would personally feel comfortable working with a client under such circumstances. Rather, the principles of beneficence and nonmaleficence trump all other considerations.

Carefully identify what option you truly believe would be in the best interests of the client involved. Would a potential client who approaches you for treatment of depression with ACT with a co-occurring problem being treated by another mental health professional be better off being seen by you or by being advised to seek services for depression from this other service provider? To arrive at an answer, you may find it necessary to obtain considerable information about the other problem as well as how it is being treated and by whom from both the potential client and, with his or her permission, from the other health care professional as well. As suggested, some types of concurrent treatment, such as attendance at AA meetings by a depressed client with a history of alcohol abuse, appear to be quite compatible with the overall purposes and approach of ACT and therefore are likely to be in the best interests of the client. Other concurrent treatment scenarios, like accepting for treatment a client with a history of taking Xanax for generalized anxiety disorder, may not be, particularly if both the client and the prescribing physician are not open to collaboratively working with you in examining how the pharmacotherapy involved can be integrated with ACT within a comprehensive treatment plan for the client.

Summary

In this chapter, we have covered several issues and challenges that you may encounter in applying ACT with clients who present themselves for treatment of depression. You may find yourself faced with some of the concerns, such as concurrent treatment issues, more frequently than others. The probability that you may encounter some of the issues discussed in this chapter more often than others is itself likely determined by the nature of your practice, among other variables. For example, you may be more likely to have to deal with concurrent treatment issues if you provide services as a staff member at a rural mental health center where clients have limited access to other forms of mental health as well as general health care. You may have little choice but to offer services to any clients who show up at your facility's door, despite whatever types of comorbid problems they present. On the plus side, however, you may also be in a relatively good position to collaborate with your colleagues in designing and implementing a comprehensive treatment plan for your depressed clients.

The types of clients and the most common associated challenges they present to you, by contrast, may be quite different if you have a solo practice in a large urban area with a specialty in treatment of depression. A disadvantage is that you may find it more difficult to consult with peers in managing some of the issues and concerns we have addressed in this chapter. Alternatively though, you may also be in an environment where referrals to other health care providers are more readily available and in which you have somewhat more discretion over which potential clients you accept for treatment with ACT.

Some of the other challenges discussed in this chapter, such as homework noncompliance and forgiveness issues, are presumably less likely to vary as a function of your particular practice niche and are likely to arise across a wide spectrum of clients who struggle with depression. Regardless of whatever challenges you encounter most frequently in applying ACT in your work with depressed clients, I hope that you will find it helpful to refer back to this chapter from time to time for suggestions in how to effectively manage and respond to them.

CHAPTER 11

Wrapping It Up

This chapter marks the end of a trip—that of using ACT with depression. If you are a clinician whose primary concern is effective treatment of clients with depression, the preceding chapters hopefully have provided you with a sufficient foundation in both the theory and application of ACT to do what you want to do—that is, help your clients achieve a vital and vibrant life.

The trip of using ACT with depression, however, is itself embedded in the larger ongoing journey of both ACT and RFT. Some clinicians may want an even fuller picture of ACT—both in where it's come from and where it's going. That is what I seek to offer in this chapter.

Before doing so, however, I'd like to first reiterate how ACT itself is most usefully understood. In particular, the perspectives on where ACT has been and where it is headed may be determined by whether ACT is more usefully thought of as a set of therapeutic techniques or as an integrated paradigmatic approach to the alleviation of human suffering within which such techniques are themselves situated. I will argue for the latter.

ACT as a Paradigmatic Approach

The term "paradigm" is being used here in the Kuhnian (1962) sense of referring to a scientific worldview or conceptual framework within which scientists work. What primarily distinguishes one paradigmatic approach from others are philosophical differences. Accordingly, the extent to which ACT can be regarded as a paradigmatic approach is ultimately dependent upon distinct fundamental assumptions it makes about the nature of psychological science itself and human behavior that distinguish it from other conceptual frameworks within which the alleviation of human suffering can be approached. However, as Hayes (1978) has argued, paradigms within behavioral approaches to clinical psychology can be usefully thought of as encompassing multiple levels of analysis that, while based on differing underlying philosophical positions, extend beyond them to also entail conceptual, methodological, and technical differences as well.

Philosophical Level of Analysis

As we discussed in chapter 1, ACT is philosophically grounded in functional contextualism (Hayes, 1993). From this perspective, all behavior—including the presenting problems of your clients, your conducting ACT, as well as my writing about it and investigating it scientifically—are viewed as "acts in context" (Pepper, 1942). Stated somewhat differently, the philosophical tradition that serves as the foundation for ACT holds that all behavior is most usefully viewed as the interaction of a whole organism in and with historical and situational contexts (Hayes, 1993).

The historical context for your clients' behavior includes their past individual learning experiences and lifetime of unique personal events. The situational context in which their behavior occurs includes their physical and social environments, including your interactions with them in therapy. While you are powerless to literally change the personal histories of your clients, you nevertheless may be able within ACT to alter the functional impact that previous life events have on their behavior by helping your clients retell the stories that they have constructed about them. You are also unlikely to be able to directly change the external world of clients. However, you may be able to indirectly effect changes in the physical environment of your clients through the impact of your in-session behavior upon that of your clients. As noted, your behavior as an ACT therapist is part of the situational context of which the behavior of your clients is a function. Alter your behavior, and that of your clients may also change.

There are certainly philosophical perspectives other than functional contextualism, such as descriptive contextualism (Hayes, 1993) or mechanism (Hayes & Brownstein, 1986), in which ACT could be grounded. Moreover, the selection of one "ism" over others for this purpose cannot be justified or rationalized on the basis of any standards or criteria that somehow transcend a philosophical level of analysis (Hayes, 1993). In effect, you could freely choose to think about ACT from a differing philosophical perspective, although doing so has rather profound implications. This is because the array of differing philosophical positions upon which ACT could be based each have their own distinct truth criteria that define them as separate, identifiable paradigms (Pepper, 1942). The truth criterion for contextualism more generally is "successful working" (Pepper, 1942). Functional contextualism, as opposed to descriptive contextualism, is even more explicitly pragmatic in its focus in identifying the ability to predict and influence behavior (Hayes, 1993) with adequate scope, precision, and depth (Biglan & Hayes, 1996; Hayes, 1995; Hayes, Follette, & Follette, 1995; Hayes & Hayes, 1992) as its truth criterion. By contrast, for example, the truth criterion of mechanism is "correspondence-based" (Pepper, 1942) in that it evaluates an explanation of behavior by how well it maps onto what is already known and is subsequently "discovered" about that particular behavior.

Functional contextualism is not better than mechanism, for instance, in any meaningful sense of that term, but it is clearly different (Zettle, 1990). In effect, a mechanist would appropriately judge a theory, such as RFT, based upon the degree to which it accurately makes predictions about cognitive phenomena. For example, how well does the model that RFT presents about human language explain what is known about the cognitive development of children? An alternative model that affords more accurate predictions about the way the world of human language and cognition are arranged would justifiably be viewed as being superior to RFT. By contrast, the critical question for the functional contextualist about RFT centers on the degree to which it better enables us, for example, to teach language and cognitive skills to populations with developmental disabilities (Carr, 2003). Note that the same standard applies to ACT in that it must, and will, ultimately be judged on its pragmatic ability to alleviate human suffering more generally and depression in particular. Because RFT provides the conceptual account of human language upon which ACT is based and both were developed alongside each other (Zettle, 2005, 2006), any practical limitations on ACT from a functional contextualistic perspective also have repercussions for the status of RFT.

Conceptual Level of Analysis

Many therapeutic approaches have their own unique terms and concepts that are used in talking about clinical phenomena, and ACT (as you have perhaps painfully realized by now) is no exception. The differences in how proponents of divergent therapeutic approaches talk about what they do themselves do not occur by mere happenstance, but rather can be linked back to differences at a philosophical level of analysis. ACT is quite understandably based upon RFT as it offers a functional contextualistic account of human language and cognition. You can certainly talk and think about ACT differently than it has been presented in this book, and you in fact should if you are to remain faithful to any philosophical perspective that differs from functional contextualism. What you would be talking about, however, at least at both philosophical and conceptual levels of analysis, would no longer be ACT as the functional contextualist knows it.

Certainly RFT does not represent the only set of terms and principles that uniquely define ACT, although it clearly constitutes the most comprehensive as well as complex conceptual framework that can be used in talking about ACT. Other ACT-specific terms and concepts involve, but are not limited to, the hexaflex itself as well as the processes, such as defusion and the contextual self, that comprise it. Regardless of whether single concepts such as experiential avoidance or more complex networks of them, such as RFT itself, are involved, all talk about ACT and its perspective on human suffering are merely more grist for the functional contextualistic mill.

Recall, as just discussed, that functional contextualism views all behavior, even the languaging of relational frame theorists and the seemingly esoteric ways of writing and talking about ACT, through its pragmatic lens. From this perspective, all words and even scientific concepts are regarded as merely tools that have been created to perform certain jobs. RFT was not "discovered" in the sense that it somehow preexisted in an independent reality until it was stumbled upon. Rather, it was created and constructed as a more useful way to think about thinking and must be evaluated by this same truth criterion. If they continue to be useful, both ACT and RFT will have some staying power. If not, they will be replaced by other, more pragmatic ways of talking about languaging and how to maximize its benefits while minimizing its "dark side." Even if they are not ultimately replaced, both ACT and RFT will still have to be modified and to evolve over time if progress in understanding and in alleviating human suffering is to continue. In fact, it is entirely possible that some of what I have written in this book will be obsolete by the time you read it. For example, the hexaflex seems to be a useful way to presently conceptualize the key processes that contribute to psychological flexibility, but adding to or subtracting some processes from it may ultimately prove to be more functional. Tools get replaced by new and improved versions of them that can do a better job of doing what they were designed to do. RFT may replace Skinner's (1957) interpretation of verbal behavior not because he was wrong, but because RFT is shown to be a more useful way of talking about talking.

Methodological Level of Analysis

As it applies to therapeutic approaches, this level of analysis involves certain general and strategic ways of making contact with the world of abnormal behavior and human suffering (Hayes, 1978). Methodologically, ACT is not unique among therapeutic approaches in its relative reliance upon the use of metaphors, analogies, logical paradoxes, and experiential exercises to reduce psychological rigidity and promote psychological flexibility. However, ACT relies upon such strategies for therapeutic change certainly to greater extent than most other cognitive behavioral approaches, particularly those that emphasize first-order change.

Such methodological differences across even seemingly similar approaches to therapy do not occur by mere chance. Rather, differences at a methodological level of analysis exist because of distinctions at a conceptual level of analysis. ACT accordingly emphasizes the therapeutic methods it does because of the account of human language provided by RFT. If human suffering is an inevitable by-product of relational framing, trying to contact and alleviate it through primary verbal means is likely to make the problem bigger rather than smaller. The phenomenon of thought suppression is a simple yet powerful example of this (Wegner, 1994). As should be obvious, especially as seen in chapter 9, ACT does not eliminate all verbal interactions between you and your clients. However, the use of advice, instructions, and rule following are kept to a relative minimum in favor of nonverbal ways of weakening the negative effects of language. Metaphors and logical paradoxes, for example, are both presented verbally but constitute particularly effective ways of undermining the normal tendency to take words literally. Moreover, experiential exercises, such as that involving the Chinese finger cuffs, can be useful even with very little being said between you and your clients. Sometimes saying little speaks volumes.

Technical Level of Analysis

This level of analysis is more concerned with the specific ways in which therapeutic strategies within ACT are enacted. For example, there are any number of techniques such as the Milk, Milk, Milk and Revocalization exercises that can be used to promote defusion from automatic thoughts. As Hayes (1978) pointed out, the potential overlap across therapeutic paradigms increases as movement occurs from the philosophical and conceptual levels of analysis to those involving treatment methods and techniques. ACT has created some of its own techniques but has also borrowed methods, such as the use of metaphors, as well as specific techniques, such as the Observer Exercise from the psychosynthesis of Assagioli (1965), from other paradigmatic perspectives and will quite likely continue to do so. The purpose in using techniques within ACT that have been developed by other therapeutic traditions, however, is often quite different. For example, progressive muscle relaxation (PMR) is often included as a treatment component to control anxiety within traditional forms of behavior therapy (Brown, O'Leary, & Barlow, 2001; Craske & Barlow, 2001). PMR could also be incorporated within ACT but as a way to promote mindfulness rather than minimize anxiety. That is, clients could be encouraged, for instance, to just notice changes in their bodily sensations and other private events as they transition from the nonrelaxed to relaxed states.

Other techniques that ACT for depression may share with other therapeutic approaches have been designed and developed independently of each other to serve different strategic purposes. For instance, ACT, cognitive therapy, and behavioral activation all include behavioral homework as an integral part of treatment. The intended function of such assignments, however, differs considerably across the three approaches. Behavioral homework is used within ACT to enact values, within cognitive therapy to restructure dysfunctional thoughts and beliefs, and within behavioral activation to regulate mood. From a paradigmatic perspective, techniques within ACT should never be viewed as mere tools that exist independently of the strategic purposes for which they can be used.

ACT as a Paradigmatic Approach: A Summary

ACT can either be viewed as a set of therapeutic methods and related techniques or as a paradigmatic approach that is uniquely defined by its grounding in functional contextualism and RFT. The choice is yours to make. While I obviously prefer the latter perspective, from the standpoint of functional contextualism, my choice can only be defended on pragmatic grounds. It is my belief that ACT can be used more effectively and creatively if it is seen as a paradigmatic approach. In short, I contend that you will likely be a more flexible and skillful practitioner of ACT if you hold it as being much more than a mere collection of metaphors and experiential exercises. At the same time, to my knowledge it has never been demonstrated that "ACT technicians" are any less effective than those Acceptance and Commitment therapists who endorse functional contextualism and are fluent in RFT.

Looking Backward

Looking backward—from the point we've come to in this book itself and in the development of ACT more generally and ACT for depression more specifically—may be useful not only to better appreciate what ground has already been covered, but also to sharpen our focus in looking forward as we seek to navigate the territory still ahead of us. What is now known as ACT developed over the last quarter century from what was initially known as "comprehensive distancing" (Zettle, 2005, 2006) and somewhat later as "contextual therapy" (Zettle & Rains, 1989) or a "contextual approach" (Hayes, 1987; Zettle & Hayes, 1986). The use of the terms "acceptance and commitment therapy" (Wilson, Khorakiwala, & Hayes, 1991) and "ACT" itself (Wilson & Taylor, 1991) first occurred in two presentation titles in 1991 and did not initially appear in a publication until three years later (Hayes & Wilson, 1994). It is thus easy to understand why some might mistakenly misperceive ACT as a therapeutic approach that is somewhat of a novelty and "new kid on the block," especially in light of the increased visibility it has received more recently (Cloud, 2006; Haaga, 2004; Hayes & Smith, 2005; Hayes & Strosahl, 2004).

Another factor that probably contributes to the impression that ACT has a much shorter history than it does stems from the considerable gap that existed from the time of the initial outcome research comparing an early version of it to cognitive therapy of depression in the mid to late 1980s (Zettle & Hayes, 1986; Zettle & Rains, 1989) until the publication of the 1999 book (Hayes et al.) a decade later. In retrospect, these two comparative outcome studies were probably ahead of their time or, at the very least, ahead of additional work needed to further articulate and develop the philosophical and conceptual levels of analysis for ACT to emerge as a fully integrated paradigmatic approach. Nevertheless, their overall findings suggested that there might be something there worthy of further pursuit.

The Transitional Period

The development of functional contextualism and RFT as the philosophical and conceptual bases, respectively, for ACT occurred during a transitional period (Zettle, 2006), roughly running from around the mid to late 1980s until the turn of the century and publication of the first ACT (Hayes et al., 1999) and RFT books (Hayes et al., 2001).

Philosophical Developments

Contextualism, more generally, was initially offered as a philosophical alternative to mechanism (Hayes & Brownstein, 1986; Hayes et al., 1988). Hayes (1993) subsequently further sharpened the philosophical foundations of ACT by differentiating functional contextualism from both the descriptive contextualism of Kantor's (1959) interbehaviorism and what he regarded as the implicit contextualism of Skinner's (1953) radical behaviorism. ACT should ultimately be judged on its pragmatic ability to prevent and alleviate human suffering. These goals themselves are embedded in values that can be explicitly stated but not justified.

Conceptual Developments

The process of developing a functional contextualistic account of human language and cognition that would culminate in the publication of the RFT book (Hayes et al., 2001) began with a 1985 paper by Hayes and Brownstein. They not only used and defined "relational frames" for the first time, but also outlined a research program for training and testing for relational framing that subsequently stimulated a program of basic research in this area (Devany, Hayes, & Nelson, 1986; Steele & Hayes, 1991). In addition, Hayes and Brownstein departed from Skinner's views of verbal behavior (1957) and rule-governance (1969) in reconceptualizing verbal behavior as "speaking and listening" (p. 22). Additional conceptual publications by Hayes and his colleagues in this transitional period (Hayes & Hayes, 1989; Hayes et al., 1989) in the area of rule-governance would result in it being ultimately conceptually subsumed within RFT (Hayes et al., 2001).

Looking Forward

While additional conceptual refinements to ACT are likely to continue for it to function and further develop as a paradigmatic approach to the prevention and alleviation of human suffering, a greater share of the work in the future is likely to be empirical in nature. In particular, more comparative outcome, treatment utility, and process research are all needed for ACT to continue to progress.

Comparative Outcome Research

One effect of the movement within psychology to recognize the efficacy of some interventions as empirically supported (Chambless et al., 1996, 1998; Task Force, 1995) has been to increase the importance of comparative outcome research for an intervention such as ACT for depression. In effect, for ACT to enjoy the same recognition and empirical status as cognitive therapy (Beck et al., 1979), interpersonal therapy (Klerman et al., 1984), and behavioral activation (Jacobson et al., 1996, 2001) it must be shown in several independent studies to be just as efficacious in treating depression as these other approaches. Such acknowledgment has not only scientific but also practical and financial implications to the extent that managed mental-health-care organizations may increasingly require system providers to offer empirically supported interventions for depression (Sanderson, 2003). While it might also be useful for both scientific and political purposes at some point to compare ACT for depression versus antidepressants alone, and the two in combination with each other, clearly the more pressing need at the moment is to further evaluate ACT against other empirically supported psychotherapies for depression.

Unfortunately, the process of determining the empirical status of a given intervention's efficacy is disorder specific, which works to the relative disadvantage of a transdiagnostic approach such as ACT. That is, the status of an *entire* approach—whether it be ACT, cognitive therapy, or behavior therapy—is not determined to be empirically supported, but it is instead based upon an approach's relative efficacy in treating each *DSM-IV* (1994) diagnosis on a disorder-by-disorder basis. Thus, the empirical status of ACT (for instance, in alleviating suffering in clients with generalized anxiety disorder) within this recognition system has no implications for its acknowledgment as an efficacious treatment of depression.

While this approach has a certain undeniable logic to it—an intervention that is effective with one disorder might be inefficacious or even harmful with another—it is hostage to a diagnostic system that differentiates one disorder from another on the basis of topographical features rather than functional properties of behavior (Hayes et al., 1996). Moreover, with an ever-expanding diagnostic system (Follette & Houts, 1996), the task of documenting a treatment approach's efficacy on a disorder-by-disorder basis becomes virtually interminable. An alternative system that placed more emphasis on the identification of empirically supported principles of change (Rosen & Davison, 2003) would not only be friendlier to ACT but also would quite likely be more pragmatic in ultimately advancing the science of clinical psychology and our ability to effectively address a broad range of abnormal behavior and human suffering. We will further discuss the need for additional process psychotherapy research in general and that specifically pertaining to ACT for depression after first considering the potential benefits of treatment utility research.

Treatment Utility Research

At least one-third of depressed clients fail to show a favorable response even when treated with an empirically supported treatment such as cognitive therapy (Hollon et al., 2002). Thus, even if the findings of additional comparative outcome research are consistent with those from earlier studies (Zettle & Hayes, 1986; Zettle & Rains, 1989), for instance, in suggesting that ACT is comparable to cognitive therapy in alleviating depression, it would be only a relative accomplishment. I believe we can and must do better in assisting clients who struggle with depression. One way of accomplishing this goal may be through treatment utility research.

Treatment utility is concerned with the degree to which psychological assessment contributes to an intervention's outcome and is a natural extension of applying a functional contextualistic perspective to assessment more broadly (Hayes et al., 1987). For example, the use of a specific inventory, such as the PVQ (Blackledge & Ciarrochi, 2005) or VLQ (Wilson & Groom, 2002), or even a more strategic approach to guide ACT, such as the case-conceptualization approach recommended in this book, could be said to have treatment utility if ACT was reliably shown to be more effective when such assessment practices were performed versus when they were not. To the degree that the assessment in question purports to evaluate psychological processes contributing to human suffering, or those involved in potentially alleviating it, treatment utility studies of this sort can also be construed as a type of process research that may help elucidate mechanisms of therapeutic change.

Unfortunately there has been an overall lack of treatment utility research in general and within the assessment and treatment of depression in particular (Nelson-Gray, 2003). I know of no publishable treatment utility research involving ACT, and with few exceptions (McKnight, Nelson-Gray, & Barnhill, 1992; Zettle, Haflich, & Reynolds, 1992; Zettle & Herring, 1995), also no investigations pertaining to cognitive therapy of depression. This should not be surprising in light of testing standards endorsed by the American Psychological Association (American Educational Research Association, 1999) that make no mention of treatment utility as an alternative to psychometric standards in evaluating the quality of psychological assessment.

One area in which treatment utility research might prove useful would be in providing a better understanding of the processes that contribute to responsivity versus nonresponsivity to differing therapies for depression. For example, it may well be that the one-third of depressed clients who fail to respond to cognitive therapy may not be the same as the one-third who fail to respond to ACT. Perhaps measures designed to assess processes critical to each approach, such as the DAS (Weissman & Beck, 1978) for cognitive therapy and the AAQ (Hayes, Strosahl, & Wilson et al., 2004) for ACT, could be used to identify at pretreatment depressed clients who are more likely to respond to one of the approaches than the other. If the nonresponsive subgroups to each approach do not completely overlap, our overall ability to efficiently and efficaciously alleviate depression should be enhanced. In effect, depressed clients who may not be good candidates for cognitive therapy may be more responsive to ACT and vice versa. Whether these possibilities constitute realities must await further research. My lab is currently involved in a collaborative project designed to provide at least some initial answers to these questions, but as this is being written, it is not far enough along to even report any preliminary findings.

Process Research

Process research that extends beyond that examining treatment utility is likely to be required if the identification of empirically supported principles of change is to be successful. The hope is that such mechanisms of change could then be maximized by perhaps better focusing and strengthening treatment strategies and techniques that target them. There are two challenges as I see it that must be met if further process research within ACT for depression is to realize this possibility. One is hardly unique to ACT, whereas the other, at least relative to other cognitive behavioral approaches for the treatment of depression, is.

Explicit vs. Implicit Measures

Thus far, the most widely used measure to investigate the mechanisms of change that may account for therapeutic improvement within ACT has been the AAQ (Hayes et al., 2006). While the AAQ is often construed as an index of experiential avoidance, it seems more useful to view it as providing a broadband measure of psychological flexibility. Regardless of how the AAQ itself is conceptualized, research that has used it as a process measure has produced a cumulative body of findings that is broadly supportive of the process model upon which ACT is based (Hayes et al., 2006).

As mentioned previously, measures have not yet been developed to assess all of the processes that are thought to contribute to psychological flexibility/inflexibility. Accordingly, measures that are more process specific than the AAQ will need to be designed If the relative degree to which separate mechanisms of change contribute to overall therapeutic improvement in ACT is to be more fully understood. This issue, however, is overshadowed by the concern that all of the measures to my knowledge that have been used thus far, including the AAQ, to assess ACT-related processes are explicit in nature. The AAQ, for example, is a self-report measure whose items are at least semitransparent, especially to subjects who may be asked to complete it after some exposure to ACT. Consequently, the AAQ appears to be susceptible to demand characteristics in that subjects, for example, may answer it at posttreatment in a way that they believe their Acceptance and Commitment therapist would like them to. To the extent that subjects can also discern what it is apparently assessing, the AAQ and other possible process measures (such as the PVQ and VLQ) may be further vulnerable to outright faking (either good or bad) on the part of subjects.

One way of addressing this concern is to use overt behavioral and/or physiological measures that may be less susceptible than paper-and-pencil inventories to demand characteristics and response sets to assess therapeutic process variables. Dermot Barnes-Holmes and his colleagues (Barnes-Holmes et al., 2006; Barnes-Holmes, Healy, & Hayes, 2000) have recently developed yet another strategy based upon RFT, the Implicit Relational Assessment Procedure (IRAP), that may show even greater promise in assessing processes of relevance to ACT. Specifically, like the Implicit Association Test (IAT; Greenwald, McGhee, & Schwartz, 1998) to which it is sometimes compared, the IRAP similarly presents subjects with a computer-based task that requires them to respond as quickly but also as accurately as possible. As implicit measures, both the IRAP and IAT are based on the premise that subjects can respond faster to stimuli that are closely associated with each other, such as "tulip" and "love," than those that are not, such as "spider" and "love." However, because the IRAP, unlike the IAT, can assess not only the strength of the association between concepts but also the nature of that relationship, it is likely to be more useful in ultimately developing implicit measures of some of the same processes that are thought to contribute to psychological flexibility and therapeutic change within ACT.

The potential promise of the IRAP for developing implicit measures of process variables relevant to ACT is suggested by two recent studies. In one, an IRAP designed to assess self as concept yielded predictable differences when it was administered to undergraduates and two groups of prisoners (Vahey, Barnes-Holmes, Barnes-Holmes, & Stewart, 2006). Specifically, undergraduates and prisoners incarcerated under less restrictive conditions because of good behavior evidenced higher levels of self-esteem as assessed by the IRAP than prisoners who had not yet earned such privileges. These differences also paralleled those seen when self as concept was assessed with an explicit, self-report measure.

Implicit measures such as the IAT and IRAP should ideally not only be significantly correlated with an explicit measure of the same variable under conditions where demand characteristics and biasing response sets are minimized, but also be demonstrably less vulnerable to them when they are present. Research that has evaluated the susceptibility of the IAT to faking has been somewhat inconsistent with at least one study reporting no effect (Egloff & Schmukle, 2002), while three others have indicated that the IAT can be successfully faked, especially when subjects have prior experience with the procedure and are instructed in how to fake their responses (Fiedler & Bluemke, 2005; Kim, 2003; Steffens, 2004). By contrast, a second recent study by Barnes-Holmes and his research group (McKenna, Barnes-Holmes, Barnes-Holmes, & Stewart, 2006) suggests that the IRAP, unlike the IAT, cannot be faked even when subjects are told how to do so.

It should be noted, however, that the specific IRAP procedure evaluated in this study was not being used to assess a clinically relevant measure. A next logical step in the development of implicit process measures that are ACT relevant is to evaluate whether the IRAP is similarly immune to faking when it is specifically used to assess such variables.

Some work of this sort is currently underway in my research lab but has not progressed far enough as of this writing to report any preliminary findings.

Therapeutic Outcome Measures

The primary measures of therapeutic outcome considered in determining the empirical status of interventions for depression (Chambless et al., 1996, 1998; Task Force, 1995) have reflected symptomatic relief, such as pre- to posttreatment reductions in BDI-II scores (Beck et al., 1996). For this reason, future comparative outcome research involving ACT must also continue to use such symptomatic measures if it is to ever be recognized as a well-established intervention for depression. However, the analysis of treatment effects should not be limited to such measures given that ACT is somewhat unique among cognitive behavioral approaches in recognizing that therapeutic improvement should go beyond mere symptomatic relief to also include changes in valued living. From this perspective, a demonstrated reduction in level of depression is necessary, but not sufficient, in determining the intended therapeutic impact of ACT.

As witnessed by the relatively recent growth of "positive psychotherapy" (Seligman, Rashid, & Parks, 2006), ACT is not the only approach that has recognized the advantages of expanding therapeutic outcome measures to include growth in leading a valued and meaningful life. An immediate challenge is to identify or develop measures that capture such changes that can be used along with those that reflect reductions in the signs and symptoms of depression to evaluate the relative therapeutic impact of ACT. It may well be that existing measures developed either independently of ACT, such as the Satisfaction with Life Scale (SWLS; Diener, Emmons, Larsen, & Griffin, 1985), or in close association with it, like the VLQ (Wilson & Groom, 2002), will be found to be useful for this purpose. If not, further quality-of-life type measures will need to be developed.

The current lack of demonstrable measures that reflect psychological growth in leading a more valued life unfortunately presents a challenge to process as well as comparative outcome research involving ACT. This is because changes in therapeutic processes ultimately must be evaluated within the context of more global improvements in psychological flexibility and valued living as outcome measures. For example, finding that changes in the AAQ mediate reductions in BDI-II scores would certainly provide some support for the model upon which ACT for depression is based. However, more definitive support would be dependent upon showing that changes in ACT-specific process measures are reliably linked to predictable increases in valued living. From this vantage point, an instrument like the VLQ might be construed as both a process measure for depressive symptomatic relief as well as a possible outcome measure more reflective of increased psychological flexibility. In any event, therapeutic process and outcome measures cannot be meaningfully evaluated independently of each other. Because they are inextricably linked in this way, the dual challenges of developing process measures that are not susceptible to demand characteristics and outcome measures that go beyond mere symptomatic relief must be satisfactorily met if process research in ACT more generally and that specific to its application to depression is to move forward.

Summary and Conclusions

For a few of you, the end of this book will in all likelihood also mark the end of your exposure to ACT. If this is the case, I hope that what you may have garnered from reading this book will at least in some small way ultimately benefit the depressed clients with whom you work in your clinical practice. For example, ACT itself may be another therapeutic option that you may wish to try with depressed clients who have not shown a favorable response to other treatment approaches. Additionally, you may also want to strategically integrate some specific techniques or procedures covered within this book with other interventions you more commonly use.

I hope, however, that most of you by this point will have some interest in learning more about ACT and perhaps in even receiving further training in it. If so, the most useful thing for you to do at this point is to join the Association for Contextual Behavioral Science (ACBS) through its website at www.contextualpsychology.org. Membership is available at several levels, for both professionals and students, with annual dues quite reasonable relative to those of other psychological associations and organizations. At present, there are over twenty-eight hundred members in ACBS, representing twenty-four countries and varied mental health professions, thus reflecting the growth of ACT beyond its origination in this country. The internationalization of ACT and RFT is further exemplified by the ACBS sponsorship of world conferences in Sweden in 2004 and in London in 2006 with summer institutes held in this country in 2003, 2005, and 2007.

The ACBS website is the place to go if you wish to pursue further training in ACT. It routinely posts workshops and other training opportunities in ACT as well as clinical resources, presentation materials, treatment manuals, and ACT videos. While the majority of ACBS members are Acceptance and Commitment therapists, the website also serves as a resource for those who have a further or primary interest in RFT. For example, an RFT tutorial is accessible as well as a listing of updated research and publications in the area.

Another convenient way to learn more about ACT and/or RFT is through joining separate Listservs available for each (accessible only to ACBS members). You can pose questions to other members, make comments, or if you prefer, simply monitor the postings of others.

There is, however, yet another Listserv, ACT_for_the_Public@yahoogroups.com, available that does not require ACBS membership and which can also serve as a learning tool for those of you who wish to become more acquainted with ACT. As its name suggests, this Listserv functions primarily as a forum in which nonprofessionals from the public and even clients can post questions and comments to be addressed by Acceptance and Commitment therapists.

I hope that there may yet be a third and final subgroup of readers of this book—those of you who may not only wish to receive further training in ACT or learn more about it and RFT, but may also have an interest in contributing in some way to the scientific support of ACT. The opportunity, resources, and support to do so are clearly greater for those of you who have academic appointments at research universities than those of you who are mental health professionals. However, even those of you who are full-time psychotherapists can still make a valuable contribution to the scientific base of ACT. In particular, as Hayes (1981) has pointed out, the use of single-subject designs can be readily integrated with effective clinical practice. For example, a series of AB designs, where A represents a pretreatment baseline and B denotes a treatment course of ACT, could be compiled in a multiple-baseline fashion, with the BDI-II administered weekly across both phases to monitor client changes in depression over time. In addition, an instrument such as the VLQ could also be administered at pre- and posttreatment as a quality-of-life measure to evaluate therapeutic improvement that extends beyond mere symptomatic relief. While AB designs alone are not recognized by the task force responsible for identifying empirically supported treatments (Chambless et al., 1996, 1998; Task Force, 1995), other single-subject experiments in which ACT would be compared to another intervention are. Thus, those of you who see a fair number of depressed clients in your clinical practice have an opportunity to engage in research that could potentially further our evaluation of the empirical status of ACT for depression.

Obviously it is easier to look backward to see the pathways that what is now known as ACT has taken to arrive at where it is today than to have a clear vision of where it is headed. In this concluding chapter, I have suggested three somewhat different yet related directions—involving comparative outcome, treatment utility, and process research—that I believe will be useful for ACT to increasingly move toward if it is to reach its ultimate goal of preventing and alleviating human suffering, in general, and that which comes from struggling with depression, in particular. Whether ACT can move forward with equal success in all three directions and whether what may be learned in the process of doing so will prove to be useful in realizing this objective can only be determined as the ongoing journey that ACT has been on continues. It is a journey on which all fellow travelers are welcome.

APPENDIX A

ACT Initial Case Conceptualization Form

<table>
<tr>
<td>1.</td>
<td>Presenting problem(s) in client's own words:
Client initial goals (What does he/she want from therapy?):
ACT reformulation of presenting problem:</td>
</tr>
<tr>
<td>2.</td>
<td>What core thoughts, emotions, memories, sensations, situations is the client unwilling to experience?

Thoughts

Emotions

Memories

Other</td>
</tr>
<tr>
<td>3.</td>
<td>What does the client do to avoid these experiences?

Suicidality (e.g., thoughts of suicide, previous attempts)

Internal control strategies (e.g., rumination, worrying, thought suppression)

External control strategies (e.g., "self-medication," eating, shopping)

Situationally specific control strategies (e.g., behavioral passivity, social withdrawal)

In-session control strategies (e.g., changing the topic, evasiveness)</td>
</tr>
</table>

4.	Relevant motivational factors (e.g., what is the cost of this behavior in terms of daily living, client's experience of unworkability, clarity of values, therapeutic relationship):
5.	Environmental barriers to change (e.g., negative contingencies, unsupportive home/social environment, unchangeable circumstances, financial circumstances, costs of changing):
6.	Factors contributing to psychological inflexibility (e.g., excessive rule-governance, "being right," reason giving, figuring things out, low distress tolerance, lack of present-moment awareness, excessive attachment to the conceptualized self):
7.	Given the above, what core processes and related ACT interventions may need to be addressed and emphasized in treatment?
8.	Client strengths:
9.	Initial ACT treatment plan:

APPENDIX B

Taking Inventory

Instructions: Use this form to make a list of your reactions to circumstances, events, or situations that you find depressing. The circumstances may include simply thinking about something that occurred in the past (like recalling the death of a loved one) as well as some event that just happened (such as having a disagreement with your spouse).

Triggering Event or Circumstance

In the space below, write down the event, situation, or circumstance that you found depressing.

_____

_____

_____

_____

_____

_____

_____

Thoughts

In the space below, list all of the thoughts you have in reaction to the triggering event or circumstance. Preface each thought with "I have the thought that [and then the specific thought]."

_____

_____

_____

_____

_____

_____

_____

_____

Emotions

In the space below, list all of the feelings and emotions you have in reaction to the triggering event or circumstance. Preface each feeling with "I have a feeling of [and then the specific feeling]."

_____

_____

_____

_____

_____

_____

_____

Bodily Sensations and Feelings

In the space below, list all of the bodily sensations and physical feelings you have in reaction to the triggering event or circumstance. Preface each feeling with "I have a sensation of [and then the specific bodily sensation or physical feeling]."

_____

_____

_____

_____

_____

_____

_____

Memories

In the space below, list all of the memories you have in reaction to the triggering event or circumstance. Preface each memory with "I have the memory of [and then the specific memory]."

_____

_____

_____

_____

_____

_____

_____

_____

Other Reactions

In the space below, list any other unpleasant reactions (such as images or impulses) you have in reaction to the triggering event or circumstance. Preface each reaction by specifying its type, such as "I have the impulse to [and then the specific impulse]."

_____

_____

_____

_____

_____

_____

_____

_____

APPENDIX C

Reasons for Depression Exercise

Instructions: This exercise has five steps. It is recommended that you complete each in the order they are listed on this form.

Step 1: In the space below, list as many reasons as you can think of for why you are depressed. Please list each reason on a separate line and leave the space in front of each line blank for the time being.

_____

_____

_____

_____

_____

_____

_____

Step 2: In the space below, list other *good* reasons for becoming depressed even if you believe that they do not apply to you. In addition to the reasons listed in step 1, what would be some other good reasons for being depressed? Please list each reason on a separate line and leave the space in front of each line blank for the time being.

_____

_____

_____

_____

_____

_____

_____

_____

Step 3: Now go back and rate how good each of the reasons that you listed in step 1 and step 2 are for being depressed. Place your rating for each reason in the space in front of each line according to the following scale:

1	2	3	4	5	6	7	8	9	10
Fairly Good									Very Good

Step 4: In the space below, list as many *bad* reasons as you can think of for why you are depressed. Please list each reason on a separate line and leave the space in front of each line blank for the time being.

_____

_____

_____

_____

_____

_____

_____

Step 5: Finally, go back and rate how bad each of the reasons you listed in step 4 are for being depressed. Place your rating for each reason in the space in front of each line according to the following scale:

1	2	3	4	5	6	7	8	9	10
Fairly Bad									Very Bad

APPENDIX D

Writing Your Life Story

In the space below, please write the story of your life with depression. Describe how your depression first began; how you have struggled with it; and the key historical, situational, and personal life events that have contributed to your experiences with depression.

_____

_____

_____

_____

_____

_____

_____

_____

_____

_____

_____

_____

_____

_____

_____

_____

REWRITING YOUR LIFE STORY

In the space below, please *rewrite* the story of your life so that it has an entirely different ending from the initial story. In collaboration with your therapist, first underline the facts mentioned in the first writing of your life story. Take these same facts and weave them into a different version of your life story such that the outcome is not one of you struggling with depression.

_____

_____

_____

_____

_____

_____

_____

_____

_____

_____

_____

_____

_____

_____

_____

_____

_____

_____

_____

_____

_____

_____

_____

APPENDIX E

Personal Values Questionnaire (PVQ)

Instructions: Following this instruction sheet, you will find several additional pages dealing with each of the nine Values Domains (areas of your life you may find important) listed below, in order.

Values Domains

1. Family Relationships

2. Friendships/Social Relationships

3. Couples/Romantic Relationships

4. Work/Career

5. Education-Schooling/Personal Growth and Development

6. Recreation/Leisure/Sports

7. Spirituality/Religion

8. Community/Citizenship

9. Health/Physical Well-Being

On the pages that follow, please read carefully through the values domain description and write down *your* values (ways of living and doing things related to that Values Domain that are very important to you) where indicated.

After writing down each of the values, you will be presented with a series of nine questions asking different things about those individual values. Please answer each of these questions by circling the numbers that are true for you.

If you have any questions about how to complete this questionnaire, please ask the person who handed it out to you.

Remember: Your name will not be on this questionnaire, so no one will know what values you write down. Because of this, please describe your values as if no one will ever see this worksheet.

Measure developed by J. T. Blackledge and Joseph Ciarrochi.; adapted from the Personal Strivings Measure developed by Kennon Sheldon and colleagues. Adapted by permission.

Personal Value #1: Family Relationships

Instructions: Describe the type of brother/sister, son/daughter, and/or parent-child relationships you would most like to build in your life. For example, if you want closer and better relationships with your family members, it may be accurate for you to list values like "building kind, considerate, supportive, and loyal sibling relationships" or "building open, honest, and nurturing relationships with my children." Regardless of these examples, *you* should choose family relationship values that are heartfelt and meaningful to *you*.

Please write down your Family Relationships values here:

_____

_____

_____

_____

_____

_____

_____

_____

_____

_____

_____

_____

_____

_____

_____

_____

_____

_____

_____

_____

Please answer the following questions by circling the number (in the right-hand column) that is true for you:

1.	I value this because somebody else wants me to or thinks I ought to, or because someone else will like it if I do. I probably wouldn't say I value this if I didn't get some kind of praise or approval for it.	1—Not at all for this reason 2—Mostly not for this reason 3—Unsure 4—Mostly for this reason 5—Entirely for this reason
2.	I value this because I would feel ashamed, guilty, or anxious if I didn't.	1—Not at all for this reason 2—Mostly not for this reason 3—Unsure 4—Mostly for this reason 5—Entirely for this reason
3.	I value this because I view it as important, whether or not others agree. Although this value may have been taught to me by others, now it is my own heartfelt value.	1—Not at all for this reason 2—Mostly not for this reason 3—Unsure 4—Mostly for this reason 5—Entirely for this reason
4.	I value this because doing this thing makes my life better, more meaningful, and/or more vital.	1—Not at all for this reason 2—Mostly not for this reason 3—Unsure 4—Mostly for this reason 5—Entirely for this reason
5.	I value this because I experience fun and enjoyment when I am engaged in the value.	1—Not at all for this reason 2—Mostly not for this reason 3—Unsure 4—Mostly for this reason 5—Entirely for this reason
6.	In the last month, I have been this successful in living this value (in acting consistently with this value):	1—0–20% Successful 2—21–40% Successful 3—41–60% Successful 4—61–80% Successful 5—81–100% Successful
7.	I am this committed to living this value (to acting consistently with this value):	1— Not at all committed 2—Slightly committed 3—Moderately committed 4—Quite committed 5—Extremely committed

8.	How important is this value to you?	1—Not at all important 2—Slightly important 3—Moderately important 4—Quite important 5—Extremely important
9.	Right now, would you like to improve your progress on this value?	1—Not at all 2—A little bit 3—Moderately so 4—Quite a bit 5—Very much so

Personal Value #2: Friendships/Social Relationships

Instructions: What kinds of friendships would you most like to build? If you were able to be the best friend possible, how would you behave toward your friends? For example, you might value building friendships that are supportive, considerate, caring, accepting, loyal, or honest—but *choose for yourself* which qualities *you* would most like to bring to your friendships.

Please write down your Friendships/Social Relationships values here:

_____

_____

_____

_____

_____

_____

_____

_____

_____

_____

_____

_____

_____

Please answer the following questions by circling the number (in the right-hand column) that is true for you:

1.	I value this because somebody else wants me to or thinks I ought to, or because someone else will like it if I do. I probably wouldn't say I value this if I didn't get some kind of praise or approval for it.	1—Not at all for this reason 2—Mostly not for this reason 3—Unsure 4—Mostly for this reason 5—Entirely for this reason
2.	I value this because I would feel ashamed, guilty, or anxious if I didn't.	1—Not at all for this reason 2—Mostly not for this reason 3—Unsure 4—Mostly for this reason 5—Entirely for this reason

3.	I value this because I view it as important, whether or not others agree. Although this value may have been taught to me by others, now it is my own heartfelt value.	1—Not at all for this reason 2—Mostly not for this reason 3—Unsure 4—Mostly for this reason 5—Entirely for this reason
4.	I value this because doing this thing makes my life better, more meaningful, and/or more vital.	1—Not at all for this reason 2—Mostly not for this reason 3—Unsure 4—Mostly for this reason 5—Entirely for this reason
5.	I value this because I experience fun and enjoyment when I am engaged in the value.	1—Not at all for this reason 2—Mostly not for this reason 3—Unsure 4—Mostly for this reason 5—Entirely for this reason
6.	In the last month, I have been this successful in living this value (in acting consistently with this value):	1—0–20% Successful 2—21–40% Successful 3—41–60% Successful 4—61–80% Successful 5—81–100% Successful
7.	I am this committed to living this value (to acting consistently with this value):	1—Not at all committed 2—Slightly committed 3—Moderately committed 4—Quite committed 5—Extremely committed
8.	How important is this value to you?	1—Not at all important 2—Slightly important 3—Moderately important 4—Quite important 5—Extremely important
9.	Right now, would you like to improve your progress on this value?	1—Not at all 2—A little bit 3—Moderately so 4—Quite a bit 5—Very much so

Personal Value #3: Couples/Romantic Relationships

Instructions: What kind of romantic relationship would you most like to build? For example, you might value building a caring, supportive, open, honest, kind, and attentive romantic relationship, but *you* should decide for yourself what kind of qualities *you'd* most like to bring to such a relationship.

Please write down your Couples/Romantic Relationships values here:

_____

_____

_____

_____

_____

_____

_____

_____

_____

_____

_____

_____

_____

_____

Please answer the following questions by circling the number (in the right-hand column) that is true for you:

1.	I value this because somebody else wants me to or thinks I ought to, or because someone else will like it if I do. I probably wouldn't say I value this if I didn't get some kind of praise or approval for it.	1—Not at all for this reason 2—Mostly not for this reason 3—Unsure 4—Mostly for this reason 5—Entirely for this reason
2.	I value this because I would feel ashamed, guilty, or anxious if I didn't.	1—Not at all for this reason 2—Mostly not for this reason 3—Unsure 4—Mostly for this reason 5—Entirely for this reason

3.	I value this because I view it as important, whether or not others agree. Although this value may have been taught to me by others, now it is my own heartfelt value.	1—Not at all for this reason 2—Mostly not for this reason 3—Unsure 4—Mostly for this reason 5—Entirely for this reason
4.	I value this because doing this thing makes my life better, more meaningful, and/or more vital.	1—Not at all for this reason 2—Mostly not for this reason 3—Unsure 4—Mostly for this reason 5—Entirely for this reason
5.	I value this because I experience fun and enjoyment when I am engaged in the value.	1—Not at all for this reason 2—Mostly not for this reason 3—Unsure 4—Mostly for this reason 5—Entirely for this reason
6.	In the last month, I have been this successful in living this value (in acting consistently with this value):	1—0–20% Successful 2—21–40% Successful 3—41–60% Successful 4—61–80% Successful 5—81–100% Successful
7.	I am this committed to living this value (to acting consistently with this value):	1—Not at all committed 2—Slightly committed 3—Moderately committed 4—Quite committed 5—Extremely committed
8.	How important is this value to you?	1—Not at all important 2—Slightly important 3—Moderately important 4—Quite important 5—Extremely important
9.	Right now, would you like to improve your progress on this value?	1—Not at all 2—A little bit 3—Moderately so 4—Quite a bit 5—Very much so

Personal Value #4: Work/Career

Instructions: What type of work would you like to do in an ideal world? What kind of worker would you like to be with respect to your work, your employer, and coworkers? Some people value doing work that allows them to bring their unique talents to bear, work that allows them to express themselves, or work that "makes a difference" in other people's lives. Regardless of what others value, what kind of work would *you* most value doing, and what kind of worker would *you* most value being?

Please write down your Work/Career values here:

_____

_____

_____

_____

_____

_____

_____

_____

_____

_____

_____

_____

Please answer the following questions by circling the number (in the right-hand column) that is true for you:

1.	I value this because somebody else wants me to or thinks I ought to, or because someone else will like it if I do. I probably wouldn't say I value this if I didn't get some kind of praise or approval for it	1—Not at all for this reason 2—Mostly not for this reason 3—Unsure 4—Mostly for this reason 5—Entirely for this reason
2.	I value this because I would feel ashamed, guilty, or anxious if I didn't.	1—Not at all for this reason 2—Mostly not for this reason 3—Unsure 4—Mostly for this reason 5—Entirely for this reason

3.	I value this because I view it as important, whether or not others agree. Although this value may have been taught to me by others, now it is my own heartfelt value.	1—Not at all for this reason 2—Mostly not for this reason 3—Unsure 4—Mostly for this reason 5—Entirely for this reason
4.	I value this because doing this thing makes my life better, more meaningful, and/or more vital.	1—Not at all for this reason 2—Mostly not for this reason 3—Unsure 4—Mostly for this reason 5—Entirely for this reason
5.	I value this because I experience fun and enjoyment when I am engaged in the value.	1—Not at all for this reason 2—Mostly not for this reason 3—Unsure 4—Mostly for this reason 5—Entirely for this reason
6.	In the last month, I have been this successful in living this value (in acting consistently with this value):	1—0–20% Successful 2—21–40% Successful 3—41–60% Successful 4—61–80% Successful 5—81–100% Successful
7.	I am this committed to living this value (to acting consistently with this value):	1—Not at all committed 2—Slightly committed 3—Moderately committed 4—Quite committed 5—Extremely committed
8.	How important is this value to you?	1—Not at all important 2—Slightly important 3—Moderately important 4—Quite important 5—Extremely important
9.	Right now, would you like to improve your progress on this value?	1—Not at all 2—A little bit 3—Moderately so 4—Quite a bit 5—Very much so

Personal Value #5: Education-Schooling/Personal Growth and Development

Instructions: What kind of student would you be in an ideal world? What kinds of things do you value learning as a person? What qualities do you value bringing to your role as a student, in school or any other places where you learn things you feel are of great importance to you? Some people value learning to face new challenges, learning different perspectives on important issues, learning better or more efficient ways to do specific things, or learning how to grow as a person. Some people value qualities like being open and receptive to new ideas and perspectives, or making serious and careful consideration of important issues. Regardless of what others want, you should write down the kinds of things *you* really value learning and/or qualities *you* value demonstrating as a student.

Please write down your Education-Schooling/Personal Growth and Development values here:

_____

_____

_____

_____

_____

_____

_____

_____

Please answer the following questions by circling the number (in the right-hand column) that is true for you:

1.	I value this because somebody else wants me to or thinks I ought to, or because someone else will like it if I do. I probably wouldn't say I value this if I didn't get some kind of praise or approval for it.	1—Not at all for this reason 2—Mostly not for this reason 3—Unsure 4—Mostly for this reason 5—Entirely for this reason
2.	I value this because I would feel ashamed, guilty, or anxious if I didn't.	1—Not at all for this reason 2—Mostly not for this reason 3—Unsure 4—Mostly for this reason 5—Entirely for this reason

3.	I value this because I view it as important, whether or not others agree. Although this value may have been taught to me by others, now it is my own heartfelt value.	1—Not at all for this reason 2—Mostly not for this reason 3—Unsure 4—Mostly for this reason 5—Entirely for this reason
4.	I value this because doing this thing makes my life better, more meaningful, and/or more vital.	1—Not at all for this reason 2—Mostly not for this reason 3—Unsure 4—Mostly for this reason 5—Entirely for this reason
5.	I value this because I experience fun and enjoyment when I am engaged in the value.	1—Not at all for this reason 2—Mostly not for this reason 3—Unsure 4—Mostly for this reason 5—Entirely for this reason
6.	In the last month, I have been this success-ful in living this value (in acting consis-tently with this value):	1—0–20% Successful 2—21–40% Successful 3—41–60% Successful 4—61–80% Successful 5—81–100% Successful
7.	I am this committed to living this value (to acting consistently with this value):	1—Not at all committed 2—Slightly committed 3—Moderately committed 4—Quite committed 5—Extremely committed
8.	How important is this value to you?	1—Not at all important 2—Slightly important 3—Moderately important 4—Quite important 5—Extremely important
9.	Right now, would you like to improve your progress on this value?	1—Not at all 2—A little bit 3—Moderately so 4—Quite a bit 5—Very much so

Personal Value #6: Recreation/Leisure/Sports

Instructions: Write down the type of recreational life you would most like to have, including hobbies, sports, and leisure activities. Indicate how important it is to *you* to make time for these activities.

Please write down your Recreation/Leisure/Sports values here:

_____

_____

_____

_____

_____

_____

_____

_____

_____

_____

_____

_____

_____

_____

Please answer the following questions by circling the number (in the right-hand column) that is true for you:

1.	I value this because somebody else wants me to or thinks I ought to, or because someone else will like it if I do. I probably wouldn't say I value this if I didn't get some kind of praise or approval for it.	1—Not at all for this reason 2—Mostly not for this reason 3—Unsure 4—Mostly for this reason 5—Entirely for this reason
2.	I value this because I would feel ashamed, guilty, or anxious if I didn't.	1—Not at all for this reason 2—Mostly not for this reason 3—Unsure 4—Mostly for this reason 5—Entirely for this reason

3.	I value this because I view it as important, whether or not others agree. Although this value may have been taught to me by others, now it is my own heartfelt value.	1—Not at all for this reason 2—Mostly not for this reason 3—Unsure 4—Mostly for this reason 5—Entirely for this reason
4.	I value this because doing this thing makes my life better, more meaningful, and/or more vital.	1—Not at all for this reason 2—Mostly not for this reason 3—Unsure 4—Mostly for this reason 5—Entirely for this reason
5.	I value this because I experience fun and enjoyment when I am engaged in the value.	1—Not at all for this reason 2—Mostly not for this reason 3—Unsure 4—Mostly for this reason 5—Entirely for this reason
6.	In the last month, I have been this successful in living this value (in acting consistently with this value):	1—0–20% Successful 2—21–40% Successful 3—41–60% Successful 4— 61–80% Successful 5—81–100% Successful
7.	I am this committed to living this value (to acting consistently with this value):	1—Not at all committed 2—Slightly committed 3—Moderately committed 4—Quite committed 5—Extremely committed
8.	How important is this value to you?	1—Not at all important 2—Slightly important 3—Moderately important 4—Quite important 5—Extremely important
9.	Right now, would you like to improve your progress on this value?	1—Not at all 2—A little bit 3—Moderately so 4—Quite a bit 5—Very much so

Personal Value #7: Spirituality/Religion

Instructions: Understand that we are not necessarily referring to organized religion in this section. What we mean by "spirituality" is whatever that means to you. This may be as simple as connecting with nature or the world around you, meditating, or praying, or as formal as participation in an organized religious group. Whatever spirituality means to you is fine. Briefly write down the very important spiritual/religious beliefs you have and the kind of person you value being in service of these beliefs (which might include things like "acting as a loving or caring person," "working to stay connected to the people and things around me," "devoting regular time to worship, prayer, etc.," or "acting consistently with my religious/spiritual beliefs"). Regardless of what other people's beliefs are, *you* should write down what kind of spiritual/religious person *you* most value being.

Please write down your Spirituality/Religion values here:

_____

_____

_____

_____

_____

_____

_____

_____

_____

Please answer the following questions by circling the number (in the right-hand column) that is true for you:

1.	I value this because somebody else wants me to or thinks I ought to, or because someone else will like it if I do. I probably wouldn't say I value this if I didn't get some kind of praise or approval for it.	1—Not at all for this reason 2—Mostly not for this reason 3—Unsure 4—Mostly for this reason 5—Entirely for this reason
2.	I value this because I would feel ashamed, guilty, or anxious if I didn't.	1—Not at all for this reason 2—Mostly not for this reason 3—Unsure 4—Mostly for this reason 5—Entirely for this reason

3.	I value this because I view it as important, whether or not others agree. Although this value may have been taught to me by others, now it is my own heartfelt value.	1—Not at all for this reason 2—Mostly not for this reason 3—Unsure 4—Mostly for this reason 5—Entirely for this reason
4.	I value this because doing this thing makes my life better, more meaningful, and/or more vital.	1—Not at all for this reason 2—Mostly not for this reason 3—Unsure 4—Mostly for this reason 5—Entirely for this reason
5.	I value this because I experience fun and enjoyment when I am engaged in the value.	1—Not at all for this reason 2—Mostly not for this reason 3—Unsure 4—Mostly for this reason 5—Entirely for this reason
6.	In the last month, I have been this successful in living this value (in acting consistently with this value):	1—0–20% Successful 2—21–40% Successful 3—41–60% Successful 4— 61–80% Successful 5—81–100% Successful
7.	I am this committed to living this value (to acting consistently with this value):	1—Not at all committed 2—Slightly committed 3—Moderately committed 4—Quite committed 5—Extremely committed
8.	How important is this value to you?	1—Not at all important 2—Slightly important 3—Moderately important 4—Quite important 5—Extremely important
9.	Right now, would you like to improve your progress on this value?	1—Not at all 2—A little bit 3—Moderately so 4—Quite a bit 5—Very much so

Personal Value #8: Community/Citizenship

Instructions: Write about the kind of person you value being with respect to your community and your country. For instance, some people think that it is important to volunteer with homeless or elderly people; lobby governmental policymakers at the federal, state, or local level; participate as a member of a group committed to conserving wildlife; or become involved in some other community group of importance to you. Some people value getting others more involved in community and national issues important to them, and some value helping others in their community or country. Regardless of what others may value, *you* should write down the kinds of community involvement *you* value.

Please write down your Community/Citizenship values here:

_____

_____

_____

_____

_____

_____

_____

_____

_____

_____

Please answer the following questions by circling the number (in the right-hand column) that is true for you:

1.	I value this because somebody else wants me to or thinks I ought to, or because someone else will like it if I do. I probably wouldn't say I value this if I didn't get some kind of praise or approval for it.	1—Not at all for this reason 2—Mostly not for this reason 3—Unsure 4—Mostly for this reason 5—Entirely for this reason
2.	I value this because I would feel ashamed, guilty, or anxious if I didn't.	1—Not at all for this reason 2—Mostly not for this reason 3—Unsure 4—Mostly for this reason 5—Entirely for this reason

3.	I value this because I view it as important, whether or not others agree. Although this value may have been taught to me by others, now it is my own heartfelt value.	1—Not at all for this reason 2—Mostly not for this reason 3—Unsure 4—Mostly for this reason 5—Entirely for this reason
4.	I value this because doing this thing makes my life better, more meaningful, and/or more vital.	1—Not at all for this reason 2—Mostly not for this reason 3—Unsure 4—Mostly for this reason 5—Entirely for this reason
5.	I value this because I experience fun and enjoyment when I am engaged in the value.	1—Not at all for this reason 2—Mostly not for this reason 3—Unsure 4—Mostly for this reason 5—Entirely for this reason
6.	In the last month, I have been this successful in living this value (in acting consistently with this value):	1—0–20% Successful 2—21–40% Successful 3—41–60% Successful 4— 61–80% Successful 5—81–100% Successful
7.	I am this committed to living this value (to acting consistently with this value):	1—Not at all committed 2—Slightly committed 3—Moderately committed 4—Quite committed 5—Extremely committed
8.	How important is this value to you?	1—Not at all important 2—Slightly important 3—Moderately important 4—Quite important 5—Extremely important
9.	Right now, would you like to improve your progress on this value?	1—Not at all 2—A little bit 3—Moderately so 4—Quite a bit 5—Very much so

Personal Value #9: Health/Physical Well-Being

Instructions: Write down your values related to maintaining your physical well-being. Write briefly about the direction *you* want to take in regard to your own health-related issues such as sleep, diet, exercise, smoking, and so forth.

Please write down your Health/Physical Well-Being values here:

_____

_____

_____

_____

_____

_____

_____

_____

_____

_____

_____

Please answer the following questions by circling the number (in the right-hand column) that is true for you:

1.	I value this because somebody else wants me to or thinks I ought to, or because someone else will like it if I do. I probably wouldn't say I value this if I didn't get some kind of praise or approval for it.	1—Not at all for this reason 2—Mostly not for this reason 3—Unsure 4—Mostly for this reason 5—Entirely for this reason
2.	I value this because I would feel ashamed, guilty, or anxious if I didn't.	1—Not at all for this reason 2—Mostly not for this reason 3—Unsure 4—Mostly for this reason 5—Entirely for this reason
3.	I value this because I view it as important, whether or not others agree. Although this value may have been taught to me by others, now it is my own heartfelt value.	1—Not at all for this reason 2—Mostly not for this reason 3—Unsure 4—Mostly for this reason 5—Entirely for this reason

4.	I value this because doing this thing makes my life better, more meaningful, and/or more vital.	1—Not at all for this reason 2—Mostly not for this reason 3—Unsure 4—Mostly for this reason 5—Entirely for this reason
5.	I value this because I experience fun and enjoyment when I am engaged in the value.	1—Not at all for this reason 2—Mostly not for this reason 3—Unsure 4—Mostly for this reason 5—Entirely for this reason
6.	In the last month, I have been this successful in living this value (in acting consistently with this value):	1—0–20% Successful 2—21–40% Successful 3—41–60% Successful 4— 61–80% Successful 5—81–100% Successful
7.	I am this committed to living this value (to acting consistently with this value):	1—Not at all committed 2—Slightly committed 3—Moderately committed 4—Quite committed 5—Extremely committed
8.	How important is this value to you?	1—Not at all important 2—Slightly important 3—Moderately important 4—Quite important 5—Extremely important
9.	Right now, would you like to improve your progress on this value?	1—Not at all 2—A little bit 3—Moderately so 4—Quite a bit 5—Very much so

APPENDIX F

Valued Living Questionnaire (VLQ)

Below are areas of life that are valued by some people. We are concerned with your quality of life in each of these areas. One aspect of quality of life involves the importance one puts on different areas of living. Rate the importance of each area (by circling a number) on a scale of 1 to 10. One means that the area is not at all important. Ten means that the area is very important. Not everyone will value all of these areas, or value all areas the same. Rate each area according to *your own personal sense of its importance*.

Area		Not at all important	Extremely important
1.	Family (other than marriage or parenting)	1 2 3 4 5 6 7	8 9 10
2.	Marriage/couples/intimate relations	1 2 3 4 5 6 7	8 9 10
3.	Parenting	1 2 3 4 5 6 7	8 9 10
4.	Friends/social life	1 2 3 4 5 6 7	8 9 10
5.	Work	1 2 3 4 5 6 7	8 9 10
6.	Education/training	1 2 3 4 5 6 7	8 9 10
7.	Recreation/fun	1 2 3 4 5 6 7	8 9 10
8.	Spirituality	1 2 3 4 5 6 7	8 9 10
9.	Citizenship/Community Life	1 2 3 4 5 6 7	8 9 10
10.	Physical self-care (diet, exercise, sleep)	1 2 3 4 5 6 7	8 9 10

In this section, we would like you to give a rating of how consistent your actions have been with each of your values. We are not asking about your ideal in each area. We are also not asking what others think of you. Everyone does better in some areas than others. People also do better at some times than at others. *We want to know how you think you have been doing during the past week.* Rate each area (by circling a number) on a scale of 1 to 10. One means that you actions have been completely inconsistent with your value. Ten means that your actions have been completely consistent with your value.

During the past week

_____

Area	Not at all consistent with my value		Completely consistent with my value
1. Family (other than marriage or parenting)		1 2 3 4 5 6 7 8 9 10	
2. Marriage/couples/intimate relations		1 2 3 4 5 6 7 8 9 10	
3. Parenting		1 2 3 4 5 6 7 8 9 10	
4. Friends/social life		1 2 3 4 5 6 7 8 9 10	
5. Work		1 2 3 4 5 6 7 8 9 10	
6. Education/training		1 2 3 4 5 6 7 8 9 10	
7. Recreation/fun		1 2 3 4 5 6 7 8 9 10	
8. Spirituality		1 2 3 4 5 6 7 8 9 10	
9. Citizenship/Community Life		1 2 3 4 5 6 7 8 9 10	
10. Physical self-care (diet, exercise, sleep)		1 2 3 4 5 6 7 8 9 10	

APPENDIX G

Goals-Action Form

In the appropriate columns below, write down homework goals and the related actions necessary to possibly achieve them. In the "Done" column, record the date each goal was attained. In the "Barriers" column, make note of any psychological obstacles that either prevented the related action or that you encountered and had to overcome in completing the related action.

Goal	Done	Related Action	Barriers

APPENDIX H

Mindfulness Exercise Diary

In the appropriate spaces below, please record specific activities you engaged in as mindfulness exercises, when they occurred, and for how long. In the last column, please also make note of any reactions or comments you have about the exercise.

Day/Date	Exercise	Duration	Reactions/Comments

APPENDIX I

Breathing Mindfully Exercise

This handout provides you with a sequence of steps to follow in practicing the breathing exercise that was introduced to you by your therapist. It is recommended that you practice this exercise at least twice a day. Please use the Mindfulness Exercise Diary to record when you practiced the exercise and how long you practiced each time you did it.

1. Find a comfortable chair in which you can sit while practicing this exercise, preferably in a location that is relatively quiet and where you will not be disturbed.

2. Position your back straight and slightly away from the back of the chair. Rest you feet flat on the floor with your legs uncrossed. Rest your arms and hands in your lap or on the armrests of the chair.

3. Close your eyes and take up to thirty seconds to notice the parts of your body that make contact with the chair. See if you can notice where you feel your legs and buttocks press against the chair, where your feet contact the floor, and the places on your arms and hands that touch either your lap or the armrests of the chair.

4. When you are ready to do so, shift the focus of your attention to your breathing.

5. See if you can notice the exact moment when the air begins to enter your nostrils.

6. Follow the breath as it enters your nostrils and travels down through your body and into your lungs.

7. Notice how your chest and abdomen gently rise upward and slightly inward with each breath that is inhaled.

8. Notice the point where the breath has reached its end and the process of exhaling begins.

9. Follow the breath as it comes from your lungs and leaves you nostrils.

10. See if you can focus your attention on the very spot and moment when the air leaves your nostrils. Notice that the air that leaves your nostrils is just a bit warmer than the air that enters.

11. Notice the sensations in your chest and abdomen as they move slightly downward and outward as the breath leaves your nostrils.

12. Continue to follow each breath as it enters and exits your nostrils.

13. If you become distracted at any point during the exercise, see if you can first notice what distracted you. Then gently bring your attention back to your breathing. There is no way to fail this exercise no matter how many times you might become distracted. Each time you become distracted is an opportunity to practice gently redirecting your attention back to your breathing.

14. Please spend at least five minutes on the exercise each time you practice it the first day. You may want to use a timer to signal the end of the practice time. Increase the length of the practice time by two to three minutes each day so that you are practicing the exercise at least fifteen minutes twice daily by the time of your next appointment.

APPENDIX J

Watching Your Thoughts Exercise

This handout provides you with the steps to practice watching your thoughts, an exercise your therapist introduced to you. It is recommended that you practice this exercise at least twice a day. Please use the Mindfulness Exercise Diary to record when you practiced the exercise and how long you practiced each time you did it.

There are several variations on this exercise, depending upon how the thoughts that you are watching are being transported. They can be written on signs being carried by soldiers marching in a parade, on leaves floating by on a stream, or by clouds drifting across the sky. You may wish to experiment by trying all three, although it is not recommended that you switch among the different versions within the course of a single practice session.

1. Find a comfortable chair in which you can sit while practicing this exercise, preferably in a location that is relatively quiet and where you will not be disturbed.

2. Position your back straight and slightly away from the back of the chair. Rest you feet flat on the floor with your legs uncrossed. Rest your arms and hands in your lap or on the armrests of the chair.

3. Close your eyes and take up to thirty seconds to notice the parts of your body that make contact with the chair. See if you can notice where you feel your legs and buttocks press against the chair, where your feet contact the floor, and the places on your arms and hands that touch your lap or the armrests of the chair.

4. When you are ready to do so, shift the focus of your attention to your breathing. For up to thirty seconds, follow your breathing as you've already learned to do.

5. When you are ready to do so, shift your attention to the version of this exercise that you have selected. Imagine being in the viewing stand of a parade, sitting on the bank of a stream, or lying on your back in a meadow. Notice the first thought you have and imagine watching it as it is being carried by on a sign, a leaf, or a cloud.

6. Focus your attention on the stream of thoughts passing by in front of you, one by one.

7. Notice that as each thought drifts by, another arises to replace it in the flow.

8. Follow each thought until another emerges in the progression.

9. If you become distracted at any point during the exercise, see if you can first notice what distracted you. Then gently bring your attention back to your breathing. Next, shift your attention back to watching the flow of thoughts in front of you. Place any distracting thought in with the others you have been watching and observe it being carried by on a sign, leaf, or a cloud.

10. There is no way to fail this exercise no matter how many times you might become distracted. Each time you become distracted is an opportunity to practice gently redirecting your attention back to watching your thoughts.

11. Please spend at least five minutes on the exercise each time you practice it the first day. You may want to use a timer to signal the end of the practice time. Increase the length of the practice time by two to three minutes each day so that you are practicing the exercise at least fifteen minutes twice daily by the time of your next appointment.

APPENDIX K

What Is Acceptance and Commitment Therapy?

As you are probably aware, there are several different psychological approaches that have shown promise in helping people cope with depression, including cognitive therapy, interpersonal therapy, and different types of behavior therapy. You are being asked to consent to participate in a relatively new type of behavior therapy that has been developed to help address depression. It is known as acceptance and commitment therapy, or ACT.

Unfortunately there is no one therapy for depression that has been shown to work better than others for everyone. As a result, the most reasonable strategy for us to follow is to select an approach for dealing with depression that has shown promise and try it long enough to determine if it works for you. While there is no guarantee that ACT will help you more successfully cope with depression, there is also no reason to believe that it will not be of some meaningful help to you. ACT has been shown to compare favorably to cognitive therapy in dealing with depression, and the best way to determine if you will benefit from ACT is to ask you to participate in a sufficiently long "trial" of it.

Specifically, you are being asked to consent to twelve weekly sessions of ACT. The sessions will last approximately one hour each and can be discontinued at your request at any time in favor of other treatment options. While there are no risks known to be uniquely associated with ACT that are not also present with other therapeutic approaches for depression, we will also change your treatment should you experience any adverse reactions to it. At the end of the twelve sessions, or even before then if necessary; we will evaluate your progress and if appropriate discuss what other treatment options may be available.

To help you consider whether you wish to consent to a program of treatment involving ACT, it may be useful to describe it at this point in some more detail. ACT is called acceptance and commitment therapy because it emphasizes the role that both processes can play in helping you try out and develop new ways to handle the difficulties we all encounter in struggling with depression and other kinds of unwanted emotional experiences. Specifically, the acceptance side of ACT helps you better learn to tell the difference between aspects of your struggles with depression that can be controlled and aspects that may have to be accepted because they cannot be changed. The purpose of the commitment side of ACT is to help you channel the energy that has been freed up by the acceptance part of ACT into changes that help you live the type of life you want to live.

While some time will be spent in our sessions talking about both the acceptance and commitment sides of ACT, it is more important that you learn how to practice both acceptance and commitment. For this reason, some of the time in our sessions will be devoted not only to talking about ACT, but also to actually having you try it out by practicing it. To provide you with further opportunities to learn how to practice ACT, you will also be asked to complete related homework assignments between our sessions each week.

As your therapist, I will be glad to answer any questions at this point that you may have about the treatment program and approach for which your consent is being sought. I also hope that you will feel free to ask any additional questions that may occur to you at any time in our work together. This is your therapy, and my goal as your therapist is to have it be about what is most important to you.

You will be given a copy of this handout for your future reference. A copy will also be attached to the consent form that you will be asked to sign. Your signature on the consent form with this handout attached to it will document that you have read the handout and that we have discussed any questions you may have had about it.

APPENDIX L

Mood Regulation Diary

In the appropriate spaces below, please record whatever activities or efforts you have engaged in to help yourself feel better and less depressed following unwanted changes in your mood or feelings. Please make note of when the incident occurred, what the circumstances were that lead to the shift in your mood or emotions, and what you did in response to it.

Day/Date	Incident/Circumstance	Your Response

References

Abrams, J. J., Lindelof, D., Cuse, C., Bender, J., Pinkner, J., & Burk, B. (Executive Producers). (2006). *Lost* [Television series]. New York: ABC.

Achenbach, T. M. (1990–1991). "Comorbidity" in child and adolescent psychiatry: Categorical and quantitative perspectives. *Journal of Child and Adolescent Psychopharmacology, 1*, 271–278.

Addis, M. E., & Carpenter, K. M. (1999). Why, why, why?: Reason-giving and rumination as predictors of response to activation- and insight-oriented treatment rationales. *Journal of Clinical Psychology, 55*, 881–894.

Addis, M. E., & Jacobson, N. S. (1996). Reasons for depression and the process and outcome of cognitive-behavioral psychotherapies. *Journal of Consulting and Clinical Psychology, 64*, 1417–1424.

Addis, M. E., Truax, P., & Jacobson, N. S. (1995). Why do people think they are depressed?: The reasons for depression questionnaire. *Psychotherapy, 32*, 476–483.

Akiskal, H. S., Benazzi, F., Berugi, G., & Rihmer, Z. (2005). Agitated "unipolar" depression re-conceptualized as a depressive mixed state: Implications for the antidepressant-suicide controversy. *Journal of Affective Disorders, 85*, 245–258.

American Educational Research Association, American Psychological Association, & National Council on Measurement in Education. (1999). *Standards for educational and psychological testing.* Washington, DC: American Educational Research Association.

American Psychiatric Association. (1994). *Diagnostic and statistical manual of mental disorders* (4th ed.). Washington, DC: American Psychiatric Association.

American Psychological Association. (2002). Ethical principles of psychologists and code of conduct. *American Psychologist, 57*, 1060–1073.

Angst, F., Stassen, H. H., Clayton, P. J., & Angst, J. (2002). Mortality of patients with mood disorders: Follow-up over 34–38 years. *Journal of Affective Disorders, 68,* 167–181.

Antonuccio, D. O., Danton, W. G., & DeNelsky, G. Y. (1995). Psychotherapy versus medication for depression: Challenging the conventional wisdom with data. *Professional Psychology: Research and Practice, 26,* 574–585.

Antonuccio, D. O., Thomas, M., & Danton, W. G. (1997). A cost-effectiveness analysis of cognitive-behavior therapy and fluoxetine (Prozac) in the treatment of depression. *Behavior Therapy, 28,* 187–210.

Arffa, S. (1983). Cognition and suicide: A methodological review. *Suicide and Life-Threatening Behavior, 17,* 64–71.

Assagioli, R. (1965). *Psychosynthesis: A manual of principles and techniques.* New York: Hobbs, Dorman & Company.

Baer, D. M., Wolf, M. M., & Risley, T. R. (1968). Some current dimensions of applied behavior analysis. *Journal of Applied Behavior Analysis, 1,* 91–97.

Baer, R. A. (2003). Mindfulness training as a clinical intervention: A conceptual and empirical review. *Clinical Psychology: Science and Practice, 10,* 125–143.

Baer, R. A. (Ed.). (2006). *Mindfulness-based treatment approaches: Clinician's guide to evidence base and applications.* Burlington, MA: Academic Press.

Baer, R. A., Smith, G. T., & Allen, K. B. (2004). Assessment of mindfulness by self-report: The Kentucky Inventory of Mindfulness Skills. *Assessment, 11,* 191–206.

Bancroft, J., Skrimshire, A., & Simkins, S. (1976). The reasons people give for taking overdoses. *British Journal of Psychiatry, 128,* 538–548.

Bandura, A. (1997). *Self-efficacy: The exercise of control.* New York: Freeman.

Barnes-Holmes, D., Barnes-Holmes, Y., Power, P., Hayden, E., Milne, R., & Stewart, I. (2006). Do you really know what you believe? Developing the Implicit Relational Assessment Procedure (IRAP) as a direct measure of implicit beliefs. *The Irish Psychologist, 32,* 169–177.

Barnes-Holmes, D., Healy, O., & Hayes, S. C. (2000). Relational frame theory and the relational evaluation procedure: Approaching language as derived relational responding. In J. C. Leslie & D. E. Blackman (Eds.), *Experimental and applied analyses of human behavior* (pp. 149–180). Reno, NV: Context Press.

Barnes-Holmes, D., O'Hora, D., Roche, B., Hayes, S. C., Bissett, R. T., & Lyddy, F. (2001). Understanding and verbal regulation. In S. C. Hayes, D. Barnes-Holmes, & B. Roche (Eds.), *Relational frame theory: A post-Skinnerian account of human language and cognition* (pp.103–117). New York: Plenum.

Batten S. V., & Hayes, S. C. (2005). Acceptance and commitment therapy in the treatment of comorbid substance abuse and posttraumatic stress disorder: A case study. *Clinical Case Studies, 4,* 246–262.

Baumeister, R. F. (1990). Suicide as escape from self. *Psychological Review, 97,* 90–113.

Beck, A. T. (1967). *Depression: Clinical, experimental, and theoretical aspects.* New York: Harper & Row.

Beck, A. T. (1970). Cognitive therapy: Nature and relation to behavior therapy. *Behavior Therapy, 1*, 184–200.

Beck, A. T. (1976). *Cognitive therapy and the emotional disorders.* New York: International Universities Press.

Beck, A. T., & Beck, R. W. (1972). Screening depressed patients in family practice: A rapid technique. *Postgraduate Medicine, 52*, 81–85.

Beck, A. T., & Emery, G. (1985). *Anxiety disorders and phobias: A cognitive perspective.* New York: Basic Books.

Beck, A. T., & Kovacs, M. (1979). Assessment of suicidal ideation: The Scale for Suicide Ideation. *Journal of Consulting and Clinical Psychology, 47*, 343–352

Beck, A. T., Kovacs, M., & Weissman, A. (1975). Hopelessness and suicidal behavior: An overview. *Journal of the American Medical Association, 234*, 1146–1149.

Beck, A. T., Rush, A. J., Shaw, B. F., & Emery, G. (1979). *Cognitive therapy of depression.* New York: Guilford.

Beck, A. T., Steer, R. A., & Brown, G. K. (1996). *Manual for the Beck Depression Inventory-II.* San Antonio, TX: The Psychological Corporation.

Beck, A. T., Ward, C. H., Mendelson, M., Mock, J., & Erbaugh, J. (1961). An inventory for measuring depression. *Archives of General Psychiatry, 4*, 561–571.

Beck, A. T., Weissman, A., Lester, D., & Trexler, L. (1974). Measurement of pessimism: The Hopelessness Scale. *Journal of Consulting and Clinical Psychology, 42*, 861–865.

Beck, J. S. (1995). *Cognitive therapy: Basics and beyond.* New York: Guilford.

Beck, M. (2002, August). A new leash on life. *O: The Oprah Magazine, 3*(8), 57–58.

Beck, M. (2006, February). Martha Beck's guide to avoiding avoidance. *O: The Oprah Magazine, 7*(2), 73–74, 76.

Beckham, E. E., Leber, W. R., & Youll, L. K. (1995). The diagnostic classification of depression. In E. E. Beckham & W. R. Leber (Eds.), *Handbook of depression* (2nd ed., pp. 36–60). New York: Guilford.

Berglas, S. (1990) Self-handicapping: Etiological and diagnostic considerations. In R. L. Higgins, C. R. Snyder, & S. Berglas (Eds.), *Self-handicapping: The paradox that isn't* (pp. 151–186). New York: Plenum.

Biglan, A., & Hayes, S. C. (1996). Should the behavioral sciences become more pragmatic? The case for functional contextualism in research on human behavior. *Applied and Preventive Psychology: Current Scientific Perspectives, 5*, 47–57.

Blackledge, J. T., & Ciarrochi, J. (2005). *Initial validation of the Personal Values Questionnaire.* Unpublished manuscript, University of Wollongong, Wollongong, New South Wales, Australia.

Borkovec, T. D., Ray, W. J., & Stober, J. (1998). Worry: A cognitive phenomenon linked to affective, physiological, and interpersonal behavioral processes. *Cognitive Therapy and Research, 22*, 561–576.

Broderick, P. C. (2005). Mindfulness and coping with dysphoric mood: Contrasts with rumination and distraction. *Cognitive Therapy and Research, 29*, 501–510.

Brown, G. K., Beck, A. T., Steer, R. A., & Grisham, J. R. (2000). Risk factors for suicide in psychiatric outpatients: A 20-year prospective study. *Journal of Consulting and Clinical Psychology, 68*, 371–377.

Brown, T. A., Campbell, L. A., Lehman, C. L., Grisham, J. R., & Mancill, R. B. (2001). Current and lifetime comorbidity of the *DSM-IV* anxiety and mood disorders in a large clinical sample. *Journal of Abnormal Psychology, 110*, 585–599.

Brown, T. A., O'Leary, T. A., & Barlow, D. H. (2001). Generalized anxiety disorder. In D. H. Barlow (Ed.), *Handbook of psychological disorders: A step-by-step treatment manual* (3rd ed., pp. 154–208). New York: Guilford.

Burns, D. D. (1980). *Feeling good: The new mood therapy.* New York: Morrow.

Carlisle, J. C. (1938). Depressions which followed apparent success. *American Journal of Psychiatry, 95*, 729–732.

Carr, D. (2003). Effects of exemplar training in exclusion responding on auditory-visual discrimination tasks with children with autism. *Journal of Applied Behavior Analysis, 36*, 507–524.

Caspi, O., & Burleson, K. O. (2005). Methodological challenges in meditation research. *Advances in Mind-Body Medicine, 21*, 4–11.

Catania, A. C., Matthews, B. A., & Shimoff, E. (1982). Instructed versus shaped human behavior: Interactions with nonverbal responding. *Journal of the Experimental Analysis of Behavior, 38*, 233–248.

Chambless, D. L., Baker, M. J., Baucom, D. H., Beutler, L. E., Calhoun, K. S., Crits-Christoph, P., et al. (1998). Update on empirically validated therapies, II. *The Clinical Psychologist, 51*, 3–16.

Chambless, D. L., Sanderson, W. C., Shoham, V., Bennett Johnson, S., Pope, K. S., Crits-Christoph, P., et al. (1996). An update on empirically validated therapies. *The Clinical Psychologist, 49*, 5–18.

Channon, S., & Baker, J. E. (1996). Depression and problem-solving performance on a fault-diagnosis task. *Applied Cognitive Psychology, 10*, 327–336.

Chiles, J. A., & Strosahl, K. D. (2005). *Clinical manual for assessment and treatment of suicidal patients.* Washington, DC: American Psychiatric Publishing, Inc.

Chomsky, N. (1965). *Aspects of the theory of syntax.* Cambridge, MA: MIT Press.

Ciminero, A. R. (1986). Behavioral assessment: An overview. In A. R. Ciminero, K. S. Calhoun, & H. E. Adams (Eds.), *Handbook of behavioral assessment* (2nd ed., pp. 3–11). New York: Wiley-Interscience.

Ciminero, A. R., Calhoun, K. S., & Adams, H. E. (Eds.). (1977). *Handbook of behavioral assessment*. New York: Wiley-Interscience.

Cloud, J. (2006, February 13). Happiness isn't normal. *Time, 167*(7), 58–67.

Cone, J. D., & Hawkins, R. P. (Eds.). (1977). *Behavioral assessment: New directions in clinical psychology*. New York: Brunner/Mazel.

Consensus Development Panel. (1985). NIMH/NIH consensus development conference statement: Mood disorders—pharmacologic prevention of recurrence. *American Journal of Psychiatry, 142*, 469–476.

Craske, M. C., & Barlow, D. H. (2001). Panic disorder and agoraphobia. In D. H. Barlow (Ed.), *Clinical handbook of psychological disorders: A step-by-step treatment manual* (3rd ed., pp. 1–59). New York: Guilford.

Cross-Drew, C. (2002). *Final report: Dual diagnosis demonstration projects*. Sacramento, CA: State of California, Departments of Mental Health and Alcohol and Drug Programs.

Cryan, J. F., & Holmes, A. (2005). The ascent of mouse: Advances in modelling human depression and anxiety. *Nature Reviews Drug Discovery, 4*, 775–790.

Davis, R. N., & Nolen-Hoeksema, S. (2000). Cognitive inflexibility among ruminators and nonruminators. *Cognitive Therapy and Research, 24*, 699–711.

Delmonte, M. M., & Vincent, K. (1985). An overview of the therapeutic effects of meditation. *Psychologia: An International Journal of Psychology in the Orient, 28*, 189–202.

de Posada, J. (2003). *How to survive among the piranhas: Tips, techniques, strategies, and materials to win*. Bloomington, IN: AuthorHouse.

Devany, J. M., Hayes, S. C., & Nelson, R. O. (1986). Equivalence class formation in language-able and language-disabled children. *Journal of the Experimental Analysis of Behavior, 46*, 243–257.

Diener, E., Emmons, R. A., Larsen, R. J., & Griffin, S. (1985). The Satisfaction with Life Scale. *Journal of Personality Assessment, 49*, 71–75.

Dimdjian, S., Hollon, S. D., Dobson, K. S., Schmaling, K. B., Kohlenberg, R. J., Addis, M. E., et al. (2006). Randomized trial of behavioral activation, cognitive therapy, and antidepressant medication in the acute treatment of adults with major depression. *Journal of Consulting and Clinical Psychology, 74*, 658–670.

Dougher, M. J., Hamilton, D., Fink, B., & Harrington, J. (in press). Transformation of the discriminative and eliciting functions of generalized relational stimuli. *Journal of the Experimental Analysis of Behavior*.

Egloff, B., & Schmukle, S. C. (2002). Predictive validity of an implicit association test for assessing anxiety. *Journal of Personality and Social Psychology, 83*, 1441–1455.

Eifert, G. H., & Forsyth, J. P. (2005). *Acceptance and commitment therapy for anxiety disorders: A practitioner's guide to using mindfulness, acceptance, and value-based behavior change strategies*. Oakland, CA: New Harbinger.

Estes, W. K., & Skinner, B. F. (1941). Some quantitative properties of anxiety. *Journal of Experimental Psychology, 29,* 390–400.

Farber, I. E. (1948). Response fixation under anxiety and non-anxiety conditions. *Journal of Experimental Psychology, 38,* 112–131.

Feldman, R. S. (1957). The role of primary drive reduction in fixations. *Psychological Review, 64,* 85–90.

Ferster, C. B. (1953). The use of the free operant in the analysis of behavior. *Psychological Bulletin, 50,* 263–274.

Ferster, C. B. (1973). A functional analysis of depression. *American Psychologist, 28,* 857–870.

Fiedler, K., & Bluemke, M. (2005). Aided and unaided response control on the implicit association tests. *Basic and Applied Social Psychology, 27,* 307–316.

Fling, S., Thomas, A., & Gallaher, M. (1981). Participant characteristics and the effects of two types of meditation vs. quiet sitting. *Journal of Clinical Psychology, 37,* 784–790.

Follette. W. C., & Houts, A. C. (1996). Models of scientific progress and the role of theory in taxonomy development: A case study of the *DSM. Journal of Consulting and Clinical Psychology, 64,* 1120–1132.

Frankl, V. E. (1965). *Man's search for meaning: An introduction to logotherapy.* Boston: Beacon Press.

Franks, C. M. (Ed.). (1969). *Behavior therapy: Appraisal and status.* New York: McGraw-Hill.

Garland, A., & Scott, J. (2005). Depression. In N. Kazantzis, F. P. Deane, K. R. Ronan, & L. L'Abate (Eds.), *Using homework assignments in cognitive behavior therapy* (pp. 237–261). New York: Routledge.

Garst, M. L., & Zettle, R. D. (2006). *The relationship among reason-giving, experiential avoidance, and levels of depression.* Unpublished manuscript, Wichita State University, KS.

Gaynor, S. T., Lawrence, P. S., & Nelson-Gray, R. O. (2006). Measuring homework compliance in cognitive-behavioral therapy for depression: Review, preliminary findings, and implications for theory and practice. *Behavior Modification, 30.* 647–672.

Gird, S., & Zettle, R. D. (2007). *Differential response to a mood induction procedure as a function of level of experiential avoidance.* Unpublished manuscript, Wichita State University, KS.

Gortner, E. T., Gollan, J. K., Dobson, K. S., & Jacobson, N. S. (1998). Cognitive-behavioral treatment for depression: Relapse prevention. *Journal of Consulting and Clinical Psychology, 66,* 377–384.

Grant, D. A., & Berg, E. A. (1948). A behavioral analysis of degree of reinforcement and ease of shifting to new responses in a Weigl-type card sorting problem. *Journal of Experimental Psychology, 34,* 404–411.

Greenwald, A. G., McGhee, D. E., & Schwartz, J. L. K. (1998). Measuring individual differences in implicit cognition: The Implicit Association Test. *Journal of Personality and Social Psychology, 74*, 1464–1480.

Haaga, D. A. F. (Ed.). (2004). Research on acceptance and commitment therapy [Special issue]. *Behavior Therapy, 35*(4).

Haggard, M. (1966). The bottle let me down. On *Swinging doors and the bottle let me down* [Record]. Los Angeles: Capitol.

Hamilton, M. (1960). A rating scale for depression. *Journal of Neurology, Neurosurgery, and Psychiatry, 23*, 56–61.

Hayes, S. C. (1978). Theory and technology in behavior analysis. *The Behavior Analyst, 1*, 25–33.

Hayes, S. C. (1981). Single case experimental design and empirical clinical practice. *Journal of Consulting and Clinical Psychology, 49*, 193–211.

Hayes, S. C. (1987). A contextual approach to therapeutic change. In N. S. Jacobson (Ed.), *Psychotherapists in clinical practice: Cognitive and behavioral perspectives* (pp. 327–387). New York: Guilford.

Hayes, S. C. (1992). Verbal relations, time, and suicide. In S. C. Hayes & L. J. Hayes (Eds.), *Understanding verbal relations: The Second and Third International Institute on Verbal Relations* (pp. 109–118). Reno, NV: Context Press.

Hayes, S. C. (1993). Analytic goals and the varieties of scientific contextualism. In S. C. Hayes, L. J. Hayes, H. W. Reese, & T. R. Sarbin (Eds.), *Varieties of scientific contextualism* (pp. 11–27). Reno, NV: Context Press.

Hayes, S. C. (2004). Acceptance and commitment therapy, relational frame theory, and the third wave of behavioral and cognitive therapies. *Behavior Therapy, 35*, 639–665.

Hayes, S. C. (2005). An interview with Steven Hayes on *Get out of your mind and into your life*. Retrieved December 20, 2005, from New Harbinger Publications, Inc. website: http://www.newharbinger.com/client/client_pages/prev_interviews/monthinterview_HAYES.cfm

Hayes, S. C., Barnes-Holmes, D., & Roche, B. (Eds.). (2001). *Relational frame theory: A post Skinnerian account of human language and cognition*. New York: Plenum.

Hayes, S. C., & Brownstein, A. J. (1985, May). *Verbal behavior, equivalence classes, and rules: New definitions, data, and directions*. Invited address presented at the meeting of the Association for Behavior Analysis, Columbus, OH.

Hayes, S. C., & Brownstein, A. J. (1986). Mentalism, behavior-behavior relations, and a behavior analytic view of the purposes of science. *The Behavior Analyst, 9*, 175–190.

Hayes, S. C., Brownstein, A. J., Haas, J. R., & Greenway, D. E. (1986). Instructions, multiple schedules, and extinction: Distinguishing rule-governed from schedule controlled behavior. *Journal of the Experimental Analysis of Behavior, 46*, 137–147.

Hayes, S. C., Brownstein, A. J., Zettle, R. D., Rosenfarb, I., & Korn, Z. (1986). Rule-governed behavior and sensitivity to changing consequences of responding. *Journal of the Experimental Analysis of Behavior, 45*, 237–256.

Hayes, S. C., Follette, W. C., & Follette, V. (1995). Behavior therapy: A contextual approach. In A. S. German & B. Messer (Eds.), *Essential psychotherapies: Theory and practice* (pp. 128–181). New York: Guilford.

Hayes, S. C., & Hayes, L. J. (1989). The verbal action of the listener as a basis for rule-governance. In S. C. Hayes (Ed.), *Rule-governed behavior: Cognition, contingencies, and instructional control* (pp. 153–190). New York: Plenum.

Hayes, S. C., & Hayes, L. J. (1992). Some clinical implications of contextualistic behaviorism: The example of cognition. *Behavior Therapy, 23*, 225–249.

Hayes, S. C., Hayes, L. J., & Reese, H. W. (1988). Finding the philosophical core: A review of Stephen C. Pepper's *World hypotheses. Journal of the Experimental Analysis of Behavior, 50*, 97–111.

Hayes, S. C., Hayes, L. J., Reese, H. W., & Sarbin, T. R. (Eds.). (1993). *Varieties of scientific contextualism.* Reno, NV: Context Press.

Hayes, S. C., Luoma, J. B., Bond, F. W., Masuda, A., & Lillis, J. (2006). Acceptance and commitment therapy: Model, processes and outcomes. *Behaviour Research and Therapy, 44*, 1–25.

Hayes, S. C., Nelson, R. O., & Jarrett, R. B. (1987). The treatment utility of assessment: A functional approach to evaluating assessment quality. *American Psychologist, 42*, 963–974.

Hayes, S. C., & Smith, S. (2005). *Get out of your mind and into your life.* Oakland, CA: New Harbinger.

Hayes, S. C., & Strosahl, K. D. (Eds.). (2004). *A practical guide to acceptance and commitment therapy.* New York: Springer.

Hayes, S. C., Strosahl. K. D., Bunting, K., Twohig, M., & Wilson, K. G. (2004). What is acceptance and commitment therapy? In S. C. Hayes & K. D. Strosahl (Eds.), *A practical guide to acceptance and commitment therapy* (pp. 3–29). New York: Springer.

Hayes, S. C., Strosahl, K. D., Luoma, J., Smith, A. A., & Wilson, K. G. (2004). ACT case formulation. In S. C. Hayes & K. D. Strosahl (Eds.), *A practical guide to acceptance and commitment therapy* (pp. 59–73). New York: Springer.

Hayes, S. C., Strosahl, K. D., & Wilson, K. G. (1999). *Acceptance and commitment therapy: An experiential approach to behavior change.* New York: Guilford.

Hayes, S. C., Strosahl, K. D., Wilson. K. G., Bissett, R. T., Pistorello, J., Tomarino, D., et al. (2004). Measuring experiential avoidance: A preliminary test of a working model. *The Psychological Record, 54*, 553–578.

Hayes, S. C., & Wilson, K. G. (1994). Acceptance and commitment therapy: Altering the verbal support for experiential avoidance. *The Behavior Analyst, 17*, 289–303.

Hayes. S. C., Wilson, K. G., Gifford, E. V., Follette, V. M., & Strosahl, K. (1996). Experiential avoidance and behavioral disorders: A functional dimensional approach to diagnosis and treatment. *Journal of Consulting and Clinical Psychology, 64,* 1152–1168.

Hayes, S. C., Zettle, R. D., & Rosenfarb, I. (1989). Rule following. In S. C. Hayes (Ed.), *Rule-governed behavior: Cognition, contingencies, and instructional control* (pp. 191–220). New York: Plenum.

Henriksson, M. M., Aro, H. M., Marttunen, M. J., Heikkkinen, M. E., Isometsa, E. T., Kuoppasalmi, K. I., et al. (1993). Mental disorders and comorbidity in suicide. *American Journal of Psychiatry, 150,* 945–940.

Hersen, M., & Bellack, A. S. (Eds.). (1976). *Behavioral assessment: A practical handbook.* New York: Pergamon.

Hersen, M., Bellack, A. S., Himmelhoch, J. M., & Thase, M. E. (1984). Effects of social skill training, amitriptyline, and psychotherapy in unipolar depressed women. *Behavior Therapy, 15,* 21–40.

Higgins, R. L., & Berglas, S. (1990). The maintenance and treatment of self-handicapping: From risk-taking to face-saving—and back. In R. L. Higgins, C. R. Snyder, & S. Berglas (Eds.), *Self-handicapping: The paradox that isn't* (pp. 187–238). New York: Plenum.

Hollon, S. D., & Beck, A. T. (1979). Cognitive therapy of depression. In P. C. Kendall & S. D. Hollon (Eds.), *Cognitive-behavioral interventions: Theory, research, and procedures* (pp. 153–203). New York: Academic Press.

Hollon, S. D., & Kendall, P. C. (1980). Cognitive self-statements in depression: Development of an automatic thoughts questionnaire. *Cognitive Therapy and Research, 4,* 383–395.

Hollon, S. D., Thase, M. E., & Markowitz, J. C. (2002). Treatment and prevention of depression. *Psychological Science in the Public Interest, 3,* 39–77.

Holowka, D. W., Salters-Pedneault, K., & Roemer, L. (2005, November). *The role of experiential avoidance and rumination in depressive symptoms.* Poster session presented at the annual meeting of the Association for Behavioral and Cognitive Therapies, Washington, DC.

Hopkinson, J., & Neuringer, A. (2003). Modifying behavioral variability in moderately depressed students. *Behavior Modification, 27,* 251–264.

Horne, R. L., Evans, F. J., & Orne, M. T. (1982). Random number generation, psychopathology, and therapeutic change. *Archives of General Psychiatry, 39,* 680–683.

Ilardi, S. S., & Craighead, W. E. (1994). The role of nonspecific factors in cognitive-behavior therapy for depression. *Clinical Psychology: Science and Practice, 1,* 138–156.

Ivanoff, A., Jang, S. J., Smyth, N. J., & Linehan, M. M. (1994). Fewer reasons for staying alive when you are thinking of killing yourself: The Brief Reasons for Living Inventory. *Journal of Psychopathology and Behavioral Assessment, 16,* 1–13.

Jacobson, N. S., & Christensen, A. (1996). *Integrative couple therapy: Promoting acceptance and change.* New York: Norton.

Jacobson, N. S., Dobson, K. S., Truax, P. A., Addis, M. E., Koerner, K., Gollan, J. K., et al. (1996). A component analysis of cognitive-behavioral treatment of depression. *Journal of Consulting and Clinical Psychology, 64,* 295–304.

Jacobson, N. S., Martell, C. R., & Dimidjian, S. (2001). Behavioral activation treatment for depression: Returning to contextual roots. *Clinical Psychology: Science and Practice, 8,* 255–270.

Jones, M. C. (1924). The elimination of children's fears. *Journal of Experimental Psychology, 7,* 382–390.

Joormann, J., Kosfelder, J., & Schulte, D. (2005). The impact of comorbidity of depression on the course of anxiety treatments. *Cognitive Therapy and Research, 29,* 569–591.

Kabat-Zinn, J. (1990). *Full catastrophe living: Using the wisdom of your body and mind to face stress, pain, and illness.* New York: Delacorte Press.

Kabat-Zinn, J. (1994). *Wherever you go, there you are: Mindfulness meditation in everyday life.* New York: Hyperion.

Kabat-Zinn, J. (2005). *Coming to our senses: Healing ourselves and the world through mindfulness.* New York: Hyperion.

Kabat-Zinn, J., Lipworth, L., & Burney, R. (1985). The clinical use of mindfulness meditation for the self-regulation of chronic pain. *Journal of Behavioral Medicine, 8,* 163–190.

Kabat-Zinn, J., Massion, A. O., Kristeller, J., Peterson, L. G., Fletcher, K. E., Pbert, L., et al. (1992). Effectiveness of a meditation-based stress reduction program in the treatment of anxiety disorders. *The American Journal of Psychiatry, 149,* 936–943.

Kaelber, C. T., Moul, D. E., & Farmer, M. E. (1995). Epidemiology of depression. In E. E. Beckham & W. R. Leber (Eds.), *Handbook of depression* (2nd ed., pp. 3–35). New York: Guilford.

Kanfer, F. H., & Phillips, J. S. (1970). *Learning foundations of behavior therapy.* New York: Wiley.

Kantor, J. T. (1959). *Interbehavioral psychology.* Chicago: Principia.

Kazantzis, N., Deane, F. P., Ronan, K. R., & L'Abate, L. (Eds.). (2005). *Using homework assignments in cognitive behavior therapy.* New York: Routledge.

Kessler, R. C., Berglund, P., Demler, O., Jin. R., Koretz, D., Merikangas, K. R., et al. (2003). The epidemiology of major depressive disorder: Results from the National Comorbidity Survey Replication (NCS-R). *Journal of the American Medical Association, 289,* 3095–3105.

Kessler, R. C., Chiu, W. T., Demler, O., & Walters, E. E. (2005). Prevalence, severity, and comorbidity of 12-month *DSM-IV* disorders in the National Comorbidity Survey Replication. *Archives of General Psychiatry, 62,* 617–627.

Kessler, R. C., Nelson, C. B., McGonagle, K. A., Edlund, M. J., Frank, R. G., & Leaf, P. J. (1996). The epidemiology of co-occurring addictive and mental disorders: Implications for prevention and service utilization. *American Journal of Orthopsychiatry, 66*, 17–31.

Kim, D. Y. (2003). Voluntary controllability of the Implicit Association Test (IAT). *Social Psychological Quarterly, 66*, 83–96.

Klerman, G. L., Weissman, M. M., Rounsaville, B. J., & Chevron, E. S. (1984). *Interpersonal psychotherapy of depression*. New York: Basic Books.

Klinger, E. (1975). Consequences of commitment to disengagement from incentives. *Psychological Review, 82*, 1–25.

Kohlenberg, R. J., & Tsai, M. (1987). Functional analytic psychotherapy. In N. S. Jacobson (Ed.), *Psychotherapists in clinical practice: Cognitive and behavioral perspectives* (pp. 388–443). New York: Guilford.

Kohlenberg, R. J., & Tsai, M. (1991). *Functional analytic psychotherapy: Creating intense and curative therapeutic relationships*. New York: Plenum.

Kolligan, J., & Sternberg, R. J. (1991). Perceived fraudulence in young adults: Is there an "impostor syndrome"? *Journal of Personality Assessment, 56*, 308–326.

Kornblith, S. J., Rehm, L. P., O'Hara, M. W., & Lamparski, D. M. (1983). The contribution of self-reinforcement training and behavioral assignments to the efficacy of self-control therapy for depression. *Cognitive Therapy and Research, 6*, 499–528.

Kuhn, T. S. (1962). *The structure of scientific revolutions*. Chicago: University of Chicago Press.

Lal, H. (1966). Conflict induced fixation of stereotyped lever pressing responses. *Psychonomic Science, 6,* 333–334.

Lapp, J. E., Marinier, R., & Pihl, R. O. (1982). Correlates of psychotropic drug use in women: Interpersonal problem solving and depression. *Women & Health, 7,* 5–16.

Leitch, D[onovan]. P. (1973). Saint Valentine's angel. On *Essence to essence* [Record] New York: Epic.

Lewin, R., & Foley, R. A. (2004). *Principles of human evolution*. Malden, MA: Blackwell Science.

Lewinsohn, P. M., & Gotlib, I. H. (1995). Behavioral and cognitive treatment of depression. In E. E. Becker & W. R. Leber (Eds.), *Handbook of depression* (pp. 352–375). New York: Guilford.

Lewinsohn, P. M., Hoberman, H. M., & Clarke, G. N. (1989). The coping with depression course: Review and future directions. *Canadian Journal of Behavioural Science, 21*, 470–493.

Lillis, J., & Luoma, J. B. (2005). *ACT initial case conceptualization form*. Unpublished manuscript, University of Nevada, Reno.

Linehan, M. M. (1993a). *Cognitive-behavioral treatment of borderline personality disorder*. New York: Guilford.

Linehan, M. M. (1993b). *Skills training manual for treating borderline personality disorder*. New York: Guilford.

Linehan, M. M., Goodstein, J. L., Nielsen, S. L., & Chiles, J. S. (1983). Reasons for staying alive when you are thinking of killing yourself: The Reasons for Living Inventory. *Journal of Consulting and Clinical Psychology, 51*, 276–286.

Lyubomirsky, S., Caldwell, N. D., & Nolen-Hoeksema, S. (1998). Effects of ruminative and distracting responses to depressed mood on retrieval of autobiographical memories. *Journal of Personality and Social Psychology, 75*, 166–177.

Lyubomirsky, S., & Nolen-Hoeksema, S. (1993). Self-perpetuating properties of dysphoric rumination. *Journal of Personality and Social Psychology, 65*, 339–349.

Lyubomirsky, S., & Nolen-Hoeksema, S. (1995). Effects of self-focused rumination on negative thinking and interpersonal problem solving. *Journal of Personality and Social Psychology, 69*, 176–190.

Lyubomirsky, S., Tucker, K. L., Caldwell, N. D., & Berg, K. (1999). Why ruminators are poor problem solvers: Clues from the phenomenology of dysphoric rumination. *Journal of Personality and Social Psychology, 77*, 1041–1060.

MacKinnon, D. P. (2003, November). *Mediator and moderator methods*. Paper presented at the annual meeting of the Association for the Advancement of Behavior Therapy, Boston, MA.

Mahoney, M. J. (1974). *Cognition and behavior modification*. Cambridge, MA: Ballinger.

Maier, N. R. F. (1949). *Frustration*. New York: McGraw-Hill.

Malott, R. W., Whaley, D. L., & Malott, M. E. (1991). *Elementary principles of behavior* (2nd ed.). Englewood Cliffs, NJ: Prentice-Hall.

Maltsberger, J. T. (2003). Can a louse commit suicide? *Crisis: The Journal of Crisis Intervention and Suicide Prevention, 24*, 175–176.

Maris, R. W., Berman, A. L., Maltsberger, J. T., & Yufit, R. I. (1992). *Assessment and prediction of suicide*. New York: Guilford.

Mark Twain quotes. (n.d.). Retrieved October 6, 2006, from http://www.brainyquote.com/quotes/quotes/m/marktwain128157.html

Marshall, P. (Executive Producer/Director). (1992). *A league of their own* [Motion picture]. United States: Sony Pictures Entertainment.

Martell, C., Addis, M., & Dimidjian, S. (2004). Finding the action in behavioral action: The search for empirically supported interventions and mechanisms of change. In S. C. Hayes, V. M. Follette, & M. M. Linehan (Eds.), *Mindfulness and acceptance: Expanding the cognitive-behavioral tradition* (pp. 152–167). New York: Guilford.

Martin, D. J., Oren, Z., & Boone, K. (1991). Major depressives' and dysthymics' performance on the Wisconsin Card Sorting Task. *Journal of Clinical Psychology, 47*, 684–690.

Martin, G., & Pear, J. (2007). *Behavior modification: What it is and how to do it* (8th ed.). Upper Saddle River, NJ: Pearson Prentice Hall.

Mathers, C. D., & Loncar, D. (2005, October). *Updated projections of global mortality and burden of disease, 2002–2030: Data sources, methods and results.* Evidence and Information for Policy Working Paper. Geneva: World Health Organization.

McDaniel, E. A., & Zettle, R. D. (2006). *The relationship among spirituality, happiness, and experiential avoidance.* Unpublished manuscript, Wichita State University, KS.

McKenna, I. M., Barnes-Holmes, D., Barnes-Holmes, Y., & Stewart, I. (2006). *Testing the fake-ability of the Implicit Relational Assessment Procedure (IRAP): The first study.* Manuscript submitted for publication.

McKnight, D. L., Nelson-Gray, R. O., & Barnhill, J. (1992). Dexamethasone suppression test and response to cognitive therapy and antidepressant medication. *Behavior Therapy, 23*, 99–111.

McNeese, C. A., & DiNitto, D. M. (2005). *Chemical dependency: A systems approach.* New York: Pearson.

Meditation. (n.d.) In Wikipedia. Retrieved October 17, 2006, from http://en.Wikipedia.org/wiki/Meditation

Meichenbaum, D. H. (1977). *Cognitive-behavior modification: An integrative approach.* New York: Plenum.

Meichenbaum, D. H. (2005). 35 years of working with suicidal patients: Lessons learned. *Canadian Psychology, 46*, 64–72.

Miller, J. J., Fletcher, K., & Kabat-Zinn, J. (1995). Three-year follow-up and clinical implications of a mindfulness meditation–based stress reduction intervention in the treatment of anxiety disorders. *General Hospital Psychiatry, 17*, 192–200.

Miller, W. R., & Rollnick, S. (Eds.). (1991). *Motivational interviewing: Preparing people to change addictive behavior.* New York: Guilford.

Miller, W. R., & Rollnick, S. (Eds.). (2002). *Motivational interviewing: Preparing people for change* (2nd ed.). New York: Guilford.

Mineka, S., Watson, D., & Clark, L. A. (1998). Comorbidity of anxiety and unipolar mood disorders. *Annual Review of Psychology, 49*, 377–412.

Mitchell, J. G., Pyle, R. L., & Hatsukami, D. (1983). A comparative analysis of psychiatric problems listed by patients and physicians. *Hospital and Community Psychiatry, 34*, 848–849.

Mueser, K. T., Noordsy, D. L., Drake, R. E., & Fox, L. (2003). *Integrated treatment for dual disorders: A guide to effective practice.* New York: Guilford.

Murray, C. J. L., & Lopez, A. D. (Eds.). (1996). *The global burden of disease and injury series, Vol. 1: A comprehensive assessment of mortality and disability from diseases, injuries, and risk factors in 1990 and projected to 2020.* Cambridge, MA: Harvard University Press.

Nakken, C. (1996). *The addictive personality: Understanding the addictive process and compulsive behavior.* Center City, MN: Hazelden Foundation.

Neese, R. M. (2000). Is depression an adaptation? *Archives of General Psychiatry, 57*, 14–20.

Neimeyer, R. A., & Feixas, G. (1990). The role of homework and skill acquisition in the outcome of group cognitive therapy for depression. *Behavior Therapy, 21*, 281–292.

Nelson-Gray, R. O. (2003). Treatment utility of psychological assessment. *Psychological Assessment, 15*, 521–531.

Nolen-Hoeksema, S. (1990). *Sex differences in depression.* Stanford, CA: Stanford University Press.

Nolen-Hoeksema, S. (2000). The role of rumination in depressive disorders and mixed anxiety/depressive symptoms. *Journal of Abnormal Psychology, 109*, 504–511.

Nolen-Hoeksema, S., Larson, J., & Grayson. C. (1999). Explaining the gender difference in depressive symptoms. *Journal of Personality and Social Psychology, 77*, 1061–1072.

Nolen-Hoeksema, S., & Morrow, J. (1991). A prospective study of depression and post-traumatic stress symptoms after a natural disaster: The 1989 Loma Prieta earthquake. *Journal of Personality and Social Psychology, 61*, 115–121.

Nolen-Hoeksema, S., Parker, L. E., & Larson, J. (1994). Ruminative coping with depressed mood following loss. *Journal of Personality and Social Psychology, 67*, 92–104.

Olfson, M., Marcus, S. C., Druss, B., Elinson, L., Tanielian, T., & Pincus, H. A. (2002). National trends in the outpatient treatment of depression. *Journal of the American Medical Association, 287*, 203–209.

Olfson, M., Marcus, S. C., Wan, G. J., & Geissler, E. C. (2004). National trends in the outpatient treatment of anxiety disorders. *Journal of Clinical Psychiatry, 65*, 1166–1173.

Osborn, A. F. (1953). *Applied imagination.* New York: Scribners.

Paykel, E. S., Ramana, R., Cooper, Z., Hayhurst, H., Kerr, J., & Barocka, A. (1995). Residual symptoms after partial remission: An important outcome in depression. *Psychological Medicine, 25*, 1171–1180.

PDR drug guide for mental health professionals (1st ed.). (2002). Montvale, NJ: Thomson.

Penner, L. A., Shiffman, S., Paty, J. A., & Fritzsche, B. A. (1994). Individual differences in intraperson variability in mood. *Journal of Personality and Social Psychology, 66*, 712– 721.

Pepper, S. C. (1942). *World hypotheses: A study in evidence.* Berkeley, CA: University of California Press.

Perez-De-Albeniz, A., & Holmes, J. (2000). Meditation: Concepts, effects and uses in therapy. *International Journal of Psychotherapy, 5*, 49–58.

Petersen, C. L. (2007). *Treatment of comorbid depression and alcohol use disorders in an inpatient setting: Comparison of acceptance and commitment therapy and treatment as usual.* Unpublished doctoral dissertation, Wichita State University, KS.

Pilgrim. D., & Bentall, R. (1999). The medicalisation of misery: A critical realist analysis of the concept of depression. *Journal of Mental Health, 8*, 261–274.

Piper, W., Hauman, G., & Hauman, D. (1978). *The little engine that could*. New York: Grosset and Dunlap.

Pyszczynski, T., & Greenberg, J. (1987). Self-regulatory perseveration and the depressive self-focusing style: A self-awareness theory of reactive depression. *Psychological Bulletin, 102*, 122–138.

Reda, M. A., Carpiniello, B., Secchiaroli, L., & Blanco, S. (1985). Thinking, depression, and antidepressants: Modified and unmodified depressive beliefs during treatment with amitriptyline. *Cognitive Therapy and Research, 9*, 135–143.

Reese, H. W. (1968). *The perception of stimulus relations: Discrimination learning and transposition*. New York: Academic Press.

Regier, D. A., Farmer, M. E., Rae, D. S., Locke, B. Z., Keith, S. J., Judd, L. L., et al. (1990). Comorbidity of mental disorders with alcohol and other drug abuse: Results from the Epidemiologic Catchment Area (ECA) Study. *Journal of the American Medical Association, 264*, 2511–2518.

Reinecke, M. A. (2006). Problem solving: A conceptual approach to suicidality and psychotherapy. In T. E. Ellis (Ed.), *Cognition and suicide: Theory, research, and therapy* (pp. 237–260). Washington, DC: American Psychological Association.

Rimes, K. A., & Watkins, E. (2005). The effects of self-focused rumination on global negative self-judgements in depression. *Behaviour Research and Therapy, 43*, 1673–1681.

Ringel, E. (1976). The presuicidal syndrome. *Suicide and Life-Threatening Behavior, 6*, 131–149.

Roberts, J. E., Gilboa, E., & Gotlib, I. H. (1998). Ruminative response style and vulnerability to episodes of dysphoria: Gender, neuroticism, and episode duration. *Cognitive Therapy and Research, 22*, 401–423.

Robinson, E. A. (1921). *Collected poems*. New York: Macmillan.

Robinson, M. D., Wilkowski, B. M., Kirkeby, B. S., & Meier, B. P. (2006). Stuck in a rut: Perseverative response tendencies and the neuroticism-distress relationship. *Journal of Experimental Psychology: General, 135*, 78–91.

Ronan, K. R., & Kazantzis, N. (2006). The use of between-session (homework) activities in psychotherapy: Conclusions from the *Journal of Psychotherapy Integration* special series. *Journal of Psychotherapy Integration, 16*, 254–259.

Rosen, G. M., & Davison, G. C. (2003). Psychology should list empirically supported principles of change (ESPs) and not credential trademarked therapies or other treatment packages. *Behavior Modification, 27*, 300–312.

Rosenberg, M. (1965). *Society and the adolescent self-image*. Princeton, NJ: Princeton University Press.

Sanderson, W. C. (2003). Why empirically supported treatments are important. *Behavior Modification, 27*, 290–299.

Sanderson, W. C., & Wetzler, S. (1993). Observations on the cognitive-behavioral treatment of panic disorder: Impact of benzodiazepines. *Psychotherapy: Theory, Research and Practice, 30*, 125–132.

Segal, Z. V., Williams, J. M. G., & Teasdale, J. D. (2002). *Mindfulness-based cognitive therapy for depression: A new approach to preventing relapse.* New York: Guilford.

Seligman, M. E. P. (1975). *Helplessness: On depression, development, and death.* San Francisco: W. H. Freeman.

Seligman, M. E. P. (1990). Why is there so much depression today?: The waxing of the individual and the waning of the commons. In R. E. Ingram (Ed.), *Contemporary psychological approaches to depression: Theory, research, and treatment* (pp. 1–9). New York: Plenum.

Seligman, M. E. P., Rashid, T., & Parks, A. C. (2006). Positive psychotherapy. *American Psychologist, 61*, 775–788.

Shellenbarger, S. (2005). *The breaking point: How female midlife crisis is transforming today's women.* New York: Henry Holt & Company.

Shimoff, E., Catania, A. C., & Matthews, B. A. (1981). Uninstructed human responding: Sensitivity of low-rate performance to schedule contingencies. *Journal of the Experimental Analysis of Behavior, 36*, 207–220.

Silberman, E. K., Weingartner, H., & Post, R. M. (1983). Thinking disorder in depression: Logic and strategy in an abstract reasoning task. *Archives of General Psychiatry, 40*, 775–780.

Simons, A. D., Garfield, S. L., & Murphy, G. E. (1984). The process of change in cognitive therapy and pharmacotherapy of depression: Changes in mood and cognition. *Archives of General Psychiatry, 41*, 45–51.

Simons, A. D., Murphy, G. E., Levine, J. L., & Wetzel, R. D. (1986). Sustained improvement over one year after cognitive and/or pharmacotherapy of depression. *Archives of General Psychiatry, 43*, 43–48.

Skinner, B. F. (1953). *Science and human behavior.* New York: The Free Press.

Skinner, B. F. (1957). *Verbal behavior.* New York: Appleton-Century-Crofts.

Skinner, B. F. (1969). *Contingencies of reinforcement: A theoretical analysis.* New York: Appleton-Century-Crofts.

Skinner, B. F. (1974). *About behaviorism.* New York: Knopf.

Smith, J. M., Hughes, M. E., & Alloy, L. (2006, May). *Rumination increases risk of depression through experiential avoidance.* Poster session presented at the annual meeting of the Association for Psychological Science, New York.

Smith, M. T., Perlis, M. L., Park, A., Smith, M. S., Pennington, J., Giles, D. E., et al. (2002). Comparative meta-analysis of pharmacotherapy and behavior therapy for persistent insomnia. *American Journal of Psychiatry, 159*, 5–11.

Snyder, C. R. (1990). Self-handicapping processes and sequelae: On the taking of a psychological dive. In R. L. Higgins, C. R. Snyder, & S. Berglas (Eds.), *Self-handicapping: The paradox that isn't* (pp. 107–150). New York: Plenum.

Steele, D. L., & Hayes, S. C. (1991). Stimulus equivalence and arbitrary applicable relational responding. *Journal of the Experimental Analysis of Behavior, 56*, 519–555.

Steffens, M. C. (2004). Is the Implicit Association Test immune to faking? *Experimental Psychology, 51*, 165–179

Storr, A. (1988). *Churchill's black dog, Kafka's mice, and other phenomena of the human mind*. New York: Grove Press.

Strosahl, K. D. (2004). ACT with the multi-problem patient. In S. C. Hayes & K. D. Strosahl (Eds.), *A practical guide to acceptance and commitment therapy* (pp. 209–245). New York: Springer.

Strosahl, K. D., Hayes, S. C., Wilson, K. G., & Gifford, E. V. (2004). An ACT primer: Core therapy processes, intervention strategies, and therapist competencies. In S. C. Hayes & K. D. Strosahl (Eds.), *A practical guide to acceptance and commitment therapy* (pp. 31–58). New York: Springer.

Tanouye, E. (2001). Mental illness: A rising workplace cost. *The Wall Street Journal* (pp. B1, B6).

Task Force on Promotion and Dissemination of Psychological Procedures. (1995). Training in and dissemination of empirically-validated psychological treatments: Report and recommendations. *The Clinical Psychologist, 48*, 3–23.

Thase, M. E., & Callan. J. A. (2006). The role of homework in cognitive behavior therapy of depression. *Journal of Psychotherapy Integration, 16*, 162–177.

Thoreau, H. D. (1995). Walden, or life in the woods. In W. Harding (Ed.), *Walden: An annotated edition*. New York: Houghton Mifflin. (Original work published 1854.)

Thwaites, R., Dagnan, D., Huey, D., & Addis, M. E. (2004). The reasons for depression questionnaire (RFD): UK standardization for clinical and non-clinical populations. *Psychology and Psychotherapy: Theory, Research and Practice, 77*, 363–374.

Titchener, E. B. (1926). *A text-book of psychology*. New York: MacMillan.

Vahey, N. A., Barnes-Holmes, D., Barnes-Holmes, Y., & Stewart, I. (2006). *The Implicit Relational Assessment Procedure (IRAP) as a measure of self-esteem in prisoners and university students*. Manuscript submitted for publication.

Valentine, E. R., & Sweet, P. L. G. (1999). Meditation and attention: A comparison of the effects of concentrative and mindfulness meditation on sustained attention. *Mental Health, Religion and Culture, 2*, 59–70.

Wagner, C. C., & Sanchez, F. P. (2002). The role of values in motivational interviewing. In W. R. Miller & S. Rollnick (Eds.), *Motivational interviewing: Preparing people for change* (2nd ed., pp. 284–298). New York: Guilford.

Ward, A., Lyubomirsky, S., Sousa, L., & Nolen-Hoeksema, S. (2003). Can't quite commit: Rumination and uncertainty. *Personality and Social Psychology Bulletin, 29*, 96–107.

Ward, N. G., Bloom, V. L., & Friedel, R. O. (1979). The effectiveness of tricyclic antidepressants in chronic depression. *Journal of Clinical Psychiatry, 40,* 83–89.

Wardle, J. (1990). Behaviour therapy and benzodiazepines: Allies or antagonists? *British Journal of Psychiatry, 156,* 163–168.

Waterhouse, G., & Strupp, H. (1984). The patient-therapist relationship: Research from the psychodynamic perspective. *Clinical Psychology Review, 4,* 77–92.

Watkins, E., & Brown, R. G. (2002). Rumination and executive function in depression: An experimental study. *Journal of Neurology, Neurosurgery and Psychiatry, 72,* 400–402.

Watkins, E., Moulds, M., & Mackintosh, B. (2005). Comparisons between rumination and worry in a non-clinical population. *Behaviour Research and Therapy, 43,* 1577–1585.

Watkins, E., & Teasdale, J. D. (2001). Rumination and overgeneral memory in depression: Effects of self-focus and analytic thinking. *Journal of Abnormal Psychology, 110,* 353–357.

Wegner, D. M. (1994). *White bears and other unwanted thoughts: Suppression, obsession, and the psychology of mental control.* New York: Guilford.

Wegner, D. M., & Zanakos, S. (1994). Chronic thought suppression. *Journal of Personality, 62,* 615–640.

Weisner, C., Greenfield, T., & Room, R. (1995). Trends in the treatment of alcohol problems in the US general population, 1979 through 1990. *American Journal of Public Health, 85,* 55–60.

Weissman, A., & Beck, A. T. (1978, November). *Development and validation of the Dysfunctional Attitude Scale.* Paper presented at the annual meeting of the Association for the Advancement of Behavior Therapy, Chicago, IL.

Wenzlaff, R. M. (1993). The mental control of depression. Psychological obstacles to emotional well-being. In D. M. Wegner & J. W. Pennebaker (Eds.), *Handbook of mental control* (pp. 238–257). Englewood Cliffs, NJ: Prentice-Hall.

Wenzlaff, R. M., & Luxton, D. D. (2003). The role of thought suppression in depressive rumination. *Cognitive Therapy and Research, 27,* 293–308,

Wenzlaff, R. M., Wegner, D. M., & Klein, S. B. (1991). The role of thought suppression in the bonding of thought and mood. *Journal of Personality and Social Psychology, 60,* 500–508.

Wenzlaff, R. M., Wegner, D. M., & Roper, D. W. (1988). Depression and mental control: The resurgence of unwanted thoughts. *Journal of Personality and Social Psychology, 55,* 882–892.

Williams, D. C. (2006). Taking religion seriously. *Journal of Constructivist Psychology, 19,* 97–101.

Wilson, K. G. (2005, July). *Acceptance and commitment therapy pre-institute advanced workshop.* Presented at the meeting of the ACT Summer Institute, Philadelphia, PA.

Wilson, K. G. (2006, March 5). Escape avoid? Message posted to http://acceptanceand commitmenttherapy@yahoogroups.com.

Wilson, K. G., & Byrd, M. R. (2004). ACT for substance abuse and dependence. In S. C. Hayes & K. D. Strosahl (Eds.), *A practical guide to acceptance and commitment therapy* (pp. 153–184). New York: Springer.

Wilson, K. G., & Groom, J. (2002). *The Valued Living Questionnaire*. Unpublished manuscript, University of Mississippi, Oxford.

Wilson, K. G., Hayes, S. C., Gregg, J., & Zettle, R. D. (2001). Psychopathology and psychotherapy. In S. C. Hayes, D. Barnes-Holmes, & B. Roche (Eds.), *Relational frame theory: A post-Skinnerian account of human language and cognition* (pp. 211–237). New York: Plenum.

Wilson, K. G., Khorakiwala, D., & Hayes, S. C. (1991, May). Change in acceptance and commitment therapy. In K. G. Wilson (Chair), *Radical behavioral psychotherapy process research*. Symposium presented at the meeting of the Association for Behavior Analysis, Atlanta, GA.

Wilson, K. G., & Murrell, A. R. (2004). Values work in acceptance and commitment therapy: Setting a course for behavioral treatment. In S. C. Hayes, V. M. Folette, & M. M. Linehan (Eds.), *Mindfulness and acceptance: Expanding the cognitive-behavioral tradition* (pp. 120–151). New York: Guilford.

Wilson, K. G., & Taylor, N. (1991, November). Why the "acceptance" in acceptance and commitment therapy (ACT)? In S. C. Hayes (Chair), *Acceptance as change: Acceptance as a strategy of clinical intervention*. Symposium presented at the meeting of the Association for Advancement of Behavior Therapy, New York.

Wolpe, J. (1958). *Psychotherapy by reciprocal inhibition*. Stanford, CA: Stanford University Press.

Wulfert, E. (1994). Acceptance in the treatment of alcoholism: A comparison of Alcoholics Anonymous and social learning theory. In S. C Hayes, N. S. Jacobson, V. M. Follette, & M. J. Dougher (Eds.), *Acceptance and change: Content and context in psychotherapy* (pp. 203–217). Reno, NV: Context Press.

Yates, A. J. (1970). *Behavior therapy*. New York: Wiley.

Yoda quotes. (n.d.). Retrieved October 6, 2006, from http://en.thinkexist.com /quotes/yoda/

Yuille, J. C., & Sereda, L. (1980). Positive effects of meditation: A limited generalization? *Journal of Applied Psychology, 65,* 333–340.

Zettle, R. D. (1990). Rule-governed behavior: A radical behavioral answer to the cognitive challenge. *The Psychological Record, 40,* 41–49.

Zettle, R. D. (1994). On the use of acceptable language. In S. C. Hayes, N. S. Jacobson, V. M. Follette, & M. J. Dougher (Eds.), *Acceptance and change: Content and context in psychotherapy* (pp. 46–50). Reno, NV: Context Press.

Zettle, R. D. (2004). ACT with affective disorders. In S. C. Hayes & K. D. Strosahl (Eds.), *A practical guide to acceptance and commitment therapy* (pp. 77–102). New York: Springer.

Zettle, R. D. (2005). The evolution of a contextual approach to therapy: From comprehensive distancing to ACT. *International Journal of Behavioral and Consultation Therapy, 1,* 77–89.

Zettle, R. D. (2006, July). *The history of ACT/RFT: Observations from an eyewitness.* Paper presented at the Second World Conference on ACT, RFT, and Contextual Behavioural Science, London.

Zettle, R. D., Haflich, J. L., & Reynolds, R. A. (1992). Responsivity to cognitive therapy as a function of treatment format and client personality dimensions. *Journal of Clinical Psychology, 48,* 787–797.

Zettle, R. D., & Hayes, S. C. (1982). Rule-governed behavior: A potential theoretical framework for cognitive-behavioral therapy. In P. C. Kendall (Ed.), *Advances in cognitive-behavioral research and therapy* (pp. 73–118). New York: Academic Press.

Zettle, R. D., & Hayes, S. C. (1983). Effect of social context on the impact of coping self-statements. *Psychological Reports, 52,* 391–401.

Zettle, R. D., & Hayes, S. C. (1986). Dysfunctional control by client verbal behavior: The context of reason-giving. *The Analysis of Verbal Behavior, 4,* 30–38.

Zettle, R. D., & Hayes, S. C. (1987). Component and process analysis of cognitive therapy. *Psychological Reports, 64,* 939–953.

Zettle, R. D., & Hayes, S. C. (2002). Brief ACT treatment of depression. In F. W. Bond & W. Dryden (Eds.), *Handbook of brief cognitive behaviour therapy* (pp. 35–54). Chichester, England: Wiley.

Zettle, R. D., & Herring, E. L. (1995). Treatment utility of the sociotropy/autonomy distinction: Implications for cognitive therapy. *Journal of Clinical Psychology, 51,* 280–289.

Zettle, R. D., Hocker, T. R., Mick, K. A., Scofield, B. E., Petersen, C. L., Song, H., et al. (2005). Differential strategies in coping with pain as a function of level of experiential avoidance. *The Psychological Record, 55,* 511–524.

Zettle, R. D., Petersen, C. L,, Hocker, T. R., & Provines, J. L. (2007). Responding to a challenging perceptual-motor task as a function of level of experiential avoidance. *The Psychological Record, 57,* 49–62.

Zettle, R. D., & Rains, J. C. (1989). Group cognitive and contextual therapies in treatment of depression. *Journal of Clinical Psychology, 45,* 438–445.

Index

cognitive defusion. *See* defusion

cognitive fixation, 46-47

cognitive therapy, 2, 5, 17-19; ACT distinguished from, 18-19; mindfulness- based, 19-20; research comparing ACT to, 17-18

combinatorial entailment, 10

commitment: nature of, 127; partial vs. full, 129-130; superordinate process of, 13

committed action, 16, 126-133; assessment of, 66-67, 72; barriers to, 131-133, 187, 190-192, 212; clarifying object of, 130; goal setting and, 126-127, 188, 189, 192-193, 194; homework noncompliance and, 212; instigating, 187; managing success and failure of, 194-198; nature of, 189-190; partial vs. full, 129-130, 189-190; psychological flexibility and, 127-128; questions for evaluating, 72; reframing success and, 128; self as context and, 148; trying vs. doing in, 129; values and, 130

comorbidity issues, 218-219; concurrent treatment and, 222-223; presenting problem and, 75-76

comparative outcome research, 233-234

Compass Metaphor, 124-125

comprehensive distancing, 19, 231

conceptual level of analysis, 229-230

conceptualized self, 15, 27, 69; assessment of, 72; depression and, 27-28; formal measure of, 73; fusion with damaged, 52-53; questions for evaluating, 72

conceptualizing cases. *See* case conceptualization

concurrent treatment, 220-223; of comorbid problems, 222-223; of depression, 220-222; ethical considerations about, 225

conditioned suppression, 41

conflicting values, 123-124

contextual therapy, 232

contextualism, 6, 232

control. *See* experiential control

coping self-statements, 5

core processes of ACT, 11-12; psychological flexibility and, 11-13; questions for identifying, 88; targeting in case conceptualization, 87-88

costs: of depression, 1-2, 80-81; of therapeutic change, 82

costs/benefits evaluation, 80-81

counterpliance, 118, 210-211

creative hopelessness, 58-60; experiential avoidance and, 58-59, 105; initial induction of, 163-166; metaphors for inducing, 105-107; titrating approach to, 59-60

D

"dark side" of language, 13-15

daydreaming, 61

dead-man test, 104, 135

decentering, 19

decisional balance, 79

defusion, 14, 92-104, 113; acceptance distinguished from, 94-95; acquisition of, 93-94; of automatic thoughts, 97-101, 174-175; explanation of, 92; methods of promoting, 95-104; mindfulness and, 135; of reason giving, 101-103, 177-178; of storytelling, 103-104; working with existing, 94

deliteralization, 94-95

depression: alternative pathways to, 31-36; benefits associated with, 81; clean vs. dirty pain and, 23-24; conceptualized self and, 27-28; concurrent treatment of, 220-222; costs associated with, 1-2, 80-81; *DSM- IV* diagnosis of, 30-31; environmental factors and, 84-86; experiential avoidance and, 35; goals and values and, 31-34; identifying pathways to, 58; life stories and, 35-36; normal mood fluctuations and, 23; pathogenic processes in, 38-54; prevalence of, 1; primary pathway to, 22-29; reactive vs. endogenous, 31; rule-governed behavior and, 32-34; rumination and, 24-27; success, 31,

32, 115; suicide and, 28-29, 59, 204; treatment of, 2; values and, 115-116

depressive disorder NOS, 30

derived stimulus functions, 97

descriptive contextualism, 228

dialectical behavior therapy, 2

diary exercise forms: Mindfulness Exercise Diary, 273; Mood Regulation Diary, 280

direct shaping process, 93

dirty pain, 14, 24, 110

discrepancy analysis, 83

distancing, 19

drug abuse, 61

DSM-IV diagnosis of depression, 30-31

Dysfunctional Attitude Scale (DAS), 18, 235

dysphoria, 23-24

dysthymic disorder, 30

E

eating mindfully, 140-141

emotional control strategies, 60-63, 71; external, 61-62; in-session, 62-63; internal, 61; situation-specific, 62. *See also* experiential control

emotional reasoning, 14

emotions: accepting unwanted, 175; increasing tolerance of painful, 206-207; strategies for controlling, 60-63, 71. *See also* feelings

empty-chair technique, 214, 216

endogenous depression, 31

environmental barriers: analysis of, 84-86; committed action and, 131, 187; questions related to, 86

Epitaph Exercise, 122, 183

ethical considerations, 223-225; concurrent treatment, 225; informed consent, 224; management of suicidality, 224-225

evaluation of experiences, 200

experiential avoidance, 14, 48-49, 200; analyzing strategies of, 78-79; assessment of, 58-63, 71, 73; creative hopelessness and, 58-60; depression

as form of, 35; emotional control strategies and, 60-63; formal measures of, 73; identifying content of, 77-78; questions for evaluating, 71; suicidality and, 59, 205-206; thought suppression and, 49. *See also* experiential control

experiential barriers, 131, 187

experiential control: futility and costs of, 169-171; mindfulness interventions and, 138-139; pervasiveness and normalcy of, 168-169; strategies of, 60-63, 71; weakening, 105-109; willingness as alternative to, 171-172. *See also* experiential avoidance

explicit process measures, 235-236

external control strategies, 61-62, 71

extreme rigidity. *See* psychological rigidity

F

fading, 137-138

failure: fear of, 211-212; managing, 196-198

Falling in Love Metaphor, 170-171

FEAR acronym, 200-201

feelings: accepting unwanted, 175; mindfulness of, 145-147, 185, 186; sitting with, 112-113, 135, 136, 175. *See also* emotions

financial contingencies, 85

first wave of behavior therapy, 5

first-order change, 5

Flat Tire Metaphor, 103, 178

flexibility. *See* psychological flexibility

forgiveness issues, 213-216; forgiving oneself, 215-216; forgiving others, 213-215

forms: ACT Initial Case Conceptualization, 240-241; Goals-Action, 272; Mindfulness Exercise Diary, 273; Mood Regulation Diary, 280; Reasons for Depression, 245-246; Taking Inventory, 242-244; Writing Your Life Story, 247-248. *See also* handouts; questionnaires

frame of coordination, 9

free operant situation, 50

full commitments, 129-130, 189-190

functional analytic psychotherapy (FAP), 2, 62, 211

functional contextualism, 6, 228-229, 232

Furniture in the House Metaphor, 148, 156, 182

fusion, 13-14, 48, 200; assessment of, 57-58, 67-68, 71, 73; formal measures of, 73; questions for evaluating, 71

future, preoccupation with, 52

G

Gardening Metaphor, 197

Gazing at the Clouds Exercise, 145-146

Get Off Your "Buts" Intervention, 156, 178-179

goals: of ACT, 11-13; committed action and, 126-127, 188, 189, 192-193, 194; graduated setting of, 125; identification of, 186-187; process vs. outcome, 76-77; therapeutic, 162-163, 183; values related to, 31-34, 63-65, 115-116, 120, 124-126, 162-163

Goals-Action Form, 125, 188, 189, 192-193, 194, 198; sample of, 272

graduated goal setting, 125

H

Haggard, Merle, 219

handouts: Breathing Mindfully Exercise, 274-275; Watching Your Thoughts Exercise, 276-277; "What Is Acceptance and Commitment Therapy?," 161, 224, 278-279. See also forms; questionnaires

hexaflex model, 11-12, 230

homework assignments: Breathing Mindfully Exercise, 185, 186; Goals-Action Form, 188, 189, 192-193, 194, 198; Mindfulness Exercise Diary, 141, 180, 183, 185, 187, 192, 194, 198; Mood Regulation Diary, 166, 167; noncompliance with, 209-212; Reasons for Depression Exercise, 176, 177; Rewriting Your Life Story Exercise, 183, 184; Taking Inventory Exercise,

176, 177; Thoughts on Cards Exercise, 172, 173; values questionnaire, 185; Writing Your Life Story Exercise, 180, 181

hopelessness: suicide and feelings of, 52. See also creative hopelessness

hot cognitions, 58, 68

I

Implicit Association Test (IAT), 236

implicit process measures, 236-237

Implicit Relational Assessment Procedure (IRAP), 236

incentive-disengagement theory, 23, 41

indirect values assessment, 119-123, 182-183

inflexibility. See psychological inflexibility

information processing guidelines, 74-75

informed consent, 158-160, 224

in-session control strategies, 62-63

integrative behavioral couples therapy, 2

internal control strategies, 61, 71

interpersonal therapy, 2

interviewing, motivational, 79-80

iterative approach, 56

J

Joe the Bum Metaphor, 194-196

Jump Exercise, 129-130, 189-190

K

Kabat-Zinn, Jon, 53, 69, 135, 137, 140

Kentucky Inventory of Mindfulness Skills (KIMS), 73

King, Martin Luther, Jr., 121

L

language: "dark side" of, 13-15; "light side" of, 15-16

learned helplessness theory, 32

Leaves on a Stream Exercise, 136, 145

life stories, 35-36; assessment process and, 57-58, 68; defusion process and, 103-104; depression and, 46-47; obtaining from clients, 162

life worth, 28
"light side" of language, 15-16
Lillis, Jason, 75
Lindsley, Ogden, 104
listening to music, 141-142
Listserv resources, 238
Lost (TV show), 122
Luoma, Jason, 75

M

Magic Pill Metaphor, 197-198
major depressive disorder, 30
Man in the Hole Metaphor. *See* Person in the Hole Metaphor
management: of challenging behavior, 203-218; of extreme rigidity, 212-218; of failure, 196-198; of homework noncompliance, 209-212; of success, 194-196; of suicidal behavior, 206-209
martyr role, 217-218
mechanism, 228
medications: antianxiety, 222-223; antidepressant, 2, 220-221
meditation: selection guidelines, 137. *See also* mindfulness
methodological level of analysis, 230
Milk, Milk, Milk Exercise, 77, 97-98, 175
Mind in the Third Person Technique, 97, 174
mindfulness, 69, 135-147; acceptance and, 135; assessment of, 69, 72, 73; breathing and, 143-145, 184; cognitive therapy components of, 2, 19-20; considerations in promoting, 136-140; daily activities and, 142-143, 181-182; definition of, 69, 135; defusion and, 135; eating and, 140-141; formal measure of, 73; interventions based on, 136-140; presenting the rationale for, 138-140; progression of exercises in, 140-147; selecting meditations for, 137; self as context and, 147-148; self-forgiveness and, 215-216; shaping and fading related to, 137-138; thoughts/feelings and, 145-147, 185, 186

Mindfulness Exercise Diary, 141, 180, 183, 185, 187, 192, 194, 198; form used for, 273
mindfulness-based cognitive therapy (MBCT), 2, 19-20; ACT distinguished from, 19-20; distancing/decentering in, 19-20; meditations used in, 137
mood fluctuations, 23
Mood Regulation Diary, 166, 280
motivational analysis, 79-84; costs/benefits evaluation, 80-83; motivational interviewing, 79-80; questions related to, 83-84
motivational interviewing (MI), 79-80
motivative augmental, 82
music, listening to, 141-142
mutual entailment, 9

N

Nietzsche, Friedrich, 207
normal mood fluctuations, 23

O

Observer Exercise, 151-155, 156, 185, 215, 231
observer self, 70
operant conditioning, 5
outcome goals, 76-77

P

pain: of absence, 80-81; clean, 23-24, 110; dirty, 14, 24, 110; emotional, 206-207; of presence, 80
paradigmatic approach, 227-231
parental influences, 117 118
partial commitments, 129-130, 189-190
Passengers on the Bus Metaphor, 131-133, 190
past, preoccupation with, 52
pathogenic processes, 38-54; cognitive fixation, 46-47; damaged conceptualized self, 52-53; dominance of verbal control, 50; experiential avoidance, 48-49; fusion, 48, 52-53; living in the past/future,

52; perseverative thought/behavior, 41-43; reason giving, 44-45; rumination, 43-44; storytelling, 45-46; uncommitted action, 51

perseverative thought/behavior, 41-43

Person in the Hole Metaphor, 60, 61, 105, 163-166, 221

Personal Values Questionnaire (PVQ), 73, 116-117, 185, 234; sample form, 249-269

pharmacotherapy, 220-221, 222-223

philosophical level of analysis, 228-229

Physicalizing Exercise, 60, 78, 111-112, 175

plan-availability-lethality triangle, 204

pliance, 33-34, 50, 118

Polygraph Metaphor, 169-170

positive psychotherapy, 237

presence, pain of, 80

presenting problem, 75-77; comorbidity issues, 75-76; process vs. outcome goals, 76-77; questions related to, 77; verifying with clients, 162

present-moment awareness, 135-147. *See also* mindfulness

pretreatment issues, 158-161; assessment options, 160-161; informed consent, 158-160

priority of being right, 35-36

problem-solving skills, 208-209

process goals, 65, 76-77

process research, 235-237; explicit vs. implicit measures, 235-237; therapeutic outcome measures, 237

progressive muscle relaxation (PMR), 231

prompt dependence, 138

psychoeducational programs, 2

psychological flexibility, 3, 11-13; assessment of, 57, 73; committed action and, 127-128; core processes contributing to, 11-13; definition of, 11; formal measure of, 73; psychological inflexibility vs., 39-40

psychological inflexibility: cognitive fixation and, 46-47; extreme rigidity and, 212-218; factors contributing to,

86-87; forgiveness issues and, 213-216; martyr role and, 217-218; perseverative thought/behavior and, 41-43; psychological flexibility vs., 39-40; reason giving and, 44-45; rumination and, 43-44; storytelling and, 45-46; types of, 40-47

psychological rigidity, 212-218; forgiveness issues and, 213-216; martyr role and, 217-218

psychotherapy, 222

Q

questionnaires: Acceptance and Action, 39, 73, 235-236; Automatic Thoughts, 17-18, 73; Personal Values, 73, 116-117, 185, 234, 249-269; Reasons for Depression, 45, 73; Response Styles, 44, 73; Valued Living, 73, 116-117, 185, 234, 237, 270-271. *See also* forms; handouts

Quicksand Metaphor, 107-108, 163

R

Raisin Exercise, 140-141, 179-180

reactive depression, 31

reason giving, 36, 44-45, 201; defusing, 101-103, 177-178; identifying, 68, 71, 73

Reasons for Depression Exercise, 102, 176, 177; form used for, 245-246

Reasons for Depression Questionnaire (RFD), 45, 73

Reasons for Living Inventory (RFL), 206

reinforcement for depression, 84-85

relational frame theory (RFT), 7-10, 12, 228-230, 232

relational framing, 8-10, 232; nature of, 8; properties of, 9-10

relational networks, 9

religious conversions, 32

research: comparative outcome, 233-234; process, 235-237; treatment utility, 234-235

response fixation, 41

162-163, 183; reactions to terminating, 199-200; values influenced by, 119

third wave of behavior therapy, 2, 5-6

Thoreau, Henry David, 34

thoughts: automatic, 68, 71, 97-101; defusing, 97-101, 174-175; mindfulness of, 145-147, 185, 186; perseverative, 41-43; ruminating on, 25-26; suppression of, 49, 61, 73

Thoughts on Cards Exercise, 99, 135, 172, 173

tracking, 32-33

transformation of stimulus functions, 10

treatment: concurrent with ACT, 220-223; formulating plans for, 90; pretreatment issues, 158-161

treatment utility research, 234-235

Trying vs. Doing Exercise, 129, 189

Tug-of-War with a Monster Metaphor, 60, 105-107, 139, 163

Twain, Mark, 127

twelve-session protocol, 157-202

12-step programs, 89, 223

Two Scales Metaphor, 110, 171-172

U

uncommitted action, 51

unipolar depression. *See* depression

V

value-congruent goals, 34, 115-116

Valued Living Questionnaire (VLQ), 73, 116-117, 185, 234, 237; sample form, 270-271

value-incongruent goals, 31-34, 115

values, 16, 115-126, admired others and, 121, 183; assessment of, 50, 63-66, 72, 73, 116-117, 119-123, 186; childhood wishes and, 120-121; clarification of, 117-119; committed action and, 130; conflicts related to, 123-124; depression pathways and, 115-116; formal measures of, 73, 116-117; goals related to, 31-34, 63-65, 115-116,

120, 124-126, 162-163; homework noncompliance and, 210; indirect identification of, 119-123, 182-183; parental influence on, 117-118; prioritization of, 126; questions for evaluating, 72; self as context and, 148; social/cultural influence on, 118-119; suffering related to, 65-66, 119-120, 182; suicidal clients and, 207-208; therapist influence on, 119

Values Assessment Rating Form, 116

Values Narrative Form, 116

valuing, 16, 63-66, 115-126, 207-208

verbal action, 29

verbal control, 50

victim role, 217-218

W

Walking Exercise, 142, 181

Watching the Mind-Train Exercise, 145

Watching Your Thoughts Exercise, 276-277

What Do You Want Your Life to Stand For? Exercise, 121-122

"What Is Acceptance and Commitment Therapy?" handout, 161, 224, 278-279

White Bear Suppression Inventory (WBSI), 73

Why, Why, Why? Exercise, 178, 190

willingness, 14, 201; barriers to, 200-201; experiential control and, 171-172; explanation of, 92-93; forgiveness and, 214; methods of promoting, 109-113. *See also* acceptance

Wilson, Kelly, 62

Wisconsin Card Sorting Test (WCST), 42, 43

Writing Your Life Story Exercise, 180, 181; form used for, 247-248

Y

Your Mind Is Not Your Friend Exercise, 95-97, 174, 207

Robert D. Zettle, Ph.D., is associate professor in the Department of Psychology at Wichita State University. He completed his predoctoral internship at the Center for Cognitive Therapy in Philadelphia, conducted the first comparative outcome study on what is now known as ACT as part of his dissertation under the supervision of ACT founder Steven Hayes, and has published both basic and applied research relating to rule governance, experiential avoidance, and ACT for depression for more than twenty years.

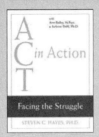

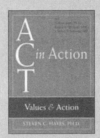